The Abingdon Preaching Annual 2013

The Abingdon Preaching Annual 2013

Compiled and Edited by
The Reverend David Neil Mosser, Ph.D.

Assistant Editor Ronda Wellman

Abingdon Press
Nashville

THE ABINGDON PREACHING ANNUAL 2013

This book is printed on acid-free paper.

ISBN 978-1-4267-4136-4

ISSN 1075-2250

12 13 14 15 16 17 18 19 20 21—10 9 8 7 6 5 4 3 2 1

MANUFACTURED IN THE UNITED STATES OF AMERICA

To the memory of my exceedingly Wesleyan uncle,
Russell A. Mosser, a longtime and faithful member of
First United Methodist Church, Lawrence, Kansas

CONTENTS

FEBRUARY

MARCH

SEPTEMBER

OCTOBER

NOVEMBER

DECEMBER

III. APPENDIXES

INTRODUCTION

Not long ago one of my colleagues telephoned with a question. She called because she knows that I know more preachers than most people (Do "not pick out the good from the bad" Leviticus 27:33). She wanted to know a preacher who could preach a first-rate set of sermons for a clergy gathering. After tossing out six or seven names of those whom I considered to be top-quality and faithful preachers, both men and women, she dismissed each one in rapid sequence. I began to get annoyed and thought of Jesse, for whom each son was paraded in succession by Samuel, unworthy to be Israel's next king (see 1 Samuel 16:1-13). Finally, out of annoyance I simply asked her, "What is wrong with these names?"

Then the caller came clean. "I'm sorry," she said, "none of your names is famous enough." It struck me as an odd thing. Can you imagine that Paul or John Chrysostom or Peter Cartwright or Charles Haddon Spurgeon or Martin Niemöller would have not had enough of a reputation in some quarters to elicit an invitation to preach the gospel? In our twenty-first century sometimes what is most essential is the status of the presenter rather than the person's competency or that the person is a faithful gospel witness. At times it seems like it is all about celebrity.

For this reason, I offer a word of appreciation to the scores of preachers who labor under relative anonymity and produce faithful sermons to feed their congregations each week. To them I say a grateful word of thanks. I find it a comfort as "a quintessential non-famous person" to know that some of the best preachers in our country today are people whom we have never heard of—and likely never will. Yet the preaching task remains central regardless of notoriety or its absence. The mission of preaching is why we labor to produce *The Abingdon Preaching Annual (APA)*. We all need to be in conversation with a lot of truly good preachers whom no one has ever heard of!

Perhaps you are like many preachers. As we preach week in and week out, we are aware that the work sometimes places us on a lonely path. To repair this homiletical isolation, many of us preaching pastors assemble with colleagues who share our preaching journey. Sometimes preachers gather weekly or monthly in "study clusters" or "lectionary groups." Yet for many rural preachers, maybe even urban preachers too, assembling regularly with others in this fashion is neither convenient nor feasible. Happily, with the Internet we can hear other preachers practice the art of homiletics. Yet listening to many sermons tends to be time consuming—a luxury that few of us have. To provide preachers a venue by which to delve into texts and ideas with other preachers is the intention behind the 2013 *APA*. The *APA* employs *The Revised Common Lectionary* for half its entries, while sermon series comprise the other half. Thus for each Sunday of the calendar year—January through December—and other high holy days (e.g., Good Friday and Thanksgiving), each preachable day's section offers not only a one-thousand-word sermon on one of the three primary lectionary texts for the day, but also a sermon that is part of a sermon series as well.

We continue to try to respond to readers' feedback. This year, while you will find many of the features introduced in the past several years, we have eliminated the additional CD-ROM and incorporated some Pre-sermon, Offertory, and Pastoral Prayers that used to be found on the disc. We have again included a classic sermon for inspiration and an at-a-glance table of the lectionary readings for the year. What you will not find this year are classical and contemporary prayers and affirmations of faith and the annotated bibliography that we introduced a few years ago.

Many of the biblical excerpts in the sermons are taken from the new *Common English Bible*, or CEB. The full text of the lectionary verses can be found online at http://www.commonenglishbibe.com. We are excited to introduce this new resource to you in the *APA*.

The aim of the *APA* is to help preachers plan a full yearly schedule for preaching the biblical good news. Each preacher, of course, has her or his own method for planning a preaching program for individual congregations. This book in your hands allows preachers to sketch a preaching agenda from January through December, or any segment of the year. Some may use the lectionary exclusively; some the series; others a combination. One way or another, the *APA* can be a useful contribution to a planning method.

Perceptive preachers might ask, "Who is the target audience for the *APA*?" The answer would be those preachers who want to be in conversation with other preachers who take the preaching task with a kind of seriousness that biblical exposition calls forth. Consequently, the kinds of preachers who may benefit from this book may be old or young, novices or experienced, rural or urban. The *APA*'s intention is to stimulate biblical discourse. We all know that faithful preachers need and want this kind of spiritual and cerebral stimulation.

Each pastor and congregation has an exacting and sacred association that no other person can imitate. In fact, I know many pastors who do everything else that they do (administration, pastoral care, fund raising, and so on) in order to preach God's word.

Consequently, we trust that no authentic preacher will be so lifeless or lacking in zest as to let the enticement for shortcuts weaken preaching's effectiveness. At the same time, the preaching task is so difficult we can never do it by ourselves. The *APA* merely attempts to be one of the voices that the preacher listens to with discernment. Naturally we all bring our own gifts in preparing a unique word for our distinctive congregations. With our individual gifts used in concert with the insights of others, faithful preaching can and does happen.

In an earlier era, preachers steadfastly read what other preachers might write in newspapers, books, and periodicals. Today, many shun the reading of sermons. We don't have the time to read, it seems. Yet to walk through a text and experience it with a sister or brother in the ministry is often a helpful way to learn as we go. No preacher is ever a finished product. We all continually learn from others and from our own small victories as well as our large mistakes. In these kinds of conversation, both we and the church are blessed. "You too heard the word of truth in Christ, which is the good news of your salvation. You were sealed with the promised Holy Spirit because you believed in Christ" (Ephesians 1:13)!

24 May 2011—Aldersgate Day in the
United Methodist/Wesleyan Tradition
The Rev. David N. Mosser

I. GENERAL HELPS

FOUR-YEAR CHURCH CALENDAR

	2013	2014	2015	2016
Ash Wednesday	February 13	March 5	February 18	February 10
Palm Sunday	March 24	April 13	March 29	March 20
Holy Thursday	March 28	April 17	April 2	March 24
Good Friday	March 29	April 18	April 3	March 25
Easter	March 31	April 20	April 5	March 27
Ascension Sunday	May 12	June 1	May 17	May 5
Pentecost	May 19	June 8	May 24	May 15
Trinity Sunday	May 26	June 15	May 31	May 22
World Communion	October 8	October 5	October 4	October 2
Thanksgiving	November 28	November 27	November 26	November 24
First Sunday of Advent	December 1	November 30	November 29	November 27

LITURGICAL COLORS

If the gospel can be proclaimed visually, why should it not be? Color helps form general expectations for any occasion. Traditionally, purples, grays, and blues have been used for seasons of a penitential character such as Advent and Lent, although any dark colors could be used. White has been used for events or seasons with strong christological meaning such as the Baptism of the Lord or the Easter Season. Yellows and golds are also possibilities at such times. Red has been reserved for occasions relating to the Holy Spirit (such as the Day of Pentecost or ordinations) or to commemorations of the martyrs. Green has been used for seasons such as the Season after Epiphany or the Season after Pentecost. The absence of any colored textiles from Maundy Thursday to the Easter Vigil is a striking use of contrast. Colors and textures can be used most effectively in textiles for hangings on pulpits, on lecterns (if any), for the stoles worn by ordained ministers, or for ministerial vestments.*

Advent: Violet (purple) or blue

Christmas: Gold or white for December 24-25. White thereafter, through the Baptism of the Lord. (Or, in the days between January 6 and the Sunday of the Baptism, green may be used.)

Ordinary Time (both after Epiphany-Baptism and after Pentecost): Green

Transfiguration: White

Lent Prior to Holy Week: Violet. Black is sometimes used for Ash Wednesday.

Early Holy Week: On Palm-Passion Sunday, violet (purple) or [blood] red may be specified. For the Monday, Tuesday, and Wednesday of Holy Week, the same options exist, although with variations as to which color to use on each day.

Triduum: For Holy Thursday, violet (purple) or [blood] red may be used during the day and changed to white for the evening Eucharist. Then the church may be stripped.
Good Friday and Holy Saturday: Stripped or black; or [blood] red in some churches on Good Friday.
Great Fifty Days: White or gold. Or gold for Easter Day and perhaps its octave, then white for the remainder of the season until the Vigil of Pentecost.
Day of Pentecost: [Fire] red
Annunciation, Visitation, and Presentation of Jesus: White
Commemoration of Martyrs: [Blood] red
Commemoration of Saints not Martyred: White
All Saints: White
Christ the King: White**

* James F. White, *Introduction to Christian Worship* (rev. ed.; Nashville: Abingdon Press, 1990), 85-86.

** Laurence Hull Stookey, *Calendar: Christ's Time for the Church* (Nashville: Abingdon Press, 1996), 156-57.

LECTIONARY LISTINGS 2013
THE REVISED COMMON LECTIONARY

Sunday	*First Lesson*	*Psalm*	*Second Lesson*	*Gospel Lesson*
01/06/13	Jeremiah 31:7-14	Psalm 147:12-20	Ephesians 1:3-14	John 1:1-9, 10-18
01/13/13	Isaiah 43:1-7	Psalm 29	Acts 8:14-17	Luke 3:15-17, 21-22
01/20/13	Isaiah 62:1-5	Psalm 36:5-10	1 Corinthians 12:1-11	John 2:1-11
01/27/13	Nehemiah 8:1-3, 5-6, 8-10	Psalm 19	1 Corinthians 12:12-31a	Luke 4:14-21
02/03/13	Jeremiah 1:4-10	Psalm 71:1-6	1 Corinthians 13:1-13	Luke 4:21-30
02/10/13	Isaiah 6:1-8, 9-13	Psalm 138	1 Corinthians 15:1-11	Luke 5:1-11
02/13/13	Joel 2:1-2, 12-17	Psalm 51:1-17	2 Corinthians 5:20b-6:10	Matthew 6:1-6, 16-21
02/17/13	Deuteronomy 26:1-11	Psalm 91:1-2, 9-16	Romans 10:8b-13	Luke 4:1-13
02/24/13	Genesis 15:1-12, 17-18	Psalm 27	Philippians 3:17-4:1	Luke 13:31-34 or 9:28-36
03/03/13	Isaiah 55:1-9	Psalm 63:1-8	1 Corinthians 10:1-13	Luke 13:1-9
03/10/13	Joshua 5:9-12	Psalm 32	2 Corinthians 5:16-21	Luke 15:1-3, 11b-32
03/17/13	Isaiah 43:16-21	Psalm 126	Philippians 3:4b-14	John 12:1-8
03/24/13	Palms: ———	Psalm 118:1-2, 19-29	———	Luke 19:28-40
	Passion: Isaiah 50:4-9a	Psalm 31:9-16	Philippians 2:5-11	Luke 22:14–23:56
03/28/13	Exodus 12:1-4, 5-10, 11-14	Psalm 116:1-2, 12-19	1 Corinthians 11:23-26	John 13:1-17, 31b-35
03/29/13	Isaiah 52:13–53:12	Psalm 22	Hebrews 10:16-25 or 4:14-16, 5:7-9	John 18:1–19:42
03/31/13	Acts 10:34-43	Psalm 118:1-2, 14-24	1 Corinthians 15:19-26	John 20:1-18
04/07/13	Acts 5:27-32	Psalm 118:14-29	Revelation 1:4-8	John 20:19-31
04/14/13	Acts 9:1-6, 7-20	Psalm 30	Revelation 5:11-14	John 21:1-19
04/21/13	Acts 9:36-43	Psalm 23	Revelation 7:9-17	John 10:22-30
04/28/13	Acts 11:1-18	Psalm 148	Revelation 21:1-6	John 13:31-35
05/05/13	Acts 16:9-15	Psalm 67	Revelation 21:10, 22–22:5	John 14:23-29

* This list represents one possible selection of lessons and psalms from the lectionary for Year C (January 1–November 28) and Year A (November 29–December 31). For a complete listing, see *The Revised Common Lectionary*.

Sunday	*First Lesson*	*Psalm*	*Second Lesson*	*Gospel Lesson*
05/12/13	Acts 1:1-11	Psalm 93	Ephesians 1:15-23	Luke 24:44-53
05/19/13	Acts 2:1-21	Psalm 104:24-34, 35b	Romans 8:14-17	John 14:8-17, (25-27)
05/26/13	Proverbs 8:1-4, 22-31	Psalm 8	Romans 5:1-5	John 16:12-15
06/02/13	1 Kings 18:20-21, 30-39	Psalm 96	Galatians 1:1-12	Luke 7:1-10
06/09/13	1 Kings 17:17-24	Psalm 146	Galatians 1:11-24	Luke 7:11-17
06/16/13	1 Kings 21:1-21a	Psalm 5:1-8	Galatians 2:15-21	Luke 7:36–8:3
06/23/13	1 Kings 19:1-15a	Psalm 42; 43	Galatians 3:23-29	Luke 8:26-39
06/30/13	2 Kings 2:1-2, 6-14	Psalm 77:1-2, 11-20	Galatians 5:1, 13-25	Luke 9:51-62
07/07/13	2 Kings 5:1-14	Psalm 30	Galatians 6:1-16	Luke 10:1-11, 16-20
07/14/13	Amos 7:7-17	Psalm 82	Colossians 1:1-14	Luke 10:25-37
07/21/13	Amos 8:1-12	Psalm 52	Colossians 1:15-28	Luke 10:38-42
07/28/13	Hosea 1:2-10	Psalm 85	Colossians 2:6-15, 16-19	Luke 11:1-13
08/04/13	Hosea 11:1-11	Psalm 107:1-9, 43	Colossians 3:1-11	Luke 12:13-21
08/11/13	Isaiah 1:1, 10-20	Psalm 50:1-8, 22-23	Hebrews 11:1-3, 8-16	Luke 12:32-40
08/18/13	Isaiah 5:1-7	Psalm 80:1-2, 8-19	Hebrews 11:29-12:2	Luke 12:49-56
08/25/13	Jeremiah 1:4-10	Psalm 71:1-6 or Psalm 103:1-8	Hebrews 12:18-29	Luke 13:10-17
09/01/13	Jeremiah 2:4-13	Psalm 81:1, 10-16	Hebrews 13:1-8, 15-16	Luke 14:1, 7-14
09/08/13	Jeremiah 18:1-11	Psalm 139:1-6, 13-18 or Psalm 1	Philemon 1-21	Luke 14:25-33
09/15/13	Jeremiah 4:11-12, 22-28	Psalm 14 or Psalm 51:1-10	1 Timothy 1:12-17	Luke 15:1-10
09/22/13	Jeremiah 8:18–9:1	Psalm 79:1-9	1 Timothy 2:1-7	Luke 16:1-13
09/29/13	Jeremiah 32:1-3a, 6-15	Psalm 146	1 Timothy 6:6-19	Luke 16:19-31
10/06/13	Habakkuk 1:1-4, 2:1-4	Psalm 37:1-9	2 Timothy 1:1-14	Luke 17:5-10
10/13/13	2 Kings 5:1-3, 7-15c	Psalm 66:1-12	2 Timothy 2:8-15	Luke 17:11-19
10/20/13	Jeremiah 31:27-34	Psalm 119:97-104	2 Timothy 3:14–4:5	Luke 18:1-18
10/27/13	Joel 2:23-32	Psalm 65	2 Timothy 4:6-8, 16-18	Luke 18:9-14

* This list represents one possible selection of lessons and psalms from the lectionary for Year C (January 1–November 28) and Year A (November 29–December 31). For a complete listing, see *The Revised Common Lectionary*.

Sunday	*First Lesson*	*Psalm*	*Second Lesson*	*Gospel Lesson*
11/03/13	Daniel 7:1-3, 15-18	Psalm 149	Ephesians 1:11-23	Luke 6:20-31
11/10/13	Haggai 1:15b–2:9	Psalm 145:1-5, 17-21	2 Thessalonians 2:1-5, 13-17	Luke 20:27-38
11/17/13	Isaiah 65:17-25	Psalm 98	2 Thessalonians 3:6-13	Luke 21:5-19
11/24/13	Jeremiah 23:1-6	Psalm 46	Colossians 1:11-20	Luke 23:33-43
11/28/13	Deuteronomy 26:1-11	Psalm 100	Philippians 4:4-9	John 6:25-35
12/01/13	Isaiah 2:1-5	Psalm 122	Romans 13:11-14	Matthew 24:36-44
12/08/13	Isaiah 11:1-10	Psalm 72:1-7, 18-19	Romans 15:4-13	Matthew 3:1-12
12/15/13	Isaiah 35:1-10	Psalm 146:5-10	James 5:7-10	Matthew 11:2-11
12/22/13	Isaiah 7:10-16	Psalm 80:1-7, 17-19	Romans 1:1-7	Matthew 1:18-25
12/25/13	Isaiah 52:7-10	Psalm 98	Hebrews 1:1-4, 5-12	John 1:1-14
12/29/13	Isaiah 63:7-9	Psalm 148	Hebrews 2:10-18	Matthew 2:13-23

* This list represents one possible selection of lessons and psalms from the lectionary for Year C (January 1–November 28) and Year A (November 29–December 31). For a complete listing, see *The Revised Common Lectionary*.

II. SERMONS AND WORSHIP AIDS

JANUARY 6, 2013

Epiphany

Readings: Jeremiah 31:7-14; Psalm 147:12-20; Ephesians 1:3-14; John 1:(1-9), 10-18

Light in the Darkness

John 1:(1-9), 10-18

The first Sunday of the New Year dawns with Epiphany Day. By church tradition Epiphany is the day we celebrate the arrival of the wise men who come to worship the newborn Christ. The Gospel text is John's great symphonic opening. With all the grandeur of Beethoven's Ninth Symphony, the text presents us with the full glory of the incarnation. "And the Word became flesh and lived among us, and we have seen his glory, the glory as of a father's only son, full of grace and truth" (NRSV). The phrase "lived among us" means literally that the Lord pitched his tent in our midst.

On one level we give casual allegiance to this great truth. On another level, it is easy for the best of Christians to forget the full impact of the gospel's great claim. God is not out there at a distance watching us but living in our midst. Faithful preaching on the text from John's Gospel challenges us to embrace again, as if for the first time, this great truth. God incarnate (in the flesh) in the person of Jesus has taken up residence in our neighborhood—next door. This is not an invitation to a Pollyannaish ignorance of evil, destruction, and pain. Nor is it a whistling by the graveyard. Evil strides across the world. War still rages. Disease, hunger, prejudice, and death are still real. The difference, the huge difference, is that if we understand 2013 as A.D. (*Anno Domino, the year of our Lord*), we can embrace the New Year with grace and truth guiding us. Is the birth baby we celebrated twelve short days ago the inauguration of a new age or an interlude in the harsh chaos of life? Consider two true stories.

The first is the well-known story of Delta Airlines Flight 253 preparing to land in Detroit on Christmas Day in 2009. As a terrorist attempted to set off a bomb, heroic passengers threw themselves on the terrorist to extinguish the flames and save the plane. By all accounts it was a chaotic scene. Reporting on the incident, *Time* magazine, notes that as some aided in subduing the terrorist and putting out the flames, "Other passengers screamed; some ran to other cabins. 'I don't want to die! I want out!' yelled one." ("The 4 Lessons of Flight 253," *Time* magazine, January 11, 2010, p. 28).

The second story comes from personal experience. Worshiping on the first Sunday of the New Year in 2010, the congregation celebrated Holy Communion. My wife and I were sitting close to the front and were among the first to take the sacrament. After returning to our seats, I sat listening to the beautiful music and meditating. My quiet reverie was broken by a young family that knelt at the altar rail. The two little girls (probably ages seven and five) enthusiastically took part in a winsome way that evoked smiles. Finishing, the family turned and walked back down the center aisle to their seats. The girls walked on either side of their father holding his hand. The five-year-old on the dad's left broke into a huge smile and started skipping down the aisle. Somehow she got incredible joy from Communion and worship that we more serious adults had trouble embracing.

Now I ask you, of the two stories, which one best captures the essence of the gospel? Which one brings us into the New Year with the fullness of what has just taken place at Christmas? Which one recognizes that this is A.D. 2013?

Before us is a question of perspective. Do you scream, "I want out of here!" or do you skip down the aisle? I must confess I have sometimes felt like running down the aisle yelling, "I want out!" In my more faithful living, however, I embrace the joy of the skipping little girl.

Epiphany Day we celebrate the light of God entering the darkness of our lives in the person of Jesus. Faithful proclamation invites us to once again embrace both the word and way of God.

"In the beginning was the Word, and the Word was with God and the Word was God. The Word was with God in the beginning" (John 1:1-2). This is not a static sentence. It recalls how the Bible opens—"In the beginning" (Genesis 1:1 NRSV). So too, this great gospel—great good news—opens with a reminder of the creative life-giving God at work.

The text pulses with action. The term "Word of God" translates the Greek term *Logos*. New Testament scholar A. M. Hunter put it this way: "It meant the ruling fact of the universe and that fact as the self-expression of God" (A. M. Hunter, *The Gospel According to John* [Cambridge: Cambridge University Press, 1965], 16). God is active in our world and in our lives!

"What has come into being in him was life, and the life was the light of all people. The light shines in the darkness, and the darkness did not overcome it" (John 1:3b-5 NRSV). The biblical image of creation is that it comes from primordial soup. Again, recall Genesis, "The earth was a formless void and darkness covered the face of the deep, while a wind from God swept over the face of the waters. Then God said, 'Let there be light'; and there was light" (Genesis 1:2-3 NRSV). Life and light are God's creative genius at work.

But don't miss this. Darkness and chaos are real, both at creation and now; both at the beginning of year 1 and at the beginning of the year of our Lord 2013. They are real, but not evil. The earth was just a formless void. Now darkness and chaos represent the pain, the evil, the sin, the anguish in this world and in our lives. We know darkness. We know the terror of chaos. We know it in us and around us. We know darkness in the haunting legacy of greed and prejudice. We know darkness in the anguished hurt of death and the sting of broken lives. We know it in the reality of divorce and the struggles facing all families, in our own country or in countries around the world. We know darkness in the hate of a terrorist sitting in a plane trying to blow up himself and others.

"The light shines in the darkness, and the darkness did not overcome it." By way of analogy, imagine yourself in pitch darkness. Years ago we walked through Carlsbad Caverns National Park for the first time. In a certain very narrow, short corridor, the ranger had us stand still and then turned off the lights. We couldn't even see our hands in front of our eyes. Then he flicked on a powerful flashlight. Its beam shot out, literally overcoming the darkness. Something like that is the image the Gospel writer is reaching for. John is saying: Look, I know the darkness of life is real. But from God there is life and light that overcomes darkness in the person of Christ through the presence and power of the Holy Spirit. God in Christ triumphs over darkness, pain, and evil. We can skip down the aisle of life after we have partaken in the body and blood of Christ. (Mike Lowry)

Lectionary Commentary

Jeremiah 31:7-14

This is a text of restoration and celebration. It is also a prayer—"Save, O LORD, your people, the remnant of Israel" (v. 7 NRSV). Throughout the text the primary actor is God. The Lord alone ransoms and redeems God's people. Human response to God's powerful action is joy and praise.

There is an unmistakable connection-of-restoration theme with the Epiphany joy of the Gospels. God in Christ acts to redeem the new Israel—the church. The light comes to the Gentiles, to "all nations." Tertullian connected this passage with the Pentecost. Other early Christian writers linked the themes of ransom and redemption for all nations to the great commission and the church as the spiritual Israel. Rejoice, for the Lord has acted, is the order of the day. It is at once reflection on current reality and future promise. God has acted and is acting to save people. The Light shines in the darkness.

Ephesians 1:3-14

Along with John 1:1-18, this passage from Ephesians is a grand, sweeping overture of the gospel of salvation. Verses 3 through 14 are a lengthy opening prayer of thanksgiving and praise to God. There is exultant emotion conveyed in the prayer offering. The opening thrust of verse 3 is lifted in celebration throughout the passage (and the whole letter). The true God has lavished divine love on us through the person and work of Christ the Son. The high christological emphasis pours forth. God in and through Christ has acted in love on our behalf. Christ's actions leap off the page and can form the foundation of a sound doctrinal sermon—blessing (v. 3), chosen (v. 4), adoption (v. 5), grace (v. 6), ransom and forgiveness (v. 7), wisdom and understanding (v. 8), and purpose and inheritance (vv. 10 and 11). Epiphany is the revealing of God to the Gentiles, and this is done through Christ. Let the faithful preacher lift up Christ as Lord and Savior.

The careful reader and preacher will note the deep sense of plan and purpose that breathes through the words. In Christ, we encounter the one true God in action for us and our salvation. It is worth carefully noting that "our salvation" is for the higher purpose of redeeming all creation (v. 10—"to bring all things together in Christ, the things in heaven along with the things on earth."). All this is sealed by the Holy Spirit as a pledge of inheritance and redemption. (Mike Lowry)

Worship Aids

Call to Worship (Based on Psalm 147:12-15)

Praise the Lord, O Jerusalem!
Praise your God, O Zion!
The Lord blesses your children within you.
The Lord grants peace within your borders:
The Lord fills you with the finest wheat.
The Lord sends out his command to the earth.

Prayer of Confession

Lord God, we gather at the precipice of a new year with an unfounded confidence in our own goodness. Forgive, we pray, our unmerited pride in our accomplishments. We confess before you in our silence our errors, failures, and misdeeds of this past year. (*Pause for silence.*) Open our eyes again to see by the light of your grace upon grace. Open our hearts again to love through your greater love. Guide us this new year to live by the light of your revelation in Christ Jesus our only Lord and Savior. Have mercy upon us and grant us your blessing. This we pray in the name of the one true God who reveals himself for us, Father, Son, and Holy Spirit. Amen.

Words of Assurance

Come on this Epiphany Day and receive again the great news of God's mercy and love. The Lord God lives among us! "We have seen his glory, glory like that of a father's only son, full of grace and truth" (John 1:14). Enter this new year of our Lord as recipients of God's overflowing grace and love! Amen. (Mike Lowry)

Back to the Future

First in a Series of Two on Beginning a New Year with the Lord's Prayer

Jeremiah 29:1-11

Epiphany is considered "ordinary time." It is the time between Christmas and Lent, the time when life is as "normal" as it can be. A new year has begun, and everyone speaks of expectations, hopes, and dreams. This is a new year. The calendar changed, and we expect that at some point this year our lives will change. There can be newness of life in this year. We are excited about the possibilities. There are new projects to complete, new goals to achieve, and new horizons to look over.

Yet for many persons, the ordinariness of life means that the new year begins just as the last year ended. Nothing has changed; nothing is different. Our worries and uncertainty remain, and we exist in ordinary time, lacking the excitement of a major event or experience. Someone is still trying to adjust to a devastating diagnosis. Someone is still looking for a job. Someone is longing for the conflict in a relationship to end. For some people, the New Year is simply last year warmed over.

I have experienced this myself. With job cuts and hiring freezes, life had become uncertain. But as I reflected on God's promises, I knew God would not abandon me in my time of need. I knew God had a future and a plan for me. I needed to revisit my days in Sunday school and the lesson of "Jesus loves me, this I know." I had to remember my days in young adult Bible study, where I learned that God provides in times of need. I had to go back to my call to ministry and remember the assurance I received that when God calls, God also qualifies. In looking back I could move forward.

I invite you "back to the future." Remember the blockbuster movie series from the 1980s? A mad scientist named Doc Brown experiments with time travel. One of his students, Marty (played by Michael J. Fox), joins him in his adventures. Marty meets Doc Brown at a time when Marty's family is dysfunctional, his school life is difficult, and his sense of direction and purpose are nonexistent. With Doc Brown, Marty moves back in time and finds his parents as teenagers getting to know each other. He interferes with his parent's planned meeting and, in a panic, Marty must try to reestablish what he messed up to ensure his own existence. Over the course of the trilogy of movies, Marty and Doc move back and forth from past to future and back to the present. They try desperately to reconnect events so that the future happens as it should.

All of us have a future that we need, at one time or another, to "get back to." We lose our way, we mess up our relationships, we become misguided and misdirected trying to do things our way. When we go back, our vision can be cleared for the future ahead. By going back, we can reclaim what we've lost and recapture a future that excites us in the ordinary time. Come back to God's future.

Jeremiah writes of a time of exile in the lives of the Hebrew people. They have lost their homes, their jobs, and many of their traditions. They have strayed from God's future for them. Nebuchadnezzar has carried away prophets, priests, elders, and others from their homes in Jerusalem to Babylon. Jeremiah, writing to those exiled, offers them words of comfort and hope as they face the future. Jeremiah's words from God tell the people to increase rather than decrease, to adjust to their circumstances, to be hospitable to their captors, and to pray for the land. Jeremiah tells the people that God has plans for them. God's plans will see to their prosperity and their peace. God's plans will not cause them harm. God's plans will recapture their hope and their God-ordained future. Jeremiah invites the people to look beyond their present circumstances back to God's future.

I believe that same invitation is extended to us this day. Come back to God's future. Look beyond your present circumstances, look back at the time you separated from God, stopped believing in God's work on your behalf, and then reenvision God's future for you. That future is exciting even in ordinary time. That future is secure even in times of psychological insecurity. The plans God has are for peace and prosperity, not for harm or evil. Come back to God's future.

Jeremiah understood the necessity of prayer. Prayer is always in order. Prayer can change minds and people. Prayer can change you and me. Prayer covers the soul with power and blankets uncertainty with confidence in God. I invite you to come back to God's future and pray for our world, for those who are good and evil, and for the journey we take together back to God's future. Come back to the prayer most familiar and hopeful: the Lord's Prayer. Remember and revisit this model prayer given to the disciples and to us, that our ordinary time might be filled with the extraordinary grace and hope of God's future through Jesus Christ. (Jacquetta Chambers)

Worship Aids

Invocation

Great God of creation, create anew in us this day desire to know you, willingness to follow you, and boldness to proclaim your word. Amen.

Call to Worship

We have come from far and near to meet our God who awaits us. Our hearts are open, our minds clear. Holy God, speak words of life, messages of hope, and stories of a future yet unknown in our worship today.

Benediction-Unison

Our Father, who art in heaven, hallowed be thy name. Thy kingdom come, thy will be done on earth as it is in heaven. Give us this day our daily bread. And forgive us our trespasses, as we forgive those who trespass against us. And lead us not into temptation, but deliver us from evil. For thine is the kingdom, the power, and the glory forever and ever. Amen. (*The United Methodist Hymnal* [Nashville: The United Methodist Publishing House, 1989], 895. Used by permission.) (Jacquetta Chambers)

JANUARY 13, 2013

Baptism of the Lord

Readings: Isaiah 43:1-7; Psalm 29; Acts 8:14-17; Luke 3:15-17, 21-22

Baptism of the Lord: Encounter at the River

Luke 3:15-17, 21-22

Today's text neatly breaks into two sections. The first part, Luke 3:15-17, is an encounter at the river between seekers for a savior and John the Baptist. The second section, Luke 3:21-22, is an encounter at the river with the Holy Trinity—God as Father, Son, and Holy Spirit. Full faithfulness impels the embrace of both encounters.

In the first encounter at the river, deep need pours forth in great longing. Scripture tells us "the people were filled with expectation." They long for a Messiah, a savior. The crush of life, the press of sin, the confusion of chaos surround them. They come to the river that day as spiritually parched people.

A story is told from the legend of Lawrence of Arabia about how, after capturing the strategic port city of Aqaba, he traveled with two young Bedouin guides across the desert to Cairo. On the way they suffered terrible hardship in a driving sandstorm and lost much of their water. One of the young Bedouins was lost in the storm and presumably died. Lawrence and the other young guide made it safely to Cairo. They staggered into the British Officer's Club half dead from dehydration and thirst. Walking up to the bar, Lawrence ordered lemonade for the parched lad, who inhaled the tall drink. Something like that level of deep longing and spiritual dehydration leads the people to seek out John at the River Jordan and ask "whether [he] might be the Messiah."

We are not that different. Our need for a savior is just as great. Our expectations are perhaps even higher. The thoughtful preacher will explore what brings us to the river of encounter seeking a savior. Casual claimants to the throne are plentiful. Recent political campaigns give vexing cry to our need for a savior (political or otherwise). The voracious consumer greed that devours our society echoes in its own distorted way our clamor. Symbolically we gather at the river of life and ask if this—money, possessions, power, pleasure, and the list goes on—is the savior we are looking for.

The answer we receive is the same answer John gave those seekers so long ago. "I baptize you with water, but the one who is more powerful than me is coming. I am not worthy to loosen the strap of his sandals. He will baptize you with the Holy Spirit and fire." To untie the sandals of another is the work of a slave. John is asserting that he is not even good enough to do a slave's work! Steadfastly, with passion, he points beyond himself. With an economy of words, John pushes us away from human solutions and directs us to the divine answer.

The baptism emphasis is on the Holy Spirit. Writing after Pentecost, Luke intends the reader to see the link to Pentecost. The divine rule of the Messiah dawns not with drums and loud clashing; he comes among us not with the pyrotechnics of a modern rock band but with the inhabitation of God's very presence in Holy Spirit and fire.

Verse 17 must be read in light of verse 16. The cleansing is not a nuclear exchange but eradication of the chaff of life, our overreliance on possessions, power, and pleasure.

Part two of the reading provides the answer to the one spoken of and referenced in the first part. The encounter at the river is with God in Christ through the power and presence of the Holy Spirit. Faithful proclamation must not miss the Trinitarian emphasis embedded in the baptism of Jesus.

Jesus Lord and Savior presents himself at the river in solidarity with us humans. The ancient Christian writers had a saying, "He (Jesus) became like us that we might be like him." In baptism the one human being who is also fully divine stands where we stand in submission to God. In baptism the blessing is poured out on him—"You are my Son, the Beloved; with you I am well pleased" (v. 22 NRSV). In baptism we encounter the God as Father, Son, and Holy Spirit.

Recall the old, faded children's sermon where the pastor calls the kids to the front and excitedly proclaims that he has something new to share with them. Smiling, cheery faces greet the pastor. "What," he exclaims, "is small and furry, has a big tail that often goes straight up, and runs around the yard gathering nuts?" One attentive little boy timidly raises his hand. "Yes, Jimmy," says the pastor. "Well," Jimmy hesitantly begins, "I know the answer is Jesus, but it sure sounds a lot like a squirrel."

The youngster is right. The answer is Jesus. But we have made it sound a lot like a squirrel. No one joins a church to keep the institution going. People come to church to meet God. They want to walk with Christ. They hunger to experience life in the Spirit. They long to live a life of great purpose in service to the Lord's kingdom-building work that will transform this battered and broken world. Unfortunately, we are often running around the yard picking up nuts.

We as the people of God proclaim this truth with an unapologetic call to a high Christology. The encounter at the river is an encounter with God in Christ through the Holy Spirit. The close relationship between Jesus and God is imprinted in the opening line. The heavens open while Jesus is praying. The Holy Spirit descends as the heavens open. It is significant that the Holy Spirit descends in bodily form. It is as if Luke wishes to insist that this is no mere casual action but rather a deeply intertwined relationship. The voice speaks of an all-embracing connection. "You are my Son, the Beloved; with you I am well pleased." *Son* can be also translated as "servant." This blessing is a sending. Jesus is about God's mission to the world.

Jesus is not simply a learned teacher or wonderful prophet. In this encounter at the river, God is present in each aspect of the Holy Trinity—Father/Creator, Son/Savior and Lord, Holy Spirit/Presence and Power. The encounter at the river posits the decisive question that must be answered again and again. Who is our Savior and Lord? To whom do we give our greatest allegiance and offer our deep obedience?

The text is clear. All of us have encounters at the river of life. In that encounter, to whom do we turn and whom do we follow? It is reported that the Christian theologian and philosopher Dallas Willard is often asked by students why he (as a philosophy professor) is a follower of Christ. Dr. Willard is reported to answer with the response—"Can you think of anyone better to follow?"

Lectionary Commentary

Isaiah 43:1-7

The words "Fear not!" ("Don't fear") ring out over this text. For Christians this is a precursor of the often-repeated angelic message to the shepherds of Luke 2. The context is important. It is spoken in a time and to a culture experiencing loss and defeat and facing a future with much to fear. We are not to fear because we have been redeemed (notice the past tense). God has acted and is acting on behalf of a people named and claimed. While the text is addressed to the nation as a whole, it has an intimate, relational character. Verse 2 may give reference to the deliverance of the exodus "pass through the waters." Verses 3 and 4 state the larger geopolitical claim of God at work in the world to save and redeem. With a sweep that encompasses nations, there is also a tender sense of intimate love—"Because you are precious in my eyes, / you are honored, and I love you. / I give people in your place, / and nations in exchange for your life." The passage's majestic sweep and emphasis calls us to place our trust in God even (especially!) in a dangerous and unknown future full of threats and fears.

Acts 8:14-17

This brief passage from Acts seals the connection of baptism with the descent of the Holy Spirit. Baptism is the sign of the Spirit's presence. The text lifts before us the importance and role of the Holy Spirit. As such, it is a twin invitation to both preach on the doctrine of the Holy Spirit and proclaim the Spirit's indwelling baptism. In this passage Luke connects the baptism of Samaritans with the baptism of Jesus in Luke 3.

A number of other insights are suggested in the text. First, the Samaritans were an often-despised enemy. Their baptism with the Holy Spirit signifies true unity through the Spirit's presence. None are excluded from the good news of God's love. Second, the baptism also reminds the faithful of Pentecost. In baptism by the Holy Spirit, the Samaritans are brought into full communion in the church. There are no second-class Christians. There are obvious lessons on how newly baptized members of a local church are to be brought into the center and not the edge of Christian fellowship. The Spirit evokes radical hospitality for all! (Mike Lowry)

Worship Aids

Call to Worship (Adapted from Isaiah 43:1-7)

Thus says the Lord God, do not fear, for I have redeemed you.
The Lord has called us by name and we are God's.
Do not fear, for God is with you!
We are precious in the Lord's sight, honored, and loved.
Together we come to worship the greatness and love of God.
Together we come before the Lord in joy and celebration!

Prayer (Source unknown)

Lord, as I enter the water to bathe, I remember my baptism.
Wash me by your grace. Fill me with your Spirit.
Renew my soul.
I pray that I might live as your child today and honor you in all that I do.

Benediction

As the Holy Spirit descended upon our Savior so long ago at the River Jordan, may the same Spirit descend upon you this day. Remember your baptism, and in remembering know the love of God with you and with all this day forever more. Go into the world with the sure conviction that God goes with you as Father, Son, and Holy Spirit. Amen. (Mike Lowry)

Lord's Prayer II

Second in a Series of Two on Beginning a New Year with the Lord's Prayer

Matthew 6:5-15; Luke 11:1-4

This is our second message on praying the Lord's Prayer. We turn our focus to the request of the disciples, "Lord, teach us to pray, just as John taught his disciples." This request was not out of line or foreign to Jesus. Jesus constantly modeled prayer. He often went aside to pray. He prayed on mountains and before healings, and he admonished his disciples to stay awake and pray.

What are we to make of the reference to John's teachings on prayer? The Bible does not give us examples of these teachings, but we know of John's upbringing in a devoted and religious family. As the son of a priest, John would be familiar with the traditions of prayer in the temple. Jesus' disciples want to follow the lead of this charismatic religious leader. As followers of Jesus, they wanted to know how to pray. They were concerned about the proper way to pray. They wanted to know just how to pray so that their prayers could be effective. What Jesus offers them retains tradition while refining prayer to its fundamental parts.

Jesus promotes first the two most important aspects of prayer. These are primary, prioritized, and placed first in the model prayer. In Matthew's version (vv. 9-10 NRSV): "Our Father in heaven, / hallowed be your name. / Your kingdom come. / Your will be done, / on earth as it is in heaven." The model prayer begins with a statement of adoration and praise. The prayer Jesus uses to teach his disciples how to pray begins with praise for our God. What a significant point for all of us who long to know how to pray. Prayer begins with adoration and praise. Even when we have issues, needs, and requests, they do not come before our praise. What a wonderful opportunity we have to begin our prayer with praise. Think of it as acknowledging who God is and honoring God's presence on earth. We honor and bless God's name when we pray. Beginning with praise also enables us to focus on something other than ourselves. Praise invites the calmness and peace of seeing our blessings. It provides the opportunity to look at what we have rather than what we need. This year will be enriched as we learn how to pray.

The second aspect of prayer is a petition for divine intervention. Verse 2 of Matthew's version says, "Your kingdom come. / Your will be done, / on earth as it is in heaven." This is a desire and a request for God's reign, God's reality, and God's will to come into our midst. Jesus taught his disciples that prayer should include a sincere yearning for God's presence and power, and all of the possibilities they bring. When we ask for God's presence, we hunger and thirst for God's righteousness. As we ask in prayer, we will be filled. We will receive fulfillment of that hunger (see Matthew 5).

The prayer includes, along with petition for divine presence, the willingness to surrender. The model prayer asks that God's will be done on earth as it is in heaven. Within that request is a perceived willingness to surrender to God's will. Jesus taught his disciples that in prayer we must seek the will of God. We might not know what that will is, but we can be assured it is for our good and God's glory. Lord, let your will be done.

Here is a story of steadfast prayer: Bill, a man in his eighties arose every morning about six o'clock and prayed. He began his prayers by looking out of his window and praising God for the sun or the rain, the clouds or the storms. Whatever the weather on that day, Bill praised God for it. One day his great-grandson awakened to hear his grandfather praising God. The boy looked outside and saw storms, and he asked, "Grandpa, why are you thanking God for the rain? We can't go to the park." Bill told his great-grandson, "On days like today, I thank God for thinking of the grass and crops and animals that need rain. I know that real soon God will think about us again, and I can wait." What an awesome testimony to surrendering to God's will! At times it may seem that God is not thinking about us, about our situations or our circumstances. We can trust that as God attends to the needs of others, God knows what we need, and God cares. Amen. (Jacquetta Chambers)

Worship Aids

Call to Worship (Luke 11:1-4)

Jesus was praying in a certain place. When he finished, one of his disciples said, "Lord, teach us to pray, just as John taught his disciples."
Jesus told them, "When you pray, say:
[All:] 'Father, uphold the holiness of your name.
Bring in your kingdom.
Give us the bread we need for today.
Forgive us our sins,
for we also forgive everyone who has wronged us.
And don't lead us into temptation.' "

Pastoral Prayer

Holy God, this day, we praise your name, we honor your presence with us and we seek your will for our lives. We gather this day relying on your guidance and your direction to help us make decisions and live God-fearing lives. You know the needs of this community. You know the hurts and pains, difficulties and desires of each of us. God, please meet us at the deepest places of our needs and provide healing. Restore our faith in you, your church, and your ministries. Challenge us when we become too comfortable, and comfort us when we are weighted down with challenges. Hear our prayers, O God, our Savior and Lord. Amen.

Benediction

Go forth now in the name of our God. Transform the world with prayer. Teach others to pray, and believe that God answers prayer. Amen. (Jacquetta Chambers)

JANUARY 20, 2013

Second Sunday after Epiphany

Readings: Isaiah 62:1-5; Psalm 36:5-10; 1 Corinthians 12:1-11; John 2:1-11

Vindication, Restoration, and Salvation

Isaiah 62:1-5

Navajo people can identify with the Israelites of Isaiah more easily than they can the dominant culture. After years of poor relations with the Spanish, the Apaches, and the U.S. government, it was determined the best solution was to remove the Navajos from their native land to a reservation located 450 miles away and overseen by the U.S. Army. After a final standoff at Canyon de Chelly, the Navajos surrendered to Kit Carson, and they began the "long walk" to Bosque Redondo in northeastern New Mexico. In January 1864, eight thousand five hundred men, women, and children left Arizona to walk to their "new reservation." After inhabiting more than 3.5 million acres, they lived on forty square miles for four years. To them it was a prison camp; they were in exile from their land and their four sacred mountains.

Throughout their ordeal, they kept their culture alive. They spoke Navajo. They told their creation story to their children. They sang their songs. They practiced their spiritual ways as much as they could. And they always looked forward to the time when they would be back on the land given to them from the beginning of time.

The Israelites had been in captivity in Babylon for seventy years. They told the creation story to their children. They sang their songs. They practiced their spiritual ways as much as they could. And they always looked forward to the time when they would be back on the land given to them from the beginning of time. They wanted to tell their stories, sing their songs, and hold their festivals on their own land.

On June 18, 1868, the remaining Navajos, a remnant, left Bosque Redondo to return to their homeland. Their homes had been destroyed. No crops were growing. Their herds were gone. For many, even their families were gone. All the time they had been exiled, they dreamed of coming home, but now the hard work of rebuilding their lives began.

The Israelites came back to a city where the temple was in ruins. The walls were falling down. Their spiritual center was in pieces. So their hard work began. And they did well for a while—but it was a renovation project.

While our children were in junior high, we began a renovation project on the parsonage. We were dependent upon church members for the labor, and most of them were only available on the weekends—which means Saturday in a preacher's life. It was exciting in the beginning, even fun. But after a few weeks, the project seemed to grow, the mess got bigger, and we had fewer workers. Everyone got discouraged and tired, not only of the project but of being dirty and tired. The dream with which we started grew dim.

What we needed was to hear the words Isaiah told to the Israelites. "You will be a splendid garland / in the LORD's hand, / a royal turban in the palm of God's hand" (v. 3). Compared to rebuilding a culture and a city, our project was tiny, but we still felt the loneliness and the overwhelming feeling that there was no end.

Isaiah reminds the Israelites that Zion will be restored and their salvation achieved as promised. They are Yahweh's chosen people, and soon their "vindication" will "[shine] out like the dawn" (NRSV). Israel's salvation, restoration, and vindication will come through Yahweh's power and grace, not the hard work of the people. They will be transformed and given a new name.

Life is difficult. It seems that no matter how much money one makes, how new her car is, how big his home is, how healthy they are, there is always something that could be better. Perhaps our children are having difficulty, or our parents. Or someone is struggling to hold a marriage together or to recover from a divorce. Or disease has overtaken a person, and all she or he can see is more and more treatments. We do the best we can, and we see so little progress.

This is when we need to hear Isaiah's words. There is only so much we can do with our own hands. We are human, created in the image of Yahweh, but still just flesh and bones. We must trust in the grace and power of one who loves us and wants only the best for us. Scripture tells us that Yahweh is the same yesterday, today, and tomorrow (see Hebrews 13:8). Doesn't that mean Yahweh wants us to have what Yahweh wanted for those Israelites—restoration, salvation, and vindication?

Isaiah didn't tell the Israelites to quit building the temple. He didn't say, "It's all right if you chase foreign idols like others have." Isaiah didn't excuse them from holding Yahweh's festivals or keeping Sabbath. He didn't say Yahweh's covenants were broken. He said while you keep on doing what is right, remember that your vindication will come as a bright light. You will be restored and your salvation is promised.

Tomorrow is Martin Luther King Jr. Day—a day in which North Americans commemorate the fight against racial discrimination in federal and state laws. Those who experience discrimination will tell you the battle is not over; it is perhaps more subtle but still present. Will the day come when we truly know equality? Will we see one another as Yahweh sees us, each one unique and each one with different gifts to offer? As a world, we have a long way to go.

The Navajo were sent to Bosque Redondo in an attempted ethnic cleansing. When they returned from exile, their population and land had been reduced. The lament had to begin again. Today they are the largest Native nation and have successfully enlarged their land to over sixteen million acres. Their life is still hard; some parts of the reservation have no running water or electricity. Alcohol, diabetes, and high unemployment affect all areas of the reservation. A remnant still carries on, keeping the traditions, speaking the language, and teaching their children in the face of assimilation.

The Israelites returned from seventy years in Babylonian exile to destruction and ruin in Jerusalem. The remnant had to begin again. They kept their culture alive and even now, it is thriving and has spread beyond the borders of Israel.

Our lives will go on, with and without difficulties. We will do what we can and do what is right, remembering that our vindication and our restoration are waiting for us. (Raquel Mull)

Lectionary Commentary

1 Corinthians 12:1-11

Corinth was filled with idols, Dionysus, Isis, and Artemis to name a few. It would be easy to see how the people could be tempted to worship another deity. Paul writes that they, the ones who call Jesus Lord, are to be united by the Spirit. No gift is better than another and all gifts are not given to one person. Each gift is given by the Spirit for one purpose, for the common good.

John 2:1-11

A wedding customarily lasted at least a week, and it was the groom's responsibility to provide the wine for the event. Scripture does not tell us what day of the wedding this was or how many guests were in attendance other than Jesus, his mother, and his disciples. We do know the wine ran out, but not why Jesus' mother thought he could fix the problem.

The first of several miracles to show Jesus as the Messiah, this story is an example of how the ordinary can be transformed into the extraordinary. The resulting wine, six jars of good wine, also shows Yahweh's generosity for his people. Others have connected the setting of a wedding as an illustration of Yahweh's concern for families. (Raquel Mull)

Worship Aids

Call to Worship

Come into the presence of the Lord.

We have left the safety and warmth of our homes to be in your presence.

Come, may your steps be steady and purposeful.

We have come to hear your word and hear the direction for our lives.

Come; raise your voices in praise and worship.

All: We come to bless you and to hear your promises as we strive to do what is right in your sight.

Benediction

Go, walking in God's light; doing what is right and knowing your salvation and restoration are promised; in the name of the Father, Son, and Holy Spirit. Amen.

Words of Assurance

Lord, we are reminded that even if we feel different from those around us, we are loved. Regardless of our skin color, our political views, even our past, your forgiveness and love are given to us. We are redeemed! (Raquel Mull)

Parents Teaching

First in a Series of Three on Home Improvement

Deuteronomy 6:4-9

It must be a common experience for new parents. At some point as your child grows, you notice that he or she is imitating you. I had been a father for two or three years when I saw that my son, who many people had said resembled me, was mimicking me. I found that not so much cute as sobering, maybe even a little intimidating.

During my late teens and early adulthood, I had been what I now consider a nominal Christian, and had gotten serious only after marrying and formally joining a church with my wife. The idea that my son would be following and imitating me led me to seek God's help in earnest, so that the life I would lead thereafter would be a positive example for one who could closely observe it.

I feel certain that this desire to follow God more closely while we are being followed by our biological offspring is itself a gift from our creator. It is a great gift, because for many adults it also provides the impetus to return to church after having wandered away from it at the time we moved out of our parents' homes.

When we pick up the Bible and look for examples and advice to guide us in our task of parenting, what do we find? Not surprisingly, there is quite a bit of good advice to be found. The scripture I am most likely to quote is Proverbs 22:6 (NRSV), "Train children in the right way, / and when old, they will not stray." The book of Proverbs clearly tasks parents with teaching their children, and instructs children to listen to and heed their parents: "Hear, my child, your father's instruction, / and do not reject your mother's teaching" (1:8 NRSV).

When Moses instructs Israel in how to conduct themselves once they come to possess their promised land, he tells them that they must love the Lord and teach their children to do the same, talking to them when they are at home (Deuteronomy 6:4-9). This passage, the beginning of the *Shema*, places the education of the chosen people's children at home, in the house of their parents, with the parents instructing them.

I remember being asked to serve on a school district committee a little over twenty years ago. We were asked to make recommendations regarding appropriate curriculum for "character education." A fine idea, I thought, that we are teaching children what good character is and that they need to develop it, but when did they stop learning that at home? It is a common complaint in our American school system that teachers are expected to teach more and more in the way of life skills, on top of the academics we all expect students to learn. That expectation of teachers comes as a result of neglect by parents.

Perhaps we should not be surprised that many parents have gone to the other extreme, taking their children out of school and back into their homes, where they now teach them character and academics.

In addition to the advice to instruct, does the Bible show us examples of parenting from which we can deduce the kind of parents God wants us to be? Some positive examples come to mind. One of the first things we learn about Job is that he would rise early when the feast days were done and offer burnt offerings for each of his children because they might have sinned and cursed God in their hearts (Job 1:5).

We also see parents who go to Jesus for their children's sake. The synagogue leader Jairus pleads with Jesus to save his twelve-year-old daughter, risking his position within the Jewish hierarchy (Mark 5:22-43). In John's Gospel (4:46-54), a royal official begs Jesus to come and heal his dying son.

In Joshua 24:15, Joshua makes the choice to serve the one true God for himself and his household an example, which is held up by groups like the Promise Keepers, groups that encourage men to be a spiritual presence in their families' lives and to take responsibility for their spiritual lives. Second Timothy 1:5 gives a mother's example, as the author is reminded of Timothy's sincere faith, which first lived in his grandmother Lois, then his mother Eunice, and now in Timothy.

We normally look to Jesus for our example—since he did not become a parent, should we look to his parents? We know that Mary and Joseph were successful parents (Jesus grew in wisdom and favor in their care), but the Gospels do not tell us much about their parenting. Matthew tells of Joseph saving Jesus from Herod by fleeing with his wife and child in the night to Egypt (Matthew 2:13-15). In Luke's Gospel, we read of a trip to Jerusalem for Passover when Jesus was twelve and how Joseph and Mary then traveled homeward for a day before realizing that Jesus was not anywhere to be found among the people they had traveled with (Luke 2:41-52). They found him in the temple, discussing Scripture with the teachers. (We don't know what consequences he suffered for not letting them know where he was.)

What about God, *the* Parent? Let us come back full circle to that phenomenon of a new parent wanting to provide a godly example for children to follow. Our God-given instincts guide us well. Jesus called God "Abba, Father," and he taught and invited us to pray to God as, "Our Father in heaven . . ." (Matthew 6:9 NRSV).

If we study God in relationship with humanity, we see a parent who never stops loving the creation. God goes through cycle after cycle of humans doing evil and suffering, crying out and seeking forgiveness and rescue; of God forgiving and rescuing again and again. One of my favorite portraits of God as a parent is in the book of Jonah. God sends Jonah on a prophetic mission. Jonah proves to be not just a reluctant prophet but also a petulant, willful child. God demonstrates slowness in anger and abundant steadfast love. May we offer the same grace to our own children. (Harris Worcester)

Worship Aids

Call to Worship (Based on Psalm 36)

Your steadfast love, O Lord, reaches far and wide, high and low.
How precious is your steadfast love, O God!
All may take refuge in the shadow of your wings.
In your light we see light.
How precious is your steadfast love, O God!

Pastoral Prayer

Most gracious God, we thank you for that spirit of adoption through which your son Jesus taught us to call you Father. Thank you for your love that has remained steadfast through all the many times in which our love has failed and we have done evil in your sight. Grant us mercy again this day. Amen.

Benediction

Now send us forth, O Lord, as children of the living God, determined to be just like you. Amen. (Harris Worcester)

JANUARY 27, 2013

Third Sunday after Epiphany

Readings: Nehemiah 8:1-3, 5-6, 8-10; Psalm 19; 1 Corinthians 12:12-31a; Luke 4:14-21

A Time for Mourning or Joy

Nehemiah 8:1-3, 5-6, 8-10

I am old-fashioned; I admit it. I have even learned that I might be a tiny bit prejudiced. I have a small problem with some of the younger members of our society. Their clothes and jewelry don't bother me too much. It takes quite a bit for me to be shocked at hair color and style. I don't have to listen to their music, so I am not even taking that into consideration. No, what bothers me is their lack of manners.

I make a point of being attentive to the cashier when I am in the checkout lane because I wouldn't want someone talking on the phone when I am doing my job and because it is polite. Now, I find myself waiting in line while the customer in front of me is multitasking—fishing for her credit card and carrying on a conversation on her cell phone. I talk to people who are checking their mail, texts, and Facebook, and I wonder if they hear anything I say!

I was taught the proper response when one receives a compliment is "thank you." The correct response when thanked is "you're welcome." And if the answer is affirmative, the appropriate response is "yes," not "yeah." As a society we teach our culture to the generation that follows us. What happens when most of the culture forgets the right responses? Could the Bible be instructive here?

The people of Israel demand that Ezra bring the book of the Law of Moses to the court and read it so all the people might hear the words. He begins, and they stand for hours to listen. They give their undivided attention to Ezra; they listen properly, because they don't want to miss a word. Ezra ensures their understanding by having scholars and priests on hand to interpret so the people can fully comprehend the reading. It is crucial for the people to understand and respond properly to the reading of the law.

For Ezra, the scribe, it is not enough that the people of Israel understand; he wants them to respond properly. Although united in this demand, they have been in exile without much of their culture and religion. They have neglected the words given to their ancestors and have forgotten the proper responses. Their immediate response is to bow down and worship the Lord. Not bad. Then, as they begin to understand the Law and how far they are from keeping it, they begin to weep. Their responses are emotional.

Nehemiah and Ezra correct them, "'This day is holy to the LORD your God. Don't mourn or weep. . . . Go, eat rich food, and drink something sweet,' he said to them, 'and send portions of this to any who have nothing ready! This day is holy to our LORD. Don't be sad, because the joy from the LORD is your strength!'" Again, all the people follow these instructions. Ezra did what was asked, and he went the next step—Ezra taught them the proper response.

Preachers are in a challenging position. We not only proclaim the word but also interpret it for the congregation. People depend on preachers for the truth and correct interpretation.

Nehemiah 8:1 states that all the people of Israel wanted to hear the word. Ezra and Nehemiah may have had it easier in one sense—they were absolutely sure why the people gathered. We who represent mainline denominations do not always have that assurance. Before I preach, I often pray, "We have gathered in your name to hear your word for our lives and for this, your church." I wonder how true this is. Compare today's response to hearing the word to the response of the people of Israel; perhaps you can see my wonderment.

Do we really hear the word properly? Instead of questioning the response, perhaps we should question the preparation of our hearts and spirits to properly hear God's word. Do we really come expecting to understand, or do we feel we have heard the Scriptures numerous times and know them, forgetting they hold the power to change lives? Have we neglected them, forgetting to put them in our hearts and minds, thwarting their ability to convict us of sin and seeing the need for change? Are we, as individuals or as a church, so prideful that we believe that we are good enough, that these words are written for others?

If I were to take this scenario and apply it to the ill-mannered of our society, success would depend upon them recognizing their present state and asking for instruction. So far, that hasn't happened, and I am not holding my breath. I could be an Ezra and tell them how rude they are and what they need to do to be acceptable in my eyes, but somehow I don't see that as working effectively—it seems a better recipe for resentment and rebellion. I could offer classes in etiquette, but attendance would probably depend on grandparents forcing their grandchildren to attend, with equally poor results.

Nehemiah, Ezra, and other leaders had the interpretation of the Law of Moses ready to share. They waited until they were asked, all the while following the Commandments and reading the Law for their own understanding and edification. They practiced faith, believing that the people would eventually ask and be ready to hear.

I am reminded from another scripture in today's lectionary reading that even those who don't fit my preferences for social behavior must not be excluded from our midst. "If the foot says, 'I'm not part of the body because I'm not a hand,' does that mean it's not part of the body? If the ear says, 'I'm not part of the body because I'm not an eye,' does that mean it's not part of the body?" (1 Corinthians 12:15-16). Neither can one's ability to "properly" hear and respond to the word be a prerequisite for participating in the body of Christ. No, let judgment be done by God as we prepare our hearts to hear and respond to the word, having faith that when questioned, we will be ready. (Raquel Mull)

Lectionary Commentaries

1 Corinthians 12:12-31a

Early philosophers used the idea of a body as a picture of unity and oneness, though they were usually illustrating a society or a government. Paul describes the church as a body with many parts, all of which are needed. Specifically addressing the gifts of the spirit, Paul wants the Corinthians to accept them all and not to put more value on one than another. All gifts are given for the good of the whole and all together make it possible for the body to do more.

Luke 4:14-21

Jesus begins his public ministry in Galilee and visits the synagogue there. The Galilean Jews experience oppression, poverty, heavy taxation, and sickness under Roman rule. When Jesus reads Isaiah's words, his audience can relate to them—they want good news, release, sight, freedom; in short, they want restoration. They are looking for a leader and want to believe that Jesus is the one to lead a rebellion. Galilee was not the center of Jewish power. Jews and Gentiles lived beside each other, so Luke foreshadows the time when God will restore both communities. (Raquel Mull)

Worship Aids

Call to Worship

Dearly beloved, leave your worries and cares behind. Let not your thoughts distract you from hearing God's word. Lord, open our hearts, minds, and eyes that we may indeed hear your word for our lives. May we see where change is needed. Give us the courage to make those changes that we may better show your love. Amen.

Prayer of Confession

Dear Lord, how easy it is to judge. We confess we want people to be more like ourselves; we fail to recognize how boring the world would be if there were no challenges or opportunities to show your love to different folk. Let us remember you created people using your great imagination, and all are worthy of your love. Forgive us. When we are tested, may we be found faithful to your teachings. In the name of Christ. Amen.

Words of Assurance

Hear and understand: the Law is given that you might know unity and joy! Be of one mind and praise God. Amen.

Benediction

You have heard God's word. May it be planted in your hearts to strengthen you to love others in God's name. (Raquel Mull)

Marriage Lessons

Second in a Series of Three on Home Improvement

Matthew 7:24-27

Our "Home Improvement" series continues with the topic of marriage, and we begin by wondering if this is the right metaphor for talking about marriage. I get this uncomfortable image of an amateur fix-it guy like myself getting out an assortment of serious power tools, borrowed or unwisely purchased, studying plans I don't entirely understand, and then undertaking a job that is beyond me, attempting something that might lead me to do serious harm to the house.

If one had a serious problem with their marriage, furthermore, one might prefer the format of one of those shows in which they raze the original structure and then build a much nicer one in its place, with the help of lots of volunteers and donations. There are definitely things that couples can do to strengthen their marriages, but there is no substitute for getting it right from the start.

In Matthew's Gospel, Jesus tells us of the wise person who built his house on the rock. "The rain fell, the floods came, and the wind blew and beat against that house. It didn't fall because it was firmly set on bedrock" (7:25). In contrast, a foolish builder builds on the sand, and when the rainstorms come, the house falls.

Before entering the ministry, I was a judge for five years, and so I performed a number of weddings in my capacity as a magistrate. My first two weddings, oddly enough, were for couples who had been married before to each other, had divorced, and then had tried marriage with one or two other partners before getting another divorce and reuniting. Perhaps they were too quick to throw in the towel that first time. Or perhaps they needed the perspective that multiple spouses gave them to appreciate that first one.

I vividly remember one wedding I did not perform—in fact, none of the magistrates available would do it. The couple was probably around twenty, give or take a couple of years, and he was nicely dressed up in cowboy fashion, and she had on a pretty dress, which nonetheless seemed way too short to wear into a courthouse, much less to one's own wedding. From what the clerks were able to gather, this couple had met at a nightspot sometime in the previous 24 to 48 hours, and they were in a hurry to marry, not wanting even to sober up first. Texas has a 72-hour waiting period between the time one applies for a marriage license and the time it can be issued, and this young couple discovered they could not get any of us to perform a wedding without the license.

We all know that we need to build our marriages on bedrock, but failed marriages are so common today. We all have witnessed marriages that seemed to be stable and weren't and those that we didn't give much of a chance but that weathered many storms and still seem strong. Part of our human condition is that the earliest part of a relationship, when a couple is smitten and moves quickly toward marriage, intoxicated with love, is perhaps the time when we are least able to reflect carefully on the relationship and the quality of the ground.

There are so many variables in successful marriages. I am fifteen years older than my wife, which places us in different generations (I'm a Boomer, she's a Gen X). She was raised Pentecostal, and I was raised a Quaker. Those are substantive differences. After we married, we set about finding a church in which we would both be comfortable worshiping, and after more than a year, we joined a small United Methodist church. We joined the choir together, and we took Bible studies together, and we got involved, separately or together, but in our church.

We have built the house of our marriage on the rock of our Christian faith, and in more than two decades together we have weathered a variety of storms. We know that God made us to be together: "a man leaves his father and mother and embraces his wife, and they become one flesh" (Genesis 2:24). Just as what we do as part of the body of Christ affects the whole body, so it is with the one flesh we become in marriage. If we profane or pollute ourselves, we contaminate the body.

If we will do our best to follow Christ and love as he taught us—love God with all our heart, soul, mind, and strength, and love our neighbors as ourselves—then we will be good people in any relationship. If the two of us, husband and wife, are in an active relationship with Jesus and striving in our lives to be Christlike, then our relationship cannot help but be blessed.

I cannot stress enough how beneficial it is for a couple to study the Scriptures together. Have you ever noticed how couples classes at larger, well-established churches tend to have several couples who have been in that class together for several decades? That is no coincidence. As we study how Jesus taught his followers to have mature and healthy relationships, we learn so much we can apply in our lives. If a couple can speak the truth to each other in love, they should be able to work through any problem.

Marriage is a holy estate into which you and your spouse enter by making a covenant with each other and your God. The language is old because marriage goes back to the very beginning, when God decided that we should not be alone, but should be in relationship with a mate, and together be in relationship with God. That's just part of how much love God has shown us. Thanks be to God! (Harris Worcester)

Worship Aids

Call to Worship (Based on 1 Corinthians 12:12-31a)

This body is one, and has many members.
We, though many, are one body; so it is with Christ.
We were all baptized in the one Spirit—Jews or Greeks, slaves or free. We all drink of the one Spirit.
We, though many, are one body; so it is with Christ.

Pastoral Prayer

Most gracious God, help us construct our lives on the solid rock of your holy word, with your steadfast love to shelter us. We love you, Lord; lead us from here out into the storm, and we will go gladly. Amen.

Benediction

Those whom you have gifted, now send forth together as the body of Christ, O Lord, ready to build your kingdom. Amen. (Harris Worcester)

FEBRUARY 3, 2013

Fourth Sunday after Epiphany

Readings: Jeremiah 1:4-10; Psalm 71:1-6; 1 Corinthians 13:1-13; Luke 4:21-30

Are You Ready?

Jeremiah 1:4-10

Have you heard the expression, "Leaders are born, not made"? In contrast to this statement, many workshops, classes, and events attempt to teach leadership. Obviously, we need leaders, but can you learn that in a class? On any self-help shelf in any bookstore, religious or secular, you will find books, CDs, and magazines to instruct leaders. Franklin Covey, a company once known for daily planners to help organize time, now specializes in leadership training. They still sell calendars and even have one titled "Leadership" with inspiring quotations from a diverse set of leaders.

Jeremiah had no course in leadership. In fact, when he was called, Jeremiah learned that he was chosen to be a prophet before his birth! Jeremiah's destiny had been determined by God before his mother and father knew if their child was to be a boy or a girl.

God, creator of the universe, the One who is still creating, the One who controls the universe, still uses human beings to do God's will, people like Moses, Jonah, and Jeremiah.

Once the call is issued, an answer is required from the person called. Jeremiah's first response is "I don't know how to speak / because I'm only a child" (v. 6). When Moses received his call, he asked the Lord to send someone else (Exodus 4:13) after his excuse that he didn't speak eloquently failed. Jonah tried to run away. To each one called, a promise is given; God will not abandon us. God told Moses, "I'll be with you" (Exodus 3:12a). Jonah's pleas were heard because God was with him. Jeremiah heard, "Don't be afraid of them, / because I'm with you to rescue you" (v. 8). God gave each messenger help and encouragement to be a leader and to give God's message to God's people.

God issues the call, and we are to go forth in faith. Just as Abram was called to leave his country and go to an unknown land (Genesis 12:1), we may not be sure of our next step. God promises to be with us; what lies ahead may include danger, loneliness, rejection, and hostility. The message God asks Jeremiah to deliver is not what people want to hear. They want to hear that they are pretty good, they will be blessed and suffer no more hardship, poverty, pain, or sorrow. Instead, God's words are "repent or perish."

God's call on Jeremiah's life also includes power: "This very day I appoint you / over nations and empires, / to dig up and pull down, / to destroy and demolish, / to build and plant" (v. 10). This is tremendous power given to a young man who recognizes his inadequacies. God sees what Jeremiah cannot see in himself. Jeremiah is chosen and accepts the opportunity to fulfill his destiny in his yes to God.

God's call on Moses, Jeremiah, and Jonah is specific: "I will tell you what to say"; "I have put my words in your mouth" (NRSV). Jeremiah's calling is to bear the divine word to Judah and beyond. That is his task, not to please humans, but to be God's voice to a backsliding world.

The good news is that God has not forgotten Israel; God is still speaking to them through Jeremiah. God wants them to repent and come back to God as God's people. Jeremiah has a formidable job, and he does it, knowing that he is responsible only to deliver the message—how the people respond is their responsibility.

We also live in a backsliding nation. As a culture founded upon biblical principles, we may think we are not as bad as the corrupt nation of Judah, but when the number of believers continually decreases, is it time for a word? And from whom should it come?

You know the answer. We claim we have the truth, and his name is Jesus. We have hope for our present and for our future: Jesus. We need only watch the evening news for one night to see where hope, love, and forgiveness are needed, not across the ocean but right in our own backyards.

Look at yourself. You are not too young or too old. The excuse that you are not a good public speaker was not valid for Moses or Jeremiah, and it isn't going to work for you either. If you are not good with words, then proclaim God's word with action. Help teach a Sunday school class or provide snacks for the children's program or Vacation Bible School.

Enable another to be the voice by watching the other leaders' children while they work with the children from the community.

Jonah tried to run away. It didn't work for him, and it won't work for us now because there is too much hopelessness and need in the world. We are surrounded by people who need to hear what God expects from God's people. I know of a young woman being raised in a home of "dry alcoholics." While these folks don't get drunk, they apparently have the manipulative and angry lifestyle often found in those who do drink. Our towns and cities need role models for living a Christian lifestyle, they need to see that following Christ is not dull or restrictive, but challenging and joyful.

God does not change; God is the same yesterday, today, and tomorrow. God still calls ordinary people like Moses and Jeremiah to extraordinary jobs with supernatural results. Even these great prophets were a little reluctant at the beginning of their call, but with God's presence and guidance, they succeeded and were indeed leaders. God is calling. Are you ready? (Raquel Mull)

Lectionary Commentary

1 Corinthians 13:1-13

The love chapter of the Bible instructs us in how to live with one another. It is not surprising that this passage is often used at weddings. Paul compares the gift of love to the spiritual gifts of prophecy and speaking in tongues, which have led to division and which distract the church from its mission. Paul reminds the people that the gift of love is like God's own love in Jesus, and it never fades or ends. Paul's hope for the church in Corinth is that they will mature in their faith and not rely on outward signs.

Luke 4:21-30

This is the second part of the Luke passage begun last week. Invited by the local officials, Jesus is teaching at a Galilean synagogue. At first he is welcomed, but by the end of his teaching, the crowds are so angry at Jesus' proclamations they are intent on murder! The Galileans greet Jesus as Joseph's son, not as the Son of God; the man they reject is the Messiah. Jesus reminds his listeners that prophets of old were sent to Gentiles instead of the Israelites, implying that the Israelites did not recognize the messengers of God. (Raquel Mull)

Worship Aids

Invocation

Dear Lord, let us take a deep breath and listen to the silence. Let us enter this holy space anticipating that we will hear you calling us to be your children and your voice. Prepare us for your service, strengthened by your word and your Holy Spirit. Amen.

Prayer of Confession

Merciful God, we come before you, mindful of Jeremiah, who in his youth and fear trembled at the task before him. We, too, are fearful, more concerned with what others think of us than how we might fulfill your desires. Forgive us for assuming that others will answer your call and hoping that we might sit by in silence, even in the midst of a hurting world. Create in us a clean and sturdy heart that we might be your faithful servants. Amen.

Words of Assurance

Hear the good news! The God of Moses, Jonah, and Jeremiah is our Lord too. When God calls, God equips us to do all that God requires. Say yes to God's call; trust in God's love.

Benediction

Go, in the name of the One who created us in the image of the divine and gave us the message of hope, love, and forgiveness to share with everyone we meet. Amen. (Raquel Mull)

Really? Retire?

Third in a Series of Three on Home Improvement

Luke 19:11-27

The final installment of our "Home Improvement" series takes a look at retirement. I will not attempt to advise you on how to go about setting aside the financial resources you will need. Life expectancy and the difficulty of providing for daily life in biblical times did not offer the option of living to 70 or 80, much less considering retirement.

Now we expect to live at least that long, and we hope to maintain a good quality of life as long as we are physically and mentally able. If we have a large extended family with a tradition of loving the Lord and each other and a tradition of care for elders, then we have a pretty good chance to live out in happiness the years God grants us. If our families are broken and distant and our resources are scarce, then we may find ourselves living in poverty and hoping to receive help from strangers.

Those who search the Bible looking for a retirement plan will find only one example. God instructs Moses regarding the Levites, who performed the priestly services in the tent of meeting, that they may begin serving at twenty-five, but that "from the age of fifty years they shall retire from the duty of the service and serve no more" (Numbers 8:23-26 NRSV). The priestly class was supported by the other tribes, so the requirement that priests stop serving at age fifty would have had no effect on their access to food and shelter.

The other biblical passage that we might consult in a discussion of retirement issues is a cautionary one, the parable of the rich fool (Luke 12:13-21). After warning the crowd to be on guard against greed, Jesus tells them of a rich man whose land produced abundantly, so much so that he did not have adequate space to store his crops. He decides to tear down his old barns and build larger ones so that he may store all his grain and goods. "I'll say to myself, You have stored up plenty of goods, enough for several years. Take it easy! Eat, drink, and enjoy yourself. But God said to him, 'Fool! Tonight you will die. Now who will get the things you have prepared for yourself?' " (vv. 19-20). Jesus concludes, "This is how it will be for those who hoard things for themselves and aren't rich toward God" (v. 21).

This lesson is about greed, not about saving for retirement—unless, of course, it is your plan to make a killing at whatever you do and then store away your money in a vault and start having a party and live off your stored booty as long as it lasts. A plan that consists of saving now to establish an income stream adequate to support you in future years is not the same. For one thing, you can make plans for that income to include your tithe. You can take John Wesley's approach of making as much as you can and saving as much as you can in order to have as much as possible to give away to the poor and to the church. Perhaps that would make you "rich toward God," to use Jesus' phrase.

I recommend that you consider a different parable as you contemplate retirement: the parable of the ten pounds (Luke 19:11-27; see also Matthew 25:14-30). A nobleman leaves the country on a mission to gain royal power for himself, and before leaving he entrusts ten servants each with ten pounds, which money they are to trade and do business with in his absence. When he returns, the ones who have traded and made more money are rewarded with proportionally greater responsibilities. The one who wrapped his money up and hid it is scolded, and his sum taken from him and given to the one who had made ten more pounds.

Our responsibility for the gifts God has given us is the stewardship issue to consider anew as we retire. Figure a portion for the church in your income calculations and projections, but also include a generous portion of the time you will have to give.

If you have managed your resources so well that you are able to retire at an earlier age, with your health intact, then celebrate that blessing by making the most of opportunities to use your gifts for building up God's kingdom. Perhaps you can put administrative skills to use for the church or for a nonprofit agency. Perhaps you know a second language and can serve as an interpreter on mission trips or during mission efforts at your church. Perhaps you can mentor a child who does not have the benefit of that kind of support from his or her parents. Perhaps you have a passion for a mission that you will start and lead for your church. Remember that when you do well, God will increase the responsibility with which you are entrusted.

I have known many retired couples who say with surprise and amusement that they are busier in retirement than they were before they stopped "working." What I have not seen is such a person or such a couple who did not seem happier, more fulfilled, and more blessed by the godly business undertaken in their new lives. Now *that* is being born again. (Harris Worcester)

Worship Aids

Call to Worship

The world teaches us to build bigger barns,
Teach us to be rich in you, dear Lord.
The world teaches us to hoard our treasure and throw a party,
Teach us to build our treasure in heaven, O Lord.
The Lord has given gifts to each of us,
Teach us to use and magnify your gifts for your glory, O God, giving freely of ourselves as Christ gave for us.

Pastoral Prayer

Most gracious God, we pray that as we are able to retire from worldly pursuits you will lead us ever deeper into your service. Whether you call us to be missionaries or prophets, helpers or leaders, we pray that we will have the faith to respond, "Here am I, Lord, your servant." Amen.

Benediction

Like the heavens, Lord, let our words tell of your glory, our lives proclaim your handiwork! Amen. (Harris Worcester)

FEBRUARY 10, 2013

Fifth Sunday after Epiphany

Readings: Isaiah 6:1-8, 9-13; Psalm 138; 1 Corinthians 15:1-11; Luke 5:1-11

Who Will Know You've Been Here?

Luke 5:1-11

How will people remember you? What is your legacy? What are you leaving behind that proves you were definitely here on earth? What is your contribution to our society?

Sometimes, we get so involved in keeping up with the bills, the kids, the job, and our families, we fail to keep the big picture in mind. When my husband and I work with a couple to be married, we ask them to set goals regarding their financial future, careers, families, and personal health. Then, to help get them started, we set up a step-by-step plan so they can begin achieving their goals. That plan always includes a time for evaluation, a reminder to keep the big picture in mind; they need to look up once in a while to see where they are in relation to each other and their circumstances.

Simon sits on the beach with his boat, washing his nets, tending to his livelihood. A stranger walks up to him, climbs into his boat, and asks Simon to put out a little way from the shore. Scripture says this stranger was accompanied by a crowd, but Simon is minding his own business. He doesn't leave his nets to go see what's happening. He is probably tired after being out all night and having caught no fish. He just wants to finish the job so he can get home, get some rest, and get ready to go out the next night.

After Jesus teaches the people on the shore, he asks Simon to go fishing again. Simon is reluctant at first. How would you feel if you, as a professional, were told by a stranger, obviously not a fisherman and maybe even noticeably not from this area, how and where to fish? Perhaps it is the message that Jesus delivers that gives Simon the small ray of hope that maybe there are fish to be caught. He has only two things to do: go out a little further and to let down his nets.

We know the end of the story, Simon catches so many fish that he has to call for his partners to come and help bring them all in so the nets don't break and the boat doesn't sink. Simon is so overwhelmed, he recognizes the power in Jesus and his own sinfulness. The assurance follows that from this day forward, Simon and his partners will fish for people.

Simon and his partners leave their boats, their nets, and even their fish to follow Jesus, believing in Jesus and his mission, knowing that they will contribute to it somehow. Not even understanding what they are getting themselves into, they follow.

Simon could have been left out of the Messiah's plan, if he had kept his head down and not paid attention. But he did change; Jesus recognized Simon's gifts and graces and how he could be used to bring the gospel to others.

We are invited to be a part of that story. This is not just a message or an invitation to be a missionary in a foreign country. This is a message to change our mind-set; we are called to something more, something bigger than ourselves. And we probably won't have to change our profession. We don't need to move to another continent. Jesus wants to use us where we are. He wants us to want to be a part of God's plan.

We need to raise our heads up and look around us. The kingdom is near. God is close and inviting us to work. We may answer in the church, but more likely, our yes will be seen through the eyes of a crying child, or a sick neighbor, or a lonely college student, or an alcoholic who wants another chance. Through the people God puts in our path, we are reminded of the work still to be done.

Keep in mind that the gospel message is for everyone. Who is not here? Who is missing from our midst? Is it your spouse? Your children? Those living on the edge? They may not believe in the miracles of the Bible. The Messiah who spoke to Simon Peter and convicted him of his sin may seem too far away, but you are near. Through you they can experience forgiveness. Your life can show them the fruits of repentance and faith.

So what is your legacy? I look at my daughter, who is now married and raising my two granddaughters in a way I would not have thought possible ten years ago. She is fun, loving, mature, and wise. If I were to say that my legacy is my daughter, I am proud and satisfied. True, I invested a certain amount of time in her upbringing, but I was young, fun, loving, and immature. I said a lot of prayers when she left the church for a decade, but now our granddaughters are being raised in a Christian home and school.

We remember Simon, the fisherman, as the first disciple; he was headstrong and rash sometimes and timid other times. He made mistakes, but he made crucial contributions to something bigger than he was. He answered yes to being part of the kingdom.

What is your legacy? I pray that it will be more than a great portfolio and a healthy insurance plan to be given to your heirs. I pray it will be your faith and your hope as you reach out to others where you are, offering what you have in the name of Jesus the Christ. (Raquel Mull)

Lectionary Commentary

Isaiah 6:1-8, 9-13

Isaiah prophesied during the reign of four kings of Judah, addressing continual idolatry and spiritual rebellion against God. This passage introduces the heavenly realm in complete contrast to Judah's experience. Instead of corruption and manipulation, this throne room reflects God's holiness and majesty.

One cannot impart what one does not have. Isaiah realized he was a man of unclean lips in need of cleansing and preparation for holy service. Once cleansed with the live coal from the altar of God, Isaiah responded in obedience; made holy, set apart, and ready to be sent.

1 Corinthians 15:1-11

Paul addresses the church in Corinth, reminding them that their belief in the resurrection of Christ is foundational to their faith. Paul has been a witness to the resurrected Jesus, along with Cephas, the twelve disciples, and others. His message is conditional, believe in the resurrection or your belief in eternal life is in vain. Paul's contact with the risen Christ came through Christ's voice when Paul was converted on the road to Damascus. (Raquel Mull)

Worship Aids

Invocation

Lord, we come this day to worship you. We offer our voices in song and prayer that we might bless you. We come before your throne, confident that you wait for your children. May your Spirit give us what we lack in attention, faithfulness, and courage. Grant that we may know your presence; in the name of Christ we pray. Amen.

Prayer

Lord, we repent of our fear of the unknown. Give us the words to tell others about you. Give us direction that we may act in ways that point to you. Let us remember we can be used, whoever we are and wherever we are, to be your light to those you place in our path. Thank you for your love and forgiveness and for giving purpose to our lives. Amen.

Benediction

Go, do not be afraid. There is work to be done.
We hear your invitation to work beside you,
like Simon and James and John.
Go, do not be afraid. There are others who have more fear and less hope.
We are only human, with jobs to do and families to raise,
and a future to plan for.
Go, do not be afraid. Remember my plan for humanity to be reconciled to me.
We go with courage in your name to serve those who need to know you. Amen. (Raquel Mull)

Communion

First in a Series of Two on How to Express God in Worship

Mark 14:22-26

Most theology considers a *sacrament* to be a "visible sign of an inward and spiritual grace" instituted by Jesus Christ. Protestants observe two sacraments because Jesus participated in them: baptism and the Lord's Supper. Sacraments have three elements. First, to be a sacrament, a holy act has the element of divine endorsement, which means our Lord instituted it. Second, the sacrament imparts divine favor in an exclusive way. Third, the sacrament has matter, form, and a sanctioned celebrant. The Lord's Supper, for example, has the matter of bread and wine, the form of liturgy, and a sanctioned celebrant to administer the bread and wine who is an ordained minister.

Most denominations charge their pastors similarly to the way pastors are charged by *The United Methodist Book of Discipline*. It outlines one pastoral duty this way: "to administer the sacraments of baptism and the Supper of the Lord according to Christ's ordinance" ([Nashville: United Methodist Publishing House, 2008], ¶340.b.1. Used by permission.).

Our world places excessive value on knowledge of "things": facts, data, and people. Yet faith, particularly reflected in the sacraments, reveals knowledge in different terms. The Orthodox Church, for example, refers to sacraments as mysteries. Why?—because *mystery* is as close as we can get to describing something as ethereal and powerful as the action of God in the sacraments. Objective, factual words simply fall short as descriptors of a deeply moving religious experience.

For most of us, the alternative world that the Bible opens seems mysterious when compared to the realm of scientific methodology—measurements, tests, and analysis—with which we are so comfortable. Yet, the Gospel of Mark calls us into the radical world of faith, where nothing seems exactly as we might expect. We are invited to wonder about love and hope and joy. Can we weigh these or measure their nuclear density or do toxicological screenings on their elemental components?

In Mark's Gospel we recall the story of the upper room. The disciples prepare the Passover meal; however, it is clear that Jesus prepares for the meal's proper meaning. The meal has less to do with facts than with the relationship between Jesus and his intimates. Perhaps this is a better way to understand God's work in our world, especially as Mark presents the Last Supper. We strive to be faithful disciples, but only by God's grace does anything spiritually positive happen to us and through us. Faith is not so much what we know (facts, data, and people) as it is knowing people love us because God loves them and us wholly and completely. As my friends sometimes say, "It is all about God."

This brings a story to mind. My friend and his four-year-old son moved a pile of gravel from the front of their house to a patio in the back. My friend said he struggled with wheelbarrowful after wheelbarrowful of the heavy gravel, moving it bit by bit to the rear of the house. All the while, his son carried a cupful of gravel in a coffee mug his mother had given him for the task. At the end of the project, the little boy told his mother, "Mommy, I moved the whole pile of gravel today, and I let Daddy help some too." This is a good picture of how God's kingdom breaks into our world. Christians struggle with cupfuls of the gospel, but God wields great wheelbarrows full of grace—and we rarely notice.

Mark's word of grace is a radical declaration for those raised on scientific methodology and common sense. When we awake to God's blessing, we discover that most things of lasting worth and value cannot be understood through conventional wisdom. Love and joy are prime examples. We cannot explain love; we can only experience and give love.

Mark's stark story tells us that while communing around a common table with a common loaf and cup, Jesus shared with the disciples the most important lesson of his ministry. Jesus said: "Take; this is my body.... This is my blood of the covenant, which is poured out for many" (v. 22-24). Few words; a host of meanings.

The last words of our text are instructive: "After singing songs of praise, they went out to the Mount of Olives" (v. 26). Between the hatching of the plot to kill Jesus (Mark 14:1-2) and the prayer in Gethsemane (Mark 14:32-42), Jesus stops to eat with and bless the disciples. In community we learn what is really important. In shared worship we gather to remember and to celebrate, and then we go forth to serve God's world.

Holy Communion lies beyond mystery. Yet it is a way we express how our relationship with God, and—more important—God's relationship with us functions. The Lord's Table may take hold of you, and if you let it, the table can become a life-changing experience. If you understand nothing else about the significance of the Lord's Supper, it means at least this—this table is about grace. Here we taste God's grace. Here we drink in God's grace. Here we experience God's grace. These Communion elements are not simply bread and grape juice. Here we digest God's grace—the unmerited, undeserved favor of God toward us. We do not merit a place at this table, and we certainly cannot earn it. This meal is God's free and willing feast-gift, given to us.

The table offers all of us God's unconditional love. It is a gift of divine love. No matter where you go or who you are, no one can offer you a more generous gift. And best of all, we eat it together as our expression of our worship. Amen. (David Mosser)

Worship Aids

Call to Worship

Lord, as we collect ourselves for worship, we pray that your Spirit might calm our anxieties and give us minds, hearts, and ears to know, understand, and hear your wonderful words of life. Center us on your divine call and claim on our lives. Amen.

Pastoral Prayer

Dear Lord of all People, when we ponder our lives as a community of faith, lead us to honestly confess that we do not always dwell in peace with our sisters and brothers. Separation and discord slither into our relationships in ways that confound us. Help us stamp out human pride that blocks our ideal, loving relationships. Bestow on us a new disclosure of who we are as your people, O Lord. Remind us that Jesus took the form of a servant. Help us recall that Christ freed each of us from pride. Now we can freely serve others. Let us take the example of Jesus to heart and become more Christlike—knowing we always fall far short of the mark. Give us the will to become a humble people of Christ. We pray this in the name of Jesus. Amen.

Benediction (Psalm 29:11)

May the Lord give strength to his people! May the Lord bless his people with peace! (David Mosser)

FEBRUARY 13, 2013

Ash Wednesday

Readings: Joel 2:1-2, 12-17; Psalm 51:1-17; 2 Corinthians 5:20b–6:10; Matthew 6:1-6, 16-21

Finishing with What You Have Left

2 Corinthians 5:20b–6:10

It was my privilege to run on a high school track team with a great quarter-miler who ran the last leg of our school's mile relay team. In his senior year, he set the national high school record in the quarter mile. Once when we were out of town for a meet, the team points for the championship were tied all through the weekend until the final event, which was the mile relay. Whichever team won the mile relay won the meet championship. As the final leg began, the hometown team had a very large lead as our teammate received the baton. The stands were already celebrating the win because no one could make up such a deficit in such a race. The young man who ran for our team was a person of great character and grit as well as being a most gifted runner. He also loved to run. As he received the baton, he took off with a burst of speed. He could not maintain that pace for the long distance of the final leg. By the time he had reached the far curve, he had caught the other team's runner. As they approached the straightaway, they were dead even. Midway through the straightaway he passed the other team's runner, beat him by ten yards at the finish line, and collapsed into the tape and the waiting arms of his fellow teammates, victorious. It was by far the greatest athletic accomplishment I have ever witnessed. Essential to such a victory is certainly great ability. However, more important was the heart and purpose that provided the fuel for such a spectacular run.

Paul appeals from the heart and soul of his faith in Christ to the church in Corinth to be reconciled to God on Christ's behalf. Such reconciliation must be at the heart of what drives the church to be the righteousness of

God in the world. In fellowship with them in the doing of the work, Paul pleads with them to not let the gift of grace be in vain. God has and is acting now to bring the experience and reality of salvation and its fullness to a hurting and broken world. As with the runner in the story above, the heart and soul of the church's witness must be the reconciliation of a broken world to the God who loves. The effectiveness of their witness must drive and be defined by their own experience of it as they allow that experience to inform and shape them. Certainly the runner had the ability to run a great race, but the difference in his performance was the love of running. This is what Paul longs for in the witness of the church. It is not enough for the church to talk about reconciliation. The church must work from its own empowered experience of reconciliation as a result of God's redeeming work in Christ, given freely in grace to them. The nature of such an experience is that it both focuses the witness and is its source.

To justify and help clarify, Paul describes what such witness overcomes related to living. He provides a detailed list of what is done, with what resources, in what ways as faithful witness is lived out. For each struggle or possible stumbling block, Paul boldly proclaims what the living witness of reconciliation looks like in response. It is a descriptive and powerful use of reconciled responses juxtaposed against the backdrop of life experiences with which we struggle. Paul also seeks to establish the reality of how a life reconciled to God weaves its way and its influence into even the most difficult of life circumstances. Paul wants the church to know that such living doesn't protect anyone from anything in life. What it does is equip persons to respond with confidence, regardless of what circumstances may come, that God will be not only present but also at work to bring transformation, healing, hope, love, or whatever is needed to move through the experience boldly and faithfully. The only credentials Paul offers to authenticate his ministry in this reconciling work of God is the witness of his own life and ministry. It is a powerful statement and proof of Paul's own sense of the reconciling work of God and its effect on life.

If the witness of the church is to be effective and faithful, it must surrender to the work God has for us to do, grounded in our experience of God's work of reconciliation. I recently saw an interview with a television evangelist who was boasting about never using the word *sin* in his preaching. I struggled with his statement, concerned that the church has gotten so bold as to change the words and concepts of its witness. As I listened to this well-known pastor describe his approach, it became obvious that he believes people really aren't that bad and, that a more fitting word than *sin* is needed to get at the human condition of our day. I began to wonder, if people are that good, why do we need God's reconciling work in Christ at all? The contemporary church seems to struggle to interpret the gospel message in a way that doesn't miss the whole point.

This world needs the reconciling work of God now more than ever. I wonder where most churches and most pastors would be today in relationship to the litany Paul offers as credentials for his own witness and faithfulness in interpreting and relating the reconciling work of God to the world. Have we watered the gospel down so much that no one would even know the difference?

When the final tape of the race is reached, how will our running be interpreted, measured, and defined? Each of us will be held accountable for what we have done with that with which we have been entrusted—the reconciling work of God in Christ in the world. I hope that each of us is driven by our own experience of reconciliation. One reason my high school friend finished the race as he did stemmed from the lessons of our track coach to run the race with everything he had and to finish with whatever he had left. My fervent prayer is that we will collapse through the tape into the arms of the God who called us to the work, into the arms of that great cloud of witnesses who have gone on before, victorious! (Travis Franklin)

Lectionary Commentary

Matthew 6:1-6, 16-21

This passage involves an introductory warning concerning the practice of piety followed by a contrast in the practice of true piety in the areas of alms, prayer, and fasting. The warning is that these pious disciplines are for the audience of God and God alone. When these three disciplines are kept in private between the practitioner and God, they can become the source of great power and genuine devotion. When they are used for status or show, they become the hypocritical tools of evil and can undo our relationship with God. Jesus calls for reform in a community that has lost its way in the practice of its devotion to God.

Joel 2:1-2, 12-17

Joel calls the community of faith to prepare for and then respond to disaster. The call to fasting and repentance recognizes the seriousness of the threat and then leads the people to appropriate action. Both external and internal acts are emphasized, signifying the need for the whole person to be involved in the practice of the disciplines of community penitence. (Travis Franklin)

Worship Aids

Call to Worship

We gather here honestly to open ourselves to you, O God.

Accept us as we are, where we are, O Lord.

Humbly we approach the throne of grace with broken and sinful hearts and souls.

You know our hearts, O God. Love us, refine us, purify us that we might be your people seeking to know you with all that we are always.

Prayer of Confession

We are a sinful and rebellious people, dearest Lord. We have chosen our ways over your ways, our will over your will, our idols over a living relationship with you. Our sin is ever before us, and our iniquities are exposed for what they are. We plead for mercy. We are remorseful and sorry for these our transgressions. Forgive us, we pray. Hear our confession and accept our pleas for mercy. Grant us in these sacred moments and in this holy place the redemption of sin that only you can give. Wash us clean with the blood of the lamb. Restore us to right relationship with you. Free us to once again be your children, dedicated to you and your loving in the world. In the name of our Lord we pray. Amen.

Words of Assurance

May the forgiveness of God the Father, Son, and Holy Spirit cleanse you of all sin. Accept the mercy and grace of the God who loves you with God's whole heart. Joyfully go forth to serve God with all that you are in all that you do. (Travis Franklin)

Water-washed and Spirit-led

Second in a Series of Two on How to Express God in Worship

Acts 16:13-17

She went down to the river to pray, gathering to worship with other women in the cool of the evening after a long day in the city square. Her fingertips were purple, having measured and sold bolts of cloth in the market. Lydia went with the Hebrew women on the Jewish Sabbath to worship. Their worship always soothed her soul, especially during the hard times. They worshiped a God bigger than a name or a temple. The women gathered, singing their Lord's song, remembering what God had done to save their ancestors from the hard times of Pharaoh's slave days. They thanked God for walking with them through the parched lands and desert moments of times past and asked for help in the wilderness moments of their lives in the present day. Sometimes they sang praises to the God of creation; sometimes they pleaded for help. Other times the women promised their faithfulness. Sometimes they simply sat in deep reverence, listening. Even though Lydia came from the city of Thyatira, had known other gods, and spoke a different mother tongue, the Jewish women welcomed her to join them in worship, calling her a God fearer. Her attitude and actions made her a beloved guest.

She remembered an evening when two strangers, itinerant Hebrew men, joined the women at the river's edge. The one named Paul spoke eagerly about Jesus, who he said had lived, died, and then lived again. Paul spoke of how Jesus was the means that the God they worshiped had used to insert a heavenly love into the wilderness and barrenness of the world. Paul offered the women a chance to be baptized, to wash away their old selves, receiving in its place this holy love. He didn't just mean the Hebrew women. He invited Lydia, a foreigner, a stranger. And she said yes. To be baptized meant Lydia was now a soul sister, no longer just a beloved guest, but a beloved child of the living Christ, water-washed and spirit-led.

It is appropriate on Ash Wednesday to begin our forty-day wilderness journey toward the cross at another river, the Jordan, with a look at baptism. How does baptism turn us from friends to faith family?

I love teaching a class about the history and significance of baptism in our tradition. Most participants are the parents of very young children; they somehow believe baptism to be a form of celestial insurance, a way of keeping their babies safe from strangers, accidents, and disease. The reassurance they seek is often discovered to be misplaced when they work through the biblical story of Jesus' baptism. John the Baptizer shows up first, there in our face, yelling to all who gather at the river's edge to worship that it is time to repent! Turn around, he says. Set your sights on God, he cries! And the people come to be cleansed of their lame excuses and poor choices, washed clean to follow a new path to the holy one. Jesus comes too. And God seems very, very pleased.

But something strange happens to Jesus. Baptism is no heavenly insurance against pain or hard times. Water-washed and Spirit-led, Jesus is immediately pushed out for a forty-day fasting and wilderness experience. Loneliness, hunger, thirst, and temptation all serve to prepare him for ministry. Baptism, even for Jesus, does not protect him from life's difficulties or temptations.

When a church member recently faced major health challenges, her sister wondered why God did not do a better job of protecting the baptized, the believers, the nice folks who do good things and live good lives. What is the point of baptism, she wondered, if it does not protect?

Have you ever wondered the same? I've heard, "Why did my husband die of cancer? He was such a good Christian." "Why did my loving friend get killed in a car accident?" "Why did my child, baptized as baby, raised in the church, get so depressed as an adult that he could not feel the love of God or this faith community when faced with life's temptations, leading him finally to take his life?" It seems at times the wilderness of pain and ashes is more common for the baptized than a life of joy.

Each year we come to be marked on this night with the ashes and wilderness dust that signals the beginning of our Lenten journey. As we face our own failure, we hear John cry to repent. Come get cleaned up, ready to face God. Following Jesus' lead, we promise to make time to focus on our own scars, our own pain, our own dry journeys so that God's love found in baptism can cleanse and heal us. Like for Lydia, the waters of baptism do not keep us from temptation or pain, but simply remind us of the affirming words of the apostle, that we love God because God first loved us. The waters of baptism that Jesus sought were a reminder of God's activity in the world. Baptism, even Jesus learned, provides strength for wilderness times, allowing us to face temptation with grace while remaining faithful.

Tonight as you come forward to receive the imposition of ashes, if you have been baptized, I invite you to dip your hands into the baptismal font and remember what God has done in your wilderness moments, then come receive the mark of the cross. If you have never been baptized and are seeking God's gift as we prepare for Easter, speak to a pastor. Forty days of soul preparation lies ahead. Easter's empty tomb waits. Meanwhile God is already at work in the barren, lifeless places of our world. Amen. (Marti Zimmerman)

Worship Aids

Call to Worship

Come gather to worship our God who is willing to walk wilderness moments with us.

Draw together praising God with parched lips and barren lives.
As Lent begins, let the waters of God's grace wash us clean. Amen.

A Prayer of Confession

I'm embarrassed to be back again this year, Lord, needing this season of repentance, seeking your mercy, yearning in the dust and ashes for a sign of your grace. I've been down to the river of mercy before, yet I forget the love of Christ offered and the faith family you provide. Help me walk the wilderness of this Lenten path. Lead me to new life. Amen.

Words of Assurance

Hear the good news! Even in the midst of the barren wilderness, we are not alone. God loves; God walks with us; God holds us up in grace and love. Amen.

Benediction

Having received reminders of God's grace for the wilderness, go prepare your hearts, your life, your soul as the waters of baptism prepare you to serve. Amen. (Marti Zimmerman)

FEBRUARY 17, 2013

First Sunday in Lent

Readings: Deuteronomy 26:1-11; Psalm 91:1-2, 9-16; Romans 10:8b-13; Luke 4:1-13

Choice: Gift or Curse?

Luke 4:1-13

Several years ago there was a television commercial proclaiming the benefit of a certain antacid product. The scene showed a middle-aged, slightly overweight man sitting on the side of his bed in obvious discomfort. He was saying over and over, "I can't believe I ate the whole thing." To this lament his wife sharply replied, "Face it, Ralph, you ate the whole thing." Then the commercial cuts to the product that one was urged to take in order to find relief from indigestion caused by overindulgence.

We live in a culture that is always inviting us to "eat the whole thing." Whether it is to purchase the latest technological invention or to buy the most stylish clothes or visit the most exotic of places, we North Americans are schooled by advertisers to believe we can always "eat the whole thing" and that we can have it all.

Into this culture comes the word of the church drawn straight from the Bible: You cannot have everything and at the same time have what matters most. This is certainly not an easy word for a consumer culture to receive, and often the church has been timid in offering its perspective for fear of not being taken seriously by society. But there is no way around it. There are boundaries in all relationships, and one cannot serve God and at the same time say yes to all the choices that come to us.

The Lenten journey has begun. We walk with Jesus through a wilderness of temptation, sin, and confession to the glory of Easter morning. Lent is designed to be a thoughtful time, a reflective time, a prayerful time. Lent invites us to consider what it means to be a person created in the image of God. Lent brings us to awareness of our essential uniqueness as God's son or daughter.

The clue for Lent is Jesus in the wilderness, where he was tempted by the devil. In three scenes are played out all that it means to be a human being made in the image of God. In the wilderness, Jesus shows his full humanity; he was genuinely tempted as every human being is. What Jesus does in the wilderness is make choices about what he will say yes to and what he will say no to. In this glimpse into the experience of Jesus, you and I have an understanding of what it means to be a child of God.

The text suggests that we humans must make choices. And choice is not always easy. The desire to live on automatic pilot with everything laid out in front of us is a strong urge. The desire to have everything our hearts want is compelling. Instead we are confronted with the necessity of making a choice, where we go in one direction rather than another direction, where we must lay something down in order to be able to pick something else up.

The reality of choice was present in the first moment of creation. God put Adam and Eve in a beautiful garden where everything they needed was provided by God's gracious hand. They had all they needed but could not have all that was there. Life in the garden hinged on trust. The humans must trust God and not try to have everything, which means not eating the fruit of the tree of knowledge of good and evil. They have to make a choice as to whether to trust God on God's terms or to live by their own design. We all know how that story turns out!

Then comes Jesus, and like every person, he has to struggle with how he will live, whom he will trust, what he will give his life to. He is tempted in the wilderness the way every life is tempted every day. The temptation to be relevant by making stones into bread must have been strong. The temptation to be expedient by worshiping the devil for the sake of greater gain was surely not easily resisted. The temptation to be sensational by throwing himself off the pinnacle of the temple was enticing. But to all these Jesus said, "No." He exercised his full humanity and chose the way he would follow.

We must do the same. For all the agony the reality of choice brings to us, there can be no other way. It is in the capacity to choose that we realize we are God's children. So in the season of Lent we take time to examine our lives and consider the choices we are making. We must choose to trust God instead of our schemes and plans to fill our needs. It isn't always easy, for the choices before us are often attractive. Our agony is not so much between the good and the bad as it is between the good and the better, and ultimately the best. We can only say yes to something by saying no to something else. The best is found through deliberateness, intention, and courage to make good choices. This is the sweet burden of being a human and made in the image of God.

Jesus lived a deliberate life. He did not drift and would not be swept up in the tides of trends and styles and momentary pleasure. He chose what his life would be. We should too, because the only life worth living is the life of intention and discipline. How countercultural is that? Richard Foster wrote a book some time ago with the compelling title, *Celebration of Discipline*. Just listen to that phrase. Who "celebrates" discipline? Isn't discipline a negative thing that hems us in and constricts how we can live?

Therein lies the irony. Through discipline we discover the strength and permission to do what we want to with our lives. Not choosing one thing in order to choose something else that is even better is what a disciplined life does, because it is clear that this is the way to real life.

The final verse of our text says that after Jesus had successfully resisted the devil's temptations, after he had made his good choices, the devil "departed from him until the next opportunity." It is a reminder that the struggle about what to choose goes on. In the garden of Gethsemane, Jesus was still struggling with what he would do. Choice—it is a gift and it is ever with us. Looking to Jesus, may you make the best choices for a life of rich fulfillment. (Chris Andrews)

Lectionary Commentary

Deuteronomy 26:1-11

The people of God remain the people of God through grateful remembering. Gratefulness may be most difficult in the midst of plenty because richness can create the false reality of independence and self-sufficiency. In this scriptural admonition to bring the first fruit of the ground to God, Israel is reminded that only through an attitude of gratitude on Israel's part can the covenant relationship with the Lord be sustained.

Romans 10:8b-13

The condition of salvation or wholeness is easily accessed according to Paul. One finds in Jesus a generous and gracious Lord who welcomes all who call upon his name. There is no qualifier here about religious experience, denominational loyalty, baptismal tradition, or anything else. The key word of the text is "everyone" (NRSV; "all" CEB). Jesus puts no obstacles around his saving grace. His grace is offered to everyone! The challenge of the text may be to ask us if we live lives big enough to match the largeness of God as revealed in Jesus Christ. (Chris Andrews)

Worship Aids

Call to Worship

Jesus bids us to follow him. Jesus went to the wilderness.
Must we follow Jesus there?
The wilderness is not where we want to be
or where we find comfort.
In the wilderness Jesus declared loyalty to his Father in heaven.
Then let us follow him wherever he leads,
that we might show him our unceasing devotion.

Invocation

In this Lenten season we seek your guidance, strength and wisdom, O Lord of the wilderness. As you have shown us, may we live in faithful obedience to that which is holy and beautiful and true. Lead us Lord, lead us in your righteousness and truth.

Benediction

Go forth with a thankful heart and clear mind and strong will to do the work of intention and devotion, so that Christ may be lifted up and his name glorified. (Chris Andrews)

Sin as Denial

First in a Series of Three on the Power of Sin and the Abundance of Grace

1 John 1:1-10

Who would have thought that we could learn so much about ourselves from an ancient church fight? A brilliant Christian writer produced the gift of the Gospel of John. Almost before the ink dried on the papyrus, the church fought over it, and one group used it to justify its pride. In a number of places they distorted the teaching of John's Gospel. A wise member of the church wrote the letter, or sermon, we call 1 John to try to combat these distortions. We hear his words differently than the first readers did, but the underlying sins bear some similarity. The first thing we learn about sin from 1 John is that we should guard against reading Scripture so that we simply bolster our own spiritual ego (I am indebted for the insights of this sermon and the whole series to Raymond E. Brown, *The Community of the Beloved Disciple* (New York: Paulist Press, 1979).

The Gospel of John teaches that people who sin become slaves of sin, but that "the truth will set you free" (John 8:31-36). This group within the community assumes that the freedom Christ offered as a gift is an attribute they could claim. They consider themselves free of sin. The author of 1 John challenges them by declaring, "If we say we have no sin, we deceive ourselves, and the truth is not in us" (NRSV). In one sense, the break-away group simply reads the Gospel of John wrong; they misinterpret the freedom Christ offers. In another sense, they feed a common human tendency to deny guilt, blame, responsibility, and sin.

We might not hide behind the Gospel of John to defend ourselves, and we might not come right out and claim complete sin-free status, but we deceive ourselves in other ways. We may not read the Gospel of John the way this group did, but we read ourselves in ways similar to how they read themselves.

We may not deny our sin completely, but we deny specific sins. When a spouse, a friend, a fellow believer, or a family member confronts us about something we have done, our defenses snap into place. We did no such thing! We may have done something wrong, but we bear no blame. The other person misinterpreted our actions. The other person doesn't see our side of the matter. Even now, while we sit here in church, our minds are racing about how someone else has done just these things, and we wish they could hear this sermon. Even now, we concern ourselves more with how this teaching applies to someone else, not to us. We do not deny our sin in the abstract, but we deny the specific sins we actually commit.

We deny our participation in larger sins, where we all make some contribution. Who bears the blame for the mega-sins of pollution, racism, hunger, and injustice? These sins are all like an assembly line where we each put in our part and move it along. No one person creates these sins, so we can pass the blame along too.

Even when we admit we have done something wrong, we might shrug our shoulders at the harm we actually have caused. We dismiss our cruel remark as "joking around," but the butt of our joke hurts for a long time. The "government" doesn't really need the money, so we can justify cheating on our taxes, even if it keeps money from helping real people. Our little lie to our children won't really undermine their trust.

The author of 1 John cites the Cain and Abel story as an example of sin, and we see in it the tendency to denial. Cain displaced his anger at God onto his brother and then killed him. When God confronted Cain, Cain acted innocent, denying his responsibility by asking, "Am I my brother's keeper?" (Genesis 4:9 NRSV; "guardian" CEB). When we assure ourselves that "no one will know," we forget about God. Cain wanted fairness for himself, complaining that his punishment was more than he could endure. Cain projected his own violence onto others, claiming that others would try to kill him. Cain shows us all of the dark holes we try to hide in: no one should try to hold us responsible for others; life treated us unfairly; everyone else acts as badly as we do.

When we face honestly our denial, we have to ask what lies beneath it. If we don't understand why we deny our sin, we can't absorb the forgiveness God offers for our sin and denial. We like to think of ourselves as good people, maybe even at least a little better than average. Confronting our sin knocks us off our perches. We have to look at ourselves with honest eyes, and we may fear what we see. We hate feeling guilty. We hate finding out we were wrong. When we face our guilt, we begin to realize that we have hurt someone and can't fix it. We feel helpless to change what we have done. When we face our sin honestly, the reality may scare us, grieve us. We deny our sin in part for our own protection.

If a kind of insecurity lies at the base of our sinfulness, Jesus offers us a foundation on which we can stand. Jesus has called us friends, and offers us a peace the world cannot match (John 14:27; 15:14-15). When we feel the love of the Risen Christ, and experience the peace only the Holy Spirit can offer, we find the security to face our sins. Then we can hear what the author of 1 John assures us, "If we confess our sins, he is faithful and just to forgive us our sins and cleanse us from everything we've done wrong" (v. 9).

Only when we face our own sin honestly and experience God's love, forgiveness, and peace can we go out into the world that Jesus assures us is full of hate (John 15:18). We go out into that world to offer love, healing, and peace. We go so that others can see, experience, and feel the love of God. (Chuck Aaron)

Worship Aids

Invocation

O God, who formed us as part of the church, we ask your presence as we gather for worship during this time of Lent. Enable us to see the healing potential in this season. Teach us that we can come to a deeper appreciation of the resurrection if we prepare ourselves. May this time of worship open us to the ways you can work in us by overcoming death anew in the celebration of Easter. Amen.

Prayer of Confession

We confess, righteous God, that we look everywhere we can to avoid seeing our sin. When we deny our sin, we close ourselves to what you can do in us. Empower us to face honestly the hurt we have caused, the good we have neglected, and the growth we have avoided. Forgive us and cleanse us. Amen.

Words of Assurance

Even as we speak our prayer, God empowers, forgives, and cleanses. Thanks be to God.

Benediction

Go out now as those Jesus called friends, as those offered peace, as those who bring light to a dark world. (Chuck Aaron)

FEBRUARY 24, 2013

Second Sunday in Lent

Readings: Genesis 15:1-12, 17-18; Psalm 27; Philippians 3:17–4:1; Luke 13:31-35

Passionate Boldness

Philippians 3:17–4:1

Nowhere in the New Testament is the Christ-centered life more vividly portrayed than in the letter to the Philippians. Paul, the writer of the letter, has so yielded himself up heart and soul to Christ that he can truly say, "for me, living serves Christ and dying is even better" (1:21). He is proud to be the slave of Christ Jesus (1:1), to be imprisoned for his sake (1:13), to be allowed to glorify Christ in his body, whether by life or by death (1:20), to lose all the advantages of birth and station in order that he may win Christ (3:7-8). Christ has laid hold of Paul, and now Paul's overmastering passion is to win Christ and be found in him. Paul's affirmation of his centeredness in Christ is breathtaking.

Near the end of the letter (3:17), Paul reveals his passionate boldness by saying, "Brothers and sisters, become imitators of me and watch those who live this way—you can use us as models."

Now just stop for a moment and think about what Paul is saying and how he is saying it. He invites people to "imitate" him. That is a strong statement. We often hear someone say, "Do as I say, not as I do." That we can understand for there is often a gap between our words and our actions. But Paul says, in effect, "Do as I do. Imitate me!" It is a bold person who can invite others to imitate how they live.

Paul "walks the talk." He is consumed with passion for the Lord who has claimed his life with redeeming love, and his highest ambition is to have Christ's experience—his suffering, his death, his resurrection produced in his own inner life. Paul is in prison when he writes this letter, and though his personal situation was dark with the threat of a violent death hanging over him, his undaunted courage leads him to write a letter that expresses his joyful confidence and brings comfort and encouragement to the friends he loved.

In effect Paul is saying, "Imitate my confidence in the adequacy of Jesus Christ to bring all people to the fullness of life." For Paul there is one magnetic pole to which his thoughts constantly return and that is Jesus Christ in his demonstration of self-humbling and suffering and death and resurrection. To be identified with Christ in humility and obedience is the noblest dignity to which any person can aspire, and Paul has given himself to this way of living without reserve. To reach the goal of living and breathing Christ and to inspire others to follow him was the constant ambition of the apostle Paul.

Like all churches, the Philippians had their troubles. There is no such thing as a perfect church. If there were, none of us could be members. But there is one unchangeable rule that Paul wants the church to follow, and that is to expose everything to the light that shines from the revelation of God in Christ Jesus. This is how Paul has come to live his life, and he wants his friends to imitate him. When the church shows tendencies of selfishness and pride, they should remember the example of the humility of Christ. When the church is tempted to trust in fleshly ordinances and advantages, they should consider the surpassing advantage of knowing Christ Jesus and being found in him. When the church finds itself despondent and anxious, they should rejoice in the Lord and find in Christ the peace that passes all understanding.

Paul is a man of passion, and he invites the Philippians to follow his example of living completely and totally for Jesus Christ. That is the witness of the church, and its light is never brighter than when it passionately lives the way of Christ in the world. For Paul, the church is an outpost of heaven. It is a demonstration of the power of Christ to change lives and to make all things new. "Stand firm in the Lord" in this way, Paul says.

Sometime ago our family decided to clean out and downsize our household. We had a garage sale, and what wasn't sold in the garage sale we took to the thrift store and gave away. There was some good stuff that we gave away. Clothes and appliances that still worked and yard tools and books—all went into the sale or were sent to the thrift store. I thought about that and realized that this is what Paul is urging the Philippians to imitate. He had a wonderful tradition in his Jewish heritage. He had the beauty of God's law and the assurance of God's blessing as a member of the Jewish nation. Paul knew the wonder and marvel of being called to be a people who would keep the candle of faith burning in a dark and sinful world. He knew all of that. But he was willing to give it all away in favor of the surpassing knowledge of Jesus Christ. "For to me, living is Christ," he says (1:21 NRSV).

"Everything else I give away. The tradition of my fathers, the worship of my ancestors, the covenant of blessing through Abraham, all of this is good. But I am ready to give all this up for the sake of Jesus. You should be too, and this is what I want you to imitate in me."

You see, Paul thought that if you are going to be a Christian, then you should be like Jesus. To be a Christian is to love, to care, to give, to serve, to suffer, to sacrifice as Jesus did. Though Paul would be the first to say that he has not gotten there yet, he is dedicated to making that his one, overarching life goal. Being like Jesus is the one thing on his mind, all the time. He is a passionate man. An unusual man. You may never in your lifetime meet anybody who takes Jesus that seriously, but then again, maybe you will. "You can be that person," Paul says. "Imitate me."

I think we should look at Paul today and celebrate his bold passion for his Lord. I think it would be good if we took his words to heart and really did try to imitate the way Paul lived. We will be a better church if we do; our lives will be richer, and the world will see Christ in us. (Chris Andrews)

Lectionary Commentary

Genesis 15:1-12, 17-18

This passage describes a trial in Abram's faith. Both Abram and his wife are old and still without children. God now reassures Abram and promises him a son. Abram's belief in God's promise represents his surrender to faith, and this is Abram's righteousness. His trust in God's word is what makes him "right" before God. Trust is the basis of the covenant Abram will have with God. Before knowledge there is trust.

Luke 13:31-35

The Pharisees try to scare Jesus into leaving with the threat that Herod wants to kill him. Jesus replies that he will persist in his ministry for the next three days until his work is accomplished. Then he will leave Herod's realm and go to Jerusalem, where prophets are consistently rejected. In rejecting Jesus, Israel experiences great spiritual loss and will see Jesus again only when he comes for judgment. (Chris Andrews)

Worship Aids

Call to Worship

Come, people of God, unite your voices and hearts in praise and worship.

We open our lives to the mystery of God's presence and grace.

Come, people of God, to the source of your salvation.

Ready, yielded, and free, we invite God's spirit to shape and renew us in this time of worship.

Invocation

Holy and Living God, center us on the one thing that matters: your love in Jesus Christ. Take away our lethargy and dullness of spirit. Infuse us with the living love of your Son that our hearts may be quickened and our lives and witness energized to bring glory to your name. Amen.

Benediction

Go forth to show the world what really matters. Let the love of Jesus flow from you in all that you do, now and forever. Amen. (Chris Andrews)

Sin as Lack of Love

Second in a Series of Three on the Power of Sin and the Abundance of Grace

1 John 3:14-24

Some stand-up comedians employ a telephone as a prop. We hear only one side of a conversation. We guess what the person on the other end of the line might be saying. This sermon or letter we call 1 John bears some similarity to this routine. A church has split, and the author of 1 John writes to encourage the group left behind after another group has left. The church before the split had drawn nourishment from the Gospel of John. Much of the dispute concerns how to interpret John's Gospel. This part of the book pleads for love among the people still in the church and between the two groups. Our author draws insight from the Gospel of John, where Jesus gives the disciples a new commandment, "that you love one another." Jesus goes on to identify love for one another as the true mark of discipleship (John 13:34-35 NRSV). The author of 1 John extols the virtue of love just as highly as the Gospel does. He makes a bold statement when he declares that we can mark the dividing line between passing from life to death by love. Perhaps he makes such a strong case for love because we find love so difficult.

How much hurt do we create when we fail to show love in our families? We talk a good game, but we often twist our love out of shape in our families. We don't listen as closely as we should, even when the other person wants to tell us something important. We don't hear the hurt and pain of our own families because we wrap ourselves up in our own feelings. We discipline too strictly or not strictly enough. Some of us place children at the center of our universe, which can be sentimentality more than love. Some of us don't pay enough attention to our children. We hold grudges; we manipulate to get what we want; we wrap ourselves too tightly around others, hoping to live through those people. We must speak honestly—sometimes we act abusively in our families. When 1 John calls us to love, part of that love is putting away our pride and our stubbornness so that we can truly love those closest to us. Sometimes, loving our families means seeking help to learn how to get past ourselves to love.

How much hurt do we create when we fail to show love to those in need? Our author asks a vital question: "How does God's love abide in anyone who has the world's goods and sees a brother or sister in need and yet refuses help" (see v. 17)? We cannot solve all of the world's problems, and we cannot help everyone, yet we fall so far short. According to the experts, most Christians give only a tiny percentage of their incomes to church and charity. Loving those in need means feeding the hungry, forgiving those who have made mistakes (including ourselves), and reaching out to those who feel abandoned. We reach out in love because of more than simple obedience to God. When we ignore those in need, we shut off part of ourselves. Something in us shrivels up when we neglect those in need. Loving those in need means more than writing a check. We love with our time and talents. We love with our presence. We become the presence of Christ when we love those in need. We show our love for God. We receive love in return.

How much hurt do we create when we fail to show love in times of conflict? Fights within the church can be nastier than the worst hockey match. The author of 1 John likely aims his accusations about hating a brother or sister at this church split. Disputes in the church almost always arise out of theology—overthinking our faith. The book of 1 John starts out with a description of the experience of the presence of Christ; what we have seen, heard, and touched (1:1). Christians do not argue over the experience. We argue over understanding the experience. In our author's church, the groups argued over the identity of Christ, over whether Jesus truly was God in the flesh (4:2). We cannot overstate the importance of this doctrine of the church, that Jesus was God in the flesh. Our theology matters. Yet the Gospel of John and the author of 1 John both hold up the virtue of love. We would never say that we can believe whatever we want to as long as we love, because the New Testament calls us to think rightly about God. Yet love matters as much as theology. Our passion over our beliefs can cloud our minds and our hearts. That passion can morph into anger and then into hate (2:9). In the heat of an argument, we may feel as though we need every weapon to win. If we can overcome our anger to show love, we already have won.

We see our sin in the lack of love in our families, failure to love those in need, and in the midst of church conflict. Our failure and even our inability to show true love—freely given, intended to help another regardless of our own needs—arises from many places within us. Besides just plain selfishness, our lack of love can arise from some hurt down inside us, from anger at the way the world has treated us. First John teaches something we don't hear often enough, "God is greater than our hearts" (v. 20). Pain, grief, and hurt arise in our hearts, but God is greater than our hearts. God can heal our hearts, so that we can love. We begin to love by acting in love before we feel anything inside. As we act and as we draw upon God, we experience the healing grace of God, who teaches us to love and enables us to love. (Chuck Aaron)

Worship Aids

Invocation

We read in 1 John that you are love, O God. Come among us to embody love in our worship. Embody love so that we may experience love, so that we can learn to love, so that we can share love with the world outside our doors. Enable us to love rightly, overcoming the things in us that wreck our attempts to love. In the name of Jesus Christ, who showed true sacrificial love. Amen.

Prayer for the Offering

We see the needs of the world, O God. We could not spend our money any better way than in feeding and clothing our sisters and brothers. We could not accumulate anything better than new connections made with those we have helped. As we give, teach us that we show love to you as we love those in need. Amen.

Benediction

Go out now to shower love on a lonely, desperate world. Go as those loved by God, and as those who love each other. Go to show the strength and power of love. Amen. (Chuck Aaron)

MARCH 3, 2013

Third Sunday in Lent

Readings: Isaiah 55:1-9; Psalm 63:1-8; 1 Corinthians 10:1-13; Luke 13:1-9

Passion and Purpose

Isaiah 55:1-9

Live long enough and eventually you are made aware that life is about time. Life is a bundle of moments, measurable and countable moments, like change in a pocket or pennies in a jar. Some feel their pockets are full, and others' pockets have almost emptied out. The bottom line is that life does not go on forever.

This realization makes Isaiah's words hauntingly relevant. The old prophet challenges us to pay attention to how we live, that we may live well. His words are powerful. These are focusing words; pay-attention words, because these words touch two essentials of life: passion and purpose. We need both and we want both. "Delight yourselves in rich food" (v. 2 NRSV), says the prophet. In response we say, "Show us where we can find this food and we will gorge on it!"

The French have given us a word that is descriptive of life for many in our time. The word *ennui* refers to a feeling of weariness and dissatisfaction and boredom. Without using the word, Isaiah warns against *ennui* when he calls us to "Listen carefully to me / and eat what is good; / enjoy the richest of feasts" (v. 2). There is food and drink that does not satisfy, Isaiah warns.

It is easy to drink and eat an *ennui* diet and not realize we are doing it. Watching television for two to three hours a day, wandering around shopping malls, spending time worrying about things in general, forgetting to laugh, not telling someone you love them, failing to walk outside are all ways to mix up a stew of *ennui* that leaves us feeling dull and unsatisfied. For good measure, add side dishes of rigid schedules, unpleasant relationships, and long-held grudges. If we eat and drink this diet long enough, we will stop hearing angels' songs that have been so cleverly disguised as children's laughter. We will not see the exhilarating glimpse of heaven standing before us as a full moon or a beautiful sunset or in the twinkling eyes of someone who loves us. The diet of *ennui*, of boredom, numbs the soul into thinking that a thunderstorm is only noise and rain and not a holy message for the soul, or that a breath is only the movement of air and not a gift of life, or that being alive is all about getting through a day and not being aware of the miracle of this moment.

We live in a culture that serves up *ennui* faster than a vending machine dispenses canned soda. It is easy to get sick on this diet without even knowing you are becoming ill. That may be why Isaiah hears God saying, "My plans aren't your plans, nor are your ways my ways" (v. 8).

So the prophet calls us to "enjoy the richest of feasts." Fortunately there is a different diet that we are invited to partake. There are mountains of rich food that, when eaten, really satisfy. Here are some of my favorite servings that always seem to restore health to my soul and body: take a walk in the woods, do something risky for the benefit of others, play with a child, pour your heart out to God, have a good laugh or a cleansing cry.

Isaiah reminds us that life does not go on forever, and it is the foolish person who spends life on that which fails to satisfy. It is healthy to ask, "What will people say about us after we have left this life?" Or even better, what do we want people to say about us after we are gone? Do you want someone saying you spent a lot of time at the office, or you were always worried about money, or you never missed the evening news, or you always got your car's oil changed on time, or you were one of the busiest persons anyone ever saw, or you were always talking on the phone, or you were always at the mall?

I don't think anyone would want to be remembered for these things. No, our passion and purpose is found somewhere else. It is found in the rich food of grace, whereby we live every moment knowing that all moments are God's gifts to us. Live with the awareness that God's joy is to give us the food that satisfies. Living with awareness and gratitude, we find our passion and purpose as children of God. Imagine life as a gigantic river of wonder that has been flowing forever. You are part of that river. You did not spring out of nothing. You are divine intention, part of a river that has flowed through time and space since the beginning of creation. God intended you to be.

There is no one else like you. You are a unique, one-of-a-kind wonder of God's creativity. You are capable of marvels that you cannot even imagine. Like all people you have experienced triumph and tragedy, healing and horror, fortune and failure. Within you the wisdom of the ages is dancing to the music of the spheres. You are the one Jesus called the light of the world and the salt of the earth in his one and only sermon. Don't waste this precious time called your life on that which does not satisfy.

We walk the journey of Lent in springtime, and spring is about rebirth and newness of life. Lent offers us the opportunity of diving back into that ancient river of life that faith names as God. Open your heart and mind and soul to the passion and purpose that only divine love creates. Eat the rich food of love and delight yourself in that which truly satisfies. Give yourself permission to do and live the things that bring joy to your days. It is the way God would want you to be, and it is the way that purpose and passion are discovered. (The French term for this, by the way, is *joie de vivre*, "joy of life"!) (Chris Andrews)

Lectionary Commentary

1 Corinthians 10:1-13

Paul says that the preexistent Christ (the Rock) ministered to God's redeemed people in the wilderness. However, the ancient people sinned, and this is something Christians must guard against. The lessons from the past and the urgency of the present warn us to beware. With God's help, temptation can be resisted.

Luke 13:1-9

Victims of brutality or catastrophes in nature are not more sinful than others. All people are sinners, and all need to be warned to repent or judgment will strike suddenly. This is a warning to Israel and to individuals to bring forth the fruit of repentance, faith, and obedience before judgment strikes. (Chris Andrews)

Worship Aids

Call to Worship

Stand before the table of grace and enjoy the richness of God's love.

We are hungry and thirsty for the good diet of God's amazing grace.

God offers grace to you freely and abundantly.

We will delight ourselves in God's rich food!

Invocation

O God, we stand before you hungry and thirsty and tired and worn. Be for us the rich food of grace that we have to neither purchase nor make, but only receive. We place the table of our lives before your love and ask that you set for us a meal of grace, goodness, and love. May we find in you our passion and our purpose.

Benediction

Thank you, O Holy one, for the passion of life that is your love. May we go forth to live that love in creative ways and thus come to know that our purpose always is to bless and praise your holy name. Amen. (Chris Andrews)

Sin as Fear

Third in a Series of Three on the Power of Sin and the Abundance of Grace

1 John 4:18

We have all experienced trying to calm the fears of a child. We have all seen the terrified expressions and dried the flowing tears. Sometimes a parent's touch can absorb the fear like a sponge. Children often succumb to irrational fears of things like storms or the dark. They grow wide-eyed over strange noises or imaginary creatures. Maybe we learn from them that our fears, even into adulthood, come from a deep place within us. Maybe we learn that our fears have a tight filter against rational argument. We hope children learn something from us about controlling fear, because some forms of our fears—rational and irrational—hang around our whole lives.

Where could we start talking about all the problems fear causes us? We might start simply talking about the hard time we have deciding which fears really warrant our attention. With warnings popping up all around us about our food, toxic chemicals, identity theft, and even the sun, where do we go to find some respite from fear? How do we stay reasonably safe without locking ourselves in our houses with the shades drawn? Fear protects us, but fear paralyzes us as well. Fear of rejection paralyzes us so that we retreat into ourselves, cutting ourselves off from people who could befriend us. Fear of failure paralyzes us from trying something risky that might just pay off. Fear of strangers paralyzes us from encountering people who mean us no harm.

The author of 1 John does not tell us much about fear. He devotes little space in his sermon/letter to fear. He places this one verse in the context of teaching about love. As we have said the previous two weeks, the author wants to promote love to a fractured church. What he says here seems almost a side comment, but thank God for it. We need all the help with fear we can receive. He writes specifically about fear of God, especially fear of God's judgment. Even with our gratitude that he touches upon this topic at all and gives us insight, we might wish he had said more. Our fear about God, our fear of God, proves as tricky as all of our other fears.

The Bible teaches us about fear of God, and we know that this *fear* really means a healthy respect for God. "Wisdom begins with the fear of the LORD" (Proverbs 1:7). The ancient sages do not want us cowering in terror at an angry deity but respecting the difference between us and God. Perhaps we in the church should emphasize this understanding of the fear of God more than we do. We can take such delight in the goodness of God that we forget God's majesty. We dismiss the attitude of the people in Exodus who fear God so much that they avoid even touching the mountain they associate with God, lest they die (Exodus 19:12). We don't want that kind of fear for ourselves, but we pay too little attention to God's *gravitas*. We show so little respect for God that we approach God casually, assuming we have no need to set aside time and space for God. We treat God as our personal concierge, ready to set up our successes and even recreation. Let us reflect on our understanding of the awesome power and independence of God.

As important as our reflection on a healthy respect for God might be, 1 John really wants us to focus on a true, morbid fear of God. For some of us, what should be healthy respect becomes terror of God's judgment. Every pastor has counseled people who sat as children in a pew listening to a purple-faced preacher twist the fear of God out of shape. The Bible certainly contains passages that depict God's judgment of sinners. The biblical authors did not intend those for young children. The Bible always balances God's judgment with God's grace and forbearance. Yet, some in the church cannot seem to resist exploiting the visions of judgment. Because we all carry around these deep-seated fears, and we all respond to fear, some—even in the church—will try to manipulate that fear. Fear motivates all of us, so people try to use fear to bring us to faith. If we use only fear to try to feed faith, we end up robbing people of the ability to love God. Some of those children who felt the pounding of God's wrath have trouble, even decades later, loving the God someone taught them to fear.

Even though he has little to say about fear, our author gives us a wonderful promise, "perfect love drives out fear." We don't usually think of love as the basis of our courage, but 1 John puts it there. We assume we must conjure up our own courage, conquer our own fear. Our fears grip us so tightly that we might need a love that does more than just ease our fears, that really tosses them out of us. Even though we are in church, maybe we can think of a bouncer in a bar, grabbing our fear by the coat and throwing it out the door so that it lands with a splat on the ground. We might wish God would do just that to our fears, evict them suddenly. What may more likely happen is that God will slowly ease our fears, so that little by little, we can come to know God's love.

God's love absorbs our fear like a sponge. God's gracious love heals our fear of not only punishment but also our other fears. Let us rejoice in God's love that drives out our fear. Let us open ourselves to the healing love of God, trusting God to calm and even dissolve our fear, not only of punishment and judgment, but also our fears about life and others. (Chuck Aaron)

Worship Aids

Call to Worship

We gather for worship in Lent,
 a time for reflection and examination.
We are grateful for the chance to grow and deepen our faith.
We prepare ourselves for the joy of resurrection.
Let us put away all within us that needs to die,
so that we embrace the life God gives us.

Prayer for Illumination

Inspiring God, from a broken church you brought forth a book that speaks across the miles and centuries. Enable these words written long ago to speak to our broken places, within us and within our church. Amen.

Benediction

Go out now into a world held captive by fear. Go with God's blessing to share a love that drives out fear, heals hurts, and creates community. (Chuck Aaron)

MARCH 10, 2013

Fourth Sunday in Lent

Readings: Joshua 5:9-12; Psalm 32; 2 Corinthians 5:16-21; Luke 15:1-3, 11b-32

Oh, Brother

Luke 15:1-3, 11b-32

Welcome to First Church of the Elder Brother. I know that's not the name on the sign, but it might well be. "Elder brother," or EB for short, here has nothing to do with birth order or gender. So, firstborns, set aside your resentments about spoiled baby siblings, and lastborns, set aside your feelings about bossy older siblings. Elder brother, like prodigal son, is a spiritual type in Jesus' parable.

Two traits characterize us EB: (1) We didn't reject home, family, faith, country, and culture. We may have left home geographically, but not relationally. (2) We didn't squander our family's most cherished resources. Prodigal sons did both. A few years of wild sorority or fraternity life do not make you a prodigal. Did you graduate with a degree?—EB!

Parents want their sons and daughters to marry us EBs—and we know why. We are responsible, respectable, and reliable. While few of us say it out loud, many EBs think if the world just had more people like us, it would be a lot better off. Prodigals don't think that.

Jesus spent so much time and energy on the lost, sinful, disgraced, and broken, it can seem as if the gospel is good news only for prodigals. At the 2010 Festival of Homiletics, Craig Barnes shared how he grew up in a church of prodigals led by a redeemed prodigal, his father. It was a Southern Baptist church on Long Island (Barnes points out that on Long Island only prodigals dare show up in a Southern Baptist church). "I once was lost but now am found" was their life story. When Craig approached his teens, pressure mounted for him to be baptized. His father asked him if he'd had a conversion experience. "Conversion from what?" Craig wondered. "Do you believe Christ died for your sins?" his father asked. "Of course," Craig replied, "just as you taught me." The "lost and found" paradigm of salvation didn't fit the elder brother-ish son of the redeemed prodigal. So when Craig became a pastor, he was sympathetic to the parishioner who wondered what the good news was for people like him: born into a Christian family, baptized as an infant, confirmed as a teen, nurtured in Christian faith, regular in church participation, diligent in prayer. "Do I have to get lost so I can get found?"—the question EBs ask at the doorway to the prodigal son's homecoming party.

Elder brothers struggle with grace—no matter how long we have been in church—probably because we see grace as what other people get. In our own minds, EBs don't need grace. We just need what we have coming. Elder brothers hear "grace" and think "unfair." "You have never given me even a young goat so I may celebrate with my friends" (v. 29b NRSV). In the course of making his complaint, the biblical EB reveals something deep and poignant. "For all these years I have been working like a slave for you" (v. 29a NRSV). Working with and for his father is a privilege, but he has turned it into imprisonment. His responsibilities are a token of trust, but he has tasted only bitterness and resentment. Are we EBs in mortal danger of turning the gift of Christian faith into "Let's Make a Deal"?

Good news comes to the elder brother through the father. It comes before he says a single word. He leaves the banquet the whole village is relishing at his expense, the banquet he has hosted to express his joy, the banquet where he belongs at the head table, in order to plead with his sulking son who insults him by refusing to enter. Why? Because he loves him so, and shameless sacrifice is the currency of love. And what does he say? "Son, [not slave] you are always with me, and all that is mine is yours" (v. 31 NRSV). Can you hear the befuddlement in his voice? "Son, how can I give you more? You have and always have had me and all my stuff. What more is there to give?" Can you hear the sadness in his voice? "It breaks my heart that what I thought was love and trust and intimacy you have felt as slavery."

The good news Christ offers us EBs is that our lives are a sacred gift from a loving giver. God promises to continue to give us whatever we really need to have a fabulous life. We EBs are invited to put down life as a burden, as a battle to win, as a project we must constantly work on, as a task that is all up to us. We are invited to stop worrying that if our vigilance wavers for one moment, it might all come crashing down around us.

Millard Fuller was the EBs' EB. Seven-figure yearly income. Business powerhouse. Competent, competitive, reliable. But Millard was troubled, "his health, integrity, and marriage suffered. These crises prompted Fuller to re-evaluate his values and direction. His soul-searching led to reconciliation with his wife and to a renewal of his Christian commitment. The Fullers [Millard and wife, Linda] then took a drastic step: They decided to sell all of their possessions, give the money to the poor and begin searching for a new focus for their lives. This search led them to Koinonia Farm, a Christian community located near Americus, Georgia, where people were looking for practical ways to apply Christ's teachings" (http://www.habitat.org/how/millard.aspx, accessed July 5, 2011). They had to stop acquiring and start giving. Millard had to go from captain of industry to servant of the least, from power to sacrifice. They decided to commit all of themselves—their abilities, experience, connections, time, energy, and accumulated wealth—to building houses for the homeless. And from that emerged Habitat for Humanity. But here's the word for us EBs. From that emerged for them joy that they never imagined was possible, joy that came only when they surrendered what they thought they'd earned.

The escape hatch out of anxious calculation, out of self-imposed slavery, out of brutal competition, out of toxic bitterness, out of unrelieved fatigue is the doorway into the joyous feast celebrating the resurrection of our good-for-nothing prodigal brother. God does love irony, doesn't God? Will we EBs join the party? Or will we require a payoff for being close to God other than being close to God? The door to the joy of the banquet is wide open. Our place at the table is reserved. All we have to do is get over what we think our virtue has earned and sit next to our prodigal siblings. God is waiting on us outside the party God has paid for in full, pleading with us to join the joy of celebration. How long would we have God wait? (Bill Obalil)

Lectionary Commentary

Joshua 5:9-12

These spare verses are extracted from a rich context: crossing the Jordan on dry ground into the promised land as their ancestors had crossed the Red Sea into the wilderness of freedom; the communal circumcision that reaffirms the identity of a called and set-apart people; and the reminder to Joshua from the commander of the army of the Lord to remove his sandals, for the ground is holy (it remains God's, even as Israel takes possession of it). Two themes within the passage are sufficiently complex to handle. One, the reproach and disgrace, the shame of Egypt is rolled away. We are not sure what that reproach is. The enduring trauma a generation later of having been enslaved, repressed, and exploited? The faithless yearning for the fleshpots of Egypt? The fear that led to forty extra years of wandering? A sensitive preacher can help people see how shame is removed only by grace from beyond us, by the enduring fidelity that God offers. As we move deeper into a post-Christendom time, and into a post-Christian society, rolling away reproach may become more prominent on our faith journeys.

Two, the passage from wilderness to fertile land moves Israel from a rather passive dependence upon God's providing to cooperation with that provision through work. How do we help people discern which side of Gilgal they are on in their exodus travels with the liberating God? How do we help people let go of manna when it is time and pick up responsibility when God fulfills God's promise?

2 Corinthians 5:16-21

Wow, there are at least five sermons in this intense passage. Maybe some Lent we might preach this passage the first five Sundays. (1) "We won't recognize people by human standards" (v. 16). Life in Christ radically transforms our perspective, the eyes through which we see our neighbors and our enemies. In *The Cost of Discipleship* (New York, Simon & Schuster, 1959, 94–101), Dietrich Bonhoeffer claimed that the Christian has no direct relationships, but they all are mediated now through Christ. How might we experience that? (2) "If anyone is in Christ, that person is part of the new creation" (v. 17). This is the Pauline prelude to John's "In the beginning. . . ." What God is doing in Christ is nothing short of new creation. Not only is there a new creature, but all creation is renewed! How do we experience that mystery? (3) "God was reconciling the world to himself through Christ" (v. 19). This is more Pauline prelude to John (3:17—God sent the Son not to condemn, but to save). God is inclined toward the world and toward each of us in love—not contempt; in grace—not rage; in promise—not threat. What will it take for us to let this good news seep into the deepest, darkest corners of our souls? (4) "We are ambassadors who represent Christ" (v. 20). The gift of new creation and reconciliation, when authentically received, impels us to share the gift. Hoarding grace works as well as hoarding manna. (5) "God caused the one who didn't know sin to be sin for our sake so that through him we could become the righteousness of God" (v. 21). Here is the mystery of atonement (at-one-ment). This is awed exclamation, not detailed dogmatics. Maybe it means at least that you can't rescue someone from a burning building without getting hot. How might we invite people into the overwhelming depth of this mystery without reducing it to a scheme that cooks the sin-accounting books? (Bill Obalil)

Worship Aids

Call to Confession

With what shall we come before the Lord, and bow ourselves before God on high, when we have tolerated injustice, sought revenge, and strutted with pride? We shall come with nothing but our need for mercy. Let us confess our sin.

Confession

Somehow, O God, our virtues can separate us from you as surely as our vices. Our dutifulness can do as much damage as our dereliction. Have mercy on us. Overwhelm our disordered hearts with your peace. Win us by your grace to the joy of your kingdom.

Assurance of Pardon

God's love is unconditional. God runs down the road to embrace the desperate, broken, and ashamed. God goes out to invite the petulant, proud, and self-righteous. God waits for our return before we know we've left. We are forgiven. Thanks be to God. (Bill Obalil)

God in a Brown Paper Bag

First in a Series of Three on Spiritual Geography: Finding God in Unusual Places

Matthew 3:1-17

Go to any church services, contemporary or traditional, and you will find the experience basically formal. Baptisms, especially, are performed in elaborate settings, ranging from baptismal pools showcased with lighting effects, music, and the candidates parading single-file (similar to the formations in a graduation ceremony) to baptismal fonts designed in the form of fountains of water cascading over crosses or marble walls. I visited one parish church where the waterfall proceeded to meander through the nave of the church and culminated in something similar to a wading pool. The candidates for baptism wore exotic white robes while ballet dancers performed to a Bach piece as the candidates made their way into the pool one by one and were baptized by the bishop, who wore an extraordinary silk vestment of gold linen over a shiny robe. In these days, finding God in a twenty-first century church setting is a grand and elaborate occasion.

"In those days John the Baptist appeared in the wilderness of Judea proclaiming, 'Repent for the kingdom of heaven has come near'" (v. 1-2 NRSV). Matthew describes the setting as one far less formal and elaborate than those we know. John showed up along a murky, dangerous river that contained many whirling pools and deep crevices that could sweep a wader under, never to be seen again. The water was nasty, and its pigment could leave ugly traces on the skin and even infectious sores on anyone who had open sores. The crowd that day was populated largely by the *hoi-polloi*, the masses of people the religious establishment deemed unclean or unworthy to be in God's presence. The majority of people among the crowd that day were those we would call today the blue-collar contingency. These were the folks who knew what it was like to be without work and a decent, livable wage. Their wilderness was unemployment, disfavor, and impoverishment. They were the folks who had to pay taxes above and beyond what was expected and were always being taken advantage of. Here and there among them were the very perpetrators of oppressive action. No wonder we find a priest who was more comfortable in the wilderness than in the adorned confines of the religious establishment. John, the priest in this setting, wore clothes that sound to us like a costume from the Flintstones, and his diet was the desert's fast-food—locusts and wild honey. Probably his hair was long and uncombed, and a scraggly beard covered his face. Put simply—in current, showbiz vernacular—he wasn't anyone's "eye candy." The scene in Matthew's Gospel flies in the face of what most of us would deem appropriate to current worship contexts. If we are honest, most of us wouldn't be caught keeping company with such folks.

But let us focus on one word in the text and that word is *wilderness* (NRSV; *desert* CEB). In the Greek, the word means a "wild, uncultivated, uninhabited region." Is this where we usually expect to find God, in the "wild, uncultivated, uninhabited regions" of our lives? Recently, I have become friends with a person who has spent a significant number of his thirty-three years on the streets, living under bridges and living on handouts and any other means of income that he could secure from passersby.

His wilderness has been the city streets. His history of running afoul of the authorities in one misdemeanor after another has plagued his current attempts to reenter into the mainstream. In some parlance, particularly of the political realm, he could be described as one who has been living in "a state of disfavor." I believe this is the state of the majority in the crowd in Matthew's version of Jesus' baptism. We, like the religious authorities who crept into the crowd to observe John's actions, don't expect to find God among those who live in a state of disfavor.

But the Gospels fly in the face of such expectations. John knows that the kingdom of God's presence defies human expectations. His posture on this matter is exemplified by the one term he magnifies that day, *repentance* ("change your hearts and lives" CEB). To repent means to intentionally choose a path in life that sets one on course to seek God's insight on all of life's matters. For Matthew, *repent* and *righteous* are synonymous. In the act of repentance, deciding that one's life choices are in conflict with God's ways, is already to have chosen the "right" way to continue one's life. To choose selfish, self-serving, and destructive ways of living is to find one's self in "wild, uncultivated, uninhabitable regions." It is at this place anybody can decide he or she needs to make a 180–degree turn and begin a new journey where God's ways help us recover and get back on track in life. These junctures in life are inhabited by people from all realms of society. John must have looked around and realized that everyone in the motley crew that populated that portion of the Jordan River needed to encounter something we all seek in this life—to be in the presence of God. From that day forward, such a presence could be encountered in the life of Jesus of Nazareth, who put no boundaries on where God could be encountered. That's why I believe we could describe Jesus as "God in a brown paper bag." Whether in socially and religiously acceptable settings or in the streets, we all still seek to find the kingdom of heaven where our station in life does not define us or make us acceptable or pleasing to God, but where we experience the grace to move in and out of all circles of social, political, and religious life knowing that God is not offended by our company. (Mike Childress)

Worship Aids

Invocation

God of Grace, fill the emptiness we bring to worship today. May the waters of our baptisms remind us once again you have claimed us for life, now and eternally, and that we may start afresh today. May our worship be pleasing to you and inspire us to do your will. Amen.

Pastoral Prayer

O God, we need your empowering grace to help us recognize that all are welcome in your presence. Take away our tendency to withdraw from those who do not fit our image of worthiness, for none of us is worthy and all are in need of your rescuing love. In the name of Jesus we pray. Amen.

Benediction

Let us rise and go back into the world from which we came. Let us throw off all that separates us from our neighbor that we might help make God's world a better place for humankind to live in. In the name of the Christ we pray. Amen. (Mike Childress)

MARCH 17, 2013

ঔঔঔ

Fifth Sunday in Lent

Readings: Isaiah 43:16-21; Psalm 126; Philippians 3:4b-14; John 12:1-8

Leap of Faith?

John 12:1-8

Our first parsonage was built into the slope of a hill, so both the front door and the basement door were at ground level. Only the diaper service delivery man used the front door. Everyone else came in through the basement. That was okay, because the screen door down there was sprung so tightly, it slammed behind anyone entering, giving ample warning to us upstairs.

When I entered late one afternoon (and the slamming door announced my arrival), I heard our two-year old daughter shriek, "Daddy's home!" As I made my way to the narrow, dimly lit staircase, I heard the "tap-tap-tap-tap" of her feet running through the house to the kitchen, where the stairs emerged. While I was on the bottom step (both arms laden with books, briefcase, bundles, and I-can't-remember-what), she flung open the door, saw me at the bottom of the stairs, and leapt into thin air toward me. I dropped everything (including a few heartbeats) and managed somehow to catch her as she hurtled into me. She wrapped her arms around my neck, squeezed with all her might, and squealed with glee. "I love you, Daddy!" she celebrated.

Every time I remember, I smile. I know it could have turned out very differently. She could have miscalculated her jump and cracked her head on the steps. I could have dropped her when she slammed into me. She could have broken her neck and become a quadriplegic. Then she would never have taken ballet lessons or thrown herself into gymnastics, softball, and basketball. Then she would never have been a cheerleader. Then our walk together down the aisle at her wedding would have been different (assuming she'd have still met her wonderful husband). Every time I remember these other moments, I smile as well. If she had been hurt in that leap, could I still use the moment as a sermon illustration of absolute faith? I do not know.

Yet, even as I ponder that tragic possibility, I cannot resist being captivated by her unrestrained exuberance. These two women give me pause, stop me in my tracks, and demand my attention: my daughter's leaping; Mary prodigally pouring precious ointment on Jesus' feet and kneeling to wipe those feet with her hair! Have I ever done anything so wanton, so uncalculated, so over-the-top? If not, am I missing something, or am I better off? When is extravagance simply wasteful and needlessly risky? When is extravagance absolutely essential to be genuinely human and authentically faithful? When is it neither, but somehow just holy, so full of wonder and delight it's not to be missed?

I have no formula through which to crunch the details of some specific situation and grind out a reliable answer. I just have this strong sense that a life without such extravagance, a life dominated by caution, careful calculation, and cost-benefit audits, is terribly sad and constricted—actually, the word that comes to mind is *constipated.* How can we hang around Jesus for very long and not catch this spirit of reckless abandon? Jesus called the Zebedee boys away from their boats, nets, and family—and they went! Jesus counseled the ardent young man to sell all his possessions, revolutionize his life, and follow Jesus—but "prudent calculation" stopped him. Jesus offered the honor of his company to the swindler Zacchaeus (instead of to any of the honorable folk), and Zacchaeus responded by promising to pay back fourfold whatever he had cheated anyone of (which was going to leave Zacchaeus with little). Jesus was warned that Herod was gunning for him, but Jesus immediately dismissed the warning and stayed his course. A few days after accepting and praising Mary's lavish gesture of love, Jesus gave his disciples his last commandment—to love one another in the same manner that he had loved them, and indicated that the measure of that love is to lay down one's life. Over the top! Always over the top! How can we be under the influence of Jesus and not be extravagant?

What might I yet do that some other preacher could use as the illustration in his or her sermon? Might I give a year's worth of income to relieve the suffering of the poor that we always have with us—although in the United States we have worked very hard to geographically insulate ourselves from them? Would that fill the world with the fragrance of love for Jesus? Might I surrender to the urge to become a foster parent and receive one of those hard-to-place children with a traumatic past and troubled present, even though that would tax my energy, patience, finances, and wisdom and would unalterably change my retirement? Would that plunge express trust in Jesus to catch me? What do I do, what do we do together, that makes absolutely no sense unless Jesus is Lord? And if Jesus is Lord, what wild and crazy thing can we not help but do?

Maybe I shouldn't even be asking such questions? Maybe they tend to turn what is the natural expression of a heart full of love into a carefully calculated strategy to make myself righteous. Maybe I should just sing songs like "More love to thee, O Christ," and "Joyful, joyful, we adore thee," and "Melt me, mold me, fill me, use me." Maybe I should just sing such songs until the rest of me follows my tongue and I'm too engaged leaping and pouring to ask many questions. It's high time I get me some nard to waste for love of Jesus. (Bill Obalil)

Lectionary Commentary

Isaiah 43:16-21

Israel's present languishing in exile is, in the poet's imagination, sandwiched between the memory of the exodus from Egypt and the hope of a new exodus from Babylon. What evidence is offered for such extravagant hope? Only a word, the word of God, apparently heard only by the prophet. Absolutely nowhere but in the prophet's announcement is that hope actualized on the stage of history. It's not a bad paradigm of faithful preaching.

Only those with a faithful memory can swallow such a call to hope without choking on its implausibility. Faithful memory recalls how incredible are all the promises of God, including the ones that have already been fulfilled. Once spoken, the audacious proclamation of hope creates a new situation for the hearer. The hearer must now decide whether to trust the promise and live by the vision or trust average experience and live only by observation. We are in that situation at every moment. We have heard the promise of the kingdom of God, glimpsed the vision of shalom and the age to come, and seen it embodied in Jesus of Nazareth. Will we, who are exiles from the realm of peace and justice, trust the gospel proclamation and live in coherence with the life of Jesus Christ, or will we trust in the power of arms and wealth and clout and live chiefly by such wisdom as "look out for number one"? Live into God's future or adapt to what already is? That is the critical decision in every age for people addressed by God's word.

Philippians 3:4b-14

Caution is called for in dealing with Paul's dismissal of his Jewish faith credentials (given the church's history of anti-Semitism) and with his embrace of suffering (given the counsels of submission church leaders have issued to women, the oppressed, and the powerless). Better for us to name our own cherished pedigrees (self-reliance, success, personal righteousness, believing the right religion), rather than Paul's Judaism, to regard as loss and rubbish in the light of knowing Christ. It is crucial for us to recognize that suffering itself is not the point, that suffering has no intrinsic value. What is valued is the courage and stamina to remain true to Christ's way of life despite the costs, the losses, and the suffering that such fidelity risks. There is no Christian discipleship without some relinquishment (even for birth-to-grave Christians), but not all relinquishment is Christian discipleship. The struggle, sometimes long and uncertain and agonizing, to discern what cherished things must be released in faith is itself a gift of God's love. We are cast into that struggle "because Christ Jesus has made [us] his own" (v. 12 NRSV). The courage to let cherished things go even when we are uncertain that God requires it comes from the confidence that our relationship with God is not a matter of us getting it all right. Our relationship with God is a matter of God's grace. Christ making us his own transforms our values. Gains become losses. The same old things look quite different because they have been reframed. One question persists beneath it all: Do we desire to know Jesus Christ more than we desire anything else? (Bill Obalil)

Worship Aids

Call to Worship

Let us dare to worship God with abandon.
Sing with shameless gusto.
Pray with urgent intensity.
Speak with holy passion.
Keep silence with awed humility.
Give with joyous generosity.
All: Let us give ourselves without reserve to the praise of God.

Invocation

Lord Jesus Christ, you have called us here, and in faith we have gathered. Meet us here and make this time holy. Let the reckless abandon of your love rub off on us. Lead us into those deep and mysterious places where only faith in you will let us go.

Benediction

Go forth as those who have made an unconditional surrender to Jesus Christ. Let the love of God control you, not the fear of how you look nor the anxiety of what others think. Let the Holy Spirit set your hearts on fire. (Bill Obalil)

Thorn Bushes and Monarch Butterflies

Second in a Series of Three on Spiritual Geography:
Finding God in Unusual Places

Genesis 22:1-19

We all have quirky ways of interpreting God's presence in matters of life. Whether it is reading Scripture or noticing certain phenomena in our lives, we try to sense God with us along life's journey.

I recall needing to sense God's presence during a particularly stressful time while living in North Carolina. Trying to take care of one's health when experiencing chronic stress is important, so I began a walking program to deal with the pressure I was under. While walking, I quoted Scripture to help buoy up my faith that God was with me and to avoid feeling severe loneliness and the dreaded thought that I was not going to survive my dilemma. One favorite was Psalm 121, which depicts the psalmist seeing God's steadfast presence in the majestic hills surrounding him. He realizes that it is not the beauty of the mountains but his creator God from whom his strength surfaces during his stressful, even despairing moments.

One day on my walk, I noticed a monarch butterfly floating in the near distance. Its golden-yellow body trimmed in black shimmered in the sun's rays, and I was awestruck by its beauty. It disappeared from view, and I couldn't help but think of the creature as I meandered through the neighborhood. About two blocks into my walk I noticed the monarch coming toward me. It stayed with me, floating in and out of my presence for the remainder of my walk. For a moment, a brief, fleeting moment, it seemed the butterfly was bringing some assurance that God was with me. I recalled a bit of Chinese wisdom that we are not to chase the butterfly but to remain still and let the butterfly come to us. That thought brought reassurance of God's presence on a day when I was unsure of my faith in God's help. This phenomenon repeated itself for weeks, even months, whenever I found myself in deep stress. And it would happen in the most peculiar, unusual places. For example, when sitting at a stoplight in the downtown area of Salisbury, North Carolina, the weight of my economic situation covered my consciousness like a foreboding cloud. At that very moment, a monarch butterfly gently crossed the windshield. This kind of occurrence continued for months, not frequently, but consistently. Rather than shrug it off as inconsequential, I accepted such moments as symbols of God's assurance that things were going to work out. I would just need to keep going forward, doing my part in bringing resolution to a very painful, depressing time in my life.

Perhaps this is what Abraham was going through in his own dilemma. His vision of God's presence in his life became the motivating factor for the rest of his life and the life of his people. God provided all he needed to get through the rough and sometimes faithless moments in his life. I would call this vision a partnership between God and Abraham. God is limitless when it comes to providing us with the assurance that we are not alone in this life. Numerous accounts in the Bible reflect such a presence. Elijah, while going through a severe depression and escaping into the mountains, came to the conclusion that God is not in the storm or any other phenomenon. God is within us and can use things like lambs caught in thorn bushes, mountains, storms, even monarch butterflies to give us the assurance we need in order to grow our faith and embark on a faith partnership. (Mike Childress)

Worship Aids

Invocation

O God, we offer to you our worship. Please accept our offering as a way to give you thanks for life, life here and life eternal. May our worship reveal to us the immeasurable depths of your love and so inspire us to love our neighbor unswervingly. Amen.

Confession

O God, we often do not know how to pray. Life's demands and uncertainties leave us searching for words to tell you how much we need your guidance. We fill the air with words and yet leave our prayer feeling that you didn't hear a word we said. Forgive us. Empower us to keep following your Christ and his teachings. In good times and bad, may we seek your face in all of our concerns. Amen.

Assurance

Know today that the God who reached out to Abraham is the God who sent Jesus of Nazareth to reach out and heal all our unrighteousness. Receive the forgiveness of God through Jesus Christ. Amen. (Mike Childress)

MARCH 24, 2013

Palm / Passion Sunday

Palm Readings: Luke 19:28-40; Psalm 118:1-2, 19-29
Passion Readings: Isaiah 50:4-9a; Psalm 31:9-16; Philippians 2:5-11; Luke 22:14–23:56

The Way of the Cross

Luke 22:14–23:56

If Luke were a screenwriter, the passion narrative would be the climactic battle scene of his film. The future of earth and humanity hangs in the balance. Jesus vs. Caesar. A rag-tag band of peasants with maybe a couple of swords vs. the vaunted Roman legions with state-of-the-art weaponry (a little like furry Ewoks vs. Imperial Stormtroopers). The prospects seem bleak for one side. I know where the oddsmakers are betting their own cash. And Jesus indeed is the one who ends up dead—not Caesar, not Pilate, not the crucifying soldiers. So, depending on how you define victory, it looks like the oddsmakers were right. Yet the Christian church has insisted that the cross of Jesus is a victory, not a defeat. How can that be?

Of course, there is the resurrection, which we will celebrate next week. Jesus is sprung from death's grip and is thereby vindicated. But even before the resurrection, the cross of Jesus is in some mysterious way a victory of God—a victory of the power of God engaged with the power of Caesar (the current exemplar of normal human rule).

This struggle brews from the beginning of Luke's Gospel. In the wilderness after Jesus' baptism, the devil offers him a coaching session on this power business, "Since you are God's Son," the devil mentors Jesus, "command this stone to become a loaf of bread." Use your power to satisfy your own wants and needs. Armies fight on their stomachs. Jesus opts for a more mysterious power. "*People won't live only by bread.*" The devil proceeds to lesson two and counsels Jesus to do whatever it takes to seize glory and authority. Even rulers have to serve the powers that establish their rule. Jesus again declines. "*You will worship the Lord your God and serve only him.*" The devil tutors Jesus in the power of manipulative spectacle. Jesus stays the course. "*Don't test the Lord your God*" (Luke 4:1-12).

The gospel struggle is not just between two competitors using the same weapons against each other to see who comes out on top, like a fencing match or a war. The gospel struggle is between two totally different kinds of power, one of which looks more like weakness to us than power. So where earthly monarchs plot to kill their enemies, Jesus schemes to love them. Where authorities punish those who hate them, Jesus plans to do them good. Where rulers take revenge on those who hurt them, Jesus prays for them (see Luke 6:27-28). Jesus reigns through compassion, not coercion.

We would have noticed this contest of opposite forms of power in almost every scene of Luke's Gospel film, even the comic ones. The ancient emperors stamped the image of stately trees on their coins—cedars and oaks—to symbolize the majesty of their dominions. As the emblem of his kingdom, Jesus picks an invasive weed—the mustard bush (not even a little tree)—mocking the pretension of earthly powers. "I am the king of the mustard seed empire." If you have to explain the joke, don't bother.

The argument about real power cannot remain *sotto voce* forever. Screenwriter Luke dropped a foreshadowing hint in the wilderness of temptation: "When the devil had finished every test, he departed from him until an opportune time" (4:13 NRSV). The opportune time arrives in Jerusalem, and Jesus is again assaulted by testing. The suspense of Luke's penultimate scene is not whether Jesus will live. Early on it is pretty clear he will not. The suspense is will Jesus, under the crushing grip of Caesar's power, renege? Will he give up on his commitment to embrace only God's power that looks more than ever like weakness?

At the table sits the one who will betray Jesus, but Jesus does not banish him. Jesus serves him. In argument, Jesus' friends succumb to the seduction of lording it over others. Jesus reminds them he is one who serves, and then confers on them his kingdom—the kingdom of God's hidden dominion. The prospect of the pain Caesar's power can exact moves Jesus to ask to be let out of his commission, but even as Jesus anguishes he also surrenders to the mysterious working of God's rule. When the temple police come to grab him by night, Jesus' disciples want to fight fire with fire and strike with the sword. Jesus thunders, "No more of this!" and heals the bloody victim (vv. 49-51). Under Caesar's authority the soldiers mock Jesus, flog him, and nail him to a cross. Under God's authority, Jesus forgives them. In this life-and-death struggle, one is tempted to say Jesus does not fare well. But the truth is Jesus emerges victorious. Caesar and his agents throw every power they have at Jesus, but they cannot get him to legitimate their kind of power. Jesus remains faithful to God's holy power of love to the end.

His fidelity saves us and challenges us. Will we decide with Jesus this Monday and the following Monday to stake our lives on God's power, or will we bow to Caesar's power along with just about everyone else?

On which power will we stake our lives—the power of Caesar or the power of God? From the cross, God got Jesus' answer. God waits eagerly for our answer. (Bill Obalil)

Lectionary Commentary

Luke 19:28-40

In John, when Pilate interrogates Jesus about his kingly aspirations, Jesus answers, "My kingdom doesn't originate from this world. If it did, my guards would fight so that I wouldn't have been arrested by the Jewish leaders. My kingdom isn't from here" (John 18:36). In Luke, Jesus acts out this truth instead of speaking it. The church, wanting to acclaim Jesus as king, has seized on the palm procession as a ticker tape parade, a celebration of the glory of Jesus. Bibles with section titles call it "Jesus' Triumphal Entry into Jerusalem." And it is, if seen through the eyes of mature faith. But look at it askance, out of the corner of the eye. Does it not look more like a parody of earthly displays of power and glory? Caesar and his agents (like Pilate, who just a few days earlier had probably entered Jerusalem from his seaside palace) ride into capital cities astride great horses or in chariots. Jesus enters Jerusalem on a colt. Caesar is ushered in by the Roman legions. Jesus is ushered in by the "whole throng" (how large was that?) of the disciples (peasants). That Jesus believes the stones would shout out if his disciples were silenced indicates he has full confidence his is a truly royal and holy entrance—one that mocks the grand displays of normal kings. If Jesus is not just a comic king, if he is God's authorized one, then he punctures the pompous pretensions of the rulers we're used to. It would be grand guerilla theater, hilarious political satire—if so much were not at stake: the life of Jesus, and the life of the world. And if we still struggle to set aside the triumphalism of Palm Sunday, let us remember the very next verse in Luke: "As Jesus came to the city and observed it, he wept over it" (v. 41). That ought to sober the party.

Isaiah 50:4-9a

The great scandal of the earliest Christians was identifying a crucified person as God's Messiah. It was a contradiction in terms, not just for their neighbors, but for them. They searched their scriptures for help in dealing with this paradox and came across the evocative Servant Songs in Isaiah, of which this is a fragment. Remember it is a song, not a treatise. It rehearses the mystery that God's faithful servant suffers in service. It does not explain it in some cosmic debt-cancellation scheme. The song is not a lament. It celebrates fidelity and praises God. Only because God has been faithful to the servant could the servant be faithful to God and fulfill the call "to sustain the weary with a word" (v. 4). God is the subject of the active verbs: "awakens my ear" (v. 4), "will help me" (v. 7), "will declare me innocent" (v. 8). The servant narrates what he does not do: "rebel . . . turn my back" (v. 5), "hide my face" (v. 6), "be ashamed" (v. 7). The song does not celebrate the popularity, success, or effectiveness of the servant. It celebrates the steadfast persistence and loyalty of the servant made possible by God's grace. Facing the horrid mystery of human suffering, we can sing songs of faithfulness without endorsing suffering as the will of God. More people are carried into the arms of God by songs and poems than by arguments and explanations.

Philippians 2:5-11

A friend calls this Christological hymn "the Christian swoosh," linking humiliation and exaltation, death and life. Math majors see in it the Christ parabola: beginning at the top in the form of God, descending through slavery to death, and ascending again to the status of Lord. Notice the agency of the verbs. Jesus does not exploit equality with God, empties himself, takes the form of a slave, humbles himself, obeys to death. With death, the Jesus action is over. He is powerless to do anything more. If anything more is to come of it all, Jesus is as dependent upon God as we are. God: highly honors Jesus, gives him the name above every name (to which everyone will bow and every tongue confess). Jesus does not achieve these things. He receives them, and not for his glory, but for God's. Paul uses the hymn as a model of Christian discipleship. We are to live the downward arc of the parabola and trust God for the rest. You know, if it was good enough for Jesus . . . The hymn presses us to examine if we in any way have followed Jesus to work a bargain, to manipulate out of God some exalting for ourselves which Jesus never sought. Whatever that is, it's not the mind of Christ. Following Jesus on the swoosh means emptying, serving, humbling, obeying, and dying. The rest is up to God. (Bill Obalil)

Worship Aids

Invocation

We have come to follow your son, our savior, Jesus Christ, even when his way leads to Golgotha. Meet us here, O God, and remain with us, or we will stumble off the path. Amen.

Confession

You call us to serve alongside Jesus. We chase after status. You call us to stand with Jesus. We run in fear. You call us to forgive like Jesus. We condemn. Forgive us, God of mercy. Deepen our faith in Jesus until we have the faith of Jesus. Amen.

Assurance of Pardon

Our confession does not make God's forgiveness possible. God's forgiveness makes our confession possible. Before we can face the truth about ourselves, before we can confront how much we need God, we must trust God's love is there for us. In Christ we know it is. Thanks be to God. (Bill Obalil)

Breaking Out of Our Personal Tombs

Third in a Series of Three on Spiritual Geography: Finding God in Unusual Places

Mark 8:26-39

The wildernesses of our lives take on many characteristics. They are the wild and uninhabitable regions in life. They are not the places we immediately expect to find (or to be found by) God. One such place is the tombs in this story where a deranged man finds refuge. Whether it was schizophrenia or some other mental health issue in his life, he has been deemed unworthy to live in the mainstream of his community.

Jesus was always finding what I would call "learning moments" whenever human need arose in his company. The disciples were not always quick to catch on to what he was trying to teach them. Many times they were silent and befuddled. In this story, their silence is deafening. At no point in this episode do we find any communication going on between Jesus and his disciples. Not even Peter, impetuous Peter, has anything to say. Undoubtedly, the screaming, wild, naked maniac has them frozen in their tracks. I can imagine them slowly backing up and getting ready to get into the boat and head back across the lake. Furthermore, to make matters worse, they are in Gentile territory and clearly out of their ethnic comfort zone.

This is what can happen to us when we find ourselves in uncharted territory along life's journey. We are quick to retreat and return to the places in our lives that are comfortable, manageable, and reasonable. In uncharted waters, we feel totally vulnerable, even helpless. But it is precisely in such times that we need to stand our ground and meet such challenges head-on. We, with God's help, can learn through such times how to greet life with an unflappable faith. I would go so far as to say that to deny ourselves the opportunity to grow our faith through such events is to stop learning, growing, and developing our faith in God's presence. This stalwart posture is evident in Jesus' demeanor and how he faces the situation. When you and I find ourselves in similar circumstances, may we use such a story to help face the situations? I believe so. But let's look at several aspects of this story to see what we may learn.

First, Jesus is unafraid of going to places he's never been before. We don't know if he had been there before. Perhaps he had heard about the man and went to check on him. For whatever reason, his visit is timely. I believe he intended to find the man and help him. Faith is something that has to be nurtured, cultivated, and exercised. We, like Jesus, need to prepare ourselves to expect the unexpected. When we do, we find the strength to face our challenges with the resolve that God will see us through.

Second, we may see the situation for what it really is. Jesus engages the man, who is startled that anyone would want to help him. I can see Jesus greeting the man, not with a stern and emotionless face, but with compassion and love; he meets the man before addressing the man's need. I experienced this once when taking our son to the pediatrician. One day, following one of many visits related to a chronic disease, the doctor asked that I remain in the room for a chat. He had learned that I was entering seminary and wanted to share something. He told me that the first and foremost thing he always does with a patient is to listen. He said you will learn in ministry to cultivate one of the essential components in helping people—listening and getting to know the person. As I think back, I realize why our son trusted this doctor—the doctor was interested in Matt first. The doctor also said to look people in the eye. A lot can be learned about a person when they know they have our full, undivided attention.

After many years in ministry, I find that his wisdom has been proven true. The tragic man in Mark's story runs to Jesus because he senses Jesus' true interest in him. Almost immediately, a trust develops. He knows he can trust Jesus. When situations entomb us, we need to seek out those we trust in order to deal with what's bothering us.

Finally, we can learn to loosen the grip of a situation on our lives. The chains fall from the man when he realizes he can survive his ordeal. First to fall are the emotional, psychological chains. Fear is one such link in the chain of events that develops in tough, seemingly insurmountable, situations. The man no longer fears his situation because someone took the time and effort to help. I imagine he is more than glad to reach out and help others when he encounters a friend or stranger going through tough times. He is able to pay it forward as a result of being empowered by God's love to loosen the grip of his situation on his life and return to the mainstream. (Mike Childress)

Worship Aids

Call to Worship

Let us come into God's presence with words that come from our hearts and souls and not just our lips. Let us prepare to be empowered to be the people of God in our time and place. Let us throw off everything that hinders our worship. In the name of Christ we pray. Amen.

Invocation

O Holy God, we come to worship realizing our unholiness. Yet, to whom shall we turn in our time of need? Only you can restore our faith. Through worship give us faith enough to move the mountains of despair that have separated us from you and from one another. In the name of the Father, Son, and Holy Spirit. Amen.

Benediction

We have worshiped the living God!
We have responded to the grace of God!
Let us pick up the mantle of faith and meet a new day!
With God's help, we will share this grace with all people. Amen. (Mike Childress)

MARCH 28, 2013

Holy Thursday

Readings: Exodus 12:1-4, (5-10), 11-14; Psalm 116:1-2, 12-19; 1 Corinthians 11:23-26; John 13:1-17, 31b-35

A Lesson Offered

1 Corinthians 11:23-26

The church in Corinth was struggling with its understanding and practice of the Lord's Supper. This passage is situated in the context of both correction and instruction in the purpose and the significance of the Lord's Supper and its place and practice in the early church. In the verses preceding the text for our consideration, Paul alludes to some apathy and misuse surrounding the celebration of Communion at the church's gatherings. In the verses for our consideration, Paul seeks to clarify and mandate the practice in the way and in the sacred experience that it must be in order for the church to realize why Jesus shared it on that first evening and why the church continues the practice.

Paul begins this passage by giving the meal its authority. This meal was received from the Lord in order to be passed on to the worshiping community. Paul wants this young, fledgling group of believers to realize that this meal was an act that Jesus began and an act of the community of faith that must be received from him to be shared with others. In the same way that it symbolized for Jesus the sacrificial nature of his living and his dying, so too it must continue to serve as a reminder to those who follow of the sacrificial nature of their own witness and faithfulness.

The apostle seeks to establish a liturgy that will empower and bring a new and holy significance to the practice of this sacred meal in helping to move the community beyond misunderstanding and misuse of it in their life together. The church in Corinth was divided, perhaps on socioeconomic terms that were beginning to find expression even in the way the fellowship sought to share and practice the Lord's Supper. Paul seeks to retrain this community by helping them understand the sacredness of this meal and its observance as an act created and instituted by the Lord. He wants to educate and inspire deeper understanding of a divine mystery that had its origin and experience in the very life of Jesus. Jesus sought to establish a way for his followers to remember his death—its power, expression, sacrifice, and purpose—by connecting with everyday elements of nourishment and the Jewish Passover. The symbols of the bread and the cup are reinterpreted by Jesus in such a way that the reenactment of the meal can become a way and a means to remember and share once again in the sacred mystery of Jesus' life and his death. For Paul it becomes a sacred proclamation of the sacrifice Jesus made on the cross for the sins of the whole world as he offers redemption and wholeness in the place of sin and despair.

I remember an opening worship service at an elementary summer camp one year. As we worshiped we continued to notice the misbehavior of one blond-headed kid on the first row. He was very disrupting. The next opportunity for worship later in the day, it was the same story. We finally began to try to understand what was going on with this child. We learned that he and his brother were spending the summer with their grandparents. Their mom was recently divorced, and the boys had been sent to the grandparents for some much-needed support and change of scenery. The grandparents had sent them to camp for the week. As far as we could determine, the boys had never been to church. We began to understand Adam's behavior, and we partnered him with a senior-high support counselor also named Adam (not their real names). We instructed "big" Adam to help "young" Adam understand why we did some of the things we did at worship. It changed everything. On the final evening of worship, we shared Communion. Each camp "family" picked two persons from their group to serve Communion to the other members in the final worship service. As young Adam's group came forward, I asked for the two persons to come join me at the altar to receive the elements to serve to their family. Young Adam was one of those chosen. I served him and the other student, and then I handed the elements to them to serve their family. Tears filled my eyes as I watched this young student serving the sacred elements and saying the sacred words to his family. I will never forget that Communion service.

Paul wants to set a young church straight about its misguided practice of the Holy meal. He seeks to help them realize the roots of its authority in Jesus and the practice of its expression in remembering and symbolizing the death of our Lord and the redemption it offers a hurting and sinful world. Paul leads the Corinthians to realize that what they are doing in this in-between time is the proclamation of Jesus' victory over death and all that it means for sinful humanity.

Paul demonstrates for us once again the role of teacher and instructor. Paul boldly seeks to help correct misdirected spiritual practices for a struggling new church. As I reflect upon young Adam and a sacred time we shared, I am reminded that we take too much for granted in the church related to where people are and what people understand. My prayer is that young Adam never forgot that experience either. In the midst of his own brokenness and pain, he learned about and experienced that the power of Jesus is in the midst of life experience. Isn't that why we are here? Isn't that what we are called to do? (Travis Franklin)

Lectionary Commentary

Exodus 12:1-4, (5-10), 11-14

These verses share the story of the institution of the Passover meal for the Jews, a most appropriate passage for Maundy Thursday. The heart of this story is God's deliverance of God's people from slavery in Egypt. This text gives specific instructions for the Passover meal and the purpose and symbolism of the meal. There is no ceremony or celebration more central to Jewish life and faith than Passover. In remembering the experience and day of Passover, the Jewish people recognize and proclaim as a community of faith that God is the one who sets people free and claims them as God's own.

John 13:1-17, 31b-35

John differs from the other Gospels about the details of the last meal Jesus had with the disciples. John places the last meal before the Passover and does not provide a retelling of the institution of the commemorative meal. The central act of Jesus in John's Gospel is the washing of the disciples' feet. This act makes a theological statement about the true nature of the identity and purpose of Jesus. In washing their feet, Jesus seeks to pass on to the disciples what the role of the church is to be in its work, scope, and purpose. Like Jesus, the church is created and formed to serve. Like Jesus, the church is to serve God, one another, and the world. The communal nature of the footwashing speaks to the communal nature of the church. Some congregations make a sacred ritual of the practice, invoking God's presence and providing an authentic expression of the mystery of grace. Present in the act is also the powerful idea of cleansing. The church lives through the cleansing act of Jesus. Humility and service become the benchmarks of the church's identity and purpose. (Travis Franklin)

Worship Aids

Call to Worship

We gather in this place and in this time to remember and to celebrate the freedom and deliverance God seeks to offer us as God's people.

In humility we gather to be open to God's most Holy Spirit as it seeks to move among us.

God is with us in the sharing of the bread and the cup.

Thanks be to God for God's love and God's mercy.

Prayer of Confession

Lord, we come before you tonight as a humbled people. In light of your most gracious and merciful love shown in the death of your son, Jesus, may we be honest before you in these moments together. In this time of reflection, we admit our many sins of omission and commission. Remembering them is painful, and we realize the misery and pain they have brought to you, O God. Pardon and deliver us from ourselves and the sinfulness of our living. Grant us a new beginning and form within us clean and righteous hearts that we might be the people you have redeemed us to be. Lead us in the way that leads to everlasting life. In the name of Jesus our Lord we pray. Amen.

Words of Assurance

As certain as the sun rises each morning and sets at the evening hour, so shall your sins be forgiven. Receive the redemption of God offered to you in Christ our Lord. Let God's forgiveness and love so fill you that you go forth and serve with compassion all who suffer. You are free to be fully God's person in all that you say and do! (Travis Franklin)

Anonymous

First in a Series of Three on Heroes of Lent

Mark 14:12-16

In literary terms, a hero is the protagonist of a story who embodies the virtues of the reader's culture. They may be strong, gracious, and morally pure. They are often valiant warriors. Sometimes they may be cunning, or wise-cracking, or have other endearing flaws.

By its nature, Lent is not something we associate with heroism. Lent is a time of self-denial, of recognizing our moral flaws, repenting, and recommitting to following Jesus. So the heroes of Lent do not fit our conventional notions of heroism.

At the beginning of every play we typically find a list of characters and a short description: Romeo, son to Montague. Juliet, daughter to Capulet. Major characters are listed before minor characters: first and second watchmen, citizens of Verona. If you are the kind of person who sits through movie credits to the very end, you read the names of actors who played "Girl on Subway #1," or "Sandwich-eating Man," characters who never get named, but who either stand in the background or have one or two lines of dialogue. They are the ones who simply point to the sky and say, "Look! Is it a bird? Is it a plane?" Sometimes they are merely what the movie industry calls "extras," yet without them the action is flat. They give voice to what the audience sees and wonders. They direct our attention to the action on the stage. Sometimes they deliver news of a key plot point.

So who is the guy with the water? How does Jesus know to direct his disciples to find him? Is it just divine intuition, something that Jesus knows mysteriously because he is the son of God? Or is it a prearranged signal, something that Jesus had orchestrated beforehand out of earshot of the disciples? Carrying water, some scholars say, was typically work reserved for women. Was the man one of the sect of Essenes, religious reformers who believed in celibacy? Was he a slave? And who is the owner of the house? The owner is clearly a follower of Jesus. Jesus sends a message to him with regal authority: "Where is my guest room?" (v. 14). "My," Jesus says, as though everything the anonymous man owns belongs to Jesus. The owner shows the disciples to a large room, furnished and ready for the Passover feast.

It's fun to speculate and theorize about these two anonymous people and their connection to Jesus. I imagine them as two unnamed disciples, part of the crowd who heard Jesus' teaching and resonated with his descriptions of a coming kingdom. Like the unnamed women who stood at a distance at the cross, or the unnamed woman who washed Jesus' feet, they are the followers who stepped up when the inner circle of named disciples fell away, the "understudies" who were minor characters until the main ones decided not to show up. So, as the authorities in Jerusalem begin putting up "Wanted" posters around Jerusalem for Jesus of Nazareth, these two individuals realize they have the opportunity to offer Jesus and his follower's safe sanctuary within the city. Jesus and his inner circle will be able to celebrate the Passover within Jerusalem, the hope of every observant Jew of their day. Through their arrangements, these two characters provide Jesus with the shelter that enables him to break bread with his disciples right under the noses of the people seeking his death. Perhaps they are also the same ones who allow the disciples to huddle behind their locked doors after Jesus' crucifixion in John 20:19.

This is not the first time that Jesus has apparently arranged things quietly beforehand. In John 11:2, before Jesus ever enters Jerusalem, he sends disciples ahead to retrieve a colt so that he may ride it into Jerusalem. While it's possible to read these instructions as mystical, divine foreknowledge, I prefer to see it as a hint of Jesus' life outside the view of the narrator. Jesus has a life that extends outside the scope of the text. In John 13:27, Jesus tells Judas, "What you are about to do, do quickly." The other disciples assume that Judas has private instructions from Jesus to take care of some business, something apparently so in keeping with Jesus' character that they never question it until later. I love hearing this side of Jesus because I like to imagine what his activities might have been outside of the biblical text. He had a real life, with acquaintances like Peter's mother-in-law, Nicodemus, Joseph of Arimathea, and Mary Magdalene, of whose stories we catch only snippets.

I was part of the generation that grew up with Star Wars. I loved pretending to be the hero, Luke Skywalker, locked in battle with the villain Darth Vader. I loved the eye-popping special effects and the amazing diversity of alien life from uncharted worlds. And, like others of my generation, when the long-awaited prequel movies came along, I was disappointed and frustrated. Part of the reason for my disappointment was that while the first movies opened up new worlds and allowed space for my imagination to play, the later movies closed those worlds, tied up loose ends, and made the imaginative universe much smaller. Good stories, well-told, feel like real life. There always remain untold stories, loose ends, and unfinished business, minor characters who appear on the scene and move the action forward. Perhaps they are not heroes. Their role is too small, their dialogue too brief. But you know from the role they play that they may be heroes in a different story.

This is the way that real heroes operate. An anonymous stranger bangs on doors during an apartment fire and gets everyone out of the building.

A woman pulls a child out of the undertow, and the grateful parents realize they never asked her name.

The two individuals who stepped forward to offer housing to this would-be Messiah who was constantly on the run, who had nowhere safe to lay his head, who was born in a manger because there was no room elsewhere; these persons risked their own necks to shelter an outlaw. Without them we might not celebrate the Lord's Supper the same way. Every time we break bread and tell the story, we owe a debt of gratitude to Water-carrying Man #1 and House Owner, the minor characters who became heroes. (Dave Barnhart)

Worship Aids

Invocation

Author of life, you are the director of the cosmic drama of redemption. You are also the main character, and the chorus, the stagehand, and audience. God of all, we come to celebrate your performance, and we heed your call to come and participate in your great work.

Pastoral Prayer

Lord, we often feel that our burdens, our desires, and our prayers are overlooked. We are minor characters in a drama in which we feel that our voices would not be missed. Yet you give us a role to play without which the action of your redemptive work cannot move forward. Let us be willing to offer ourselves and our resources for your use.

Sending Forth

We leave this place mindful of our roles in the story of God. God gives us each a persona in God's great drama of salvation. Go forth and play your part not as an extra, but as a hero whom God has called into service! (Dave Barnhart)

MARCH 29, 2013

Good Friday

Readings: Isaiah 52:13–53:12; Psalm 22; Hebrews 10:16-25 or 4:14-16, 5:7-9; John 18:1–19:42

Just Another Day!

John 18:1–19:42

John offers a very different telling of the crucifixion of Jesus than that of the other Gospels. John makes bold and declarative proclamations as to who Jesus is, what God is doing through Jesus, who the world is in the involvement of God's work in Christ, and who the church must be as a result. Throughout the telling of the story Jesus is in control of each part of the drama as it unfolds. Jesus is portrayed as very aware and very purposeful in his playing out of the role God has called him to play. Because the hour has come, Jesus allows the arrest to be made.

Even in the interrogation by Pilate, Jesus is in charge. Pilate is portrayed as worried, skeptical of his own role in it all, uneasy and failing at every turn to try to negotiate for Jesus' release. In the end, the only thing he successfully accomplishes is a confession of faith out of the Jewish religious leaders as to the kingship of Caesar. Even at the cross Jesus carries his own cross, quotes scripture so as to define what God is doing in this event, making arrangements for the care of his mother, and finally, willingly, gives up his spirit. John wants all to know that Jesus is the one who controls and interprets what is really going on in the story as it unfolds.

John also seeks to portray those representing the world in religion, politics, and the "crowd" as completely rebellious and out of touch with what God is doing among them. The religious leaders are seen only as bit players in the unfolding drama. Pilate is unsure of how to handle Jesus, but finally gives in to the wishes of the mob. The crowd continues to cry out for Jesus' blood. The soldiers beat him and mock him. Even the disciples struggle and finally deny and forsake him. It is as though John wants the reader to realize that the world is against Jesus in every way. The irony of this reality is laced throughout the story. One of the most poignant moments is illustrated cleverly when—in the season of Passover, at the anniversary of freedom from Pharaoh—the Jews choose "Pharaoh," the emperor (19:12). Jesus is alone against a broken and rebellious world. Even those closest to him have now turned their backs on him in his time of trial.

John is more preacher than historian throughout this narrative. He tells the story in such a way that truths about who people are, who God is, and the relationship between the two become powerfully evident. The sinfulness and brokenness of the people are woven throughout. Power, misunderstanding, manipulation, pride, fear, hatred, control, pain, suffering, and humiliation all find their way into this telling of the tale. Jesus knows who is in control of these moments in history.

In the closing episode, the disciples remove Jesus' body from the cross. Even here, John employs deep symbolism and evidence of God's plan. Jesus died as the Passover lamb, and his body was treated as such. John, the preacher, wants us to know that this was the Passover of all Passovers. These events are used by God to proclaim a new exodus, not from the bondage in Egypt, but from the bondage of sin and death.

In one year I lost my marriage, my best friend to a brain tumor, my sister to drug rehab, a position in a ministry I truly loved and had served faithfully for twelve years, and had my salary cut in half as I served an interim church. It was by far the worst year of my life, and the suffering I experienced is beyond description. However, throughout that year I also experienced the presence of God in a way I never had before. I saw some of the worst in humanity and yet, I saw God working in powerful and transforming ways that changed me forever.

Isn't that what this story is about? Regardless of how we may experience or perceive life, even in our worst moments God is moving, working, redeeming, loving, creating, and transforming history. John portrays that truth with vitality and purpose. The drama is "so us," and it is "so God." We seem to bumble along, so caught up in the foolishness of our lives that we lose touch with where God is and what God is doing. We miss the beauty and wonder of all that God is giving and all that God is doing in our midst. What happened to me in a year marked by one crisis after another is that I was finally humbled enough that, for a short time anyway, I simply began to realize just how present God is in my life. The issue is never God; the issue is always us.

On that day in Jerusalem, as the great celebrations were being shared and preparations were under way for God's day, an individual was crucified on a cross at Calvary. It was just another day. God always comes when we least expect it. It was anything but just another day! This was the day and because of this day the world would never be the same again! Thanks be to God! (Travis Franklin)

Lectionary Commentary

Isaiah 52:13–53:12

The text from Isaiah comes from the fourth Servant Song in "Second Isaiah." It is a powerful text to share in the community of faith on Good Friday. The passage portrays the exultation of God for the work of the suffering servant and the surprised response of nations and kings. The central section of the work has a third party reporting on the life and death of the servant and the response to them. The final section declares the meaning and effect of the servant's suffering and the exultation of the servant for the work that was done through his suffering. The text of this work identifies the meaning of all that the servant does and establishes through his suffering: God will exalt and make right his suffering, God's power and might find their most powerful expression through weakness, the suffering is for the benefit of others, and others do not have to pay the price because the servant has already paid it. Through the ages, Christians have found comfort and purpose in these passages related to the death and the resurrection of Jesus.

Hebrews 10:16-25

This reading begins by quoting Jeremiah 31:33-34. Its powerful imagery appeals to the Christian community to be assured in its expression of faith as it remains steadfast in hope and leads all to express love and to do good works. It builds confidence. It promises a new covenant in which God is present in our hearts and minds and our sins are not held against us. It reinforces that the work of Christ in redeeming the world from its sin is authentic. Christ becomes the reason and purpose for community. Christ also enables intimate relationships between God and sinners. (Travis Franklin)

Worship Aids

Call to Worship

We dare to gather on this dark and sinister day to remember.

We remember our sin and our need for redemption.

We boldly look and see the suffering of your Son
and the horror of such dying.
We remember his love and the price he has paid
that we might be forgiven and freed.

Prayer of Confession

Dearest Lord, the reality of our sin is clear to us. We have the scars on our hearts and souls to prove it. We come together as a sinful and broken people. We do not have the capacity to save ourselves from ourselves. Sin has brought pain, suffering, death, and despair to us, those we love, and to our world. Forgive us for our inclination to sin. Pardon us from the sin that has infected all that we know and experience. Liberate us from this present evil that cleverly deceives all that you have given to us. Lead us to the light of your salvation. Make us ever obedient to your will and your will only, not only today but every day. In the name and spirit of Jesus Christ our Lord we pray. Amen.

Words of Assurance

Hear these words, for they are trustworthy and true: Christ came that we might be a forgiven people. Through his suffering, death, and resurrection we have been given new life. Pardoned and delivered from our sin, we claim this new beginning. In the name of Jesus we are forgiven. Hallelujah and Amen! (Travis Franklin)

Peter

Second in a Series of Three on Heroes of Lent

Mark 14:66-72

Peter is perhaps a too-obvious choice for a Lenten hero. He seems to jump into the spotlight every time Jesus turns around. He misses his cue or comes in early or misinterprets Jesus' lines or says the wrong thing. At the climax of the story, when he stands in the courtyard of the high priest, he fails to deliver the lines he has practiced. "If I must die alongside you, I won't deny you," he told Jesus in Mark 14:31. He's been fantasizing about playing the martyr and being faithful until the end, yet when the moment arrives and he has a chance to play the hero, the wrong words come out, "I don't know this man you're talking about."

Peter gets a bum rap. He is the whipping boy for the failure of all of us to follow Jesus, and he bears our Christian sins of naive enthusiasm and cowardice. We have heard from thousands of pulpits that he is alternately heroic and weak, faithful and inconstant, insightful and stupid. The stories of Peter read like a litany of bravado and missed opportunities. We see in him a picture of our own shame and a reminder of all the ways we fail Jesus.

I do not know how many times I have daydreamed of being the hero myself. Witnessing a car wreck, I'm the one who braves the flames to cut an unconscious victim from the seatbelt and drag him from the wreckage before it explodes into a fireball. I'm the one who sprints through gunfire (timed, as in the movies, so that no bullets actually hit their targets) to rescue a child. Afterward, when I'm interviewed for the local television news, the breathless reporter asks me how it feels to be a hero, and I reply, "I just did what anyone else would do." And yet I remember a night when I witnessed a drunk driver turn his car end-over-end into a ditch after nearly missing my rear bumper. I remember gripping my steering wheel, too panicked to move, speak, or do anything constructive. I slowed the car to a crawl long enough to make sure that other cars stopped to help. I did not. I drove to a pay phone and called my parents to bring me home. I was only sixteen, I tell myself. I was inexperienced. I have a long list of excuses. The simple fact is that I failed to be a hero. I cannot pretend that I am less cowardly today.

When I hear the story of Peter, I can feel the panic rising in his gut. "Aren't you from Galilee? Your accent sure sounds Galilean," someone asks. "I left Galilee years ago," he replies. "I never knew Jesus." "I'm pretty sure I saw you with him," the serving girl says. "You're wrong," he answers, "You mistake me for someone else." Perhaps as the words escape from Peter's lips, he remembers Jesus' words from Matthew 10:33: "everyone who denies me before people, I also will deny before my Father who is in heaven." So we can sympathize with Peter. He seems a lot like us.

Is he really, though? Peter has the courage to follow Jesus, after all, even though he risks his life to do so. Most of the other disciples were too afraid to follow as far. Peter walks right into the lair of the enemy, right into the courtyard of the High Priest. Most courtyards were located right in the middle of the house, so he was within the very walls of power. Sure, his words may betray Jesus, but his actions do not. Jesus tells a parable like this in Matthew 21:28-31: A man who had two sons asked them both to go work in the vineyard. The first son said he would and did not. The second son said he would not but then changed his mind and went. "Which one of these two," Jesus asks the religious leaders, "did his father's will?" Although Peter denies Jesus with his words, he continues to follow at great personal risk. Would I even walk so far? Or would I be with the other disciples, hiding behind locked doors in some other part of the city?

Other stories of Peter also demonstrate his courage. When he sees Jesus walking on the water, he is the one who asks Jesus to command him to walk on the water too. He is the one who speaks boldly even when giving the wrong answer. Like other faith heroes of the past—Abraham, Moses, David—he has the gall to argue with God. He has the courage to try. It is hard to fault him for failure.

In contrast, how many of us claim to know Jesus but do not follow him? Far from imitating Peter and standing vigil with those awaiting execution, many of us who call ourselves Christian pretend such travesties of justice never happen. We timid Christians never follow Jesus as far as the courtyard; we shirk confrontations with power and spiritualize our faith to the point that it's completely nonthreatening to us or to the rulers of this world. Those of us who do carry Jesus' name on our lips into the courts of power will face persecution and tough decisions. Modern-day versions of Caiaphas and Pontius Pilate throw around Jesus' name as if he were their best buddy. Religious and political leaders often claim to know Jesus even as they turn their backs on the people Jesus identified with most: the imprisoned, the sick, and the poor. It is easy to claim to know Jesus when nothing of ours is at stake.

There are modern-day Peters, of course. I recently met South Koreans in Seoul who had been missionaries in China and North Korea, places where following Jesus can mean physical danger. Some have had the opportunity to relive Peter's crisis.

I'm impressed with anyone who has the courage to step into the spotlight, to deliver his or her lines with boldness even when he or she might be wrong. Those who take the stage and say the wrong thing or forget their lines are to be commended because they choose to do what most of the audience will not. After the resurrection, Jesus returns to the very ones who turned their backs on him, and they will have more opportunities to speak his name and risk their lives to do so. The director, Jesus himself, is always willing to give them another chance. (Dave Barnhart)

Worship Aids

Invocation

Jesus, hero of our faith, defender of the weak, teacher and friend, be present with us as we learn to be faithful. Inspire us to follow you boldly. Let us hear your call to take up our crosses and to imitate you. We ask these things in your name and by the power of your Holy Spirit. Amen.

Confession

God, how we crave the spotlight. Yet at the same time we want anonymity. We humbly confess our cowardice in the face of wrong and our complicity in injustice. We recognize too easily our own denial of you in Peter's words. Yet you construct your church out of rocks such as these, and use broken instruments as tools for your glory. Forgive us and use us in spite of our fear.

Words of Assurance

Our God is a God of second chances, and we know by the power of the empty tomb that Jesus returns to the very ones who betrayed him. Congratulations! We are forgiven because his love is greater than our fear, and he continues to call us to follow him. Amen. (Dave Barnhart)

MARCH 31, 2013

Easter

Readings: Acts 10:34-43; Psalm 118:1-2, 14-24; John 20:1-18; 1 Corinthians 15:19-26

How Do We Come to Easter Faith?

John 20:1-18

Today's lesson from the Gospel according to John enables us to reflect upon the question, "How do we come to the Easter faith?" First, we come to the Easter faith through the testimony of the first witnesses who themselves saw and believed. John tells of Mary Magdalene coming to the tomb and seeing the stone rolled away. She runs to tell Peter and the other disciple, the one Jesus loved. These two then run back to the tomb. Peter enters the tomb and sees the linen wrappings that had held the body of Jesus. Then, the other disciple goes in: "He saw and believed" (v. 8). Although the resurrection took them totally by surprise, those who witnessed the empty tomb and those who would later witness the appearances of the risen Christ became living witnesses to the reality of the resurrection. Those who knew Jesus best and were most disillusioned by his death would now come to life as fearless witnesses to the resurrection. Their testimony is made all the more powerful to us because of their legacy of faithfulness "in spite of dungeon, fire, and sword" (Frederick W. Faber, "Faith of Our Fathers," 1849). We come to the Easter faith first through the testimony of those who found the tomb empty and then discovered that Christ now filled their lives.

In verse 9 we find another answer to the question of how we come to the Easter faith. When the other disciple enters and comes to believe, John adds, "They didn't yet understand the scripture that Jesus must rise from the dead." How true that is. They would come to understand many Hebrew scriptures in a new way. Their own Bible would come alive to them as they read the scriptures with resurrection eyes and found that in

Jesus the scriptures had been fulfilled. We too can say that we come to Easter faith through our growing understanding of the scripture. This certainly has been true in my own experience. In the early years after seminary, I busied myself with the daily and weekly round of pastoral duties. After three years of ministerial study, it was exhilarating to be practicing ministry every day. But after about three years, I began to wonder how all the diverse roles of a pastor actually fit into a meaningful whole. I wrestled with the question, "What is the golden thread that ties together the preaching, teaching, visitation, counseling, and administration?" The more I wrestled, the less progress I seemed to make. Early one morning I was studying the scriptures, reading the first chapter of Ephesians in the *New English Bible*. That, in itself, is remarkable since I almost never use the NEB. When I came to Ephesians 1:9-10 I read these words: "He has made known to us his hidden purpose—such was his will and pleasure determined beforehand in Christ—to be put into effect when the time was ripe: namely, that the universe, all in heaven and on earth, might be brought into a unity in Christ." I have never forgotten the thrill of that moment, although it occurred thirty years ago. Through the scriptures, God revealed to me that God's purpose is to heal the brokenness of the universe through Christ Jesus our Lord. For me, that passage became a witness to Easter as the Risen Christ spoke to me through the words of Ephesians. I experienced a resurrection of my own call to ministry. In the same way, those who take *DISCIPLE Bible Study*, or other biblical studies, can provide their own testimony to the way in which our growing understanding of scripture brings us to the Easter faith in ways we would never have believed possible.

The second part of today's lesson is the story of how Mary stood weeping beside the tomb after Peter and the other disciple had left. So great was her grief that she was not particularly inspired by the two angels that spoke to her, and she did not recognize Jesus as he stood beside her. But when Jesus called her name, Mary came to life and went and announced to the disciples, "I've seen the Lord." This encounter reminds us that we also come to the Easter faith through the personal experience of the presence of the Risen Christ.

We come to Easter faith through the powerful testimony of the first witnesses who encountered the resurrection and came to believe. We come to Easter faith through our own growing understanding of the scriptures. We come to Easter faith through personal experience of the Risen Christ in the ordinary moments of our lives. In the testimony of the earliest witnesses, in the study of scripture, and in the daily round of life, the Risen Christ is with us. Praise the Lord! (Lawson Bryan)

Lectionary Commentary

Acts 10:34-43

This remarkable story finds Peter, a Jew, in the home of Cornelius, a Gentile, in the city of Caesarea. Peter states plainly the strangeness of this meeting, "You all realize that it is forbidden for a Jew to associate or visit with outsiders. However, God has shown me that I should never call a person impure or unclean" (10:28). Indeed, this entire chapter of Acts is about God at work across all boundaries of race, religion, culture, and nationality. Both Cornelius and Peter learn that God brings them together so that Peter can share the message of Jesus Christ. But this meeting is possible because Cornelius has already demonstrated that he is seeking God's truth and is open to a fresh revelation of that truth. This passage is full of insight for today's world in which we have more contact than ever before with the great diversity of race, religion, culture, and nationality in our world.

Easter is an excellent time to celebrate the way Acts 10:34-43 is presently being fulfilled on every continent. God is working among devout persons in every nation to spread the gospel. Christianity is growing rapidly in Latin America, Africa, and Asia. Truly, God shows no partiality. The astounding growth calls us to celebrate the fact that Easter is occurring all over the world. The missionary outreach of the Christian faith through the power of the Holy Spirit is bearing fruit of biblical proportions. Surely, this will give to us the same zeal that we sense in Peter's pronouncement in Acts 10.

1 Corinthians 15:19-26

The new playground constructed on our church property is surrounded by a handsome green metal fence. Each day the preschool children enjoy the freedom of rambling over that playground. They always wind up standing beside the fence, holding on to the upright bars, and looking at what's going on beyond the fence. The bars are close enough together that the children cannot squeeze through and get out—though they certainly try to do so again and again. Curiosity is a powerful urge. One day a child found the one area where two bars were a little farther apart than all the others. He pushed his little body all the way through the fence and got out. Another child saw what had happened and yelled, "Look, Jacob got out. Let's go!" Fortunately, the teachers retrieved Jacob and prevented more children from leaving the playground and moving into danger. On Easter we sing of how Jesus "tore the bars away" and rose victorious over sin, evil, and death. Using all the resources at our disposal, we shout, "Look, Jesus got out. Let's go!" That is Paul's focus throughout the fifteenth chapter of 1 Corinthians as he reminds us, "If we have a hope in Christ only in this life, then we deserve to be pitied more than anyone else" (v. 19). In other words, do not limit the Christian faith to a self-help religion that assists us in living out our days on earth with a little positive reinforcement and a spiritual pep talk every now and then. It is much more than that. Like Jacob on the playground, Jesus tore the bars away so that "In the same way that everyone dies in Adam, so also everyone will be given life in Christ" (v. 22). That is good news in life, in death, and in life after death. (Lawson Bryan)

Worship Aids

Call to Worship (Based on Psalm 118)

O give thanks to the Lord, for God is good;
God's steadfast love endures forever!
The Lord is my strength and my might;
God has become my salvation.
The stone that the builders rejected has become
the chief cornerstone.
This is the Lord's doing; it is marvelous in our eyes.

Invocation

Merciful God, as we celebrate the resurrection of Jesus, send your Holy Spirit to tear away the bars that imprison us in sin, evil, and death. Fill us with the power of the resurrected Christ so that we may be his faithful disciples in life, in death, and in life beyond death. In the name of him who is the resurrection and the life, even Jesus Christ our Lord, we pray. Amen.

Benediction

Go forth in the name of the Risen Christ and may the same Easter faith that has come to us now come to others through us. (Lawson Bryan)

The Women

Third in a Series of Three on Heroes of Lent

Matthew 28:1-10; Luke 24:1-12

Heroes inspire us to be like them. We tell their stories because the virtues they embody are the virtues we want to possess. But when Jesus tells us who we should aspire to be, the people he holds up as examples don't sound very heroic. "Become like this little child" (Matthew 18:3), Jesus says. In other words, he asks us to become like one without power. He also says, "many who are last will be first" (19:30), and "Whoever is least among you all is the greatest" (Luke 9:48). So perhaps it isn't surprising that Jesus' first resurrection appearance is to a group of first-century women, whose testimonies were considered less worthy than those of men, and whose initial reports were dismissed as "nonsense" (Luke 24:11).

Even two thousand years later, in our supposedly more-enlightened time, we get hung up on the gender of these first witnesses. For many years, people assumed Mary Magdalene was a former prostitute. In novels, she has been portrayed as Jesus' love interest. In musicals, she pleads for the disciples and Jesus to be less argumentative, and when she is cast in movies she is almost always young, thin, and attractive. She is never dumpy, or hairy, or missing teeth, or walking with a limp. It's almost as if, two thousand years after these women preached the first gospel message, they still have to justify their presence and their place as Christian leaders by conforming to our gender prejudices.

In the three synoptic Gospels (Matthew, Mark, and Luke), we can almost detect the embarrassment over how Jesus chose to appear alive to his disciples. They stumble over the details. In Matthew, it's Mary Magdalene and "the other Mary" (the mother of James). In Mark, it's these two plus Salome, and in Luke it's the three named women plus "other women." Although Paul often acknowledges women leaders in his letters, he omits the women in the resurrection story altogether, saying that Jesus "appeared to Cephas [Peter], then to the Twelve" (1 Corinthians 15:5). John, on the other hand, focuses his attention on Mary Magdalene. In his story, not only does Jesus appear first to a woman, he actually waits until the men have left (John 20:10)!

So why a group of women? Again, a woman's testimony was not worth as much as a man's in the ancient world. The Gospels report that the male disciples were reluctant to believe the women. Yet this group of women gets to be the first to proclaim the gospel, speaking the first news of the resurrection on record. Does Jesus have an agenda in choosing them to be the first witnesses? Is this Jesus' way of making a point?

We certainly find plenty of precedent for the inclusion of women in Jesus' ministry. He heals Peter's mother-in-law (Matthew 8:14). He accepts Mary, Martha's sister, as an equal in his inner circle, allowing her to sit and learn at his feet (Luke 10:38-42). He even compares God to a woman (Luke 15:8). Luke lists several women who traveled with Jesus and the twelve: Mary Magdalene, Joanna, Susanna, and "many others" (Luke 8:2-3). These are not "minor characters" in the Bible, any more than other members of the twelve, like Thomas or Nathaniel, are minor characters. In fact, some of these women have more words devoted to them than the twelve men.

In addition, Jesus has a long conversation with a Samaritan woman (John 4), and it is as if for the first time she realizes that God watches her, cheers for her, and wants the best for her. She learns that God is not hung up on the fact that she does not belong to the right religion, ethnicity, or gender. She goes on to spread the word to her whole community and begs them to come meet the man who told her everything she had ever done, and "Many Samaritans in that city believed in Jesus because of the woman's word when she testified" (4:39).

Jesus' choice to appear to a group of women firmly connects his resurrection with the whole tenor of his ministry. Whereas most of contemporary Western Christianity makes Jesus' death and resurrection all about *my* sin and *my* hope for eternal life, focusing on individual salvation and ignoring most of Jesus' preaching on the kingdom, Jesus' appearance to a group of women makes it clear that the resurrection is a continuance of the ministry he outlines in Luke 4:18-19: to bring good news to the poor, proclaim release to the prisoners, to let the oppressed go free, and to proclaim the year of the Lord's favor. He chooses his first preachers to be women because that's the way God operates.

The early church understood that Jesus had introduced a new social order. We are no longer defined by our social expectations, our disabilities, our gender, or any other accidentals. When we encounter the resurrected Jesus, we are defined by our new relationship with our Lord. For the early church, that meant recognizing in Jesus "that God doesn't show partiality" (Acts 10:34; also see Romans 2:11), a God in whom there was no longer "Jew or Greek . . . slave or free . . . male and female" (Galatians 3:28 NRSV). The resurrection of Jesus means that the doors of the kingdom of God have been thrown open, and that a radically inclusive invitation has gone out to all people to join God in this new movement in the world.

Perhaps some people in the early church knew Mary, Joanna, or Susanna personally. Like some of the other named characters in the Gospels—Rufus, Nicodemus, Mary, and Martha—when they heard the names they whispered to each other: "Is that our Mary? Our Salome?" "Have you heard her tell this story?" "I once met her in Joppa, and she was amazing." Perhaps the children of that early church heard the story of that resurrection morning, and a girl tugged on the hem of her father's tunic and whispered to him, "Daddy, when I grow up I want to be like Mary. I want to tell people about Jesus too." (Dave Barnhart)

Worship Aids

Invocation

Lord, the news of the empty tomb is too good to be true. Our faith is too weak to believe it on our own. Your presence and the sound of your voice calling our names give us hope. Be present as we hear your Word read and proclaimed, and help us become bearers of your good news. Amen.

Pastoral Prayer

Jesus, some of us come to worship to feel your presence but feel only your absence. We carry the burdens of the world with us—broken relationships, financial worries, anxiety about your world and its direction. Yet you are as close as the voice of a stranger asking, "Who are you looking for?" Let us recognize your presence, give our burdens to you, and feel the lightness that you offer us.

Benediction

Congratulations! Jesus invites you to be a hero and calls you by name. Go forth into the world and keep your eyes open so that you may see the Lord working and moving, calling attention to all the ways that God is building the kingdom around you and through you. Amen. (Dave Barnhart)

APRIL 7, 2013

Second Sunday of Easter

Readings: Acts 5:27-32; Psalm 118:14-29; Revelation 1:4-8; John 20:19-31

Easter Vision: Priests

Revelation 1:4-8

On Easter we sing, "He tore the bars away" (Robert Lowry, "Up from the Grave He Arose," 1874). Jesus came out of the tomb. And we rejoice that because he overcame sin, evil, and death, we too can be set free. But now the question is: Set free for what? What next?

That question is answered in today's lesson from the book of Revelation. This book is a vision Jesus gave to John to provide what we need for living with Easter vision; the resurrected Jesus showed us how to see life from the perspective of Easter.

John, on an isolated island, needs this revelation. The authorities think that by sending him into exile they can keep him out of circulation. But they had not counted on the ability of the risen Christ to find him there.

In verse 6 we learn that this revelation is from Jesus Christ, who is "the firstborn from among the dead"—Resurrection. Then in verse 7, "Look, he is coming with the clouds!"—*Parousia,* Second Coming. What happens in between?

"To the one who loves us and freed us from our sins by his blood, who made us a kingdom, priests to his God and Father" (vv. 5-6). This is where we come in: we are described by Jesus as a kingdom of priests. This brings to mind the phrase from the Protestant Reformation—"the priesthood of all believers." I have often heard this phrase invoked in a negative tone: "I don't have to pray to God through a priest, I can pray directly to God through Jesus Christ." Now, that is very true. But the tone usually suggests to me that the speaker thinks we are better off without priests. That, however, misses the meaning of this powerful phrase. It is about increasing the number of priests in the world, understanding that all Christians are called to the priesthood of Jesus Christ.

This is not a new vision. It has been God's vision from the beginning. In Exodus 19:5-6 God gives Moses these words for the people of Israel: "So now, if you faithfully obey me and stay true to my covenant. . . . You will be a kingdom of priests for me and a holy nation." A kingdom of priests was God's vision from the start—for the sake of the whole world.

This vision continues in the New Testament when we read in 1 Peter 2:5, 9-10: "You yourselves are being built like living stones into a spiritual temple. You are being made into a holy priesthood to offer up spiritual sacrifices that are acceptable to God through Jesus Christ. . . . But you are a chosen race, a royal priesthood, a holy nation, a people who are God's own possession. You have become this people so that you may speak of the wonderful acts of the one who called you out of darkness into his amazing light."

Priests have a twofold function—they represent people to God and God to people. As priests we bring with us the needs of humanity when we come to worship, the joys and sorrows of human life. Then, having drawn near to God, heard God's word addressed to us and to our world, we go forth to live as priests by representing God's love to the world.

To be God's priests means we are given a place in the drama of divine redemption. Once we were nothing, and now we are children of God. This refers to all members of the church; we find here no distinction between laity and clergy.

One of the best examples of this priesthood of all believers was revealed recently at the funeral service for one of our church members. Jim (not his real name) was a faithful member of the congregation. Few of us knew that he had worked with a Stephen minister for the past two years. Stephen ministers are church members who are trained to be confidential Christian friends who offer prayer and support to those going through difficult times.

One day, Jim needed to go to the emergency room, but his relatives were out of town. His Stephen minister took him. The attendant at the emergency room got the information needed from Jim and then asked Jim if the man who brought him in was a relative. Jim replied, "Oh, no; he's my minister!"

And that was the truth. This layperson in our church was Jim's minister. Now, that's the priesthood of all believers. Jim saw that clearly because he had Easter vision. (Lawson Bryan)

Lectionary Commentary

Acts 5:27-32

The apostles have been arrested for teaching in the name of Jesus after the authorities had warned them not to do so. Their response, "We must obey God rather than humans" (v. 29) shows how far they have come from their earlier abandonment of Jesus when he was arrested and crucified. Throughout this episode, and others like it, we get a glimpse of the radical transformation that has occurred in the apostles. The source of their transformation is "the Holy Spirit, whom God has given to those who obey him" (v. 32). This is the fulfillment of Jesus' promise in John 15:26, "the Spirit of Truth who proceeds from the Father—he will testify about me."

John 20:19-31

The disciples who were present when the risen Jesus appeared in the upper room are filled with conviction. They know what they saw, heard, and experienced. But when they share their testimony with Thomas, he rejects their witness. Then something truly remarkable occurs, "After eight days his disciples were again in a house and Thomas was with them" (v. 26). This community of faith made an unbeliever feel so welcome that a week after rejecting their witness he is still with them. This community becomes the creative environment in which Thomas experiences his own encounter with the risen Jesus. This is a vision of the kind of community of faith we want to be for the sake of those who have not yet come to know Christ. (Lawson Bryan)

Worship Aids

Call to Worship (Based on Psalm 150)

Praise the Lord! Praise God in the sanctuary;
praise God in the mighty firmament!
Praise God with tambourine and dance;
with strings and pipe!
Praise God with clanging cymbals;
with loud clashing cymbals!

Let everything that breathes praise the Lord!
Praise the Lord!

Invocation

Lord Jesus, as you entered the upper room through locked doors, come now and enter the locked doors of our own lives. Find the hidden places of shame, hurt, and brokenness; breathe your life-giving Holy Spirit on us and live your resurrection life in us and through us. This is our prayer. Amen.

Benediction (Revelation 1:5-6)

To the one who loves us and freed us from our sins by his blood, who made us a kingdom, priests to his God and Father—to him be glory and power forever and always. Amen. (Lawson Bryan)

Christ Alive!

First in a Series of Three on Transformed by Christ's Resurrection

1 Corinthians 15:1-11

A youth pastor inherited the Easter sunrise service as part of his responsibilities and he—with a small contingent of teenagers—put together a service, breakfast, and Easter egg hunt for the whole congregation. The weather cooperated brilliantly with a beautiful dawn, the service went off without a hitch, the breakfast fed literally hundreds, and then dozens of children raced around the church grounds looking for eggs. Everyone seemed pleased except for one young girl who marched across the lawn bawling her eyes out. Inconsolable, the child could hardly articulate her distress. Her mother and the youth pastor attempted to calm her down.

"Honey, look, you have lots of eggs in your basket. Isn't that wonderful?" asked the mother.

"Maybe she got stung by something," mused the confused young pastor.

After another few minutes, the child calmed down enough to say what she was so upset about. With a protruding lower lip, she explained, "You said Jesus came back today, and I keep looking for him, but all I can find are these stupid eggs!"

The metaphor may be a bit of a stretch, but often on Easter morn we lose sight of what we should really be seeking—the risen Christ—and instead we settle for eggs. The amazing, miraculous event of the resurrection of Jesus the Christ is one of the truly defining events in our entire faith system, yet for many it is just another in a long string of "interesting" stories about Jesus. "Jesus, back from the dead? Big deal. I knew it was going to happen all along!" seems to be a common attitude. The story has somehow become ordinary. Think of it. The conquest of the grave, taken for granted. How could we let such a thing happen?

Well, part of it is all the chicks, and bunnies, and colored eggs, and chocolate treats, and all the rest that have turned a religious celebration into yet one more Hallmark holiday. But even more important than that, Easter just doesn't mean as much to people who live in the grace and glory of God's abundance as it did to those who were oppressed, poor, meek, and marginalized. In the first century, the Christ was the hope of all hopes, the promise of a new life, and a new world order. The sight of Jesus crucified on the cross was devastating, and unlike millions of us today, on that first Easter morning no one was certain how things would turn out but God and Jesus. For the waiting world, hope had been buried in a tomb, and the promise of a new age was broken. What an amazing and unbelievable message was spread that first Easter—Christ is alive.

For days, for weeks, for months people struggled with the news. Yet, it was the testimony of witnesses that resurrected hope and joy. Paul taught the church in Corinth that the risen Christ appeared to Peter, then to the twelve, then to over five hundred men and women. He appeared to his brother James and the rest of the growing number of apostles, and Paul then says the risen Christ appeared to him—one untimely born. It was these appearances—this miracle of all miracles—that transformed the hearts and minds of the disciples and propelled the church toward Pentecost.

Perhaps we have it too easy today. Few of us live in fear for our lives or wonder where our next meal is coming from. It allows many today to scratch their heads and say, "So what? What is the big deal? God did an amazing thing, but it truly is old news." It is difficult to place in context the immensity of the resurrection of Jesus the Christ. Many taught as Jesus taught. Many healed as Jesus healed. Others performed miracles. Others displayed mighty acts of spiritual power. But how many came back from the dead? How many turned the laws of nature on their heads and did what is still today considered impossible? People do not come back from the dead. Skeptics worldwide develop elaborate scenarios to discredit and debunk the resurrection event. (*The Da Vinci Code*, anyone?)

Had Jesus not returned, none of us would be sitting here this morning. Had the resurrection of the Christ never happened, countless ministers—both clergy and lay—would never have served in his name. Billions of acts of compassion, kindness, selflessness, sacrifice, and love would never have occurred. We are today the body of Christ, empowered and guided by his Holy Spirit, because he rose from the tomb.

Paul wrote to his friends in Corinth to "think of us in this way, as servants of Christ and stewards of God's mysteries" (1 Corinthians 4:1 NRSV). There may be no greater mystery, no higher miracle, than the resurrection of the Christ. In this one act, the truth of Jesus' teaching, the manifestation of God's will, and the enduring power of the Holy Spirit are all confirmed. Well into the game of life, God changed the rules. God made the impossible possible and the unreal real. Truly, we are "Easter" people, but only if we live in the light of this amazing miracle. Jesus who died, God raised to life. The Christ lives forevermore. We should be stunned. We should be incredulous. We should be jubilant!

Such is the story of Jesus, but what does it mean to each of us? How does the specific resurrection of the Son of God relate to a general resurrection of "normal" human beings? What happens to us when we die? Theologians through the centuries have wrestled with this mystery. A significant question of the early church was this, "Does the resurrection of Jesus mean that we will be raised with him?" Is resurrection a historical event of the Christian faith or is it a reality into which each and every Christian will one day enter? This will be the focus of the second part of this series, "Talking Ourselves to Life." (Dan Dick)

Worship Aids

Pastoral Prayer

Gracious and loving God, we place before you the deepest concerns of our hearts. That which is beyond us, we entrust to you. May you send the Spirit of healing and comfort into the lives of those who need you most, and help us trust that there is nothing you cannot do.

Invocation

We are a people made new by the resurrection of Jesus the Christ. That which was darkness is now light. That which was desperate now gives hope. That which caused us to doubt and fear is lifted from us. Thanks be to God. Amen.

Benediction

Christ is alive, in Spirit and in truth. Christ lives in us, so we must live in Christ to be Christ for the world. Go from this place as Easter people, transformed in the light of Christ to be a blessing to everyone you meet. (Dan R. Dick)

APRIL 14, 2013

Third Sunday of Easter

Readings: Acts 9:1-6, 7-20; Psalm 30; Revelation 5:11-14; John 21:1-19

Easter Vision: Worship

Revelation 5:11-14

Today's epistle lesson continues the reading of the book of Revelation. This revelation was given to enable Christians to avoid becoming confused about their own faith in the midst of rejection and persecution. It introduces us to the new clarity, the new vision that Easter makes possible in our lives.

Last week, we read in Revelation 1:4-8 of the vision Christ had given John of Christians as a kingdom of priests. We focused on the word *priests*. We searched Scripture for a fresh vision of what it means to be a kingdom of priests. Without this Easter vision, it is likely that our understanding of what it means to be a Christian will be skewed by individual definitions or cultural assumptions about the priesthood of all believers.

The same is true with today's reading from Revelation 5. Actually, the scene begins in chapter four as John sees a door open into heaven. This is a way of saying this scene reveals what reality is like in the kingdom of God. John looks and sees the throne of God surrounded by twenty-four elders with golden crowns on their heads, reminders of the twelve tribes of Israel and the twelve apostles of Jesus. Also around the throne are four living creatures: one like a lion, one like an ox, one like a human being, and one like an eagle (wild animals, domesticated animals, humanity, and animals above the earth).

Then John sees a scroll sealed with seven seals. An angel asks: "Who is worthy to open the scroll and break its seals?" (5:2). But no one can be found until a Lamb appears—the Lamb of God who takes away the sin of the world—and takes the scroll.

This revelation of the one who is worthy to open the scroll leads to great jubilation in heaven. John's description of the scene includes thousands of angels singing "Worthy is the slaughtered Lamb / to receive power, wealth, wisdom, and might, / and honor, glory, and blessing" (v. 12). In response to this glorious ascription of praise to God, the four living creatures shout "Amen" and the twenty-four elders fell down and worshipped (v. 14).

If the word last week was *priests*, then the word that comes to us loudly and clearly in this passage is *worship*. Indeed, Revelation is sometimes referred to as the book of worship in the Bible. Many passages get a lot of attention because they speak of the battle between good and evil. But the dominant theme that ties together all the parts of the book is worship.

In scenes like this one we are given a new vision—an Easter vision—of worship. If asked why we place such high importance on worship, we might talk about a sense of awe and wonder, the majesty of God, excellence we offer God, connecting with history and tradition, anchor, rooting, grounding, silence, fellowship, familiarity, and music.

Each of these is a good reason to value worship, but look at the Easter vision of worship in Revelation. As we listen to the elders, the four living creatures, and the myriad of angels praising God, we hear other voices—all in heaven, on earth, under the earth, and in the sea—all creation joining the worship of Jesus Christ.

In other words, we learn that worship is the future toward which we are headed. When we worship, we are living in God's future. It is God who calls us forward to worship. It is God who forms us through worship: practicing unity, compassion, forgiveness, mercy, love. It is God who scatters us from worship to live as Christ's representatives in the world. We are called together for worship. We are transformed by worship. We are sent from worship.

How does worship accomplish this glorious work of unifying all creation in the praise of Christ? Revelation speaks of worship as trinitarian—God who is Father, Son, and Holy Spirit. This is a very particular understanding of God as Creator, Redeemer, and Sustainer. When worship is focused on God, then our lives are given great strength and a sense of eternal purpose.

In verse 12, all of heaven sings. When we listen to someone else sing, we can remain passive, a detached observer. But as soon as we start singing ourselves, we become part of the song and the song becomes part of us, transforming us. Something happens to those who sing powerful words of praise genuinely and authentically. We don't watch worship; we do worship, and we are transformed. Without Easter vision we miss this understanding of worship as living in the future right now.

To worship is to go way beyond respecting and appreciating; to worship is to focus our lives on someone or something. Worship becomes very dangerous when what we are worshiping is something less than the triune God. But when we join this trinitarian worship, uniting our voices with the twenty-four elders, the four living creatures, the myriad of angels, and all the rest of creation—then we too become part of God's future. (Lawson Bryan)

Lectionary Commentary

Acts 9:1-6, 7-20

The is the story of Saul's Damascus Road encounter with the risen Christ, complete with lightning flash, a voice from heaven, and temporary blindness. So powerful are the details of the story that one is tempted to overlook the importance of verse 10, "In Damascus there was a certain disciple named Ananias." As it turns out, Ananias is the one whom the Lord sends to lay hands on Saul that he might regain his sight. Furthermore, the Lord reveals to Ananias that though Saul has persecuted the Christians in Jerusalem, nevertheless, Saul will be God's instrument to bring the gospel to the Gentiles. While Ananias's initial skepticism about Saul is understandable, these faithful disciples do indeed go and lay hands upon Saul, saying: "Brother Saul, the Lord sent me—Jesus, who appeared to you on the way as you were coming here. He sent me so that you could see again and be filled with the Holy Spirit." The story of the great apostle Paul begins with a faithful disciple named Ananias. What Ananias has, God brought into our lives. How have we been shaped and formed in the Christian faith by such faithful disciples?

John 21:1-19

This resurrection appearance of Jesus occurs to seven of the disciples, including Peter. Interestingly, it happens after they have been fishing all night and have caught nothing. Jesus shows himself to them and leads them to cast their nets one more time. This time they haul in a net filled to overflowing. In every age, it is the presence of the risen Christ that keeps prompting the church to cast nets in anticipation of a great harvest of disciples for the kingdom of God. The passage concludes with the restoration of Peter's relationship with the Lord and a clear reminder that each new disciple will need the shepherding care of those more mature in the faith, "Feed my lambs.... Take care of my sheep.... Feed my sheep" (vv. 15-17). (Lawson Bryan)

Worship Aids

Call to Worship (Based on Psalm 30)

I will extol you, O Lord, for you have drawn me up,
  and did not let my foes rejoice over me.
O Lord my God, I cried to you for help,
  and you have healed me.
You brought up my soul from hell and restored me to life.
Sing praises to the Lord, O you faithful ones,
  and give thanks to God's holy name.

Invocation

Gracious God, we thank you for the precious gift of music that lifts our hearts to you in praise and thanksgiving. Open us to every evidence of your presence in this service. Give us ears to hear and hearts to understand what you are saying to us today through the words and music of the Christian faith. In the name of the risen Christ, we pray. Amen.

Benediction

Go now in the joy of the Lord and may the words and music of the Christian faith sound forth in your life this week. Amen. (Lawson Bryan)

Talking Ourselves to Life

Second in a Series of Three on Transformed by Christ's Resurrection

Acts 20:7-12

Most of us can relate to being "bored to death" by preachers, but few of us can relate to Eutychus, who was literally preached to death, then raised from the dead so he could be preached at some more. It is a brilliant story. Paul comes to town, has a meal, then he starts talking. The scripture emphasizes in a number of ways that Paul is talking on and on and on, from early evening until midnight. In what appears to be a courtyard wall, are windows at multiple levels, and people are sitting in the windows to listen. One young man, sitting about three stories up, fights valiantly to stay with Paul, but sleep overtakes him. It is one thing to doze in a church pew, but Eutychus falls fast asleep in his upstairs window and pitches out, falling to unyielding stones below, where he is pronounced dead. It would make sense that this would cause quite a stir, and perhaps end the evening's festivities, but Paul isn't done talking yet. He walks over to the dead boy and pronounces him alive again. Eutychus resuscitates, and Paul continues talking until dawn. It is one thing to talk a person to death, but it helps if you can also talk them to life, as well! Undoubtedly, Paul's audience stayed awake and paid even closer attention than before.

After the resurrection of Jesus from the dead, the whole concept of death changed in the early church. Certainly, there were stories of Jesus raising people from the dead, and there were tales of miraculous healing and resurrection in the Hebrew Scriptures, but in the advent of Jesus' return from the grave, death became a lot less scary. Death, according to Paul in his letters to Corinth and Rome, lost its power, lost its sting. That which caused mortals to live in bleak despair became irrelevant in the wake of Jesus' resurrection. Paul even took things a significant step further by promising that, "If the Spirit of him who raised Jesus from the dead dwells in you, he who raised Christ from the dead will give life to your mortal bodies also through his Spirit that dwells in you" (Romans 8:11 NRSV). For Paul, the significance of Jesus' resurrection is that it paved the way for all who believe in him to share in his eternal kingdom. This was a radical teaching in the face of a divided Judaism where many teachers and leaders did not believe in eternal life.

Such teaching created controversy and debate. What form would such a resurrection take? For one freshly dead, like Eutychus, it was no problem. The body that died was the body that was reanimated. But what about those in the ground a few days? A few months? Grandma and Grandpa, decades deceased? What about the aged and infirm and crippled? Would they really want their bodies back? Surely, God wouldn't be so cruel as to trap us in broken and corruptible bodies. Some, like Paul, speculated that we would be "changed," that we would be given an upgrade to a premium model body. Others decided that our resurrection would be spiritual—that we would not have a physical vessel, per se, but would hold some form beyond our earthly comprehension. Still others believed that we would be returned to our very best body—the earthly vessel we possessed at our halest and most hearty. Such discussions, debates, disagreements, and downright fights raged in the early church. Early confessions and creeds attempted to codify specific beliefs, such as our own Apostle's Creed that clearly affirms that we believe "in the resurrection of the body." This was one of the earliest efforts to "prove" once and for all (by establishing it as orthodoxy) that the physical meat, muscle, and bone of earthly life will become our eternal home. Even such clear statements did not settle the issue.

To this day, people question, "What happens when we die?" With all we have learned about biology, physiology, neurology, and cognitive development, we still struggle to understand what makes us, well, us. Where does the soul reside? What is physical and what is metaphysical? What are the boundaries of body, mind, and spirit—and how are they connected? Is what we have now all there is, or is there something more? These are eternal questions—questions that probably will never be answered in our earthly existence. Their ubiquitous ambiguity is the reason we have faith. We believe that which we cannot prove. We embrace that which gives us hope and meaning and purpose. We will never receive the clear assurance of a Eutychus, who died and was resurrected and got to go home to think about it.

No, we walk by faith and not by sight. As Christian disciples we must make a faith choice—to believe that the God who raised Jesus from the dead extends to us a similar fate and future. We no longer have to worry about what comes after. Through the assurance of our faith, our future is in God's loving hands. For us, the main question is not "What happens after we die?" but "What does God need from us now?" If we are raised into the resurrection of Christ, then we are given the great commandment of Christ—to love God with all our heart, mind, soul, and strength, and to love our neighbor as ourselves.

A woman lay dying in a hospital bed, no one nearby to comfort her. A nurse stopped to see if she needed anything, and she asked, "Where are your people, honey?" The woman responded, "I outlived them all. I have no living children, no living friends, but I have my loving Lord." The nurse shook her head and said, "You shouldn't have to die alone, dear." The woman smiled and said, "I have never been alone, and it doesn't much matter to me how I die. All that matters is that I lived, and I hope in my living, I made God glad."

In the third part of this series, we will think more deeply about what resurrection means in "The Immortal Christ." (Dan R. Dick)

Worship Aids

Prayer of Confession

Forgive us, O Lord, for the times we live in doubt rather than faith. Too often we worry about the future and end up wasting the present. Fill us with the assurance that in all things you give life and hope and purpose. And help us be the people you most need us to be. Amen.

Words of Assurance

"We were saved in hope" (Romans 8:24). We know that God is with us, filling us with the Holy Spirit, calling us to do God's good work and will. God will never forsake us or leave us. In Christ, we are made one, to be the hands and heart and voice of Christ for the world. Thanks be to God. Amen.

Benediction

Friends, we have been given a glorious gift—we are made one with Christ, one with each other, and one in service to all the world. There is no place on earth that God does not go with us. We have the promise of God's eternal love—a love we can share with all we meet. (Dan R. Dick)

APRIL 21, 2013

Fourth Sunday of Easter

Readings: Acts 9:36-43; Psalm 23; Revelation 7:9-17; John 10:22-30

Hard of Hearing

John 10:22-30

There's an old question in my family: Is my father, now in his 60s, going deaf, or does he have what doctors (usually marriage counselors) call "selective hearing?" Actually, that's an old question (or joke) in many families, isn't it? And it is so pervasive because all of us—not just aging men who are set in their ways—hear what we want to hear. Sometimes "Honey, could you take out the trash?" goes unnoticed, but then, as we see in today's Gospel lesson, so do the words and actions of Jesus.

In John 10 Jesus is talking and has been teaching for quite some time, but no one seems to be listening. The people say, "How long will you test our patience? If you are the Christ, tell us plainly." "I have told you," he says, "but you don't believe" (vv. 24-25). God has been speaking to these first-century Jews, and they don't seem to absorb what he is saying. Rather, they have been hearing what they wanted to hear.

Do we share this sort of selective hearing with these first-century people? The disciples were notorious for not listening at the pertinent times, even falling asleep in the garden of Gethsemane when they were supposed to be praying for Jesus and themselves on their last night with their friend and Lord. What if we, too, "tune out" to the voice of the Lord when God says something that has little to do with our versions of "success" and much to do with sacrifice, commitment to the least of these, or the call to perform a thankless task? What happens when an "uncomfortable truth" emerges? Flannery O'Connor writes that "the truth does not change according to our ability to stomach it emotionally" (*The Habit of Being: Letters of Flannery O'Connor* [New York : Farrar, Straus, Giroux, 1988], 100). If we find something unpalatable, do we simply dismiss it?

What if we aren't listening at all? I often say that I am waiting for God to speak to me about doing this or that, but what if God has been speaking all along, and I have too much noise and clutter around me to pay much attention? For many of us, if God were to speak up, we might miss it because when we do get a bit of time away from the office or the children we bury ourselves in our cell phones or worry about our status at work or on the social scene. Sometimes we worry about our status at church, too, concerned first and foremost about showing off our wit and knowledge.

Neither form of deafness is a good thing, and if the followers and opponents of Jesus had either of these diseases—true deafness or selective hearing—then they were in real trouble in this scene. Jesus answers here the New Testament's most important question: "Are you the Christ?" *Christ* means "the anointed one." It occurs in the Old Testament to describe the one who will represent the people in the presence of God. It is used to describe prophets, priests, and even some kings. When the definite article is used, however, it refers to the one who will liberate Israel forever. And so, the Jews in the crowd want to know if Jesus is *the* anointed one. Jesus' answer, though he already answered clearly, is "I and the Father are one" (v. 30). His answer to their question is yes.

Did you hear that? Are you sure? Because even though "I and the Father are one" may seem like a clear answer, it has caused many to miss the real point of this passage. Centuries have been spent arguing over the doctrine of the Trinity, some using the phrase "I and the Father are one" and some, in opposition, lifting up "the Father is greater than me" (John 14:28). But such a christological argument is another example of cluttering up this passage with things that would prevent us from hearing what Jesus is saying to us: "I am the Messiah."

I am. Jesus says "I am" seven times in this Gospel: the bread of life, the true vine and so on. He has been trying to tell them in all the ways he can that he is Messiah. But they do not hear. Or they do not believe. Or they do not want to believe that which they think just might be true. Is such willful deafness a form of unbelief?

Most us know how to follow Jesus. We know the texts, the commandments, and the stories. The trouble is not that we encounter a Jesus we can't figure out or our inability to make sense of the Trinity. Rather, the trouble for most of us is listening to a Jesus who calls us into radical faith. We often talk and sing as though we want to hear the voice of the shepherd—"Teach Me Your Ways, O Lord"—but do we? Just as many in the time of Jesus wanted to maintain the status quo, we are quite comfortable, and we fear what change would mean for us.

In this, the fourth week of Easter, may we remember that we celebrate a resurrected Lord, and remember that if we truly believe in this resurrection, if we truly believe that Jesus and the Father "are one," then there is no tuning him out. For persons who have already placed their faith in something as odd as the resurrection, there is no call too radical. So hear him when he calls you to "take up your cross," when he calls you to "feed the sick," when he says "visit my prisoners," when he says "do this in remembrance of me." He is Messiah, the anointed one. In the words of the Lord as Jesus stood in the presence of Moses and Elijah at the transfiguration: "This is my Son, whom I dearly love. Listen to him!" (Mark 9:7). (Scott Bullard)

Lectionary Commentary

Acts 9:36-43

Acts tells us a powerful story of resurrection. Peter faithfully and without hesitation rushes to the aid of a neighbor. This all must be seen against the backdrop of Acts 2, when the Holy Spirit was given to the church. Acts 9:31 confirms this. None of Peter's acts here—his decision and desire to help, his powerful act of resurrecting Tabitha—can be separated from the work of the Spirit. This story meshes well with the Gospel lesson for today.

Revelation 7:9-17

That every tribe and nation are represented in the gathering around the throne of God in this heavenly scene will link up nicely with the Psalm readings for the next two weeks, since both proclaim that Yahweh wants to be the God of all people. However, this week the psalm focuses upon God as a shepherd, leading and gathering Israel not only out of exile but into the house of the Lord. Such an earthly gathering, however, is merely a foretaste of what is depicted here—eternal worship of, and rest in, the one true God. This is the end for which we were created. (Scott Bullard)

Worship Aids

Hymn

"I Hear Thy Welcome Voice" (Lewis Hartsough)

Prayer

God the great revealer, you have much to say to us, and yet we spend so much time talking, doing, running—anything but listening. Quiet our bodies and hearts and minds, Lord. Help us be still and know. Attune our ears to your voice, O Lord, that we may truly listen for it.

Bulletin Quote for Reflection

"The challenge for most mainline Christians is not following Jesus. We've been taught pretty well about that. The challenge for us is recognizing Jesus' voice." (David Ewart, http://www.holytextures.com/John-10-22-30.pdf, accessed July 6, 2011). (Scott Bullard)

The Immortal Christ

Third in a Series of Three on Transformed by Christ's Resurrection

1 Corinthians 15:50-58

A woman came to a pastor for counseling. She sat nervously in his study, unable to make eye contact with him. Finally she blurted out, "I don't believe in heaven or hell or resurrection or any kind of afterlife!"

The pastor asked her why she felt this way.

"I watched a special on television last night and a whole bunch of scientists said they have proven there is no heaven or hell and that when a person dies, they are dead and that's all."

"And what proof did they give?" asked the pastor.

"They said that there is no evidence of heaven or hell and that no one has ever come back from being truly and totally dead, and that people who say they see a white light or loved ones waiting for them are deluded or brainwashed," she explained.

"And that proves to you that there is no possibility of life after death?" the pastor inquired.

"Well, do you have any proof they exist?" challenged the woman. "The men on TV said that the only people who can believe in religion are ignorant, mentally challenged, or fooling themselves. They say that we have no proof for anything we say we believe."

"Well no, not the kind of proof you mean. Do I believe in an afterlife? I think I do, though I must agree that I don't think heaven is a place in the clouds with angels flying around and people playing harps, and I don't think hell is a stinky pit with fire and devils with pitchforks. But I do believe that there is more to reality than what we can see with our eyes and touch with our fingers. I 'believe' in resurrection, and I 'believe' in an afterlife, and I trust in God. That's good enough for me. But you know what? I am really not as concerned with what happens when we die as I am with what we do while we're alive. If we don't live well, I'm not sure I want to think about what comes next!"

Questions about eternity and immortality are speculative at best. Paul took a stab at explaining eternal life in his letters, though his descriptions are somewhat sketchy and contradictory. This is to be expected. Paul didn't know for sure, and early in his ministry he believed Jesus would return before too many people died. As years passed, Paul had to rethink his beliefs. The exact description of what the afterlife was like changed, but his belief in resurrection never flagged. For Paul, it was the promise of a life well-lived and a faith well-performed. Interestingly, Paul came to much the same conclusion as the pastor in this morning's story—beyond speculation of what might be was Paul's instruction, "Therefore, my beloved, be steadfast, immovable, always excelling in the work of the Lord, because you know that in the Lord your labor is not in vain" (v. 58 NRSV). To be raised with Christ, one must be one with Christ—serving the world as Christ served. The goal of the believing Christian is not to "prove" resurrection or eternal life, but to live life as though we know resurrection and eternal life to be true.

This is the highest testimony to what we believe—to live in such a way that everything we say and do is a witness to our assurance that God's promises are true. We don't know what will happen when we die. We might be "changed" as Paul indicates. We might be given a physical body or a spiritual essence. We might become something beyond our comprehension. We might be converted to pure energy. Those who choose to believe that we merely become fertilizer have every right to do so, but their belief is no better or worse than anyone else's. Certainly, the idea of eternal life defies reason and common sense. It deals with the metaphysical, not the physical. It calls us to think outside the box, so to speak, and see new possibilities. Quantum physics is taking human knowledge to undreamed-of realms with limitless possibilities, some of them touching on the very edges of faith.

There will always be critics. We will always have opponents to faith that point out how ignorant and irrational it is. But perhaps it is not as irrational as it seems. A professor of physics speculating on infinite universes and realities claimed that one day we would discover everything anyone ever imagined exists somewhere. A student timidly raised her hand and asked, "Does that mean that we will find God?" Pausing for a moment, the professor scratched his head, realized he had talked himself into a corner, laughed, and said, "Well, I guess we will!"

Do Christians know what will happen when they die? No. This is where faith comes in. We believe in the resurrection of Jesus Christ. It is, for us, a fact of faith. We believe it to be "true," in the deepest sense of the word. Can we prove it? No. Do we need to? Absolutely not. What a terrible waste of time, energy, resources, and opportunity to debate something that cannot be proven. In a world of terrible want and need, of injustice and violence, of poverty and disease, of hunger and homelessness, does anyone actually think we have time to squander debating where we go after we die? If we ignore the things that Jesus was passionate about, the things God calls us to address, what happens when we die is a moot point. How we die pales in significance with how we choose to live.

Let us live as resurrection people—givers of life in a dying world, voices of hope to a hopeless generation, and a Spirit of promise for a better day to come. This is the power of the resurrection to change lives—to live in such hope and trust that we can willingly give our lives to God that we might be raised together to be the immortal Christ for the world. (Dan R. Dick)

Worship Aids

Call to Worship

We are called to this place to worship God.
We lift our voices to God.
We are called to this place to be changed by God.
We offer our lives to God's service.
We are called to this place to be equipped by God.
Use us as you will, O God.
We are called to this place to be sent forth by God.
Help us be faithful servants in all we say and do, O Lord.
We are here to be God's church!

Prayer of Confession

Gracious God, we are distracted by many things. We allow worries about what might be to shift our focus from what could be. Help us attend to your will and create the future you most want us to have. Teach us to live like we truly believe what we confess. Amen.

Words of Assurance

God is working within each and every one of us to transform us from people held captive to sin and regret into people filled with the Holy Spirit and shining the light of Christ into the world. We are the new life in Christ that God promises. Let us live in this glorious truth. Amen. (Dan R. Dick)

APRIL 28, 2013

Fifth Sunday of Easter

Readings: Acts 11:1-18; Psalm 148; Revelation 21:1-6; John 13:31-35

What Do We Do Now?

John 13:31-35

In the Gospel lesson this week, Jesus refers to the conversation with some Jewish leaders that we discussed in last week's passage. Although we didn't talk about it last week, Jesus told them, "I am leaving, and you can't come with me." Today, in what many scholars call Jesus' "Farewell Discourse," Jesus tells the disciples (or perhaps reminds them at this point) what kind of people they are to be after he leaves them on earth.

Briefly, "Farewell Discourse" is not a term that can be simply taken at face value, but is actually a particular type of speech that occurs frequently in ancient literature. John has chosen to incorporate this speech in a way similar to that of many authors who have chronicled the life of ancient heroes. And with Jesus, as with others who have given famous "last speeches," the things that are most important to him are emphasized in these, his final words to his friends.

This discussion is particularly important for the disciples, for unlike other groups who follow a leader, they must not simply carry on the spirit of their teacher's movement, they must, in a sense, *be* their teacher. A few weeks after this speech is given, Jesus' body will ascend to heaven. Then, the disciples will begin to be referred to as Jesus' "body" (see, for example, 1 Corinthians 12:27). The earliest form of the church is not the second person of the Trinity, but it is called the "body of Christ." Lutheran theologian Robert Jenson even dares to say that it stands to reason that we also call the church "the body of God" (Carl E. Braaten, Robert W. Jenson, Gerhard O. Forde, *Christian Dogmatics* [Philadelphia: Fortress Press, 1984], 177).

This is lofty, and, some would say, dangerous language. But it is true. The second person of the Trinity has a body, and it is concretized, at present, in the church. This is developed in greater detail in next week's Gospel lesson, but as the Gospels and Acts (and the Apostles' Creed) spell out very clearly, Jesus will die, be buried, be resurrected, live on the earth for a few weeks more, and then ascend to the right hand of God. The Spirit will then descend to his body (the church), empowering humans to boldly wear the banner "body of Christ."

Jesus is aware that the disciples will find this an intimidating and even, as some suggest, an impossible task. So, as he bids them adieu, he also equips them. And his parting words surprise many of us. "Love one another" (vv. 34, 35 NRSV; "Love each other" CEB). This might not quite constitute the whole of the gospel, but Jesus tells his disciples to "love one another," not once, not twice, but three times in the space of only two verses. This is one of Jesus' last opportunities to speak to his body, and its importance cannot be overstated; Jesus even calls it a "new commandment."

Do you wonder why Jesus gives this new commandment? It seems there are at least three ways to get at this. First, and most simply, Jesus says the disciples are to love another just as he has loved them. That is, as imitators of their Lord and Savior, they are to love one another. Jesus was loving, and so those who follow him should be loving.

Second, the call for the disciples to love one another is evangelistic. By actively loving one another, members of Christ's body communicate to outsiders that they are followers of Jesus. Jesus says, "This is how everyone will know." The familiar saying "preach the gospel at all times, use words when necessary" has been attributed to St. Francis. While St. Francis was apparently referring to sharing the gospel with persons outside the body, it seems that here Jesus is speaking exclusively to members of the body. The message is no less evangelistic, however, as the love among members of the body will communicate to others that they are followers of Jesus.

Third, remember Jesus' bold proclamation in last week's text, "I and the Father are one" (John 10:30). If this is true, that God is one, one being and yet somehow three persons, and humanity is created in the image of the Triune God—then Christians are to embody this oneness in the world. We are to be one with one another just as the persons of the Trinity mutually indwell one another. Thus, while we modern and postmodern Christians have individualized Christianity and especially "spirituality," the apostle Paul repeatedly emphasizes that we are "baptized by one Spirit into one body" (1 Corinthians 12:13), that we are "parts of each other in the same body" (Ephesians 4:25). Jesus prays later in John that the disciples may be one just as he and the Father are one (John 17:21). In such a body, we are not so much individuals as we are parts of one another.

What does such love look like? It is not sentimental, and it is difficult to embody in a twenty-first-century context. Acts and the Pauline corpus spell this out well. Through Luke, we read that in the earliest church "all the believers were united and shared everything," that none went hungry, that they ate together daily and worshiped together frequently (Acts 2:42-46). Through Paul, we hear of people so bound up with one another that when one member suffers, the whole body suffers. When a member rejoices, so does the whole body (1 Corinthians 12:26).

This Easter season, may we truly consider what it means to follow Christ, to be a people of the resurrection. As people living by a new commandment from a resurrected Lord, let us not live as the world does, but "love one another" so that the world might believe. (Scott Bullard)

Lectionary Commentary

Acts 11:1-18

In today's passage from Acts, the Jews in Jerusalem want Peter to explain to them how he can baptize non-Jews or even associate with them. Peter, making it very clear that he is permeated by the Spirit, explains that God wants us "to go with them and not to make a distinction between them and us" (v. 12 NRSV). As we live with "the other," this is a very empowering text. It also meshes well with the psalm for this week, which similarly clarifies that all persons are created by God and called into communion with God.

Revelation 21:1-6

This week's reading from Revelation, like next week's, reveals that unity with God is indeed possible, that the redemption of the earth is not a foreign idea to the Christian narrative. To see this, we must read the entire story—the breadth of the canon—but it is there, even if Revelation 17–18 have described other cities with strong words like *prostitute*, in today's reading we see a city reunited with God. God desires to dwell with God's people (Revelation 22:3). This is also emphasized in today's other readings, from Jesus' unity with the Father in John 13, to Peter's emphasis in Acts 11 that all persons can experience such unity. Indeed, as the psalmist has described, all of creation has the capacity to praise the Lord. (Scott Bullard)

Worship Aids

Hymn

"They'll Know We Are Christians by Our Love" (Peter Scholtes)

Prayer for the Unity of the Church

Almighty Father, whose blessed Son before his passion prayed for his disciples that they might be one, as you and he are one: grant that your Church, being bound together in love and obedience to you, may be united in one body by the one Spirit, that the world may believe in him whom you have sent, your Son Jesus Christ our Lord; who lives and reigns with you, in the unity of the Holy Spirit, one God, now and forever. Amen. (*The Book of Common Prayer* [New York: Church Publishing, 1979], 255).

Benediction (2 Corinthians 13:11, 13)

"Finally, brothers and sisters, good-bye. Put things in order, respond to my encouragement, be in harmony with each other, and live in peace—and the God of love and peace will be with you. . . . The grace of the Lord Jesus Christ, the love of God, and the fellowship of the Holy Spirit be with you all." (Scott Bullard)

Keep on Trucking

First in a Series of Three on Women in Ministry

Philippians 4:4-9

"She wants to work. She wants a job, and she's coming to you asking for one," my mother sternly said to my dad when I asked to go to work for him at our family's trucking business. Dad was in no mood to listen. Mom had had enough.

For weeks, our family had been listening to Dad talk about needing another employee or two at his shop. The expansion of Interstate 30 was proving to be good for business. Dad's trucks were running almost twenty-four hours a day. Dad, his shop foreman, and mechanic needed extra hands to help keep the trucks in shape and on the road.

When I heard Dad telling Mom what he needed, I thought my ship had come in. To me, this was the perfect summer job, especially for someone of my young age. Babysitting was sporadic, and I was too young to work at the businesses in town.

I was raised in Dad's business—a grease monkey almost from birth. On days when Mom did not need me at home, I was with my dad. By the time I was eight, Dad had taught me how to clean his tools and how to work the air wrenches. I was an expert at cleaning the garage floors after a major overhaul. Dad prided himself on a shop so clean you could eat off its floors. Simple chores I did for Dad were often redone in order to be up to his standard. I didn't mind; I was with Dad, and we were accomplishing a lot.

So when I decided to ask my dad for a job, I knew what to expect, and I knew I could do it; but when I asked him to consider me for one of the positions, he blew me off. The next day, he talked about how busy they were and again I asked to be hired. I knew what he needed, was confident I could fill the job requirements, but again I was rebuffed; but this time he told me, "You can't. You're a girl." I walked toward my room wondering why being a girl would keep me from doing what he had taught me to do.

Dad spent a couple of weeks coming home around midnight. His current work schedule meant that for us to see him we would have to take him dinner and say hi.

One evening we arrived at the shop with dinner. Dad ate and Mom asked me to help put things in order in the hope of everyone going home a little earlier. I cleaned tools, swept, and helped Dad's shop foreman and mechanic roll tires to the side of the building. That night Dad was able to come home by 10:00 p.m.

The next day Dad came home in time for dinner, but when he talked again to Mom about the need for employees at the shop to help, I asked again, and again was rebuffed. The reason: I was a girl. Mom immediately asked why being a girl would hinder me from working.

She pointed out to Dad that I had helped the previous night, and my help allowed him to come home two hours earlier than expected. Dad tried a different argument, "She's too little," but Mom would not relent, "You think she's too little now, but she was just right last night." Dad replied, "That's different." To which Mom asked, "How? How is that different?" The discussion continued until Dad said, "It doesn't look right to have a girl working in a shop full of men!" "You didn't seem to mind last night!" said Mom.

Dad squirmed. His pride was wounded, and he was losing a verbal battle with his wife. With a heavy sigh from Mom, the discussion ended.

As I went to my parents' room to tell them goodnight, I was surprised by an impromptu job interview with Dad. In thirty minutes we discussed wages, duties, days, and times I would work. I would begin the next morning.

About a month later, Mom asked Dad and me how the job was going. Mom and I smiled as Dad said, "It hasn't been a big deal. I'm enjoying having help. I don't even know why I fussed about it in the first place."

Dad hit the nail on the head. What is all the fuss? That is the question that has persisted for over two thousand years.

Jesus turned culture upside down when women became his disciples. Or should I say, Jesus set culture aright for "God created humanity / in God's own image, / in the divine image God created them; / male and female God created them" (Genesis 1:27).

Paul continued what Jesus began. Thanks to Prisca (also known as Priscilla), Chloe, Eunice, Lois, Mary, Euodia and Syntyche, Junia and Phoebe, Paul was able to accomplish his ministry. Paul even tells the church at Rome of Prisca's bravery (Romans 16:3-4).

These women showed strength, wisdom, perseverance, and a faith that helped change the world. They were generous, they nurtured, they spoke out, and they prayed. These strong souls followed where God led, even to prison (Romans 16:7). These women did not follow blindly but with great faith and gratitude for the sacrifice Christ had made for them.

Paul showed that these women were not chattel, not an afterthought, but were precious and valued. Because of God's great love and grace, these women could stay neither silent nor still.

Thanks to my mother, I was able to persevere and gain not only a job but also new respect from my dad. Thanks to the foundation laid by generations of women—including my mother, grandmothers, and aunts—I am able to do the work of God with little harassment. My family in turn gives thanks for the examples laid before us. These God-fearing women and generations of women after them showed others what God knew all along, "[we] can do all things through [Christ]" (Philippians 4:13 NRSV). (Julie Worcester)

Worship Aids

Call to Worship

We live in a world of distraction and burden.

We do not worry for God hears our prayers.

We find it hard to get along with our neighbors.
We seek God's peace and are open and patient.
We can live, for the Lord is near.
Rejoice in the Lord and give thanks!

Passing of the Peace

We are assembled as the body of Christ to give thanks and praise for God's mighty works. Stand and greet your brothers and sisters with the peace of God that passes all understanding.

Benediction

Go from this place with the assurance that Christ guards your hearts and minds. Go forth and keep on doing the work of the kingdom, and may the peace of God go with you. Amen. (Julie Worcester)

MAY 5, 2013

Sixth Sunday of Easter

Readings: Acts 16:9-15; Psalm 67; Revelation 21:10, 22–22:5; John 14:23-29

Coming and Going; Going and Coming: The Necessity of the Spirit

John 14:23-29

Last week we spent a great deal of time talking about love and the way in which this is necessary both to be the body of Christ and to proclaim the gospel to persons who are not followers of Jesus. Of course, this is all easier said than done. In addition to the "high view" of the church espoused by Paul, threads also run through Scripture on sin and the human condition. The church is full of spots and wrinkles, Paul always seems to add, though Christ will present the church to God as though it were "holy and blameless" (Ephesians 5:27).

Again we come to the disciples' need for encouragement and comfort as Jesus is saying farewell. Let me say it more plainly this week than last week: the disciples know that they are sinful and feel inadequate, incapable of doing the things that Jesus is forecasting. Indeed, in the verses leading up to today's Gospel lesson, the Teacher predicts that this ragtag bunch of fishermen followers will do greater works than he has done (John 14:13).

I don't know about you, but I would have been uncomfortable with this prediction. Of course, we've already seen this crew misunderstand Jesus' statements about himself, fail to walk on water, and argue about who will sit where in the kingdom of heaven. Those things aside, however, how do you feel about yourself and your ability to comfort, to heal, or to simply speak a word of forgiveness to another person? Have you done those things recently?

The only true answer to this question is a resounding no. We do not do anything. Rather, God heals, teaches, preaches, forgives, and comforts through us. We are vessels. This is the crux of Jesus' message to the disciples in today's text: "The Companion, the Holy Spirit, whom the Father will send in my name, will teach you everything and will remind you of everything I told you.... Don't be troubled or afraid" (vv. 26-27).

This must have been of some comfort to the disciples, if indeed they understood it as we can in hindsight. "I am going *and* I am coming" makes more sense on this side of Pentecost, certainly. We must be this body because Jesus' physical body is leaving this earth—this is what Teresa of Avila meant when she said we were to be "Christ's hands and feet"—but we can only be this body if we are a Spirit-filled people.

Additionally, the Spirit will remind Jesus' followers of his words to them. Remember the lists from last week—rejoicing together, suffering together, worshiping together, and (gasp!) sharing our food and other goods? That sounds like a demanding list and difficult to remember, in addition to being a little less palatable than the individualistic, health-and-wealth gospels we can hear on our televisions. But it should challenge us—to look more like the first-century church and to rely solely on the Spirit in humility. This is the truth of Pentecost, which we'll experience next week; to be a Christ-follower after Jesus' ascension is to be a person who continually leans on the Spirit—not the gods of this world—for power.

Last week the hymn we sang ended memorably with these lyrics: "they'll know we are Christians by our love." That song begins by repeating "We are one in the Spirit, we are one in the Lord." The order of the lyrics is important, and it is instructive. The final clause is completely dependent upon the first. Without the Spirit, we can't love the way we ought to, can't be (or become) the body that we are called to be.

Thus, as we end this Easter season and rapidly head toward the Ascension and Pentecost, we are caught in the middle, looking back at Resurrection, but also forward to the oddity of the Ascension and the even odder arrival of the Holy Spirit.

"I'm going away and returning to you," Jesus says in verse 28. Where are you in all of this? Are you frightened about the future, about some impossible task you've been given? Are you prepared to live by faith in the days and weeks ahead, to breathe in and lean on the Spirit of God? Jesus says that, though we cannot do it on our own, we have a Companion ("Advocate" NRSV), a powerful and available and continually renewable resource in the Spirit. The Comforter will aid us in remembering Jesus' words and in enacting them. May God give us the strength and the awareness of our weakness to rely on him for the glory of God's name. Amen. (Scott Bullard)

Lectionary Commentary

Acts 16:9-15

In this passage, Paul continues to reach out and evangelize Gentiles. It is interesting that at this point in the lectionary, two of the last three Acts readings have dealt with the restoration of another group of outsiders—women. This relates quite well with the psalm for today, which reminds us that all persons are called to be in relationship to God, not just persons who are like us. The Acts reading relates equally well to today's Gospel lesson. Jesus, who is about to ascend, tells the disciples that they must now be his body through the power of the Holy Spirit, because his fleshly body will go to the Father. Indeed, they will carry on Jesus' mission and do even greater things than Jesus has done (John 14:12)! Here in Acts 16, Paul embodies Jesus' mission by reaching out to and baptizing Lydia and her household.

Revelation 21:10, 22–22:5

As the entire Christian canon draws to a close, the author of Revelation depicts a unique and clear vision of the divine life. This vision includes "the throne of God and the Lamb" (v. 3) and the heavenly Jerusalem. In relation to Psalm 67 and John 14, today's other readings, it is significant that "the nations" are all pervaded by the divine presence and "walk" according to that divine presence. This is the fulfillment of a promised unity that the Psalm, the Gospel lesson, and the reading from Acts have foreshadowed. (Scott Bullard)

Worship Aids

Prayer

Come, Holy Spirit, send the comfort and power that only you can provide. We are a fallen, fearful, and sometimes weak people. We know that we cannot be Christ's body without you. And yet our Lord promised that with you, anything is possible. So we ask you to come into our midst for the building up of your kingdom. Amen.

Hymn

"Spirit of God, Descend upon My Heart" (George Croly)

Benediction (sung by all):

"May the Grace of Christ, Our Savior" (John Newton; Use Tune Name: DORRNANCE) (Scott Bullard)

Know Your Place

Second in a Series of Three on Women in Ministry

1 Corinthians 14:31-36

It was a magical time for the young and independent Julie. It was two weeks before her wedding and well into the Christmas season, her favorite time of year. Julie's mind was full of hopes, dreams, love, and wonder. She was looking forward to Christmas parties, wedding showers, and time with friends and her beloved.

Julie looked forward to worship on Sundays, and especially loved the peacefulness of the sanctuary decked out in Christmas splendor. Prior to the service, she sat and chatted softly with friends, catching up on the news of the week. The service began, and Julie participated to the fullest, singing cheerfully with the choir, playing an offertory on her flute, and lifting up joys and concerns during prayer time. As the transition was made from music to sermon, she cheerfully joined her friends and looked forward to a sermon that talked of the faith walk during the Christmas season, but it was not to be.

Instead of reading the comforting scriptures talking about Mary's visit with the angel, or the continued story of Elizabeth and Zachariah, the pastor instead had the congregation open their Bibles to 1 Corinthians 14:32-35, and then began preaching on women knowing their place. The sermon was directed straight at Julie and her fiancé, who was the county judge.

For Julie and her intended, dating had taken place in a fish bowl. The entire community watched every move the young couple made. Marrying meant that Julie would live an even more active public life. Julie discovered that the choice did not sit well with her pastor.

Julie's face turned red, and she found the pastor's personalized sermon surreal. The sermon was meant to change Julie's mind, to make her call off the wedding and become less visible.

It wasn't enough that the pastor and most of the congregation were staring at Julie; to make the situation more awkward, sad, and frustrating, the pastor had prominent women in the congregation stand and speak—among them, the pastor's wife. All stood and faced Julie and gave testimony on how wonderful their life had been being quiet, behind the scenes, out of sight. They all spoke of the virtues of knowing one's place; a silent and hidden life.

As the pastor wrapped up, he turned to Julie and said that if his wife or daughter aspired to public office or public life like being a senator or governor, he would be embarrassed and his family disgraced. One of Julie's friends jokingly elbowed her and remarked, "Well, there goes your bid for president."

The sermon finally ended, and the altar call was given with the expectation that Julie would succumb to the intense peer pressure, see the light, and run to the altar crying out for a solution. Julie stayed in her seat. Not satisfied, the pastor called for extra praying time. Julie sat in the pew and prayed for her friends, her family, her fiancé, her church, for the ladies who spoke, and for the pastor.

Eventually, everyone finished praying, the last hymn was sung, and everyone headed for the exit. Julie did not rush out the door, but walked out with her group of friends. She had not made it to her car before the pastor, surrounded by staff and family members, approached Julie, shook her hand, and asked her what her decision would be. Julie replied, "There is no decision to be made." With the group still standing by, Julie pulled away from the parking lot and headed to lunch with her parents and fiancé.

Two thousand plus years of progress of inclusion in the work place and in ministry and still women battle the age-old question of whether it is appropriate for a woman to be seen, to be heard, and to lead. Where do women belong? Should women be at home, in the community, in the world?

The answer is yes, women should be at home, and in the community, and in the world. Women can and do lead, not because they are trying to take over the world, but because women know they can be another set of useful hands in the work and life of the kingdom.

While men and more than a few women grapple with questions of propriety, women everywhere have for centuries rolled up their sleeves and met needs head on. While others have stood around looking shocked, scandalized, and astonished at the nerve of the ladies, these bold women have helped with vital ministries. They have accompanied and been apostles on mission trips; they have prayed; they have fed those in need; they have used their own money and status to set up house churches; they have faced death, imprisonment, and persecution. Their example has allowed generations of women to take bold steps forward for the kingdom.

But the world then and now tells us to focus on our fears. The world encourages us to listen to our fight-or-flight mentality. If it feels threatening, then we have a right to be afraid. If we are frightened then the offending issue must be wrong, right? Often the fear is not of physical threat to our person but a perception that someone will outdo us, make us look weak and inferior. Some segments of society tell us to lash out at women and put them in their place. Society encourages those in fear to get personal, to criticize women where it will hurt the most. Criticize their looks, their dress, their socioeconomic background; insult their families, their spouses, their children, their homes, their faith.

As Christians we must remember that we are new creations. We must remember that Christ set the example. He changed the culture and showed that women were not chattel but living, breathing, active members of the body of Christ. Paul continued to show that women were important members of the body of Christ. God did not create only male but also female. Jesus ministered to, died for, and was resurrected for men and women. It is up to us as followers of Christ to live and work together side by side in peace, uplifting and encouraging one another in a world that would have us live fragmented and in darkness. Are we faithful enough and brave enough to live as Christ intended? With prayer, patience, love, and mercy we can all roll up our sleeves—men and women—and get to work. (Julie Worcester)

Worship Aids

Call to Worship

We put aside the noise of the world.
We come in love to worship the one who loved us first.
We lay down our wants and fears.
We come in love to give thanks to the one
who died to set us free.
We push aside our bad behavior.
We come in love to praise the Almighty
who knows us better than we know ourselves.

Passing of the Peace

We gather as children of the most high, full of love and joy. Stand and greet your neighbors with the peace of Christ.

Benediction

Be full of the Holy Spirit, be led where you will. Go forth with God's unending love. Go forth with the grace and mercy of Jesus our Savior. Go in peace, hope, and love that endure all things. (Julie Worcester)

MAY 12, 2013

Ascension Sunday

Readings: Acts 1:1-11; Psalm 93; Ephesians 1:15-23; Luke 24:44-53

The Ascension of Our Lord

Acts 1:1-11; Luke 24:44-53

Many of us this week are still standing at the empty tomb, scratching our heads or perhaps rejoicing with the angels there. Some of us remain locked in the Jerusalem house where Jesus appeared just after his resurrection. Indeed, the ascension narrative in Luke's Gospel begins in that locked house. There, Jesus explains to his disciples that the Christ's suffering and death and resurrection were consistent with the writings of the prophets. Eventually, Jesus leads the disciples out of that room and outside the city, where he blesses them and ascends into heaven before their eyes. We, too, must follow Jesus and the disciples beyond the resurrection and witness his ascension.

Jesus' ascension into heaven is an integral part of the gospel, the story of the divine work in and through Jesus. But what does this pair of ascension stories tell us about God?

First, Jesus does not remain on earth. After the forty-day tutorial following his resurrection, Jesus leaves the disciples, returning to heaven. Though the Son of God remained fully human and fully divine after the resurrection and into eternity, the rightful place for Jesus after performing the redeeming work for humanity is in heaven, enthroned on high. Paul states in Ephesians 1 that Jesus has been raised above all rule and authority and power and dominion. Jesus is not so much in charge of the powers of this world as he is above them. The divine agenda should not be confused with the agenda of any earthly power. Jesus sits above the squabbling that causes so much heartache and suffering in this world. There, he cannot be co-opted to fight wars or support the human agendas that may tear the world apart (although many rulers have certainly tried). Jesus is not the head of the world, but the head of the church.

Second, God wants human witnesses to the divine story. During his time with the disciples after his resurrection, Jesus tells the disciples, "You are witnesses of these things" (Luke 24:48). Later, in the Acts account of his ascension, he promises, "You will be my witnesses" (Acts 1:8). Both refer to the testimony about Jesus Christ and the proclamation of the gospel message. While Jesus certainly wants people to verify the truth about his life, death, resurrection, and ascension, he desires something more than the type of testimony a witness could give in court. God wants witnesses to all aspects of the divine story because the divine story is worked out in the human heart. Thus, the disciples can say more than, "Jesus forgives sins." They can say, instead, "We have been forgiven." They can offer more than "Jesus was crucified, is risen, and has ascended," because they are able to say, "The risen Lord taught us, blessed us, and then ascended to heaven before our eyes." More than, "there is a Holy Spirit," Jesus urges them to wait in Jerusalem so that they may testify, "We have received the Holy Spirit, who gives us hope, courage, guidance, and assurance of God's truth in Christ Jesus." God's work in us is the divine story of redemption for all humanity, played out in the human heart.

Third, Jesus Christ acts in continuity with the ways God has always acted toward humanity. Jesus walks his disciples through the law of Moses, the prophets, and the psalms (in short, the entirety of Hebrew Scripture), to point out the fulfillment of Messianic scriptures in his own life. While something new is happening in Jesus, the sacred texts of the Jews and the Jewish faith itself should be seen as a wellspring from which flows the new activity of God. Jesus does not abandon old ideas about God. Jesus inhabits them, giving them new life, and perhaps frees the old notions of God's activity from poor interpretations and distorted expectations. Unless the disciples understand Jesus' life, death, and resurrection as the fulfillment of Scripture, their witness will be inadequate.

Fourth, the presence of God is to accompany the testimony about God. We might all think that the Incarnation of Jesus might teach us this truth, but Jesus' instruction for the disciples to wait in Jerusalem for the promise of the Father nudges us further toward understanding. Jesus says the coming Holy Spirit will clothe the disciples with "heavenly power." He also describes it as a baptism. The presence of the Holy Spirit will wash over the disciples, endowing them with power and completing their witness.

Finally, God intends that the gospel story have a period of gestation in our hearts. After the disciples encounter the risen Lord, why does Jesus not go ahead and give the Holy Spirit? Why wait the ten or so additional days between ascension (forty days after Easter) and Pentecost (fifty days after Passover). In fact, by John's Gospel account, Jesus breathed the Holy Spirit into the disciples when he appeared to them in the upper room (John 20:22). The point made by the writer of Luke–Acts may be that this good news about Jesus should be processed slowly and gradually. The truth about God should age in our hearts as we meditate and mull over Jesus' activity in and for the world. Perhaps the disciples needed a period of prayerful reflection over the resurrection and ascension of Jesus. Perhaps we do too.

As we celebrate the ascension, let us meditate on what Jesus' ascension tells us about God. May we release all our earthly claims to Jesus' power, allowing him to ascend to heaven where he belongs. Let us allow God to continue working out the narrative of Jesus in our hearts, as God has done throughout the ages in the hearts of God's people. And let us wait, as Jesus said, that the presence of God may complete our witness of the good news of God. In Jesus' ascension, our Lord opens heaven to us. Let us, in our prayerful waiting, open the earth to the Holy Spirit's outpouring. Amen. (Amber Essick)

Lectionary Commentary

Ephesians 1:15-23

This prayer of blessing expresses the ascension of Jesus in cosmic and theological terms. Its Trinitarian emphasis explores the actions of God as Father, Son, and Spirit. All three persons of the Godhead have been active in the world and in the story of Jesus. The Father raised Jesus from the dead and gave him the seat of glory and is also the one gifting believers with the Holy Spirit. The Son, who once dwelled among mortals, now occupies the seat of power in the heavenly places above and beyond the power struggles of humanity and has become head of the church. The Holy Spirit, Paul asserts, provides wisdom, gives revelatory knowledge, and enlivens the hearts of Christians. While the three persons of the Holy Trinity may have different functions in this blessing, Father, Son, and Spirit all perform out of unity in purpose and being.

Jesus' ascension to the throne does not so much put him in charge of world powers as raise him above them. He is not co-opting the kingdoms of the world to his purposes, but transcending them. Jesus does, however, inhabit the church, enlivening it and filling it with purpose. (Amber Essick)

Worship Aids

Call to Worship (Based on Psalm 93)

The Lord is king, robed in majesty;
The Lord is robed, girded with strength.
God has established the world; it shall never be moved;
Your throne is established from of old;
you are from everlasting.
More majestic than the thunders of mighty waters,
majestic on high is the Lord!
Holiness befits your house, O Lord, for evermore.

Invocation

Lord Jesus Christ, who sits enthroned above all rule and authority and power and dominion, we speak your name with great reverence. We call on you, knowing that you do not come at our bidding but by your own will. We beg of your Spirit to come to us, to enliven us, and to reign over us. To your name be all glory and praise forever. Amen.

Benediction

Let us pray with the apostle Paul (from Ephesians 1:17-19 NRSV): May the God of our Lord Jesus Christ, the Father of glory, give you a spirit of wisdom and revelation so that you may know the hope to which he has called you, what are the riches of his glorious inheritance among the saints, and what is the immeasurable greatness of his power for us who believe. Amen. (Amber Essick)

Faith versus Misogyny

Third in a Series of Three on Women in Ministry

2 Timothy 1:1-7

A few minutes after the bell rang, the professor came in and sat down at his desk, looked over the group of students, and then snorted, "Almost all women." The professor called roll, then handed out the syllabus and another sheet entitled "Pet Peeves." The class viewed the handout, then we all looked at one another as the professor began his rant on things that pushed his button and ensured a failing grade.

Number one on the list told the class that we were to address him as Doctor, not Mister and not Professor. Numbers two through nine of the Pet Peeves list dealt with supposed misspellings that would mean an automatic zero, "I know what the dictionary says. It's wrong! Spell it my way or fail. Better yet, don't use the word at all."

The whole sheet had everyone bewildered, but what most struck us was number ten. We couldn't take our eyes off of number ten. The quiet consensus was that the whole paper was a joke and number ten proved it. There was a small hope that the professor would read through the paper, get to number ten, read it, and then say something like, "Only kidding," or "Surprise," or begin to laugh.

Number ten on the professor's pet peeve list: "A class where women outnumbered men." The class was puzzled; even more so when no hint of a joke was given. The lecture continued its steady pace downhill.

"Women," said the professor. "It's nice that we have allowed you to get out of the house, but it seems you are taking over. And you are now trying to educate yourselves, and for what? You will not be as successful as a male, and you'll waste what education you received as soon as you marry. Why are all of you even here? I have a class full of women overdressed and taking space from men who need the education. It is the men, not the women, who will be something in life."

I locked eyes with my friend Matt. The professor noticed the looks on our faces and asked Matt why he was so surprised. "It was about time someone spoke up and defended men from the takeover of women in the workplace," said the professor. Matt asked the professor about his fellow professors, many of whom were women. "I have no choice. I have to work with them. They cannot teach, but I can. I am generous and offer students what they could not learn from the other, so-called instructors."

Matt and I surveyed the classroom, looking at the various expressions on the faces of our classmates. Still waiting for the punch line, some sat with a smirk on their faces; others looked worried, some looked defiant. We all looked at the professor. With a Cheshire cat grin he acknowledged our awkward silence and expressions and explained that women had enough advantages and that men needed all the help they could get. He looked directly at me and said, "It's enough that we allow you to dress up and hold a job, but now you are in school when you should be at home."

I couldn't stand it any longer. I raised my hand and was met with a chilling laugh. "Ah, a brave one," he said. I asked, "Why the hostility?" His response to me, "I'm angry at the waste of time and money, my time and taxpayer money. Women do not have the capacity to learn the way men learn, and women are taking resources and jobs from those who need them." My head was swimming. A few more began to raise their hands and ask questions. The professor looked at me and said, "Look what you've done."

The bell rang, and our professor gave us an assignment that was due next class. Two class meetings later our writing assignments were returned to us. Every woman received a failing grade, while every male received a passing grade along with a nice curve.

After inquiries and complaints, many of us found out that our tenured professor had behaved this way for years, and if we filed formal complaints it would be us and not the tenured professor facing harsh consequences.

By the fifth class meeting I was the only girl left in a room full of boys. I dropped the class afterward and was disappointed but not surprised to see that all but my male friends stayed in the class. One guy told me that he was making As and Bs for the first time in his life. He would be a fool to drop it. My friend Matt did the same. It's an easy A, he told me.

During this time my mother and my dad strongly encouraged me to stick with the class as long as I possibly could. "Who knows, you might be the one to change his mind," Dad told me. As part of the morale-boosting conversations, my parents reminded me that I had been raised in and worked in areas that are dominated by men, but I had handled myself well and proven myself to be as capable as any man. In the end they knew that I would be fine. Tough lessons learned, but the growth that followed would only make me a better person.

It was my grandmother who told me that even in trying times such as this, she knew I would be okay. She explained that I was raised with a faith that keeps me strong even when I don't feel strong. Then she quoted me one of her favorite scriptures, Proverbs 22:6: "Train children in the way they should go; / when they grow old, they won't depart from it."

My grandmother explained that God was imprinted not only in my heart but in my very being. Like Timothy, I was raised well, I was raised strong, I was raised with the Spirit, and it dwells within me. Even when I was hurting, God would heal me, stretch me, and help me grow through the toughest of situations. There will always be those who, for some reason, do not like me. For women it may be our gender, but for others it may be faith, looks, jobs; the list can go on and on. There will be those who will find something to not like about me, and I will have to be okay with it. In the end God's strength and righteousness will be revealed in how I handle the situation. I will be strong enough to continue God's work, and by doing so I will continue to touch lives. One man may not like the fact that I am a woman, but God loves how I was created and that is what counts most. My job is to live out my faith and, with my experience, help others live out their faith.

My grandparents and parents reminded me that I will face tougher situations as my life continues but I am to stand bravely in the Spirit, for God did not give us a spirit of timidity, but a spirit of power, of love, and of self-control (see 2 Timothy 1:7). My grandmother ended her visit by telling me, "Go and live and be strong and be the beautiful woman God has created." It is with grace and mercy that I strive to live a strong and beautiful life every day I have on this earth. (Julie Worcester)

Worship Aids

Call to Worship

We are part of the family of God.
The Spirit dwells in us, guiding us along our journey.
We live in love and fellowship, in peace and power.
The Spirit burns within us, giving us strength to serve.
We live a faithful life, full of grace and mercy.

Words of Assurance

You are not alone. God treasures you and dwells within you. God loves you. Through the sacrifice and resurrection of Jesus you are reconciled and in relationship with the One who is creator of all things and who reigns over all things.

Benediction

Go from this place with the grace of God. Live a strong and beautiful life. Encourage one another, be patient, be kind, and may your life be a saving light in a world of darkness. Amen. (Julie Worcester)

MAY 19, 2013

Pentecost Sunday

Readings: Acts 2:1-21; Psalm 104:24-34, 35b; Romans 8:14-17; John 14:8-17, (25-27)

The Wind Blows

Acts 2:1-21; Romans 8:14-17

After Jesus' ascension, his followers remained together and devoted themselves to prayer. They were still gathered together on the day of Pentecost. Suddenly, the Holy Spirit came upon them with power and rested on each person in the house. Each believer was filled and began proclaiming the works of God in a different language. They were each given the gift of speech. Just as Jesus, in his resurrection and ascension, opened heaven for humanity, so the believers, in their openness to God, opened the earth to the Spirit of God. As Jesus promised, those who believed in him were given power from on high, which completed their witness to the activity of God on earth. We may struggle today to understand what a Spirit-filled believer looks or acts like. Still, we acknowledge our need for the Holy Spirit in our churches and in our lives. This story of Pentecost teaches us several truths not only about the Spirit of God but also about ourselves.

First, there is goodness in the human heart that only the Holy Spirit can free. In the beginning, God created humans in the divine image. God pronounced this final touch on creation, men and women, very good. We were created to be in partnership with God, caring for everything God made. Although sin damaged the close relationship between human and divine, sin did not destroy the possibilities of human creative and redemptive partnership with God. From humanity's fall onward, God has worked to redeem the divine-human relationship that sin impaired. God most fully expressed that perfect union between God and humanity in the person of Jesus. Not only did Jesus show us the image of God, but in Jesus,

God also showed us how to be fully human, fully enlivened by God's Spirit, how to be good as God is good.

Jesus told his disciples to wait for the Holy Spirit, who would empower his followers to proclaim the good news of forgiveness of sins and fellowship with God. Those who were filled with the Holy Spirit on the day of Pentecost were freed to participate in the divine work on earth. This new freedom, this participation in God's work, was experienced in the forms of fellowship, prayer, and the ability to communicate the gospel to people of all nations. God shows us humanity's potential and the Spirit's power to use it in this story.

Second, we are most human when fully surrendered to the will of God. The believers who shared fellowship in Jerusalem after Jesus' ascension devoted themselves to prayer. Their devotion to God in prayer, as well as the fact that they cast off their own agendas and plans, indefinitely waiting for the gift of God, embodied what Jesus taught them to pray: "Thy will be done on earth as it is in heaven." With all the wildness of this story, one might get the impression that the Holy Spirit commandeered these willing vessels to proclaim the works of God like holy robots. But the followers of Jesus were not hostages of the Holy Spirit (doing God's will against their own); nor were their personalities eclipsed by the indwelling Spirit of God. Instead, the Holy Spirit was working in and through them as individuals whose wills were surrendered to God's will. The disciples and their companions did not act outside of themselves. Rather, by the design of God, by the love of Jesus Christ, and through the power of the Holy Spirit, the believers became fully alive, fully human, and fully aware of their status as God's children when the Spirit came. As the apostle Paul proclaims (Romans 8:15): "You received a Spirit that shows you are adopted as his children." In the coming of the Holy Spirit at Pentecost, the believers accepted their role as heirs to God, joint heirs with Jesus. They shed on that Pentecost day the notion that human nature means brokenness and imperfection. They accepted that to be fully human is to be united to God's Spirit, doing and proclaiming the work of God in the world.

Third, the Spirit's indwelling is God's gift to all people. Both men and women were filled with God's Spirit on that day, and both Jews and proselytes from all over the world heard the gospel proclaimed in their own languages. The gospel excludes no one from blessing or judgment, nor does the gift of the Holy Spirit fall on a select few. Also, the very fact that the twofold miracle involved some speaking other languages and others hearing the gospel in their own tongues verifies that God sought to bless all humanity with the good news of Jesus, starting in Jerusalem.

Fourth, we don't make sense of the Spirit. It makes sense of us. Can we really claim to understand the Spirit of God who, according to Jesus, "blows wherever it wishes" like the wind (John 3:8)? Later in Acts, as the Holy Spirit fell upon Gentile Christians, the scene resembled the picture of the Pentecost event, but earlier in the New Testament, the Spirit of God acted very unpredictably. The Spirit overshadowed Mary (Luke 1:35); descended like a dove on Jesus at his baptism (Luke 3:22); led Jesus into the wilderness (Luke 4:1); came upon and anointed Jesus to proclaim good news, release, recovery of sight, and liberation respectively to the poor, the captives, the blind, and the oppressed (Luke 4:18); and, furthermore, filled several people so that they burst into song, including Elizabeth, Mary, and Zechariah (all in Luke 1). Perhaps this unpredictability is why the third person of the Trinity makes many people so nervous.

Though many accepted the Pentecost miracle at face value, some sneered. They could not recognize what was happening as God's generous act. Today, some groups hold meetings in which the Holy Spirit causes them to speak in unknown tongues or makes them act very strangely with rolling, laughing, or even barking. Others say that the Holy Spirit has ceased to gift people with the gift of tongues. Both attitudes (and many others) relegate God's Spirit to predictable and tame expressions that seem antithetical to the wild, surprising nature of the Holy Spirit of Scripture. We should not presume to corner, apprehend, or ascertain all there is to know about the Holy Spirit from this encounter in Acts 2.

The Holy Spirit brings understanding, clarity, and enlightenment. It assures us of our status as God's children. It teaches us how to be fully alive. We do not own or wield God the Spirit any more than we do the other two persons of the Godhead. The Spirit of the living God approached humans in Acts 2. It filled them. It empowered them to testify to the works of God in Christ Jesus. And today, the Holy Spirit reminds us of our status as the heirs of God and partners with Jesus in redemption. As we open our hearts to God's will, the Spirit can lead us in surprising new directions. A community enlivened by God's Spirit is open to possibility. May it be so among us that the Spirit finds us to be willing partners in God's creative and redemptive work in the world. Amen. (Amber Essick)

Lectionary Commentary

John 14:8-17, 25-27

Jesus, in the midst of his farewell remarks to his disciples, begins to explain both the unity between himself and the Father and how the disciples might share in it. Philip, perplexed, claims that some visual representation of God might be helpful to them all. Jesus retorts with stinging words, "Don't you know me, Philip, even after I have been with you all this time?" (v. 9). Jesus is, after all, exactly what Philip requests: God-made-flesh.

We do not know God even when we see God. Our eyes and ears need help to see the way, truth, and life, who stands before us in the person of Jesus. We do not know the way. We need God's Spirit, dwelling inside of us, to light the path, to point to Jesus, and to keep our feet from stumbling as we walk the path.

Jesus understands this and promises that the disciples will understand it when the Spirit teaches them and reminds them of his teachings. Meanwhile, Jesus tells them to believe in his unity with the Father, even if their faith is based on the power of his works. He asks them to love him in obedience, promises the same kind of love toward them, and urges them to wait for the Holy Spirit. He assures them and leaves them his peace. (Amber Essick)

Worship Aids

Prayer of Confession

Holy Spirit of the Living God, we confess that we have sinned against you this week. Our hearts are often unprepared for you. Our actions betray divided hearts; our thoughts reveal unbelief. In this moment, we ask your forgiveness and guidance. Holy Spirit, come to us, breathe on us, illumine us, that we may know your transforming presence among us. Amen.

Words of Pardon

In the name of God, who is Father, Son, and Spirit, you are forgiven. Walk now in the light of God's Spirit, who lives in you, knowing that you are indeed children of God and co-heirs with Jesus Christ. Amen.

Responsive Reading (Based on Psalm 104:31-34)

May the glory of the Lord endure forever;

  may the Lord rejoice in the works of God.

Who looks on the earth and it trembles;
who touches the mountains and they smoke.
I will sing to the Lord as long as I live,
I will sing praise to my God while I have being.
All: May my meditation be pleasing to God, for I rejoice in the Lord. (Amber Essick)

The Good Samaritan Church

First in a Series of Three on Evangelism Lessons

Matthew 25:31-46; Luke 10:25-37

Today there is so much confusion about what it is to be a Christian. Churches have defined it in many ways: how we worship, the music we use, our liturgy. Being a Christian has been defined by particular rules, such as the way we cut our hair, the garb of our clergy, and the amount of water used in baptism. In a society that has become very secular, we need to get to the point of what it is to be a Christian. Peter sought to answer that in 1 Peter 2:21: "You were called to this kind of endurance, because Christ suffered on your behalf. He left you an example so that you might follow in his footsteps."

In 1896, a Kansas pastor named Charles Sheldon was inspired by those words and wrote a novel defining what it is to be a Christian called *In His Steps*. The idea is so simple. To be a Christian is simply to ask, "what would Jesus do (WWJD)?" Several years ago, people wore WWJD bracelets, and it was popular to affirm our faith with that simple slogan. The popularity of the bracelets and slogan has waned, but the meaning is still essential. The Christian is to follow in the steps of Jesus, asking, "What would Jesus do?" in every decision.

In Luke 10, Jesus tells a story of a man attacked on the road between Jerusalem and Jericho. Some people coming down the road see he has been robbed and is injured, in a desperate condition; they are too busy to stop and help. The good Samaritan sees the man and stops to help. He goes beyond normal courtesy, even placing himself in danger. Jesus says at the end of this story that we are to go out and "do likewise." We need to be the people who help if we are going to do what Jesus would do.

As Jesus was just beginning to preach, he went back to his hometown and read aloud the scripture,

> The Spirit of the Lord is upon me,
> because the Lord has anointed me.
> He has sent me to preach good news to the poor,
> to proclaim release to the prisoners
> and recovery of sight to the blind,
> to liberate the oppressed,
> and to proclaim the year of the Lord's favor. (Luke 4:18-19)

Jesus said he was called to help people in need.

At the end of Matthew 25, Jesus makes that point extremely clear as he tells the story of judgment day. We will be divided like sheep from goats. The sheep, those who help ordinary people, get to go to heaven. Those who don't are the goats and will go to the other place. It's very clear; we are called to be like the good Samaritan.

Today, churches are declining in membership, attendance, and participation. We ask how we are to reach new people and new generations, and we are susceptible to all kinds of membership campaigns and gimmicks. In previous generations, we won new converts by telling people that the thing to do was to go to church; everyone in town went to church. Today it is not "the thing to do." In other generations, people went to church because they were scared into it. They were told that if they didn't go to church, they would go to hell. Today, people disregard our scare tactics and are not going to church. Sometimes it would help if we had the most entertaining worship; surely then people would come to church! But, when a praise band takes a job at another church or a popular youth director goes to seminary, the youth group begins to fail, and we realize that entertainment, fear, guilt, cultural pressure, or attendance campaigns will not work in the long run to create sincere relationships with Christ.

Jesus said that what will work is helping people where they hurt. "Needs-based Evangelism" is being sensitive and caring; it is helping people. The greatest mistake the church has made in recent years is not noticing the hurts of the people on the side of the road. We get so busy going to our meetings and activities that we do not have time to stop. The irony is that, by that very act, the church is dying. Churches all across the world are growing and thriving when they are sensitive to the needs of the people. Jesus says that he came to help; if we are to be his followers, that is what we must do. There will be lots of techniques for reaching new people, lots of membership campaigns that will be tried and materials that will be sold, but until we really care for and help others, the church will not grow. The answer is not simply doing a little bit of good in a world that needs so much; it is really caring; it is inviting someone to a cancer support group where there is prayer and faith and hope. It is caring enough to go to the hospital when that patient undergoes treatment or surgery. It is meeting friends and family and inviting them to join you in prayer.

To be a "Good Samaritan Church" (perhaps the best name for a vibrant church today), doing a little bit of good from time to time will not cut it; it requires really caring about each and every individual. In this way, people come to know Jesus not by some slogan that they use or an empty prayer that they say but through acts of love. Jesus set an example, and we should follow in his steps. (Bob Pierson)

Worship Aids

Responsive Reading: Matthew 25:34-40

"Then the king will say to those on his right, 'Come, you who will receive good things from my Father. Inherit the kingdom that was prepared for you before the world began. I was hungry and you gave me food to eat. I was thirsty and you gave me a drink. I was a stranger and you welcomed me. I was naked and you gave me clothes to wear. I was sick and you took care of me. I was in prison and you visited me.'...

"Lord, when did we see you hungry and feed you, or thirsty and give you a drink? When did we see you as a stranger and welcome you, or naked and give you clothes to wear? When did we see you sick or in prison and visit you?

The king will reply, "Truly I tell you, whatever you did for one of the least of these brothers and sisters of mine, you did for me."

We are committed to loving our neighbors as we love ourselves.

Pastoral Prayer

The God of all has created people who are in need and people who can help. We understand that we are called to be like the good Samaritan: available to help wherever we see the need. God, we ask for wisdom to discern where needs are real and where we can really help. We ask for creativity to find solutions that work rather than create dependency and entitlement. God, give us determination, even when we are tired and out of sorts from helping so many times, to still be enthused about following Jesus and caring for those in need. God, may we understand the truth that by giving we shall receive. May we understand that our sense of purpose and joy and excitement in life comes from helping others. In the name of Jesus. Amen.

Benediction

Go forth to love your neighbor. Stop and help wherever you see a need. The grace and power of our Lord Jesus Christ will go with you, and the Holy Spirit will indeed inspire and strengthen you. Amen. (Bob Pierson)

MAY 26, 2013

Trinity Sunday

Readings: Proverbs 8:1-4, 22-31; Psalm 8; Romans 5:1-5; John 16:12-15

Triple Play for God

Proverbs 8:1-4, 22-31; John 16:12-15; Romans 5:1-5

Each year on Trinity Sunday, we gather with high hopes. We want to understand the triune nature of God. We confess that God is three-in-one, but a satisfactory explanation of this tends to elude us. We may wonder whether God's trifold essence is inexplicable and incomprehensible to us. Often Christians find it easier to speak about the Godhead in negatives: we deny that God is three Gods. We refute the notion that God is one person wearing three masks. We stumble short of describing God in positive terms. Indeed, all our metaphors, speech, and experiences offer partial and imperfect illustrations of God. However, as believers in a skeptical world, we must come to terms with such limitations. Our God, revealed as Father, Son, and Spirit, seeks to be known. The divine identity holds gifts for humanity: unity, love, cooperation, wisdom, and inexpressible mystery. We must understand and experience the triune God in order to communicate these gifts to the world. We may find that the Holy Trinity is not as elusive as it is all-pervading, not so incomprehensible as mysterious.

What does it mean to say that God is triune? However much like a riddle it sounds, God is three persons and one being, or three "whos" and one "what." That which makes up the Godhead (God's essence) is shared among all three persons of the Holy Trinity. However, each person is distinct from the other (not divided, but distinct). In John 16, Jesus expresses unity with God the Father and with the Holy Spirit, although he speaks of three distinct persons doing three different tasks: God the Father shares with the Son; God the Son stands among his disciples, teaching them; God the Spirit communicates and interprets truth from the Father and Son. There is no metaphor in creation that accurately illustrates this concept. A divine family or council denotes more separation than exists within God. The three are unified in essence and in purpose, and they share everything. Through the Holy Spirit, God offers humanity the type of union exemplified within the Trinity. Paul notes in Romans 5 that God grants us two gifts through Jesus Christ: access to God's grace and peace with God.

The triune God is eternally a God in relationship: Father, Son, and Holy Spirit have always existed in a loving relationship with one another. Woman Wisdom declares that she was present with God at creation as God's delight, "I was having fun, / smiling before him all the time, / frolicking with his inhabited earth / and delighting in the human race" (Proverbs 8:30b-31). Her speech expresses the eternal truth of divine love among the Trinity: God's love is complete. In the familial relationship of the Trinity, God loves in a way that does not require another being. God's creation of humanity therefore expresses generosity and abundance rather than need, loneliness, or scarcity. In giving the Holy Spirit, God pours this love into the hearts of believers, as Paul explains in Romans 5. The divine love remakes our lives, forming endurance, character, and hope within us, so that we might receive and give love as God does: generously and completely. Living into the divine love through the grace of the Holy Spirit's gifts, we can live our lives out of abundance as God does.

Though Father, Son, and Spirit each have primary tasks and functions, they act in cooperation. While we must be careful in naming God solely based on divine care for humanity (as if God exists only to care for humans), it is helpful sometimes to offer praise to the Father, Son, and Spirit for their works in creating, redeeming, and sustaining the world. Many Christians refer to God the Father as the Creator, the Son as Savior or Redeemer, and the Holy Spirit as the Sustainer, Friend, Comforter, or Advocate. However, there is cooperation among the Trinity in all of God's acts. God the Father's primary task is that of creation, but as Woman Wisdom states, "I was beside him as a master of crafts" (Proverbs 8:30a). In John 16, Jesus, the teacher and redeemer, utilizes the Spirit in teaching the disciples, though the Spirit collaborates with the Father and Son. Likewise, the Spirit involves the Son and Father in the divine task of nurturing the church. All three persons of the Trinity are involved in the shared tasks of creation, redemption, and sustenance. As we experience union with God and receive God's love, humanity is drawn into cooperation in the divine tasks as partners with God.

The triune God of our faith is a mystery, revealed to us only partially and gradually. God transcends our comprehension and understanding, yet invites us to comprehend and understand, to pursue the truth. The triune nature of the one God was revealed to humanity over millennia, in the fullness of time. Not until after all the books of our Scripture were written did the church discern a doctrine of the Trinity, and that amidst conflict. While the Holy Spirit does communicate God's truth to believers, the identity and the activity of God remains partially veiled from us. Jesus expresses both the limitations and the potential for human understanding when he first tells his disciples, "I have much more to say to you, but you can't handle it now," then, "when the Spirit of Truth comes, he will guide you in all truth" (John 16:12-13). When God passes by Moses in the wilderness, Moses is shielded from seeing God's face (Exodus 33:17-23), and yet Moses had an intimate relationship with God. However, God offers understanding to all people, not an elite few. Woman Wisdom does not stay upon a mountain, remaining aloof from humanity. She descends to the streets and crossroads. She appears at the town's gate, and before we know it, she approaches us in the doorway. Wisdom calls out to "all of humanity" (Proberbs 8:4). God's Spirit actively communicates God's wisdom and truth to humanity. Making the inner mystery of God known to us is one of the primary tasks of the Holy Spirit. Though a portion of the divine identity remains shrouded in mystery, God's wisdom is a gift for all who live.

The God whom we serve is three persons and one being. God exists in eternal relationship, in the eternal giving and receiving of love. While the persons of the Trinity are distinct, there is cooperation in all the divine tasks, such that separating the persons of the Trinity based on their primary functions is not possible. Knowledge of the Triune God, partial as it may be, is available to all who will discern the expressed wisdom of God, made known to us by the Holy Spirit. The very identity of God illuminates possibilities for humanity: God's unity, love, cooperation, and wisdom become gifts for humanity, drawing us into the divine tasks as partners with God. As we receive the divine wisdom, may we even learn to see the mystery of God as a gift. May we come to rest in the mystery that is the ground of our being. Amen. (Amber Essick)

Worship Aids

Invocation

O Sacred Three in One, we enter worship with hearts lifted toward heaven. Come into our midst, we pray, that in your light we may see, in your joy we may sing, and in your love we may be formed into your people. In the name of the Father, Son, and Holy Spirit we pray, one God, now and forever. Amen.

Responsive Reading (Based on Proverbs 8:1-4; 22-31

Does not Wisdom call? Does not Understanding raise her voice?
On the heights, beside the way,
at the crossroads she takes her stand.
Beside the gates in front of the town,
at the entrance of the portal she cries out:
To you, O people, I call, and my cry is to all that live!

Benediction

May the love of God the Father find you this week. May the grace of God the Son keep your feet on the Christian path. May the wisdom of God the Spirit guide you in the way of salvation. Amen. (Amber Essick)

TELL

Second in a Series of Three on Evangelism Lessons

John 1:43-51

The mainline Protestant church today is declining. The percentage of Americans who claim to be Christian is decreasing. These trends have been happening for twenty years. These statistics ought to remind us not of a need to have a new membership campaign but to do what Jesus taught and to make disciples. Our effectiveness will be made possible by three decisions: the decision to follow his final instructions, the decision to do what Jesus taught, and, finally, the decision to tell others about Jesus Christ and how wonderful it is to follow him.

They were doing what is natural, just telling a friend about a really good deal. We do it all the time. It is called word of mouth. You find there is a bargain at your favorite department store, and you tell your friends. You hear your favorite singer is coming to town, and you tell your friends and family. There is a new television series that you really like, so you tell others, whether they like it or not. We are always telling.

John 1:43-47 shares the simple story of Philip telling Nathanael about Jesus. This "telling" others happens over and over. The book of Acts is the story of telling others about Jesus. It is so natural and simple, and yet for a Christian today to tell another about Jesus seems so hard.

The people we want to share with live in a society that has become very secular. In fact, much of our society views organized religion in a negative way. Church members are thought of as hypocritical and uncaring, arrogant and judgmental. Often the language we use to describe our faith is difficult for non-Christians to understand. We use unfamiliar metaphors and symbols. Most troublesome, we have not lived our faith very well in front of the very people we would like to share with. That being the reality, how do we share?

The letters in the word *TELL* can be a reminder of some of the principles of how to share our faith. The *T* reminds us of the *Truth* of our own lives. In order to tell the story of Jesus, we need to know that truth ourselves. It needs to be in our minds, but more than that, it needs to be a part of our experience. Some of us have known the truth of Jesus Christ since childhood; we are almost born into the faith; it has become so much a part of how we think and live that it is who we are. Others of us have become Christians along the journey of life. We have made a change and a promise to follow Jesus. We have experienced the indwelling of the Holy Spirit, and we sense the excitement of being a part of the church. We each have a story and truth about what being Christian means. Too often, we detract from that truth with fear, guilt, mistakes, and how we have changed from our worst nature. Certainly that is an important aspect of truth in all of us. But Christianity is not just about how bad we have been but about how good Jesus is. The truth is that God loves us despite our faults. Our self-esteem is secure. That's our story. It is our truth.

The letter *E* reminds us of the word *Explain*. Much of the task of telling about Jesus is to explain. A lot of misinformation is present in our society. We need to explain our beliefs. We need to be prepared to answer hard questions. Many doctrines of the church require careful study. We must have answers for these questions. We must be able to explain. This is the story of salvation for all of us, and it must be explained and understood for us to be able to enjoy it, celebrate it, use it, and tell it clearly.

The first *L* reminds us of *Living*. If a person is to understand what the Christian faith is all about, they will understand it best by the way that we live. We need to show that love, generosity, kindness, patience, understanding, integrity, and responsibility are the principles we live by. Our society seems to reward un-Christian behavior, so we must tell others about Christ through our actions in ordinary times and in times of crisis.

A young woman found she had a difficult disease. Her friends at the office were impressed with the effective way she dealt with illness. They were amazed because she seemed to have unusual strength to handle this difficult time. When they asked how she remained so strong, she shared the strength that God had given her. They saw Jesus in her behavior.

The last *L* represents *Leading*. We are called to invite someone to church and to explain salvation. We need to learn how to lead others to accept Jesus Christ as Lord and Savior.

Jesus called us to go make disciples. There is no exception to that. How we share the faith and tell the story is a critical part of our discipleship. In order to really TELL we have to spend time studying, praying, and practicing. Our real effectiveness is our deep sincerity and commitment to follow Jesus. We may not have all the doctrines of the church worked out in our minds when we have an opportunity to invite someone, but we must try our best to explain what church is about, even if we fumble. We need to remember that the truth of how we live is important as a means of invitation. We are called to tell with love what Christ has taught us. Every day we live, we are telling the story of Jesus with our own lives. (Bob Pierson)

Worship Aids

Call to Worship

God has created a world with so many opportunities for each of God's children.

We thank God for possibilities for a better life in a changed world.

Jesus taught us that we are called to invite others to this better life and to change the world by following him.

We are committed to following Jesus Christ, our Lord and Savior.

We must tell others what Jesus told us.
We must share the good news.
May God help us as we tell the story to our friends, family, and the world.

Pastoral Prayer

Jesus made it clear that we are to tell the story. Just as the disciples told their friends, so are we to tell our friends, neighbors, relatives, and acquaintances. God, sometimes we are so reluctant, so bashful, we don't say anything. Help us speak up when appropriate, in a way that is inviting, and out of an authentic desire to share. God, we share because we have found that the power of Jesus Christ brings us help, success, love, and inner peace. Dear Lord, help us share this good news, to tell. In the name of Jesus. Amen.

Benediction

Go forth and tell your friends and family, everyone you meet, about Jesus Christ.
He is our Lord and Savior. We will tell his truth to everyone.
Through the power of the Holy Spirit you are called to tell the world. (Bob Pierson)

JUNE 2, 2013

Second Sunday after Pentecost

Readings: 1 Kings 18:20-21, 30-39; Psalm 96; Galatians 1:1-12; Luke 7:1-10

We Must Be Consumed

1 Kings 18:20-21, 30-39; Galatians 1:1-12

Abundance and scarcity are often the building blocks for human stories. Stories draw on images of deluge and aridity, vagrancy or luxuriance. Post-apocalyptic stories regularly take up themes of plenitude and deficiency as a vehicle for addressing what it means to be human. Competition for valuable resources has characterized our attempts at life together in all ages, so when confronted with a story about the absence of water, it is not difficult for us to imagine how quickly various explanations, causes, and remedies for a drought would spill forth. When our interests begin to compete with the interests of others, we often invoke the divine to settle such disputes, to set things straight, and to order our common life.

For the ancients, weather patterns were assumed to reflect the mood, will, or wishes of divine beings. In 1 Kings 17 we read that Elijah's first act as a prophet of YHWH involved informing King Ahab of an impending and lengthy drought, which could be lifted only at YHWH's discretion. Apparently YHWH grew impatient with the people's insistence upon running after Baal. As 1 Kings proceeds, we find that the drought was indeed severe and that YHWH alone was responsible for any abundance of food or water. It was YHWH who led Elijah to a ravine with water and directed the ravens to care for him there. The brook eventually dried up for Elijah, though, and so YHWH turned the prophet's attention to a struggling widow and her son in Zarephath. It was there that YHWH restored the widow's son to life after Elijah had instructed her to provide YHWH's prophet with water and bread despite a scarcity of oil. These episodes signal to us that it is YHWH alone who is capable of abundance in a world of scarcity.

But nowhere is this competition between YHWH and Baal more pronounced than in 1 Kings 18, where Elijah ascends Mount Carmel to confront the prophets of Baal. He accuses the people of swinging back and forth like a pendulum between Baal and YHWH. Elijah, living up to his name—which means something like "YHWH is my God"—informs the people that YHWH is jealous and impatient. It is time to choose, Elijah pronounces, and so begins the competition.

The prophets of Baal limp around the altar in a rather strange ceremony obviously meant to call down water from heaven. Elijah joins in the event by taunting them, even suggesting that Baal appears unaware, unconcerned, or disinterested. For all the noise generated in the opening act of the competition, it ends in a deafening silence (v. 29). Elijah, on the other hand, takes time to repair the altar to YHWH, which is a sign to all present that he is marking the place again as YHWH's. He then proceeds to flood the altar with water, perhaps to symbolize rain, but the effect of seeing vast amounts of water being poured on the ground must have been a powerful reminder of what is at stake for a community in desperate need of water: nothing less than life and a future. YHWH, unlike Baal, gets involved, remembers the promises to the ancestors, and keeps the divine promise. YHWH descends upon the altar, or perhaps inhabits the sacred space Elijah has reconstructed, and consumes everything in fire. Nothing former remains.

The prophets of Baal and Elijah are engaged in competing stories that will produce a clear winner and loser, but more than the struggle is to understand reality and be swallowed up by what is true and enduring. Drought and famine and scarcity all suggest expiration and fading into nothingness. These are the things that YHWH descends to consume and devour and destroy. YHWH's acts on Mount Carmel also call attention to divine abundance, the all-encompassing provision of YHWH alone. It is not just that Baal has lost; Baal, like any and all human creations, has been utterly consumed by YHWH.

Let us remember again that all that we hold most dear must be sacrificed. All the ways of ordering our life together must be consumed on the altar of the gospel. All the ways of dividing ourselves or uniting ourselves must be consumed on the altar of the gospel. There was nothing left in that trench after God's fire fell from heaven; every remnant of the old was licked up, we are told. The gospel Paul proclaimed to the Galatians was an all-consuming piece of good news, a word that consumed and devoured all other words. Similarly, there are no scraps or leftovers in the gospel's wake. To grasp at a shred of anything else is to make room for an idol or chase after a different gospel. Indeed, allowing vestiges of old ways or other gospels to exist is idolatry and denies the divine story we've been given in the incarnation, life, death, resurrection, and ascension of Jesus. May God's story consume us all this day and every day. Amen. (John Essick)

Lectionary Commentary

Luke 7:1-10

Jesus here exhibits a willingness to heal a member of the foreign, occupying, and conquering Roman establishment. In Luke, this miracle comes on the heels of Jesus teaching a crowd of disciples about wealth, forgiveness, and the dangers of judging others (see Luke 6). Jesus' own ministry demonstrates his disregard for constructed social boundaries, evidenced not only in the healing of a Gentile but also in his apparent willingness to enter a Gentile household. That Jesus is "amazed" (NRSV; "impressed" CEB) here is also noteworthy, for this is the only occasion in any of the canonical Gospels that we read of Jesus being amazed. (John Essick)

Worship Aids

Call to Worship (Based on Psalm 96)

We have gathered to sing a fresh song and proclaim
God's marvelous deeds.
God alone is worthy of our praise.
We have gathered in fear and trembling before the judge
of heaven and earth.
God alone is worthy of our praise.
We have gathered to join our voices with the fields, the trees,
and all creation.
God alone is worthy of our praise.

Words of Assurance

The God of Abraham, Sarah, Isaac, Rebekah, Jacob, Rachel, and Elijah has heard our prayers and confessions this day. The Lord is God, and the Lord is turning our hearts back again.

Benediction

May the grace of God our Father, the peace of the Lord Jesus Christ, and the unity of the Holy Spirit be to you wings of life as you depart this place. (John Essick)

The Final Instructions

Third in a Series of Three on Evangelism Lessons

Matthew 28:16-20

It was halftime of the homecoming game. The home team was behind by two touchdowns. The coach knew his job was on the line. The team knew this was the most important game of the year. As they sat in the locker room, the coach's instructions were clear. They had a new strategy for the second half, some assignments were changed, and an attitude of determination was set. As the team went back on the field, no one questioned what they would do or when; the time was now. They had heard the final instructions, and they were clear.

The CEO was visiting the city from corporate headquarters, meeting with all of the members of this particular branch of the company. The sales force, management, manufacturing—everyone was there. As she began to speak, she told them clearly about changes that had to be made. She described the new strategy, telling them what had to be done. She ended with an enthusiastic summary. The applause was vigorous. The employees knew that, if they wanted to keep their jobs, they had to do what was said that day by the CEO who had given the final, clear instructions.

At seventy-eight years old, he had been in good health most of his life, but now he was dying of cancer. He asked for his children to come to his bedside at the hospital. All were saddened by their father's illness. They were all very emotional. As the family gathered around the room, he began to tell them things he believed in—things about life, things he wanted them to do. Then, he asked each of them to promise to do what he had reviewed. That day, they all agreed to follow his final instructions as best they could.

We've all had experiences like these, some of us in the same situations. We understand the imperative.

In each of these stories, the instructions are clear. The emotion is strong, and behavior cannot be compromised. The team has to follow the instructions—now. The corporate management strategy was an imperative. The family gathered around their dad's deathbed comes to understand what family is all about. They will do their best to do what he asks them to do.

Matthew 28:19-20 tells a similar story. Jesus asks his followers to meet him on a hillside in Galilee. They had done this many times before in the three years of following Jesus. This was not unusual; the unusual thing was that this is the last time. There is something final about this meeting. Jesus shares "The Great Commission." He makes it an imperative. As followers of Jesus, we must understand that imperative. What Jesus says to the disciples, he says to all of us. To follow his way truly, we need to follow this Great Commission.

Look at the words carefully and review this imperative. First, Jesus says, "I've received all authority in heaven and on earth. Therefore, go and make disciples" (vv. 18-19a). This is an imperative—we must make disciples of Jesus Christ, who comes to us in authority. Everything the church does—fellowship, worship, recreation, community service, and acts of social justice—must align with the imperative to make disciples. We have become immune to the phrase because we've heard it so many times. Jesus told us that our first obligation is to help people become followers of Jesus! It is the final instruction.

The second aspect as Jesus states it is to "make disciples of all nations" (v. 19b). There is no limit to whom we are reaching, those of every age, station, and situation in life. As we do evangelism, we tend to focus on certain groups—groups that are like us, those with whom we can communicate—and there's no problem with that, but we must understand that, in reality, our field is unlimited.

Jesus says that we are to baptize new believers. We are not just to tell them about Jesus' teachings or help them enjoy the music of worship and recreation in the fellowship hall. We are to lead people to accept Jesus Christ as their Lord and Savior; we are to lead people to "take up their cross and follow him"; we are to baptize them as followers of God, seen in the power of his daily presence and in his beautiful creativity.

Finally, Jesus says we are to teach them to obey all of Jesus' commands. We are to help people really understand the purpose of the gospel, take time to explain the difficult doctrines and the easy ideas. All species of the animal kingdom teach their offspring the skills necessary to survive—gathering food, providing shelter, taking care of themselves. We as "parents" of new followers of Jesus need to teach everything he taught. It's not always easy, but we are to teach the whole gospel—not just what is convenient or popular, but all of what Jesus taught. The church has a responsibility to help us all come to understand and teach it.

As the disciples walked away from that fantastic experience, and seeing Jesus ascend into heaven, they had many alternatives. They could go back to fishing or grieve in their homes because they had lost their Savior. They could go about family responsibilities—on and on, we have choices.

In the church today, there is so much to do. There are many good, important things to be involved with; there are so many things that are pressing and critical. Evangelism has gone out of style; this "Great Commandment" has been rejected by many Christians. They have clipped it out of the Bible and tossed it in the trash as not possible, not practical, and not doable. Yet if we are truly to be on God's team, working for our leader, Jesus, and are truly to be children of God the Father, we have no choice. We must make disciples! This is our imperative, the final instruction! This is our task! (Bob Pierson)

Worship Aids

Call to Worship

Jesus Christ our Lord and Savior sends us
to make disciples of all nations.
Jesus our leader instructs us.
We will baptize people
in the name of the Father, Son, and Holy Spirit
and teach what Jesus commanded.
Jesus will be with us every day until the end of the age.

Pastoral Prayer

Oh Lord, we understand your instructions to go into all the world and preach and teach the gospel of Jesus. Help us, oh God, to do what you command. Help us, oh God, to be creative, consistent, and brave in following your teachings as we seek to be the persons Jesus taught us to be, to follow his instructions, and to proclaim love throughout the world. God, we thank you for loving all of us, even though we have failed and sinned. Thank you for forgiving us and loving us enough to give us power to overcome, tenacity to keep trying, and comfort to know that you love us despite our faults. In the name of our Lord and Savior, Jesus Christ. Amen.

Benediction

Jesus said, "Go and make disciples."
We will do what he said.
Jesus said, "Go into the entire world."
We will do what he said.
Let us go and do. (Bob Pierson)

JUNE 9, 2013

Third Sunday after Pentecost

Readings: 1 Kings 17:17-24; Psalm 146; Galatians 1:11-24; Luke 7:11-17

A Pair of Prophets

1 Kings 17:17-24; Luke 7:11-17

These two readings naturally pair. Two widows. Two sons. Two widowed mothers faced with the prospect of losing their children too. Luke apparently thought these two readings dance well together, too, for in 7:16 of his Gospel, the terrified onlookers take the words right out of the mouth of the widow in 1 Kings 17 when they exclaim concerning Jesus that "A great prophet has appeared among us!" Almost everyone knows Elijah's prophetic exploits, and Luke is more likely than any other New Testament writer to describe Jesus as a prophet. Elijah raises one son from the dead by praying to God. Jesus raises a son from the dead by speaking to him. And so we have two prophets and two boys raised from the dead. Indeed, these passages anticipate and echo one another in many ways. We would do well to read them several times over if we wish to mine their meaning.

Eliljah could not keep the boy alive. The widow is desperate. Yet Israel's God, who actively controls rain in the enemy's territory, also controls life. The physical nature of the healing ritual has been the subject of speculation and its exact meaning remains unclear, but it does seem that Elijah seeks to transmit in the act some of his own life to the dead boy. Beyond stretching his own body over the boy's, Elijah implores God to restore the boy to life. The final stage of the miracle is God's response: God listens to Elijah. There is no sense here that Elijah's physical act or his prayer account for the return of the boy's life. This is no efficacious human ritual on its own; it is the insertion of the life of God into a dying world.

There is yet another, deeper aspect to this miraculous situation. The mother, who originally accused Elijah of killing her son, is now the mother who confesses faith in the God of Israel. God is at work, even in Zarephath, turning people toward life and truth and a future. And Elijah, who himself blamed God for the situation, is affirmed as God's prophet in preparation for the upcoming competition with the prophets of Baal. Elijah, this mercurial conundrum of a prophet, stands tall in Israel's history. His successor, Elisha, watched him fly away in a chariot of fire, and the Old Testament closes with the expectation that Elijah will return and usher in the "day of the LORD" (Malachi 4:5-6).

That Elijah visits with Jesus at the transfiguration is one sign, among others, that Jesus himself is the day of the Lord for which God's people have been longing. Whereas Elijah's plea for help is laced with some measure of frustration, Jesus' response in Luke's story is filled with compassion and pity. Humanity's great need greets Jesus at the city gate. The bearer of life is welcomed to this place by a corpse, an image of the limited and fleeting nature of our bodily existence. Jesus, extending the hands and voice of life, is literally able to speak life out of death. The young man, too, speaks with life as Jesus presents him as a gift to his widowed mother.

Upon witnessing death's reversal, the crowd, like the widow in 1 Kings 17, is compelled to confess faith in God and acknowledge that divine favor has indeed visited them in Jesus. In fact, Jesus notices and has compassion on a widow, a member of a vulnerable group for whom survival and sustenance was ever dependent upon the favor and protective care of others. Moreover, Jesus' compassionate act returns a means of income and stability for this widow's future. Jesus has come that we may have life and that we may live abundantly.

These stories of restoration and return speak to the delicacy of life and the power of God. We are reminded that God's creation is far from static; rather, it is flexible, open to possibility, and capable of being reborn and used at God's pleasure. These passages also beckon God's people to challenge the givenness of the world's suffering. How can Christians be more like Elijah in seeking ways to stretch their own bodies over a world in need of life and hope? How can Christians follow Jesus in embracing the world's great need with hands of compassion and a confession that divine favor has been extended to all in the person of Jesus. May this pair of prophets make prophets of us all! Amen. (John Essick)

Lectionary Commentary

Galatians 1:11-24

This section of the epistle to the Galatians provides helpful and somewhat confusing biographical details about Paul. Paul's apostleship is a primary concern in these verses, but there is disagreement as to what these details suggest about Paul's opponents and the background of the disagreements. Regardless, it is abundantly clear that Paul's own history speaks to the transforming power of the good news of Jesus Christ. Paul identifies here the revelatory moment on the road to Damascus as a crucial piece in his conversion process, a process that began in God before Paul was even born. (John Essick)

Worship Aids

Call to Worship

Gather around, people of God. Take your place in this story of old told through our worship in this place. What we proclaim to one another and the world this day is not of human origin. We have been grafted into this story revealed to us by God's Son. Proclaiming God's story is our worship. Our worship is God's story.

Words of Assurance (Based on Psalm 146)

Praise the Lord, people of God.
Praise the Lord.
Know this: it is God alone who secures your freedom
and provides justice.
Praise the Lord.
Hear this: our God opens eyes and lifts the lowly.
Praise the Lord.
Proclaim this: the Lord watches over the sojourner
and the abandoned.
Praise the Lord.

Benediction

May the word of the Lord be on our lips in our departing. May the life of God sustain us in our working. And may the unity of God compel us in our returning. (John Essick)

June 9, 2013

The Spirit of God—The Breath of Life

First in a Series of Two on the Holy Spirit in the Old Testament

Genesis 1:1-2; 2:4-7; John 20:19-23

Actors say that working in the theater is infinitely harder than television or movies, because a play is a human event in real time—things can go right or they can go wrong. The audience is present and waiting to be drawn into the story. They quiet as the curtain parts; the lights and sound work to achieve powerful special effects; actors deliver their lines to move us along with the plot. All this is vital for a seamless story, and when it works right, a play can be more than memorable, it can be life-changing.

As we read the Old Testament, that is the sense that should underlie our experience of Scripture. Rather than simply providing historical recounting or scientific explanation (to which we moderns often wish to reduce the Old Testament), the text seeks to fill us with the wonder, majesty, and power of God's interaction with humanity in the salvation drama. There are all the elements of great theater: beautiful and exotic scenery, engaging characters, plots rife with tension, and conflict and resolution. Yet rather than such a drama being contrived for an audience's enjoyment, this drama has eternal roots and timeless implications, for we are not only spectators but also participants. We are a part of the creative drama.

If this is the context, then what is the story? The Bible asks us to take the Genesis accounts seriously as historical reality and explanatory truth, but the events are expressed in a compelling narrative about the God of Creation. Yahweh creates because God loves, and that love is most fully expressed in relationships. But how Yahweh creates is critical, because it tells us about God as we watch those who respond to God's love. Yahweh is not a static creature bound by the temporal parameters of time, as are we. Yahweh is an uncreated and perfect God who creates through the agency of his own will. In the second chapter of Genesis, Yahweh shocks us by taking the simple elements of his created order and, in a blessed miracle, breathes on them with his Spirit ("life's breath" v. 7; Hebrew, *ruach*). Yahweh gives life to the human creature.

This may seem a naïve folk telling of the creation story, a way for unscientific premoderns to understand the world around them. But let's linger in the truth of this text for a moment. Have you ever seen someone die? It's a powerful, often emotionally painful experience, and unfortunately as an Army chaplain, an event at which I've sometimes had to preside. What lingers in the memory from watching another person die is the final act: it is to breathe one's last, to let go of the last vestige of earthly life. There is a timeless power in this, for we recognize then, if we've ever ignored it, that breathing is the essence of life—we cannot live without our capacity to inhale and exhale air—our bodies live only by this process and none other. So our human creation points back to the Genesis account and we learn: God breathed not only once; God breathes in me each day, and only in, through, with, and by the Holy Spirit do I have the capacity to live and enjoy a relationship with God.

In the Gospel of John, Jesus renews this timeless truth within the life of his church. As the disciples fearfully gather in the upper room after Christ's resurrection, our Lord blesses the few who will represent the renewed Israel in the world. Jesus knows that he will call them to go throughout the earth proclaiming the gospel in both word and deed, in salvation and justice. He also knows that they are not yet ready to go because they lack one thing—Jesus' blessing through the Holy Spirit. And so, he does what may seem strange to us but what is perfectly consistent with God's creative process: Jesus breathes on them, and says "Receive the Holy Spirit," giving life to his people forever. Later at Pentecost, the Holy Spirit will further manifest in power, but here the quality that Jesus offers his church through that same Spirit is peace, for the church is always to rest in the assurance that God is the great Author of Life.

Yet the gospel account teaches us a deeper truth about the God we serve: God is One in essence and purpose, and yet we know him as Father, Son, and Holy Spirit. Again, by looking to the text we learn something of the God who lies behind it. The Holy Trinity has been the agent of the created order since the foundation of human history, and though the church only gradually came to understand God is Three-In-One, yet so it has always been and remains. We, the created people of God, continue to live and grow in fidelity to glorify God the Father, bear witness to Jesus the Son, and to walk daily in the power of the Holy Spirit.

And so, we, the audience in the creation drama, now understand how we are also on the stage, under the lights, in the story. God breathed—God continues to breathe—each and every day in us, not only in a physical sense but also in a spiritual sense. If the lesson of physical life can teach us about the nature of spiritual life, that we are, as the Hebrews always understood, both body and soul, then this will have been powerful theater indeed. May the Trinitarian God continue to create the church by the Spirit, the breath of life, now and eternally. Amen. (Timothy Mallard)

Worship Aids

Prayer of Confession

Holy God, we confess that we have sinned and fallen short of your glory and righteous purpose. You yearn that we turn from ourselves toward you. Forgive and restore us to right fellowship with you through the power of Jesus the Christ; renew us through your Holy Spirit. Amen.

Words of Assurance

Hear the abundant good news! God breathes life into our lives, and we are freed and called to be the life of God in the world. Amen.

Benediction (Adapted from 2 Corinthians 13:14)

And now may the grace of our Lord and Savior Jesus Christ, the love of God the Father, and the blessing of the Holy Spirit rest and abide with you now and always. Amen. (Timothy Mallard)

JUNE 16, 2013

Fourth Sunday after Pentecost

Readings: 1 Kings 21:1-21a; Psalm 5:1-8; Galatians 2:15-21; Luke 7:36–8:3

The Word of the Lord

1 Kings 21:1-21a; Luke 7:36–8:3

One of the most meaningful moments of worship for me is the congregational response "Thanks be to God" to some variation of the lector's pronouncement of "This is the word of the Lord for God's people" after the reading of Scripture. How special it is to be reminded as a community of faith that we have just read and heard God's word, yet this moment of response is also a terrifying one for me. Am I really, in all honesty, grateful for the towering and overpowering word of the Lord? What does it even mean to be thankful for the word of the Lord? At times I am too aware and at other times too unaware that by voicing assent in that moment, we place ourselves under the weight and yoke of the divine word to us, for us, and even against us.

These two lectionary passages suggest in rather stark terms that the word of the Lord constitutes a decisive moment, a judgment. The reading from 1 Kings illustrates well the timeless tension between the fortunate and the less fortunate, the ability of the powerful to exert their will over the powerless. Naboth, a vineyard owner in Jezreel, refuses to release or exchange his inheritance at Ahab's request, so Ahab pouts and sulks. Jezebel, noticing her husband's discontent, takes matters into her own hands and orchestrates Naboth's death to secure royal access to his land. When Ahab proceeds to take possession of the land, he is confronted by the prophet Elijah, who brings the word of the Lord to bear in the situation. Ahab, surprised by Elijah's presence, exclaims: "So you've found me, my old enemy!" Elijah responds: "I found you . . . because you've enslaved yourself by doing evil in the LORD's eyes" (v. 20). Elijah's response is instructive, for it reveals the exposed nature of our entire existence before God.

Interestingly, Ahab may be at least partially ignorant of how he has come to possess Naboth's land, though he has probably learned to suspect such machinations from his pernicious spouse. Regardless of his involvement or knowledge, Ahab is culpable. The word of the Lord finds Ahab. The delivery of the word of the Lord means that his despicable actions are known. God knew all along. Elijah now knows. When the Lord speaks, Ahab knows that his jealousy and schemes and ill-gotten gains have all been found by God. When we hear the word of the Lord, we know that we have been found.

When we turn our attention to Luke 7, we find forgiving words from our Lord mixed with stinging accusations. This passage has Jesus dining with Simon, a Pharisee, when a city-dwelling woman, a sinner, joins them and makes herself rather conspicuous by wiping, bathing, and anointing Jesus' feet. Simon, apparently appalled at the spectacle, wrongly assumes that Jesus is unaware of who it is that kisses his feet; he falsely concludes that his own thoughts are hidden from Jesus. But Jesus, aware of all things, it seems, has "something to say" to Simon.

Jesus offers a short parable exploring the implications of forgiveness. It becomes abundantly clear that Jesus has something to say to both Simon and the woman. Jesus' words expose Simon's thoughts and the woman's actions. Nothing is hidden. Simon's inhospitable actions (i.e., his failure to give Jesus a kiss, wash his feet, or anoint his feet) reflect his inhospitable thoughts regarding the woman who also made her way into his home. Thus, Simon sees little need for forgiveness and has little reason to be grateful. The woman, on the other hand, understands the depth of her debt and the forgiveness that Jesus brings. She departs in a state of peace that only forgiveness can create. Note here, however, that the forgiveness made possible by God's incarnation is not exoneration. The woman stands guilty as accused in the presence of Jesus. So does Simon. They both realize they have been found out by the words of Jesus. Thanks to his words they see more of themselves than would have been possible otherwise.

True speech is revelatory. Judgment arrives when the Lord speaks. The word of the Lord is nothing if not true and honest. Forgiveness is given when we admit that we have been judged rightly. Indeed, the word of the Lord is for all people, but God's people should be particularly adept at hearing and responding. So, by the grace of God may we with due gravity respond together to the word of the Lord for God's people: Thanks be to God. (John Essick)

Lectionary Commentary

Galatians 2:15-21

This passage shifts considerably from the preceding verses in that Paul now writes in the first person plural language of "we," suggesting a shift in emphasis. Instead of standing opposite Peter as he has been doing, Paul now appeals to the convictions they both share: a person is not justified by the works of the law; a person is justified by faith in Christ. As a result, it appears that justification according to the law is set in opposition to justification in Christ. Yet the implications of dying to the law, being crucified with Christ, and Christ living in us proves difficult to agree upon and live out together in community. (John Essick)

Worship Aids

Call to Worship

We gather in this place to give thanks.
We are among those whose transgressions have been forgiven.
We have journeyed here from many places and diverse backgrounds.
We are all justified through faith in Jesus Christ.
We have found a hiding place in God.
Christ has made a home in and among us.
All: Be glad in the Lord and rejoice, O righteous,
and shout for joy, all you upright in heart.

Pastoral Prayer

Our groans and sighs we lift to you, O Lord. May they find your ears this morning. We look nowhere else for help; we call on no other name for aid. Many are those who delight in wicked and evil ways, but you, O Lord, have no patience for anything less than righteousness and uprightness. Carry us in your love this day, O Lord, that we may delight in the worship of you and make our way along your straight path.

Benediction

May the all-knowing God of forgiveness lead us all in the pursuit of the straight and narrow in the week ahead. Go now in the peace of the

Father, the Son, and the Holy Spirit. One God, now and forever. Amen. (John Essick)

The Spirit of God—The Bread of Life

Second in a Series of Two on the Holy Spirit in the Old Testament

Deuteronomy 8:1-5; John 14:25-27

Have you ever had homemade bread, hot out of the oven? Fresh flour, yeast, and water combine into a warm, crusty loaf of goodness. Mixed with other delicacies like nuts, fruits, or cheeses, it can yield a sublime experience of the senses. When you taste a slice spread with fresh butter or dipped in succulent olive oil, you feel almost like you've tasted life itself and that you need nothing else to be fully nourished.

In a real sense such a feeling is true. I've travelled extensively throughout the Middle East, and no matter what country I'm in or what group I'm visiting, all have a common experience: the baking of fresh, hearty, and life-giving bread. In fact, everywhere I've been bread is vital to life because it's the staple of each family, each tribe, and each community. It's been that way for thousands of years, and the bread that peoples make and so graciously share with strangers is indeed made from the types of flour, grains, legumes, and seeds that provide all of a body's needs.

Perhaps because bread has always been such a staple of life, God chose it to represent his life-giving spiritual presence. God knew, not just in ancient times but even today, that bread is an image that each of us readily understands as illustrating how vital God is to our eternal life. In the book of Deuteronomy, as the people of Israel begin their journey toward national identity, God reminds them of how he sustained them in the crucial part of their journey. After they have left Horeb and recounted their wilderness wanderings, after they have received the Decalogue and understood the beginnings of how Yahweh would have them order their society, God reminds them that they came from the humiliating origins of slavery in Egypt. Rather than helping them forget such tragic circumstances, Yahweh reminds them that it was God who raised up for them a prophet in Moses, it was God who patiently endured their rebellious idolatry, and it was God who sustained and led them through their desert journey toward the promised land. In the powerful central verse of this passage, which our Lord would later quote in rebuffing Satan's temptation (Matthew 4:4), Yahweh states through Moses, "He humbled you by making you hungry and then feeding you the manna that neither you nor your ancestors had ever experienced, so he could teach you that people don't live on bread alone. No, they live based on whatever the LORD says" (v. 3; or "whatever comes out of the LORD 's mouth," author's translation).

What's curious to modern ears here is the word picture of sustained speech proceeding from the mouth of God. However, to the Hebrew hearer, this image would have particular potency, for the verb root connotes a divine prerogative and power in speech: the ability to speak into being the cosmic will of God. In essence, it captures the same divine power that Yahweh used in the creation event itself, that only Yahweh—by virtue of being the one, true God—has the ability to speak and bring the physical order into being or change it outright. In essence, Moses reminds the Hebrew people that Yahweh not only spoke into being the world in which we live but also he spoke *ex nihilo* into being their very existence as a people! What those hearers would have also understood, however, is that the agent of the Almighty that brought this world-changing reality about was none other than the Spirit of God. This same image will underlie Paul's admonition to his protégé Timothy, to always rely on the Scripture because it is "God-breathed," and thus perfect for sustaining the man or woman of God in all circumstances (2 Timothy 3:16 NRSV).

Here the people of God begin to understand in a deeper way that it is the Holy Spirit of God living in us that sustains us each and every day. This is why Jesus, in the penultimate act of his earthly ministry, gathered the disciples in the upper room and gave them an impassioned and detailed explanation of the coming presence and power of the Holy Spirit. The Companion (or Advocate) will teach them about the deep things of God after Jesus has ascended to the Father's right hand. In essence, Jesus clearly and decisively places the continued life of the church as being one in relationship with our Lord, as the Father, Son, and Holy Spirit are in the divine drama of the cosmos. We shall be one as the Holy Trinity is one, and the agency of our unity will be the Holy Spirit.

Our understanding is complete: we as the people of God have been created, like the Hebrew nation of old, completely by and through the power of God, and we are sustained even today by the same. The Holy Spirit is the breath of God upon the church but, miracle of miracles, God not only creates but also sustains us in the deepest part of our individual and communal lives, our souls. The Holy Spirit sustains us daily in our spirits just as bread sustains us in our bodies. May the blessed Spirit of God, who proceeds from the Father and points us toward our Lord Jesus Christ, continue to feed, to teach, to nurture, to comfort, and thus to nourish us as God's people now and eternally. Amen. (Timothy Mallard)

Worship Aids

Call to Worship

I will praise the Lord all my life;
I will sing praise to my God as long as I live.
Blessed is he whose help is the God of Jacob,
whose hope is in the Lord.
God upholds the cause of the oppressed and gives food to the hungry.
All: The Lord reigns forever. Praise the Lord.

Pastoral Prayer

Loving Lord, we have too often asked for stones when you seek to feed us with the bread of life. Teach us to trust in your unfailing goodness and to show by faithful actions that we know you will supply our every need. Thank you for loving us in all circumstances. Amen.

Benediction

Now to God who is able to do immeasurably more than all we ask or imagine, according to God's power at work within us, to God be glory in the church and in Christ Jesus throughout all generations, forever and ever! Amen. (Timothy Mallard)

JUNE 23, 2013

Fifth Sunday after Pentecost

Readings: 1 Kings 19:1-4, (5-7), 8-15a; Psalms 42–43; Galatians 3:23-29; Luke 8:26-39

On the Wrong Side of the Tracks

Luke 8:26-39

This story has always intrigued me. Here we have a naked man bound by demons. As soon as Jesus steps out of the boat and into this non-Jewish territory, this naked, demon-possessed man approaches Jesus. The man falls at his feet and shouts at Jesus, confessing that Jesus is the Son of the Most High God. Now I'm sure that we have all encountered some interesting folks. But I dare say that few of us have ever encountered a naked, crazed man who fell at our feet, shouted at us, and begged for healing. Yet Jesus does not seem surprised, disgusted, or embarrassed. Jesus doesn't try to avoid the man or ignore him. True, the man makes it difficult to be ignored, but instead of smiling pathetically at the man and excusing himself, Jesus asks, "What is your name?"

The demons ask Jesus to cast them into a large herd of pigs, so Jesus gives the demons permission to leave the man's body and to enter the pigs feeding on the hillside. The pigs then rush down a bank into the lake and drown.

I can understand why the swineherds are upset. After all, the pigs were their livelihood. But why are the people of the city and in the country so upset? Are they angry because their supply of pork is gone? Perhaps, but I don't think so.

The people's fear and anger did not originate with the pigs' drowning. The pigs' drowning caught their attention, but didn't spark their anger. I think I would have been afraid of a bunch of pigs running off a bank and drowning, just as people were afraid when birds started dropping from the sky in Arkansas in January 2011. However, the people became afraid when they saw the man—who had once been possessed by demons—

clothed and in his right mind, sitting at the feet of Jesus. This man was healed and yet the people are afraid of Jesus. They ask Jesus to leave. Of course, this man wants to go with Jesus. Not only does he want to follow Jesus, but he probably wants to escape the scrutiny that he will face. And although Jesus granted the demons what they wanted by casting them into the pigs, Jesus does not grant the man permission to follow.

This story is mind-boggling to me. Isn't this man's life more valuable than a bunch of pigs? Unfortunately, seeing the man healed is what instilled the fear, and this is when the people ask Jesus to leave. We often get our sense of security and our good feelings about ourselves when others are oppressed. It is a terrible idea, but it is true. Why do kids bully? Why do adults exclude others from their social groups? Why do adults pay membership dues to join exclusive communities? In order to feel superior, we need to distance ourselves from others. To feel special, we feel that we must exclude.

Sometimes churches can be like this. Sure, we say we want all to join. But what if the homeless man wants to join? What about the woman with the tattoos? What about those with criminal backgrounds? What about those who are destitute? Our life is messy enough. When we come to church, we don't want to have to deal with "those kinds of people." Our world is safe as long as "those people" stay on their side of the town—in the tombs with the demoniac. Our world is safe as long as we stay on our "right" side of town. If Jesus had never crossed over into the country of the Gerasenes, then this whole mess with the naked demoniac and the pigs would have been avoided.

I know of a church that hosts an annual fall festival with carnival games, hayrides, bouncing houses, and trick-or-treat. For years the church claimed that this fall festival was a part of their outreach to the community, but they made no effort to invite the community. A newly hired minister of outreach decided that if the church was going to call the fall festival a community event then flyers would be sent to all school-aged children within the community.

What had been a church event with an attendance of approximately one hundred people became a community event of nearly five hundred people from all walks of life. The new minister thought that the church would be thrilled. Now the fall festival was actually an outreach event. Children who went to school next door would know that the church they looked at every day was a place where they would be welcomed. Instead, the new minister heard grumbling that some of the people in attendance were rough looking and some even looked scary. Some people did not fit the social, racial, and economic profile of the existing church members.

A small group proposed that the neighborhood school be excluded from the invitations for the following year, and the new minister should be more selective with the invitations. How very sad!

If Jesus had never crossed over into the country of the Gerasenes, then this whole mess would have been avoided. The swineherd would not have run off the bank and drowned nor would the people have had to ask Jesus to leave. But if Jesus had never crossed over into this country, this demon-possessed man would not have been healed. If Jesus had never crossed over, this healed man would not have been able to spread the good news of Jesus, the Son of the Most High God, to this country of the Gerasenes. Are we willing to cross over into the "wrong" part of town to bring healing to those who need it most and to share the good news of Jesus, the son of the Most High God? (Jessica Williams)

Lectionary Commentary

1 Kings 19:1-4, 5-7, 8-15a

Elijah is on the run from Jezebel, but why does he travel forty days and forty nights to Horeb? Elijah knows that Moses and the Israelites encountered God at Mount Sinai, also known as Horeb. God made the covenant with the Israelites, and God gave Moses the commandments at Mount Sinai. But perhaps more important, Moses experienced a theophany at Mount Sinai. God showed up and appeared to Moses at Mount Sinai. Mount Sinai, Horeb, the mountain of God. Elijah knows the past happenings at this place: Moses and the burning bush; God appearing to the Israelites with thunder, lightning, smoke, and the trembling mountain; and the Lord descending to the top of the mountain. Moses saw God's back at Mount Sinai. And Elijah knows that Moses' face shone radiantly because he had spoken to the Lord.

Elijah wanted to meet God on that mountain. Elijah was ready to quit. He had told God that he had had enough! He needed a theophany. True, the word of the Lord had come to Elijah before, but he needed a personal encounter with God. I think we can all identify with Elijah. We want God to speak to us in a mighty and powerful way. We need God to speak to us.

Galatians 3:23-29

It is hard to understand what it is like to live under the law that Paul is talking about in this passage. We live in a democratic society that celebrates the promise of "justice and liberty for all." In first-century Jewish culture, women were treated as property, non-Jews were less than first-class citizens. People suffering an illness or who were differently abled were outcast. Yet Paul writes that in Christ Jesus, all are children of God. If we say we are Christians, followers of Jesus the Christ, then do we treat all people as children of God? Do we love all people for who they are, daughters and sons of God? (Jessica Williams)

Worship Aids

Call to Worship

Most High God, you stand ready and want to be sought out.
But we fail to recognize you and we do not ask.
Help us be like the demoniac, recognizing who you are,
We fall at your feet and ask to be touched by you.
Don't let us miss your presence.

Prayer of Confession

Most High God, forgive us for not being more like your Son, Jesus. We have seen those in need of your healing, in need of the good news, and we shy away. We are afraid. The situation seems too complicated. Forgive us, God. Amen.

Words of Assurance

The God who calls is the God who fills us with courage and power to answer the call. We have the power of God to overcome our fear and share the good news with all the world. Hallelujah!

Benediction

You have heard the good news of Jesus Christ, the one who offers healing to all. It is time for us to leave this sanctuary and go into a world that is hurting. May we be agents of restoration and of love. Now go and share the good news of Jesus with all people! (Jessica Williams)

Do We Follow the Prescription?

First in a Series of Three on Foundations of Christian Faith: Faith, Hope, Love

Romans 12:1-2; 2 Chronicles 32:7-8; Psalm 36:7-9

When we go to the doctor for a regular physical, one of the health indicators that will be checked is our cholesterol level. The reason for this test is that high cholesterol can lead to heart disease, heart attack, or stroke. All of these can lead to death. Just because our doctor warns us about the fatal effects of high cholesterol levels does not mean that we will follow the prescription. In fact, each person's reaction reveals our faith in the research evidence, the testimony of other patients, and the authority of the doctor. In the same way we differ in our response to God.

There are several factors that contribute to high cholesterol levels. Some people are born with a genetic predisposition. Just because we are born with a certain tendency or weakness does not mean that we are victims of our disposition. We are all born with a bent toward sinning. I believe that God created us with this weakness or imperfect nature so that we would understand that we need God. Also, if we did not have this tendency to turn away from God, then our turning toward God would not be an act of choice but a foregone conclusion. God's gift of free will would not be valid if God did not also give us the gift of choice to not believe God and not trust the salvific work of Jesus Christ. But these inherited tendencies can be overcome through Jesus Christ. The death and resurrection of Christ offers us victory over the power of death when we place our trust in God.

Genetic predisposition is not the only factor in high cholesterol. We can exacerbate our nature with the allures of this world. We live the good life and indulge our lust for rich foods. We prefer the comforts of this world to the practices of discipline and exercise. For the poor who are also at risk from high cholesterol levels, the inequality of resources limits the availability and affordability of a healthy diet.

In similar fashion, we reject God because society lures us to believe that we can do it ourselves, that we are in control of our own fate, and that this is it, there is no life after death. How awful for those who believe that this cruel, unjust, violent, and sick world is all we will ever experience.

Each person reacts differently to a diagnosis of high cholesterol. There are no certainties in the statistics, which show only likelihoods and increased chances of serious health impacts. In fact, some people with high cholesterol levels live long and healthy lives. So are we right to think we are in control? Can we simply take a chance that we will be all right? Some deny the diagnosis. They prefer to play a game of Russian roulette and take their chances. They put out of their minds the possibility that high cholesterol can be life threatening. In the same way, many just put out of their minds the possibility of the existence of God and the implications of that possibility. They are willing to take their chances and hope for the best. How can believing in God make life better, lessen the pain, pay the bills, feed the kids?

God does not miraculously cure every ailment or grant every wish. God is not a vending machine. God does answer every prayer, though it is often not the the answer we want. We do not have absolute assurance of the existence and power of God; that's why we need faith.

Some accept the diagnosis but do nothing about it. They might believe that nothing they do will change their fate. Perhaps they feel that they are not worthy of a long and healthy life. Perhaps they feel that they cannot reverse the results of their choices. God wants us to know that each and every single person matters. God loves us and desires the best for us. Jesus died on the cross so that our past mistakes can be forgiven. Jesus was resurrected so that we can trust that out of our mistakes a healed life without shame can be possible.

And finally, we have a small group who believe the diagnosis and trust the doctor's prescription. This group embraces lifestyle changes. Of course, no one plan of action fits all patients, but these people learn to make good food choices, exercise self-control, and add a regimen of disciplined exercise. They study and keep themselves informed in order to make sound decisions. They attend small support groups or retain the help of a personal trainer to keep themselves focused on the goal and motivated to persevere. Faith in God should be reflected in radical changes in the life of the believer. Faith should go hand in hand with a new lifestyle that follows God's prescription for life. This is why Paul pleads with us to "be transformed by the renewing of your minds, so that you may discern what is the will of God" (Romans 12:2 NRSV). The will of God is the prescription prepared for you. But this prescription will require a radical change from the way the world thinks and acts. It requires discerning the choices we make and adding a healthy dose of spiritual disciplines. Studying the Bible informs our decisions. Worship and small groups help us stay focused and motivated. We don't even have to hire a personal trainer because Jesus has promised the Holy Spirit to be our personal guide, encourager, and strength to overcome our weaknesses and live an abundant life starting today. (Arlene Turner)

Worship Aids

Call to Worship

We come to praise God.

God has healed our wounds.

God has miraculously provided.
God has guided our steps.
God has lifted our spirits.
God has prepared a purpose.
Who else has been ever faithful?
None other than the Lord.
Forever, we come to praise God. Alleluia.

Prayer of Confession

We look at the mystery and immensity of this universe, and yet do not believe it is your handiwork, Lord. We study the intricacy and interdependence of nature, and yet dare to defy your natural laws. We feel the power of love and hope overcome obstacles, and yet do not trust your love letters to us. Help us, O Lord, to overcome our disbelief, our disobedience, and our distrust. Amen.

Words of Assurance

With grace and love, you are forgiven.
With grace and love, you are forgiven.

Benediction

Go forth and believe. Trust God's love to embrace you when you are in doubt. Trust Jesus' power to heal your hurts. Trust the Holy Spirit to strengthen your faith. Go forth and follow God's prescription for you. (Arlene Turner)

JUNE 30, 2013

Sixth Sunday after Pentecost

Readings: 2 Kings 2:1-2, 6-14; Psalm 77:1-2, 11-20; Galatians 5:1, 13-25; Luke 9:51-62

Cry to Me

Psalm 77:1-2, 11-20

When was the last time that you cried aloud to God? I mean a cry expressed out loud, demanding that God hear you, just in case God was not hearing the whispers of your prayer or the thoughts rolling through your head. When we are faced with trouble or filled with pain, do we seek God? Do we stretch out our hands in desperation to God and refuse to settle for anything less than the knowledge that God has heard our cries?

If it has been a long time since you cried out to God, truly cried out to God, the way that the psalmist did, why is that? Do we not trust God? Is it that we don't think that God works the way God did thousands of years ago? Or is it that we don't feel worthy to demand God's attention?

I think that our pride gets in the way. Our rugged U.S. individualism gets in the way. A belief that we really can't demand that God listen to us gets in the way. At one point in my life, I did not think I was worthy to cry out loud to God. I thought of it as having self-pity or lacking faith. I thought that I should accept, silently and submissively, the trouble or the pain. I blamed myself for the chaos in my life. We may shrink away from crying aloud to God. We may think that if we have said our prayers, then we have done all that we can. However, the psalmist shows us something different with this lament.

The psalmist cries out loud because the psalmist needs to know that God is listening. The cries may be tears of sadness or shouts of frustration. Whatever the emotion, it is coming from grief over a life situation and the psalmist pleads for God to listen. Just as the life situation is unrelenting, the psalmist's cries are persistent.

We don't know what the psalmist is mourning. Perhaps an illness? A rebellious child? A difficult work situation? A rocky relationship? Finances? The reality of mortality? The death of a loved one? Do any of these things sound familiar?

The psalmist has probably heard plenty of helpful responses and advice from friends, yet the psalmist's soul refuses to be comforted. The psalmist simply needs to be heard by God. Other psalms ask for rescue, but not this one. It is almost as if the psalmist has accepted the life situation, as if he is journeying through the stages of grief. He simply needs God to listen.

The psalm does have a turning point, however. It does not continue forever in mourning. Just as the other psalms of lament transition from grief to a celebration of God's mighty deeds, so does this one. We grieve. We cry out. We may even yell. However, we do not go through life wringing our hands.

The psalmist does not quietly accept the life situation, nor does he thoughtlessly accept that God is in control. We all know that when trouble or pain is all around us or swelling up inside us, a well-intentioned "There's no need to cry. God is in control" doesn't really bring the comfort that a good cry can bring. The psalmist moves from grieving and crying to recalling the good works that God has done. The psalmist looks to the God of the past and remembers that God is in control. It is almost as if the psalmist recalls how God has proven the truth of God's existence. Sometimes it doesn't seem that God is there in a situation. Of course, we know that we are to believe that God is always with us, but when those storms of life hit, we don't always feel God's presence. So the psalmist starts going back and reminding himself of God's mighty deeds.

"The waters saw you, God— / the waters saw you and reeled! / Even the deep depths shook" (v. 16)! This imagery brings to mind the creation. God brought forth creation from the chaos of the waters, but not as some kind of puppet-master or director calling all the shots from a safe location. No, God was right in the midst, lovingly forming all of creation.

If the waters—the chaos of waters—were afraid, then we do not have to continue to shudder at the chaos in our lives. "Your way went straight through the sea; / your pathways went right through the mighty waters" (v. 19). God was in full control from the beginning, bringing forth creation, and now we hear the story of the Israelites at the Red Sea. God parted the chaos of the waters at the Red Sea. The waters were still there, but God was there too. Just as before, God did not orchestrate from afar; God was right there in the midst, leading God's people like a flock.

And just as the chaos and troubles of our lives are still here, we know that God is here with us. God has been here before and God is here now. God does not watch us from afar. God gets right in the midst of our chaos, our troubles, and our pain. God does not always stop the raging sea, but God is right there with us as we walk through the chaos of waters—the pain and tragedies of life. (Jessica Williams)

Lectionary Commentary

2 Kings 2:1-2, 6-14

We would do well to follow Elisha's example in relation to his mentor, Elijah. Who is your mentor? Do you have a mentor on the job? What about a spiritual mentor? Elisha is bold. We often think of respecting our mentors by following their instructions. Yet, when Elijah tells Elisha to stay, Elisha says, "As the LORD lives and as you live, I won't leave you" (v. 6b).

We often get caught up in trying to outdo the great people around us or we shrink away because we lack confidence. However, Elisha values this relationship and wants everything that he can get from it. He even asks Elijah for a double portion of his spirit. Elisha wants to be blessed, and he is willing to ask for it. This passage encourages us to seek a spiritual mentor and to learn all we can. Let us not be afraid to seek out the spiritually mature and to ask for a double portion of the Spirit.

Galatians 5:1, 13-25

For freedom, Christ has set us free. Although Paul was writing about freedom from the law, it is easy so close to July 4 to think about the freedom that we have in the United States. Paul writes in verse 13, "don't let this freedom be an opportunity to indulge your selfish impulses, but serve each other through love." We, who live in one of the wealthiest countries in the world, can be a self-indulgent people.

With freedom, freedom from the law, and freedom as a democratic society, comes great responsibility. Do we love our neighbors as ourselves? Do we live by the Spirit, or do we gratify the desires of our flesh? To live in the freedom that we have, we need to live by the Spirit and be guided by the Spirit. And the Spirit bears the fruit of "love, joy, peace, patience, kindness, goodness, faithfulness, gentleness, and self-control" (vv. 22-23). Are these the characteristics that we embrace?

Luke 9:51-62

We see the cost of discipleship in this passage. Someone tells Jesus, "I will follow you wherever you go." Instead of saying "Come," Jesus tells the individual that "the Human One [or Son of Man] has no place to lay his head." Then Jesus tells another individual, "Follow me." But the man gives the excuse of burying his father. Jesus doesn't accept the excuse. And yet a third individual says, "I will follow you, Lord, but..." Again, Jesus doesn't accept this response.

So, what do we have going on here? If we look back to verse 53, we read of Jesus being rejected by Samaritan villagers "because he was determined to go to Jerusalem." Jesus understood what loving God and loving others would cost him—everything. Why should we think that we can have both our interests and be a sincere follower? We have to be all in! (Jessica Williams)

Worship Aids

Invocation

Creator God, we ask that you meet us here. You know that our lives are chaotic, just as the waters were chaos before creation. You are a God of wonders. Bring wonder to this hour and create something new in us. Come now. Amen.

Prayer of Confession

God, we ask that you hear our concerns. The storms of life crash in on us like waves. Following your Son is not easy. The cost of following wholeheartedly is high. We are afraid and reluctant. Forgive us, Lord. Amen.

Words of Assurance

Life is filled with joy and with hurt. Life can be difficult. Just as God created from the waters of chaos, God created each of us. God hears our cries. God leads us like a good shepherd who lovingly leads his flock through danger. Rest assured, God is forever present! (Jessica Williams)

Why Bother?

Second in a Series of Three on Foundations of Christian Faith: Faith, Hope, Love

Romans 12:3-8; Psalm 33:18-22

We all need counseling. We "all have sinned and fall short of God's glory" (Romans 3:23). Our mistakes and sins have brought shame and guilt. For these transgressions, Jesus died on the cross as a sacrifice of atonement, effective through faith (see Romans 3:25). In Jesus Christ, we have been forgiven; the file has been deleted; the record has been expunged. Through faith, "all are treated as righteous freely by his grace because of a ransom that was paid by Christ Jesus" (Romans 3:24). In Jesus Christ, we have also been liberated. We are now free to unbuckle the seatbelt and embark on a new journey with our own personal motivator, trainer, counselor, and advisor—the Holy Spirit. Together we set our course for eternal life in the presence of God. Because of Christ's resurrection, we too hope to be resurrected and share in the glory of God. All this is available to you for the fantabulous price of "nada." Yep, it is the free gift we receive when we place our trust in God. Wow! What a gift! But are we willing to unwrap it and claim it as our own?

Last week we identified faith by how we respond to the existence of God. If we trust God and follow God's prescription, we will inevitably be transformed. This week, we will dissect the human psyche and gauge our hopefulness by how we react to being healed and transformed by the Holy Spirit as we commence the Christian journey. Hope is dependent on our cooperation with the sanctifying power of God if we choose to unwrap God's gift.

Every crisis, stressor, or tragedy in our life adds to the baggage we have to unpack on this journey. As we make mistakes, hurt others, disobey, and rebel, we take on the shame and guilt of our trespasses. We might shy away from others because we fear being judged and cast out. We might try to hide what we have done and how we feel by putting on a mask. Or our lack of intimacy may alienate others. We might feel unworthy of any affections, much less of God's gift. We need to receive forgiveness and be emptied of our emotional baggage, but we are afraid to face the truth about ourselves. What if forgiveness is not enough? Could I really hope for a fresh start?

Sometimes the baggage is not of our own making, caused by the hurts and pains inflicted on us by someone else. In response, we might lash out in anger and violence, having learned to survive by preparing a plan of attack. We think we might be able to control the circumstances, so that the circumstances cannot control us. Or we build a defensive wall to hide behind, telling ourselves that we don't care what others think. We might retreat from life, fading into the background to avoid confronting the feeling that we are not of value. Can we face the truth that we are just running away? Will we remember that our God is the God of Abraham, "who gives life to the dead and calls things that don't exist into existence" (Romans 4:17)? Just as God brought life out of Sarah's dead womb, God can bring new life from the deadness in your heart. Can we really place our hope on God's love to deliver us and keep us alive in times of crisis?

It's incredible how diligently we can work to keep from facing the truth about ourselves and God. We might ignore or run away from self-reflection. It's safe and comfortable in our bubble, so why get out? Self-reflection might lead to growing up, which means growing old and boring. Even if we step out of the bubble, we try to sabotage any self-awareness and spiritual growth. Spending time to reflect on our self can be overwhelming and frightening. What if we fail? Then what is left of us? We spend so much energy trying to hold on to the old self even though "the person that we used to be was crucified with him in order to get rid of the corpse that had been controlled by sin" (Romans 6:6). It is precisely for this reason we are so reluctant to face the truth. We are afraid to lose ourselves. What if we become a cookie-cutter image of the pious monk or nun? It is difficult to understand that by letting go of the old self, God will be able to give birth to a new and improved you. It will still be the quirky, eccentric, wonderfully unique you—just better, whole, healed, and true. Of course, most Christians keep this secret to themselves, so how can the world know about this wonderful gift? If we shared about the immense difference God has made in our life, then we might be able to give up our old self.

So why should you bother with the work of self-reflection and step out in faith onto this Christian journey? Because an abundant life is a life with purpose. We all need some guidance and direction, and God is waiting to point you to your unique purpose, and God provides you with the gift and grace to fulfill your unique purpose. Are you afraid that God might call you to do something for which you are unequipped or to go somewhere unexpected? Let me reassure you, God will never call you to a ministry for which your heart has not already been prepared. Just as God prepares the way and provides the resources, God also creates the desire in your heart. Keep in mind that only you can fulfill your unique purpose. The body of Christ is realized when all its members are focused on fulfilling their purposes, individually and in community. Today, the hope of the world is that the kingdom of God on earth will be accomplished through the body of Christ. (Arlene Turner)

Worship Aids

Call to Worship

Let us remember the stories of God's power and presence.
Let us remember the ways God has provided.
Let us thank God for gifts and grace.
Let us thank God for love and care.
Let us hope in the Lord forever. Amen.

Pastoral Prayer

Lord God Almighty, help us face the truth about ourselves, help us unpack our baggage of shame, guilt, hurts, and pain. Give us wisdom to reflect and discern. Give us courage to be transformed and healed. Lead us to our purpose, to those who need our gifts, with the power of the Holy Spirit and in the name of Jesus. Amen.

Benediction

May the Holy Spirit open your eyes to see God's gifts. May Jesus Christ raise your heart and mind to hear his word. May God, the loving parent, birth a new you, with a life filled with peace, joy, love, and purpose. Go forth on your journey surrounded by God's love, grace, and mercy. Amen. (Arlene Turner)

JULY 7, 2013

ꕥꕥꕥ

Seventh Sunday after Pentecost

Readings: 2 Kings 5:1-14; Psalm 30; Galatians 6:1-16; Luke 10:1-11, 16-20

King for a Day

2 Kings 5:1-14

Imagine for a moment that you are a king or a queen. Your kingdom stretches for miles. You have servants to look after your every need. Palace walls provide a sanctuary from the chaos that consumes most of the lives of your citizens. People love you, but it is difficult to tell if their affection is for you or for what you can do for them. It's been a rather difficult few years. There is a rumor that the neighboring kingdom would like to expand its territory. In an effort to supply more troops to defend the borders, taxes have been increased. Severe heat and drought have devastated the grain crops. Grain will surely have to be imported, which will have high tariffs. The populace has become disgruntled and expects you to do something.

To add to the drama, pesky prophets are wandering through the crowds warning of God's forthcoming wrath. These prophets claim to be messengers from God, but their allegiance is wavering. How could these uncivilized human beings be the representative for the Most High? One prophet in particular, Elisha, seems to be ringleader. He walks around performing all kinds of miracles.

Today of all days, just as you are sorting through the list of tariff forms and arguing with an army leader about the lack of support on the southern border, a letter is brought to your attention. It's from the King of the Arameans. It must be something extremely important. Perhaps the king is declaring war or informing you of his intent to take over one of the cities on the border. Your finger slips under the official seal, and once you begin to read it, you cannot believe your eyes.

The king has asked you to heal one of his greatest leaders from a terrible skin disease. With all the other things on your plate, now your adversary has asked you to heal one of his men? He must be kidding. This is an impossible request and has got to be some type of ploy.

Knowing these circumstances, what would your reaction be? The king of Israel tears his clothes in an all-out temper tantrum. He yells in a tirade, "Am I God to hand out death and life?" The task is too much and like everything else, you are powerless to do anything about it.

The truth is, very few of us will be a queen or a king. But we are people who like control. We like to feel that we are in charge and have everything right where we want it. We like calendars and agendas with fifteen-minute intervals to make sure that every minute of the day is planned. Our yards, surveyed and marked with boundary lines, and our locked doors block out the chaos of the world. So in a way, are not all middle-class heads of households kings and queens of something? We have the joy of reigning over our territory, but sometimes the castle has a plumbing problem, weeds continue to encroach upon our lavish yards, and our children are not only demanding protection but require us to supply their every need.

Have you ever gotten to the point where it was too much? Like the king, you just want to tear your clothes, sling all the bills from the kitchen table in one clean swipe, and just slam the door to shut out the rest of the world. It is difficult to give up control. It is difficult when expectations are greater than our expertise.

Then some of us are like Naaman, who found the one who could heal him but needed to take a few extra steps. We think we have covered all the contingencies, and then there is one more demand that needs to be met. I am notorious for expecting things to be simple and then getting upset when they are not. My wife and I argue about my time estimation for certain home projects. I say, "It will only be a fifteen- or twenty-minute job." Two hours later I am still battling some unforeseen problem. Like the king, I feel that I am letting people down. I feel incompetent and insecure in my abilities to perform my duty. Also, like Naaman, one additional step seems to be too much trouble. I feel as though I don't have things under control when I think I should have.

But being out of control is not the theme of this story, is it? Two other characters are our real teachers. The servant girl was taken captive and now waits on Naaman's wife hand and foot. She has no control over her daily routine. Yet she is the one who remains calm, feels compassion, and has the solution for Naaman's illness. Elisha the prophet is totally reliant on the help of others and wanders through the country following God each step of the way. Yet he does not tear his clothes; he remains calm and gives instruction to Naaman.

No matter who we are, we are not in control as much as we would like to be or think we are. Like the servant girl, running at someone else's pace, can we stay calm and compassionate? It is the recognition that God is in control that saves Naaman, seen through the calm compassion of the servant girl and the practical advice from Elisha. If we read on, Naaman does eventually give credit to the God of Israel. We are not God, and we shouldn't act as if we are. When was the last time you and I gave up our illusion of control, humbled ourselves, and allowed God to heal our broken spirits? Is it worth the trouble? (Darren Williams)

Lectionary Commentary

Galatians 6:1-16

Paul is writing to the churches in Galatia with some irritation that Jewish Christians are trying to convince Gentile Christians to follow Jewish law before following Christ. The natural break at verse 10 promotes preaching each part separately.

Verses 1-10 call on the Galatians to "carry each other's burdens" (v. 2); however, each person is also told to "carry their own load" (v. 4). Paul urges the community to fight against the desires that come naturally. They need self-control and not pride. Christians need to work together for the benefit of the entire community.

Verses 11-16 remind the reader of the original debate. Gentile Christians should not be required to be circumcised before following Christ. When we have new followers to the faith, do we impose unnecessary requirements? Each denomination has different expectations and requirements. Some ask for baptism, church membership changes, new believer classes, and a range of other initiation procedures. For Paul, the outward expression of one's faith was not as important as the inward transformation. He saw Christians as being new creations.

When I read the epistles, I like to extract elements that coincide with stories from the Gospels. The epistles were written prior to the Gospels, and the common threads may be closer kin to Jesus' actual message. One example is Galatians 6:4, "Each person should test their own work and be happy with doing a good job and not compare themselves with others."

That sounds much like the message of Matthew 7:3 about the splinter in your neighbor's eye and the log in your own eye.

Luke 10:1-11, 16-20

This is the second time that Jesus sends out disciples. In Luke 9:1-6 we see a similar list of items that the twelve disciples should refrain from taking with them. He tells them not to take a staff, bag, bread, money, or an extra tunic. When Jesus addresses the larger group of seventy-two disciples in Luke 10, the list is shortened to no money belt, no bag, and no shoes. Both stories emphasize reliance on God rather than on one's own means.

In Luke 9, Jesus warns the disciples that they may come to towns that do not welcome them; he counsels them to shake the dust off their feet and keep moving. There is a stronger warning in Luke 10. Jesus now tells the disciples that he is sending them out like lambs in the midst of wolves. Yet he also encourages them to stay in towns, preach, and cure the sick when they are welcomed. He repeats the admonition to wipe off the dust and walk away when they are not welcomed. The travelers return with good news. Jesus encourages them and us to continue to follow Christ even in the face of adversity. (Darren Williams)

Worship Aids

Call to Worship

The psalmist says, "Be still, and know that I am God" (Psalm 46:10 NRSV)! In our world it is difficult to be still and let go. Our call to worship begins by slowing down, letting go of all the distractions of our week, and coming to God with open hands. Are you ready to worship?

Litany

God, from nothing you created everything.
We seek to be like God and create order out of confusion.
God, your Spirit moves across the face of the earth
desiring to make all things new.
We work so hard, but get frustrated at our inadequacies.
All: You are God, and we are not. Our trust rests in you.

Benediction

As you reenter the pace of the world, know that you are not alone. When you feel that your life is out of your control, know that it never was. One far greater is at the helm of creation with a will superior to our desires. May God be with you and bless you. (Darren Williams)

Stop, Drop, and Roll

Third in a Series of Three on Foundations of Christian Faith: Faith, Hope, Love

Romans 12:9-21; Isaiah 58:6-7; Proverbs 10:12

I remember the first time I said to my best friend: "I love you." She was taken aback by my declaration. Perhaps she had never heard those words outside of a familial or romantic relationship. I wasn't just making a statement; I was putting into words what we thought of each other and how we treated each other. The New Testament is peppered with the command that we love one another. It is imperative in the Christian journey to master loving one another. Jesus is our role model.

Two weeks ago we defined faith as the positive response to the existence of God. At one end of the continuum, there are those who believe and follow the prescription. They take the leap of faith and embark on the Christian journey. Last week, we saw how faith is graciously blessed with God's free gifts of forgiveness and abundant life made possible in Christ when we receive the Holy Spirit. These gifts initiate a lifelong process of sanctification. Our hope is quantified by how we react to the healing transformation and spiritual formation empowered by the Holy Spirit as God leads us to become disciples of Christ. If we cooperate with the Holy Spirit, then we learn how to love one another because we mature in our understanding of God. Loving one another is about keeping God's commandments. In order to know what God commands, we must first get to know God.

Do you remember the lesson from grade school in case you were on fire: Stop, Drop, and Roll? The teacher probably made you repeat it several times, and then you practiced the steps. The repetition was to reinforce the learning because it might be essential to your survival. By practicing the steps, you trained yourself to act correctly in a given situation. Let's reframe how we define love. Every interaction with another can include a measure of love. When we choose to interact in ways that affirm and uphold God's ways, then we are acting out of love. Unfortunately, it is much easier said than done. Therefore, we are going to train ourselves to be more loving by learning how to Stop, Drop, and Roll when we are on fire for the Lord.

Every interaction can be an act of love. But first we have to Stop and take notice. When you pass a person in the hallway or along the street, stop what you are thinking, saying, or doing. Ask God if this person needs your attention right now. If the answer is yes, then Drop yourself—your needs, wants, and wishes—out of the equation. In Romans 12, Paul writes that we are not to please ourselves, not to think of ourselves as better, and not to make ourselves seem smarter. This is counter to what the world tells us—to look out for number one. Instead, we are to put aside what we want, or the right answer we might suggest, or our right to go first. How we act then begins with listening, and this requires that we drop ourselves and consider the needs of the other person. Every person is made in the image of God, even if they haven't figured it out yet. Paul makes it clear in Romans that we are never to judge, because only God knows each one's heart, secrets, and sorrows.

Now Roll. Instead of picturing yourself rolling around on the ground to put out the fire, picture a roll of bread, like Communion bread. As the roll served at Communion nourishes our bodies and souls, what rolls can you serve others that will nourish their bodies, hearts, minds, and souls? Today's passage(s) point out that we should be both reactive and proactive. We react to our enemies not as the world would suggest, through revenge, reneging on our obligations, lawsuits, or slander. Instead, we patiently pray for and bless our enemies, overcome their hate with kindness, and to the best of our ability strive for peace and harmony. Of course, this is not easy, which is why the message is so often repeated in Scripture.

As we proactively serve rolls to others, we start with the body by looking for ways that we can provide for physical needs. Then we move to the heart and look for ways that we can provide for emotional needs. When we listen—sharing real joys and concerns—we become vulnerable, and it is possible to grow closer, become more intimate, and share a deeper relationship. Only after basic human needs are met can we move to the mind and look for ways to provide for rational needs, teaching and sharing the good news. Finally, we move to the soul and look for ways to provide for spiritual needs. Pray together, and share the deep joys and hopes and fears of our souls.

Remember, our faith journey is marked with opportunities to Stop, Drop, and Roll. You might be the only person who can speak to the needs of another. You might be the only Christian who will cross their path today. So, Stop, Drop, and Roll for Jesus. (Arlene Turner)

Worship Aids

Call to Worship

Let us stop and rest in the presence of the Lord. Leave behind the distractions of this world and focus on the hope and love that God offers us through the death and resurrection of Jesus Christ. Be assured that God's desire is for us to be filled with peace and joy. Therefore, let us sing and dance, praising our King and Savior for his righteousness and goodness. Hallelujah! Hallelujah!

Communion Prayer

Approach the altar cleansed from guilt and shame because the blood of Jesus has prepared the way. Come to the table expecting to feel the presence of God. With this bread we will be nourished in our bodies, refreshed in our hearts, and renewed in our souls. Allow the power of the Holy Spirit to break through our walls and transform our lives. Know that the Lord loves us and desires the best for us, now and forever. Amen.

Benediction

Go and choose to love. Choose to Stop, Drop, and Roll in the name of Jesus. Let the Holy Spirit guide you to those who need you. Let the Holy Spirit equip you with a vision of their physical, emotional, rational, and spiritual needs. Let the Holy Spirit empower you with courage, patience, and shrewdness. Go and choose to love because God first loved you. Amen. (Arlene Turner)

JULY 14, 2013

Eighth Sunday after Pentecost

Readings: Amos 7:7-17; Psalm 82; Colossians 1:1-14; Luke 10:25-37

Mine and My Neighbor's Kingdom

Luke 10:25-37

Yes, another sermon about the good Samaritan. We know the story all too well. An inquisitive lawyer approaches Jesus about how to inherit eternal life. Jesus in typical fashion answers the question with a question, "What is written in the Law?" The lawyer's reply is a recitation of the *Shema* (Deuteronomy 6:4-5) and a familiar Levitical law (19:18), "You must love the Lord your God with all your heart, with all your being, with all your strength, and with all your mind, and love your neighbor as yourself." Then the lawyer asks Jesus, "And who is my neighbor?"

So Jesus begins to tell a story. A man is traveling through a territory that has a notorious reputation for robbers. The man is attacked and hurt. A priest, who holds one of the highest positions in the Jewish ranks, walks by and does not help the man. Priests were not allowed to touch blood for a fear of being seen unclean and risking losing their jobs. Next a Levite, the lay leadership of the Jews, comes by and does nothing. The third visitor is an outsider, a Samaritan. The Samaritan is given the title of *good* by his actions. The Samaritan feels compassion, bandages the man's wounds, takes him to an inn, and pays for his room and board.

The story of the good Samaritan has been picked over by preachers more than an all-day buffet at closing time. It seems there is nothing left to glean from this text that someone else hasn't already touched. The story has become so common that it is included in secular conversation without any knowledge of the biblical reference. News reports call anyone who does a good act for someone else a good Samaritan. Yes, for many of us the story is all too familiar.

Yet we still do it, don't we? I know I do. We pass by the stranded motorist out on the freeway changing a tire in the pouring rain. I hope that the light stays green long enough to avoid being confronted by the man holding a cardboard sign, while taking a van load of teenagers on a ski trip. We avoid the elderly lady down the street walking her dog because we know that thirty minutes later she will still be talking about how hard her husband had worked to get the yard in order and now look at all those weeds. "Can't do things like I used to," she'll say.

Is the story of the good Samaritan just about guilt? Is it like the commercials that disrupt our favorite television shows and display starving children in developing countries or malnourished and abused animals? No, the story is not about guilt. The lawyer has one simple question, "Teacher, what must I do to gain eternal life?" Notice the words *I* and *gain*. Does the story of the good Samaritan stem from the root of selfish intent?

Is the lawyer's question self-centered? Is reward of eternal life the motivation for helping someone? Perhaps the Jewish understanding of eternal life was different from the idea of a mansion in heaven. Perhaps the lawyer really wanted to understand the way of righteousness. Maybe the lawyer had a similar goal of Jesus to usher in the kingdom of God. Remember the rich young ruler? He asked Jesus the exact same questions, but Jesus tells him to sell all of his possessions and give the money to the poor. There is no such command for the lawyer. Instead, the lawyer was told a story and asked to reflect on what it meant. Regardless of the meaning, apparently we can understand Jesus' interpretation of eternal life by the parable he shares.

If we have not already, we will eventually play all of the characters in the story. We will be the people who pass by. We will be the helpless, pleading for assistance. We will be the outsider trying to make sense of it all. As we read this familiar story, we need to see it with fresh eyes, like children listening for the first time. It is a story that desires to usher in a new kingdom and a better way. It gives hope for the broken and gives purpose to the powerful. It is a vision of a shared kingdom, where my neighbor and I are both working toward the same goals. If my neighbor doesn't reach the destination, then neither will I. (Darren Williams)

Lectionary Commentary

Amos 7:7-17

The prophet is on the border between the Holy and humanity, given coded visions of the future, and compelled to relay these visions to the masses. Amos had been interceding to God on behalf of Israel, but in this instance, Amos is only the bearer of bad news. God's judgment is as clear as a plumb line and allows for no deviation from the standard. The three symbols of Israel's empire—high places, sanctuary, and the house of King Jeroboam—will be laid to waste.

Amos's opposition comes in the form of the priest, Amaziah, who benefits from the protection and status quo of the kingdom. The words of Amos cut to the core of Amaziah's spirit. He wishes for Amos to go away, but Amos is only following what God has told him to do. The difficult part of this passage is there seems to be no hope. There is no intercession and no call for repentance—only a declaration of destruction. The text challenges us to wait in the midst of ruin, while compelling us to move forward and seek what lies beyond the horizon of exile.

Colossians 1:1-14

The introduction of the letter to the Colossians is a boastful exaltation of the church's success, measured in fruitfulness and growth. If we read on, we realize that the introduction is building up the spirit of the Colossians before the writer criticizes their entertainment of false teachings. The writer begins by addressing the brothers and sisters at Colossae as faithful saints. Compliments are given to their minister, Epaphras, who appears to have offered an update on the state of the church. Next, there is confirmation of intercession as prayers have been offered for God's wisdom and understanding. Words such as *strength*, *joy*, *endurance*, *patience*, and *inheritance* lead up to the one purpose of addressing their need for protection against false teachings.

The introduction is a masterful method for offering critique of someone's behavior. It appears as if almost every word is a direct path addressing false teachings. The introduction empowers the people to recognize God's past accomplishments, affirms their leadership, and provides support through prayer as added encouragement. The original readers had to affirm first or else they would not have listened to the critique. (Darren Williams)

Worship Aids

Call to Worship (Deuteronomy 6:4-7)

"Israel, listen! Our God is the LORD! Only the LORD!
Love the LORD your God with all your heart, all your being, and all your strength. These words that I am commanding you today must always be

on your minds. Recite them to your children. Talk about them when you are sitting around your house and when you are out and about, when you are lying down and when you are getting up."

Invocation

God of Compassion, we are so consumed with ourselves and getting higher on the social ladder that we neglect our neighbors. We know a better way. Help us out of the ditch of selfish desires. Open our eyes to see your kingdom. As you join us now, we also join you to bring healing to a broken world. Amen.

Benediction

Israel, listen! Go and seek your neighbor for in them you may find the kingdom of God. (Darren Williams)

The Twenty-third Psalm in Three Movements

First in a Series of Four on Celebrated Biblical Texts

Psalm 23

Have you ever seen a shepherd, or met one? Have you seen him or her leading the sheep? Have you seen a flock of sheep or been to a sheep shearing? The answer for most of us is no. We live in a part of the world where shepherds and sheep are foreign to us. My only experiences with sheep were as a child of about five. I stayed part of each day with my aunt who lived on a farm. They raised chickens and dairy cows, but they also had a small flock of sheep. One of the sheep had a lamb that it rejected. I had the opportunity to help bottle feed the lamb and watch it grow. My only other experience with sheep was on a trip to the Holy Land. There I saw shepherds and sheep primarily as I was riding on a tour bus around the countryside. We did stop at a Bedouin camp and watch them feed and water the sheep and goats.

The twenty-third psalm is often called the shepherd's psalm. It was written by a shepherd who became a king, King David. He knew all about sheep, and he also knew about music. He played a harp and wrote psalms. I enjoy music, and I can play several musical instruments. I like listening to all kinds of music, but one of my favorite genres is classical. Most classical pieces are composed in movements. Some of the movements are fast and lively, while others are slow. Some movements are bright, and others are dark and heavy. Many psalms have movements. In some psalms the writers move from laments to praise for salvation. In others the psalmist cries out for God's help and then rejoices when God hears and responds. In the twenty-third psalm I noticed three major movements.

The first movement speaks about calm, peace, and quiet. In the first three verses we read about having no wants, being completely satisfied and content. We read about green pastures and quiet waters. We read about restoration for our soul and gentle paths. Just reading these verses causes us to relax and floods us with a sense of calm.

Where do you go to experience quietness and calm? Do you have a favorite place? For some it is the beauty of the ocean and the constant crashing of the waves on the beach. For others it is the splendor of the mountains with tall trees and flowing streams. For still others it may be a peaceful shore by a lake or pond. Wherever that place may be, the shepherd leads us there to be restored and recreated. Just as the good shepherd leads his sheep to quiet places, God knows we all need places of retreat and calm.

The second movement takes us to a place of sorrow and darkness. We read about the valley of the shadow of death. This is one reason this psalm is read so often at funerals. There is comfort to know that even when a loved one has traveled through the literal valley of death they were not alone. The psalmist writes that we do not have to fear any evil even when we look death in the face. We can be assured that the good shepherd walks with us. In his hand is his rod and his staff to comfort and protect us. This psalm was written long before the birth of Jesus. The psalmist did not have the knowledge of his death and resurrection, and yet there is that same assurance that we do not have to fear death. In John 10 Jesus refers to himself as the good shepherd. "I am the good shepherd. The good shepherd lays down his life for the sheep" (John 10:11). In the twenty-third psalm we find this same assurance that the good shepherd has walked through this valley and come through on the other side and can lead us there as well.

Even when we are not facing death, we all have our own dark valleys to travel through. Sometimes they are valleys of depression. Sometimes they are valleys of illness. Sometimes they are valleys of hurt, disappointment, loss, or anger. No matter what the dark valley is, we can be assured that we are not alone. The Lord walks with us and will comfort and protect us until we come through on the other side.

The third movement speaks of the shepherd's eternal goodness and mercy. In verses five and six we read about a table that is prepared for us. I can envision a table spread with all kinds of delicious food, from fruits and vegetables to warm breads and meats. We read about being anointed with oil. One of my favorite things to do is to get a good haircut that includes a hair wash and a warm towel on the face. I imagine that's what it felt like to be anointed with oil. We read about a cup that is overflowing with goodness. I remember a commercial for a restaurant that served an all-you-can-eat pancake-with-coffee breakfast. In the commercial, as soon as the person took a drink, the coffee cup filled back up. Perhaps that is what it is like to have a cup that runs over. Finally, we read about goodness and mercy being with us all our lives and dwelling in the Lord's house forever. This is our present and our eternal reward. Again in John 10, Jesus shares that "I came so that they could have life—indeed, so that they could live life to the fullest" (v. 10). The good shepherd says, "My sheep listen to my voice. I know them and they follow me. I give them eternal life. They will never die, and no one will snatch them from my hand" (vv. 27-28). May we all experience God's abundant mercy and goodness in the present and forever. (Neil Epler)

Worship Aids

Collect

O Lord, you are the Good Shepherd of the sheep. You came to seek the lost and to gather them into your fold. Have mercy on us who have wandered away from you. Feed those who are hungry, cause the weary to lie down in your pastures, bind up those who are brokenhearted, and strengthen those who are weak. Help us rely on your care and be comforted by your love. Guide our lives to the end, in the name of Jesus. Amen.

Offertory Prayer

For good times and bad times, for all the moments in life when we are reminded that we are your creatures, we give thanks to you, O God. We share with you and your church this day a part of our lives. Never let the giving of our money be a substitute for the giving of ourselves to you and to others. Through Jesus Christ, our Lord. Amen.

Benediction

O Lord, we know your way is perfect. Help us follow you like your sheep. May we hear your voice and accept your gentle encouragement. Help us bring the lost back into the fold. Truly you are our Good Shepherd. In the name of the Father, the Son, and the Holy Spirit. Amen. (Neil Epler)

JULY 21, 2013

Ninth Sunday after Pentecost

Readings: Amos 8:1-12; Psalm 52; Colossians 1:15-28; Luke 10:38-42

Who Is Christ for You?

Colossians 1:15-28

In theology, beliefs about Jesus Christ are called "Christology." There are many Christologies. Several exist within the New Testament itself. After the New Testament was written, Christians debated the nature of Jesus Christ. Councils were held, and creeds were written. This discussion will probably never end.

This text is one of the classical statements about Jesus Christ in the Bible. The Colossians had differences of opinion about Jesus. Some of the views were troubling to followers of the apostle Paul. It was probably one of these disciples of Paul who wrote this letter.

Apparently, some of the Colossians were being influenced by Gnosticism, a popular philosophy. Gnostics believed that matter was altogether evil, while spirit was good. Since the world consists of matter, it's bad. Now, where does this put God? God is Spirit and therefore good, so God couldn't have created the material world. It was created by a distant emanation of God, not the real God.

And what does this say about Jesus? The man Jesus couldn't be the Son of God since he had a material body. Remember, material equals evil. Gnostics tried to get out of this difficulty by saying that Jesus only appeared to be human. This viewpoint led to two other conclusions: (1) Jesus wasn't unique. He was one of many intermediaries between God and humanity, and (2) Jesus wasn't the center or source of salvation.

Salvation for the Gnostics was a long process of gaining knowledge, learning secrets and passwords, and climbing a spiritual ladder. Jesus wasn't at its center. The Gnostics couldn't accept the idea that God was born as a Galilean carpenter who was executed on a town garbage heap and that his death was central to human salvation. That couldn't be.

Their Greek philosophy clashed with the Hebrew theology of the Old Testament. First, it contradicted the biblical view of creation. The Bible said that God directly created the material world and called it good. Gnostics couldn't accept this. Second, Gnosticism led to a faulty view of Jesus.

The author of Colossians proclaims who Jesus is. Jesus is supreme in both the created order and the church. He's the very embodiment of God's saving work. Our text incorporates an early Christian hymn that flashes forth several images of Jesus:

- the one in whom we have redemption and forgiveness of sins
- the image of the invisible God
- the firstborn of all creation
- the one in whom all things in heaven and on earth were created
- the one in whom all things hold together
- the head of the church
- the firstborn from the dead
- the one who has first place in everything
- the one in whom the fullness of God dwells
- the one who reconciles all things to God and makes peace

That's a mouthful! These stunning claims go against all who would minimize Jesus and his work. The author is saying that Jesus is God in flesh. Jesus is God's creative, saving work in action. Jesus is how we know God. These bold claims went far beyond the teaching that many of the Colossians were hearing.

In the 1930s and 40s Dietrich Bonhoeffer raised for Christians a central issue of Christology. He asked, "Who really is Christ for us today?" Not who was Christ for the first century or the third century? Or who was Christ for the Colossians? But, rather, who is Christ for us?

Christ is bound to be something to every one of us. To some he's just another object of speculation. But what would it mean if we made the words of Colossians central to our lives?

Take this idea that Jesus is God in human flesh. What does this actually mean to us? What ought it to mean? If I were the proverbial Martian and walked around earth and heard a billion people saying that Jesus was God in human form, I know what I'd do. I'd want to learn about him. I'd study the records of his life and teachings and join a group of people who were studying about him and trying to follow him.

I can come to only one conclusion: The reason Jesus' words have endured as they have is that they're true. They're not like any other words.

Another question: What do the words of Colossians mean for us in the church? They mean that the church isn't just a body of people who've organized themselves to perpetuate the teachings of Jesus. The church isn't a memorial society, a dead poet's society. It's a living organism of which Jesus is the living head.

When we experience Jesus Christ as the living head of the church, everything changes. We realize that the church is of God; it's not a social club—not a creation of humans. The church is meant to run on God's agenda, not ours.

Think about this: What would it mean if we Christians took all of our orders from Jesus Christ, if we put ourselves completely at his disposal? Our church programs and budgets would change.

It's not hard for us to see where Jesus' heart was, to see whom he loved. If Jesus showed up in our city today, we have good ideas as to where he would go. He would go first to those for whom he was most deeply concerned in his earthly life: the poor, the broken, the outcast—and he would surely visit us poor sinners, who need forgiveness and peace. Therefore, we ought to organize our churches to reflect these things. We ought to cling tightly to our Lord. All of our time and resources should be directed to his agenda, not ours.

William Booth, the founder of the Salvation Army, said that he gave himself completely to Christ. There had been others who were more talented or able, but from the day he had a vision of what God could do, he decided that God would have all there was of William Booth.

Today's questions are, How much does God have of us? Who is Jesus Christ for you and me? Does he live in us? If he doesn't, then this whole letter to the Colossians is a dead letter; the entire New Testament is a dead letter; all of Christian theology is a dead letter.

Is Jesus Christ the true Lord of our lives? He's either that—or he's something else. (Sandy Wylie)

Lectionary Commentary

Amos 8:1-12

The book of Amos has three sections: oracles against Israel's neighbors (chs. 1–2), indictments of Israel for its sins (chs. 3–6), and visions of

God's judgment (chs. 7–9). This text is the fourth of five visions of Israel's coming doom. The focus is on a basket of ripe summer fruit, which symbolizes the national prosperity of that day but also the imminent end of prosperity. The vision involves a word play on the Hebrew terms for "summer fruit" and "end." The people see summer fruit, but God and the prophet see the end.

There hasn't been an age in which Amos's prophecy wasn't relevant. Plutocracy and oppression of the poor have been major features of the life of every nation, ranging from brutal dictatorships to modern representative republics. The rich and powerful are always striving to increase their assets, and the poor are but tools in their quests. For this reason God and God's codifiers and prophets were always reminding Israel of its obligation to protect the widows, the orphans, the resident aliens, and the poor. This concern is always in place for God's people. The sensitive preacher faces no more difficult burden than voicing this concern effectively, especially since the values of many of our congregants are at odds with the values of the Bible.

Luke 10:38-42

Luke 9:51 is a turning point in Jesus' ministry as he sets his face to go to Jerusalem. This text is one of twenty-two lectionary Gospel readings in this Year C that are drawn from Luke's travel narrative (9:51–19:27). That narrative focuses on Jesus' death and resurrection and on the demands of discipleship. For Luke discipleship is comprised supremely of hearing and doing the word. Both hearing and doing are indispensable practices.

This story of Martha and Mary immediately follows Jesus' story of the good Samaritan. We can gain insight by bringing the two stories into conversation with each other. The first story focuses on the active doing of good to another. It closes with Jesus' admonition, "Go and do likewise." If the second story had the same focus, Martha rather than Mary would gain Jesus' greater approval. However, this story shifts focus. Its energy is in attentively hearing the word. There's a time for doing and a time for hearing. We don't need to go into overdrive analyzing the psychology or motives of Martha, Mary, or Jesus.

This story is one of several in which Luke spotlights women whom Jesus accepted as serious disciples. Women are not inferior partners with Jesus in Luke's Gospel. Many religious groups have yet to catch up with Jesus on this score. (Sandy Wylie)

Worship Aids

Call to Worship

We come out of the busyness and discord of our lives.
We come because the Christ has called us for service.
Let us raise our voices to him in thanksgiving and praise.
Let us seek his will and blessing in this day
and in all the days to come.

Invocation

O God of infinite mystery, we come before you as those who are committed to Jesus and his church. We offer up these moments of worship as part of our effort to stay focused on our commitments. Steady our minds and lift our spirits. We pray it in Jesus' name. Amen.

Benediction

May the Lord Jesus Christ go before us as we scatter into a fractured and confusing world. May his light illumine our paths, and may we be renewed in our fellowship with him and our neighbors. Go in peace. Amen. (Sandy Wylie)

What It Means to Be Truly Happy

Second in a Series of Four on Celebrated Biblical Texts

Matthew 5

Do you know someone who is struggling to be happy? Maybe you are struggling and seeking to find true happiness. There are people who spend their whole lives in pursuit of happiness, and most never find it. They move from one fad to another, thinking if they change this or that then they will be happy. They seek out one adventure and then another, only to find that the excitement did not bring true happiness. They accomplish one thing and then another, complete one quest after another, only to find the happiness wears off in a short amount of time. They pursue the things that the world claims will make them happy. They read all of the newest self-help books, and yet happiness eludes them.

In the fifth chapter of Matthew, the beginning of Jesus' Sermon on the Mount, we find new definitions of happiness and what I would consider true happiness. The happiness of this world depends on external things: people, achievements, and possessions. These things will not last. People can let us down. Achievements give momentary satisfaction, but there is always something else to achieve. Possessions wear out and become old. There is always something newer and better. Jesus shares with us things that bring eternal happiness.

In verses 3-12 we find the beatitudes. Typically they begin with the words "blessed are . . ." Some translations read "Happy are . . ." The things that bring blessing and happiness in these verses would not be the things the world tells us bring happiness. We are told that those who are poor, those who mourn, those who are humble, those who seek peace, those who are pure, those who show mercy, and those who hunger and thirst for righteousness will be truly happy. Many of these are the opposite of what the world tells us will make us happy. The world tells us that those who are powerful, those who are wealthy, those who enjoy the pleasures of life, those who can make and win wars, and those who live to party are the ones who will be happy. Again, that kind of happiness is fleeting, and we do not have to look far to see that there are those who have or pursue these forms of happiness who are miserable people. Some of the happiest people I know are not wealthy. Some of the happiest people I know have been through difficult times. They are the ones who are truly blessed and have found lasting happiness.

True happiness can be found in making a difference in our world and in the lives of others. In verses 13-16, Jesus talks about being salt and light. Salt adds zest and flavor to food. As Christians we can add zest and flavor to people's lives when we share God's love and grace with them. As Christians God calls us to be lively and joyful. Are others uplifted by your presence? Do you bring life and joy to people? Light is another sign of life and joy. Have you ever heard the saying that the light has gone out of someone's eyes? When there is no purpose in people's lives, when there is no joy in people's lives, they become shrouded in darkness. We are called to bring light. We have the light of the world in our hearts, and we need to allow that light to shine forth and dispel all the darkness and gloom. When we live salty and light-filled lives, we experience true happiness. True happiness comes from giving and sharing.

Some people seem to find happiness in holding grudges. They enjoy being angry at others, and they just wait for something bad to happen to them. They enjoy putting others down and gossiping. In verses 21-24, Jesus tells us that true happiness comes from reconciliation. He expands the commandment not to murder and tells us that hating someone in our heart is just as bad as killing them. I find that most people who harbor grudges do not hurt the person with whom they are angry, they hurt only themselves. Their anger begins to eat away at them from the inside, and they soon find that they are miserable people. Jesus suggests that even before we come to God, we go to our brother or sister who has something against us or whom we have something against and be reconciled. This is the only way to find true happiness.

Matthew 5 closes with Jesus sharing about whom we should love. In verses 43-47, Jesus encourages us to love all people, even our enemies. Some people look for happiness in revenge. Perhaps they have truly been wronged or perhaps the wrong is only imagined, but they spend all their time thinking of ways they can get back at or punish the one whom they consider their enemy. I often wonder if there is much, if any, satisfaction in seeing the criminal who has wronged you punished. Is there really any relief in seeing the person who killed a loved one die in the electric chair or be executed by lethal injection? Jesus tells us to "love your enemies and pray for those who harass you" (v. 44). He reminds us that God "makes the sun rise on both the evil and the good and sends rain on the righteous and the unrighteous" (v. 45). We are called to love the unlovable. We are called to love those who are different from us. We are called to "be perfect, therefore, as [our] heavenly Father is perfect" (v. 48 NRSV; "just as your heavenly Father is complete in showing love to everyone, so also you must be complete," CEB). It is in finding a way in our hearts to love everyone that we find true happiness.

As Christians, may we pursue the means of finding true happiness. May we not be fooled by the ways of the world. May we not be envious of others who appear happy. And may we not gloat about those who fall into despair. May God help us find the joy intended for us all. (Neil Epler)

Worship Aids

Call to Worship

When we feel low and downtrodden,
Remind us that we are blessed.
When we are sorrowful and feel alone,
Remind us that we are blessed.
When we strive to find you but feel so distant,
Remind us that we are blessed.
When people mock us and make fun of us,
Remind us that we are blessed.

Restore to us the joy of your salvation,
And bless us with everlasting peace.

Offertory Prayer

Heavenly Lord, we want to love you. We want to love one another. We want to love ourselves. Sometimes, through faith in Jesus Christ, we experience real love. Let this moment of offering be a time for us to join hands with you and one another. Help us experience your love and the love we have for one another. In Jesus' name. Amen.

Benediction

And now may you go and be salt, bringing zest and life to those you meet. May you go and be light, dispelling the darkness and gloom of this world. May you go and love others, even your enemies. In the name of the Father, the Son, and the Holy Spirit. Amen. (Neil Epler)

JULY 28, 2013

Tenth Sunday after Pentecost

Readings: Hosea 1:2-10; Psalm 85; Colossians 2:6-15, (16-19); Luke 11:1-13

Teach Us to Pray

Luke 11:1-13

Two Christians were trying to outdo each other. The conversation came around to prayer. One said, "I'll bet $20 you can't even say the Lord's Prayer." The other replied, "It's a bet." He began, "Now I lay me down to sleep..." The first man interrupted, "OK, here's your money. I didn't think you could do it."

Luke is interested in two things more than any other Gospel writer, and both of them are in today's text: Jesus' prayer life and the Holy Spirit. The disciples asked Jesus to teach them only one thing: how to pray. They didn't ask him how to preach or do much else.

There were as many different approaches to prayer then as there are now. It was common for a rabbi to give his disciples a model prayer. This seems to have been a motivation behind the disciples' request.

When people say, "Teach us to pray," what are they saying? They're saying, "Put us in touch with God." This is a universal, timeless plea. Connecting with God, knowing God, is "job one." Everything else in the religious life flows from this.

Many people today feel that the church is failing them. In the 1990s, William Hendricks noticed that thousands of people were leaving American churches every week and never going back. He investigated. His 1993 book is *Exit Interviews: Revealing Stories of Why People Are Leaving Church* (Chicago: Moody Press). Hendricks found that two-thirds of people who attended church said they didn't experience God in their worship regularly. They said that preaching was poor and worship was boring. The church was like a restaurant where hungry people came looking for food but didn't find it and walked away frustrated and still hungry. They were saying, "Teach us to pray."

Fifteen years later Julia Duin did the same kind of research. She found exactly what Hendricks had found. Her 2008 book is *Quitting Church: Why the Faithful Are Fleeing and What to Do About It* (Grand Rapids: Baker Books). Worshipers told Duin that they weren't getting decent preaching, good community, or spiritual food. The church had become irrelevant to their lives, so they were investing elsewhere. Churchgoers everywhere are pleading, "Teach us to pray. Help us know God." And it's not happening!

We know Jesus' model prayer as "The Lord's Prayer." The version that we know best is the longer version that Matthew includes in the Sermon on the Mount. Before us today is Luke's shorter version. It's probably closer to the original. Matthew's version seems to be an elaboration. Luke's version of Jesus' model prayer is brief and carefully constructed. It has four quick thrusts (vv. 2-4 NRSV):

(1) "Father, hallowed be your name. / Your kingdom come." The praise of God and God's kingdom comes before all else. The first words of Christian worship are notes of praise.

(2) "Give us each day our daily bread." God is concerned about our earthly condition. Daily bread is the most basic of our material needs, and it stands for all of the others.

(3) "and forgive us our sins, / for we ourselves forgive everyone indebted to us." If we are to live in harmony with God and neighbor, which is the foundation of our religious life, we've got to deal with our wrongdoings. We must forgive and be forgiven. This thrust deals with community—and you can't have community without forgiveness.

(4) "and do not bring us to the time of trial." In John Bunyan's *Pilgrim's Progress*, Pilgrim knows that danger lurks everywhere and that trials are unavoidable. We can't expect to escape them—nor should we want to do so, for trials strengthen us. But there's that trial that we all fear—the trial that will defeat us. It's the trial that takes from us our families, our jobs, our self-respect—even our souls. "O God, give us your Spirit so that we will not be defeated!"—that's what Jesus is saying here.

Luke attaches to this model prayer some of Jesus' teachings on prayer. These thirteen verses contain Jesus' most complete statement on prayer. The first thing that we should notice about this text is the first word of

Jesus' model prayer. That word unlocks everything. It's the word *Father*. It translates the Aramaic word *Abba* (Daddy). In the romance languages there are familiar forms of address and familiar forms of verbs that are used only in the close family circle. That's the kind of thing we're talking about here. Knowing God as Daddy gives us direct access to God on the most intimate level.

Another thing Jesus teaches is that we should be persistent in prayer. Ask, seek, knock: these are imperatives, these are action words. There's a kind of fatalism or quietism that reasons this way: "If God wants me to get this job, I'll get it." To reason that way is to misunderstand providence. It's to leave out the human part of the equation. God wants us to be active and probing in working out our lives. We must actively bend ourselves toward our goals.

It's been said that God answers prayers in four ways: (1) No, not yet. (2) No, I love you too much. (3) Yes, I thought you'd never ask. (4) Yes, and here's more. Be persistent in prayer!

Yet another thing Jesus teaches is this: God showers us with gifts. To be one of God's children is to be gifted. Gifts come in the form of different human temperaments, personal abilities, material possessions, and so on. We're all different, yet richly gifted!

In Matthew's version of this teaching Jesus says, "If you who are evil know how to give good gifts to your children, how much more will your heavenly Father give good things to those who ask him" (7:11). Matthew says "good things"; Luke says "the Holy Spirit," which is the greatest gift.

Any father knows that the best gift he can give to his children is himself. There's no substitute for a parent's love. As children of God, you and I never have to settle for substitutes. Our self-giving God never leaves us empty. We may bring our trivial desires to God in prayer, but in prayer we always receive something greater: the fellowship of one whose love for us never fails. (Sandy Wylie)

Lectionary Commentary

Hosea 1:2-10

We humans are so self-absorbed that we see almost everything in human terms. We're fixed on ourselves and only want to know how everything affects us. Is it possible that we could ever see the world from God's perspective? How might God feel about what goes on among us humans? In this text Hosea, the first of the Minor Prophets, challenges us to see the world through God's eyes. It's not a pretty picture. Hosea presents his message, as prophets often do, by acting it out in highly symbolic and shocking ways. The action is driven by a loving, passionate God who waits, seeks, finds, pleads, forgives, and saves. This God is like a long-suffering spouse who encounters never-ending unfaithfulness and rejection but whose love is so great that he or she is willing to suffer great pain and all kinds of indignities in order to win back the beloved. On down the road God is even willing to be crucified for the unfaithful ones!

Just when the drama in our text has reached its lowest point, Hosea sounds a message of incredible grace in verse 10. God cannot bear to finally abandon us unfaithful humans. Our destiny is not to be remembered as "not my people" but as "Children of the living God." If this grace doesn't touch and influence us wayward creatures, then nothing else ever will.

Colossians 2:6-15 (16-19)

In this text the author confronts his theological opponents. He names their errors in verses 8 and 16-19. His central concern is to establish a correct understanding of Christ. In Christ and only in Christ "all the fullness of deity lives in Christ's body" (v. 9). The idea that God could be embodied in human flesh was nonsense to the writer's opponents.

At verse 10, the writer addresses the relationship between Christ and believers. He begins, "You have come to fullness in him" (NRSV). Believers partake of the divine nature when they attach themselves to Christ and live in him. Verses 11-14 spell out the identification between Christ and believers. Spiritual circumcision marks those who belong to Christ, just as circumcision marks Jews. So closely are believers connected to Christ that they are buried with him in baptism and raised with him in his resurrection. There's no question as to the efficacy of Christ's redemptive power. Christ is the ruler of all creation. The redemption of believers is shown especially in the forgiveness of all of their trespasses through the cross. Christ is a savior without peer. (Sandy Wylie)

Worship Aids

Invocation

O loving God, we know you as one who always listens, one who never tires in hearing your children. Receive our many prayers in this hour as our sincere though often feeble efforts to connect with your will and purpose for us. In Jesus' name we pray. Amen.

Prayer of Confession

O God, we know that our efforts to converse with you never match your willingness to engage us. Too often we draw away from you and refuse to listen to your voice. We choose distractions rather than main events. Forgive us, we pray, and turn us to your light. Amen.

Words of Assurance

We know that God's grace is sufficient for us. There is no infirmity, no weakness that is beyond God's power to redeem. Even now God is acting in our behalf. Let us claim God's forgiveness for ourselves and each other. Amen. (Sandy Wylie)

Why God?

Third in a Series of Four on Celebrated Biblical Texts

Genesis 22

There are many passages in Scripture that are hard to understand. If I were writing the Bible, there are many things that I would leave out. I would not mention the affair between David and Bathsheba. I would not write about the incestuous relations between Lot and his daughters. And I would leave out this passage about Abraham being asked by God to sacrifice his son, Isaac. But then again, would I?

It is difficult for us to understand how a good and loving God could ask for a human sacrifice. Didn't God destroy the former dwellers of the Holy Land in part because of these practices? Isn't this something that God warned the children of Israel never to do? In Leviticus the practice of child sacrifice is strongly condemned. "You must not give any of your children to offer them over to Molech so that you do not defile your God's name: I am the LORD" (18:21). "Any Israelite or any immigrant living in Israel who gives their children to Molech must be executed. The common people will stone such a person" (20:2). One of the reasons Israel was carried away into captivity was because "[t]hey burned their sons and daughters alive" (2 Kings 17:17). Yet here we find God asking this very thing of his servant Abraham.

As I struggle with this passage I realize that a human sacrifice would become God's ultimate plan for the salvation of humanity. God would become incarnate. He would become flesh and blood in his son Jesus Christ, and offer himself as the perfect human sacrifice. What we see God asking of Abraham is what he would do for all humankind. An angel stayed the hand of Abraham and kept him from killing his one and only son, but no one stayed the hand of God while his son died upon the cross at Calvary. God's son cried out to him, "My God, My God, why have you forsaken me?" (Matthew 27:46 NRSV). Still God allowed his death so that we might be saved. The request of Abraham to offer his son as a sacrifice can be seen as a foreshadowing of what God himself would do thousands of years later.

I must believe that God knew the outcome of the request he was asking of Abraham even before it happened. In verse 1, we are told that God was testing Abraham. God knew how faithful Abraham was in following him. God asked him to leave his native country and travel to a strange and foreign land that he would show him (Genesis 12:1). Abraham obeyed God and God made a covenant with him. He told Abraham that he would possess that land to which he traveled, that he would become a great nation with descendants as numerous as the grains of sand and the stars, and that through him all the people of the world would be blessed. God repeats this covenant with Abraham later in this chapter after he passes this test. "I will bless you richly and I will give you countless descendants, as many as the stars in the sky and as the grains of sand on the seashore. They will conquer their enemies' cities. All the nations of the earth will be blessed because of your descendants, because you obeyed me" (Genesis 22:17-18). The last part of this covenant would be fulfilled in the coming of Jesus. He was a Jew, a descendant of Abraham, and through him all the nations and all peoples are blessed. He too was obedient, "obedient to the point of death, / even death on a cross" (Philippians 2:8). Because of Jesus' obedience, we now have a new covenant for all people for the forgiveness of sins.

Abraham was a patient man. Although his wife Sarah was barren, he waited for God to fulfill his promise and give him an heir. He stumbled once in taking Hagar as his wife and having a child through her named Ishmael. This happened after Sarah pleaded with him that "[m]aybe she will provide me with children" (Genesis 16:2). Thirteen years after Ishmael's birth, Abraham received heavenly visitors who promised that the next year he would have a son through Sarah. Sarah laughed at the idea that she could have a child in her old age and that is why the child was named Isaac, which means "he laughed" or "the son of laughter."

Abraham was nearly one hundred years old when his son, Isaac, was born. It was years later, when his son was at least a teenager, that God tested Abraham. What would it be like to sacrifice your one and only child? I have two sons and now a grandson, and I can't imagine the anguish of being asked to offer up one of their lives. How was Abraham able to answer his son when he asked, "Here is the fire and the wood, but where is the lamb for the entirely burned offering?" Abraham told Isaac that the Lord would provide the lamb for the offering, knowing full well the offering was his son. But God did provide the offering. After an angel called out to Abraham and told him not to harm the child, they found a ram caught in a thicket by his horns, which they offered up as a burnt offering.

God does not test us all in the way he tested Abraham. God does not call all of us to make such dramatic sacrifices. But God does call us to be willing to make sacrifices. I have known of people who gave up their careers and their homes to answer God's call to enter the ministry. I have known of people who sold all their possessions to go out on the mission field. But they have discovered that God always provides, just as God provided the lamb for Abraham. May we be willing to answer God's call to sacrifice, whatever it may be, and depend on God to provide. (Neil Epler)

Worship Aids

Confession

Almighty and most merciful Father, we have erred and strayed from thy ways like lost sheep. We have followed too much the devices and desires of our own hearts. We have offended against thy holy laws. We have left undone those things which we ought to have done; and we have done those things which we ought not to have done; and there is no health in us. But thou, O Lord, have mercy upon us, miserable offenders. Spare thou those, O God, who confess their faults. Restore thou those who are penitent; according to thy promises declared unto mankind, in Christ Jesus our Lord. And grant, O most merciful Father, for his sake; that we may hereafter live a godly, righteous, and sober life; to the glory of thy holy name. Amen. (*The Book of Common Prayer* [Boston: Massachusetts Episcopal Missionary Society, 1831], 30–31.)

Words of Assurance

The Lord hears the confession of our hearts and forgives. Thanks be to God.

Offertory Prayer

O Lord, it is just money. Yet, if it is just money, why is it so hard to part with? This money represents our work, our study, long hours, hopes, and plans. It is a part of us. Take what we give and use it to give food to the hungry, clothing for the naked, health for the sick, and concern for the prisoner. In Jesus' name. Amen.

Benediction

Lord, as we leave here this day, teach us how to sacrifice. Show us what we need to do and what we need to give and then empower us through your Holy Spirit to do it. Give us willing hearts and remind us that you will always provide. In the name of the Father, the Son, and the Holy Spirit. Amen. (Neil Epler)

AUGUST 4, 2013

ꕥꕥꕥ

Eleventh Sunday after Pentecost

Readings: Hosea 11:1-11; Psalm 107:1-9, 43; Colossians 3:1-11; Luke 12:13-21

High Fidelity

Hosea 11:1-11

Bill Cosby's book *Fatherhood* (New York: Doubleday, 1986) is about the difficulties of parenting. The first parent, says Cosby, wasn't Adam or Eve. It was God. Even God had trouble with his kids. God wasn't able to inspire much obedience or faithfulness in Adam and Eve, and they didn't have any better outcome with their children, either.

It's amazing to us parents that God would give us the most precious gift in the world, a child, and not give us a manual on how to raise that child. When you buy any kind of gadget, you get a manual. But with the most complicated gift, there's no manual.

There's nothing quite like the agony of being a parent. Our bond with our children is one of the strongest forces we ever experience. When our children hurt, we hurt. Almost nothing will cause us to give up our loyalty to them.

The eleventh chapter of Hosea is remarkable Scripture. In it the prophet pictures God as a parent. The child is Israel. This relationship is everything that our parent-child relationships are, only much more.

First of all, there's the love of the parent, love beyond measure. The Hebrew language has a special word for God's love: *hesed*. This word is sprinkled through the Hebrew Scriptures, including Hosea. Some English Bibles translate *hesed* as "constant love" or "loving kindness," but it's stronger than that. It's a love that will not quit—a love of those who are in a covenant of complete trust and faithfulness.

It's often said that the God of the Old Testament is a God of judgment, and the God of the New Testament is a God of love. Not so! Throughout much of the Old Testament, including Hosea, God is always a God of constant love.

In chapter 11 Hosea paints a portrait of God's love for Israel. It begins, "When Israel was a child, I loved him." That's the way love stories begin. In verse 4 the Lord says, "I treated them like those / who lift infants to their cheeks." I remember that as a child. Nothing was more fun than being swept up in a parent's arms and held to his or her cheek! Being whisked up that way is scary and exciting, all at the same time. Your stomach does a flip-flop, resulting in a giggle of delight.

With little touches like this, Hosea portrays the tender caring and intimacy between the Lord and God's people. But, unfortunately, all is not well. Israel is unfaithful, and this hurts.

Hosea began his ministry around 750 B.C.E. at a time when Israel was drifting away from God. In fewer than thirty years they would be conquered by the Assyrians. Hosea knew that the Lord was watching this sad spectacle.

At times Hosea could hear the Lord talking to himself. If being a parent won't get a person talking to himself, then nothing else will. Hosea 11 is a divine soliloquy in which the Lord meditates on his relationship with Israel. The Lord seems to have gone through all of the cycles of behavior that we parents go through with our children: lecturing, reasoning, shouting, warning, begging. None of the Lord's attention-getting devices has worked. He's in agony.

One of the painful parts of being a parent is that you can't intervene in everything that affects your children. Sometimes you just have to let them learn life's painful lessons.

Those of us who have read Ann Landers or Dear Abby see this type of letter from sorrowing parents at least a couple of times each year. A child has stormed out of the family and hasn't been heard from. In this open letter to the child the parents plea for some word from the child. The ache in the parents' hearts is palpable. This letter could have been written by thousands of parents in this country—thousands! Such is the love of parents.

What is the Lord's final response to wayward Israel? It begins in verse 8: "How can I give you up, Ephraim? / How can I hand you over, Israel?. . . / My heart winces within me; / my compassion grows / warm and tender."

The key line comes in verse 9: "For I am God and not a human being." This means that the Lord will continue to love his children, not because they deserve it or are lovable but because God is God. God is so full of unconditional love (*hesed*) that the New Testament proclaims, "God is love" (1 John 4:8).

Have you ever bumped into unconditional love? I tell you, it's the most wonderful thing in the world. It heals the broken-hearted and puts steel in the spines of the faint-hearted.

I heard Dave Roever speak to the troops at Fort Sill. As he told the story, he was fighting in Vietnam when a phosphorus grenade exploded six inches from his right ear. Amazingly, he survived and arrived at the burn center at Brooke Army Hospital. The day before his wife, Brenda, was to come, the man next to Dave was visited by his wife. That wife stared briefly, put her wedding ring on the night stand, and walked away. That event set up the most anxious twenty-four hours in Dave's life.

The moment finally came. He could hear Brenda's footsteps. Then there she was. She smiled and said, "Welcome home, Davey!"

All Dave could say was, "I want you to know I'm real sorry that I can never look good for you again." Brenda said, "Oh, Davey, how silly. You never were good-looking, anyway!" Such was the beginning of Dave's psychological and spiritual healing.

Where did a twenty-year-old like Brenda Roever learn to love like that? I wanted to know. I called the office of the David Roever Ministries in Fort Worth. Brenda answered. She said she grew up as a committed Christian, nurtured by the Scriptures of the church and Christian fellowship. These were the building blocks that formed her. And so when the test came, she was ready to say those words that come from the heart of God: "Welcome home."

That's the kind of love that can heal the world. The good news is that God offers it to us. All we have to do is take it. (Sandy Wylie)

Lectionary Commentary

Colossians 3:1-11

This text has two divisions. Verses 1-4 discuss believers' relationships with Christ. The relationship is one of union: believers "were raised with Christ" and "will be revealed with him in glory." The union is so complete that the writer proclaims to believers that Christ "is your life."

Verses 5-11 coach believers on the kind of conduct that their new self in Christ requires. Believers must set aside a dozen or so behaviors as they focus on "things above." One of these behaviors is greed (identified as idolatry), which is the subject of today's Gospel reading from Luke 12.

The text ends with verse 11, which boldly proclaims that believers' union with Christ is paramount and that common distinctions among believers such as race, nationality, and gender fade into insignificance.

Luke 12:13-21

This parable appears only in Luke but is found elsewhere in the lore of the Middle East and in the Gospel of Thomas. In Luke 12, it's the first in a short series of teachings about possessions that extends through verse 48. These teachings make clear that the management of wealth is a central component of Christian discipleship.

The rich man in this story deserves the title "fool." A fool talks only to himself, as does this man—not to others and not to God. He congratulates himself and plans only for himself. He's shortsighted. Consequently he loses himself, as Jesus puts it in an earlier teaching on wealth (9:25). After all, Jesus is about to point out that discipleship is not about hoarding wealth but sharing it (12:33). (Sandy Wylie)

Worship Aids

Call to Worship

Let us worship the one who created and sustains us all.
Let us glorify the one whose love endures forever and never fails us.
By grace we are vessels of God's love and doers of God's word.
Let us then worship God in spirit and in truth.

Invocation

O God of great and wondrous love, hear us as we enter this sacred hour of worship. Fill our faint hearts with love's fullness, strengthen our timid spirits with love's boldness, and guide our hands with love's steadiness. And to you we will give the praise. Amen.

Benediction

Send us out, loving God, in the fullness and strength of your spirit. Direct our voices, warm our hearts, and guide our hands as we seek to bless others. And may we discover your blessing for us in all things great and small. Amen. (Sandy Wylie)

Four Powerful Words

Fourth in a Series of Four on Celebrated Biblical Texts

John 3:16

For many of us, John 3:16 was the first scripture we ever memorized. It is one of the most widely known verses both in and outside of the church. Who can forget seeing the sporting events with someone holding up a sign that reads "John 3:16"? Maybe you learned how to say this verse by placing your name or the name of someone you love right in it, "God so loved [me or John or Martha], that he gave his only Son, so that [if I or John or Martha believe] in him, [I or John or Martha] won't perish but will have eternal life." For some people this is the only passage of Scripture they know. I always encourage people when they are witnessing to start with this passage to let people know how much God loves them and what God has done for them. As I studied this verse, I noticed four powerful words that tell us about God and how we can respond to God.

The first word is *love*: "God so loved the world." *Love* is a word that can cause a great deal of confusion. We seem to toss it around a lot these days. We talk about loving a pet, loving a favorite food, or loving a favorite sports team. Then we use the same word and say that we love a friend, a family member, or God. For some, saying the words *I love you* to a spouse or a parent or a child can be very difficult. The New Testament Scriptures usually use the Greek word *agape* when referring to spiritual love. This love is hard to define. There is no higher or more excellent love than *agape*. It knows no limits and has no boundaries. *Agape* is sacrificial and thinks of others before itself. Paul defines *agape* in 1 Corinthians 13; our lives are nothing without this love. *Agape* is patient and kind, it is not arrogant or rude; it is not easily provoked and rejoices in the truth. "Love puts up with all things, trusts in all things, hopes for all things, endures all things. Love never fails" (1 Corinthians 13:7-8). This is the kind of love God showed toward us in dying for us while were still sinners (Romans 5:8).

This kind of love calls us to action. Just as God has loved us, we are called to love God and to love others as ourselves. When Jesus was asked about the greatest commandment, he talked about love. If God so loved us, we need to love others.

The second word is *gave*: "that he gave his only son." Our God is a giving God who gave us all the beauty and wonder of creation. God gave us the breath of life and each day is a gift from God. Then God gave us the greatest gift: God's son, God incarnate. God gave himself to us and died for our sins to a pay a price we could not pay.

Just as God gave himself for us, we are called to give ourselves for others. We are called to share the many blessings that God has given us. We offer our tithes and offerings so that the work of God's church can continue and we can build God's kingdom. We offer our spiritual gifts and talents so that the church, Christ's body, can function at its full potential.

Believe is the third powerful word: "everyone who believes in him won't perish." This is the real crux of our faith. We are asked to believe that Jesus is God's son, that he died for our sins, and that he rose from the dead. Our believing is more than just a mental affirmation. In James 2:19 we read that even the demons believe and tremble. Their belief does not lead to salvation. True belief demands that we surrender our lives to Jesus and receive him as our Lord and Savior. "Because if you confess with your mouth 'Jesus is Lord' and in your heart you have faith that God raised him from the dead, you will be saved. Trusting with the heart leads to righteousness, and confessing with the mouth leads to salvation" (Romans 10:9-10).

We are called to respond to God's gift of Jesus by believing in him and giving our life to him. This is the only way we can be saved and the only way to avoid the punishment we have earned through our sin. Our belief in Christ should show itself in the way we live and the way we treat other people. True faith brings about change in our hearts and in our lives.

The last powerful word is *have*: "but [they] will have eternal life." So many people struggle with the assurance of their salvation. How can I know that I am saved and that I will have eternal life? Simply believe what the Scriptures say. In John 3:16 we are given the assurance that if we believe we will not perish and we will have eternal life. Don't allow anyone or anything to separate you from this truth. You can know that you are saved by believing that God's word is true. In 1 John 5:13 we read, "I write these things to you who believe in the name of God's Son so that you can know that you have eternal life." The Scriptures also tell us that if we believe we will be saved. We can be sure of it.

Having this gift of eternal life is not something that we keep to ourselves. We are called to take the good news out into the world and let everyone know that God loves them and that God sent his son to die for them. Use these four powerful words to proclaim the gospel today. (Neil Epler)

Worship Aids

Call to Worship

It is more, O God, this life of ours;
More than we deserve, often more than we expect.
It is more blessed, O God, these days in which we happen to be living.
We share more of the joyful celebration of life.
It is more blessed to give, O Savior, to one another and to all others.
We know this because you gave of your life
for the joy that was set before you.
It is more blessed to give than to receive, Lord Christ,
for in giving we truly receive.
In letting go we are held close to you
and our hearts are made happy,
our lives made full, and our spirits set free.

Offertory Prayer

Merciful Lord, as we bring our gifts to you, help us realize that most of us are surrounded by people with whom we have failed to share the gift of love. In this act of giving help us know that you in your goodness are giving us another chance to love and determine the destiny of others. We make our prayer through the Spirit of Jesus Christ. Amen.

Benediction

O God, as we go forth from this place, help us love you and love others. Help us give of ourselves, our time, our talents, and our treasures. Help us grow in faith and remember that in you we have eternal life. Amen. (Neil Epler)

AUGUST 11, 2013

Twelfth Sunday after Pentecost

Readings: Isaiah 1:1, 10-20; Psalm 50:1-8, 22-23; Hebrews 11:1-3, 8-16; Luke 12:32-40

A Way of Life

Luke 12:32-40

Jesus has told us through his words to the disciples that we need to prepare for the coming of the son of man ("Human One" in CEB). So many times we take this text and others like it and hold it up as some kind of threat. There are evangelists who are making a living interpreting the signs of the times and trying to pinpoint just when the son of man will come back. The earthquakes that have rocked the world the past year or two lead us to ask, "Could this be the beginning of the end?" Political issues and decisions made by our government and governments abroad have caused some to ask the questions, "Are we seeing the Anti-Christ?" "Is this the end?" And some even urge us to hurry and get busy because Jesus is coming soon.

But we need to stop and listen more carefully to the words of Jesus in this text. He begins by saying, "Don't be afraid, little flock, because your Father delights in giving you the kingdom" (v. 32). This is good news! Jesus is not trying to threaten or scare his disciples but to share with them the love that God wants to share with them. He explains this by using the example of a wedding and the return of one's master from the wedding party. This isn't the only time that Jesus uses wedding imagery to illustrate his relationship with the people.

Jesus uses this imagery so that we can understand not only the need to prepare but also the joy and excitement that preparation is meant to bring. Think about it, a bride prepares for her groom the moment she sets her eyes on him and falls in love. In fact, in our culture, the bride often dreams and plans for her wedding long before she has met the man of her dreams. But when she falls in love, when she discovers the love of her life, she begins to prepare for her wedding day. She wants it to be the most perfect day of her life. She carefully selects just the right music, the perfect gown, the perfect bridesmaid dresses, the perfect flower arrangements, and the perfect location. Everything about the day, the day that she begins living her life with him, forever in holy matrimony, will be filled with wonder and joy. The couple stands together in front of God, the guests, and the wedding party and promises to love, honor, and cherish each other. Jesus tells his disciples that God already loves us and wants to give us the kingdom; as with a bride it's up to us to prepare our hearts, minds, and souls to return that great love. Not so that we can start living in eternity sometime in the future but so that we can enjoy the blessings of God's love, grace, and mercy now.

When we realize the significance of Jesus' words, we put aside the questions of anxiety and dread and begin to ask questions of hope and anticipation. "What is God doing among us?" "How can I be part of the coming of the kingdom?" God is counting on our hands and feet to fulfill the promise.

This past summer I was reminded of this as I watched some of the adults and youth of my congregation hand out school supplies to those who were in need in our community. They had an assembly line of sorts set up in our fellowship hall. Those who were in need of school supplies would come in and sign up and receive a number. When their turn was called, they were given a new backpack, and they walked through the assembly line and picked up the school supplies that were on their child's school list. It was a long process, and some people waited for an hour or more for their turn. As I stood, watched, and marveled at the event that was taking place in front of me, one of the women we were serving came up to me. She said, "Thank you. God is so good. I have sat here this morning watching all those people get their school supplies. It's been a blessing." I just smiled and said, "You're welcome." But in my mind I was thanking God because I knew I was in the midst of God's kingdom.

Jesus' admonition to be dressed and ready for action, then, is not a threat but a promise. The other day one of my "friends" on Facebook lamented that she had been stuck in traffic for a very long time. In fact, she had seen the same traffic light turn green ten times and she still hadn't made it through the intersection. She couldn't understand why the woman who had a stalled car didn't get out and push her car off the road. We can all imagine the frustration of sitting and waiting as the light turns time after time, wondering when the road is going to clear. It seemed clear to me sitting on my couch, reading the Facebook post, that the answer for the frustration of being stranded on a busy road was to get out of your car and help the woman push her stalled car off the road. Perhaps if I had been in my car trying to get home after a long day of work, my vision would not have been so clear. But if we, as Jesus commands, prepare ourselves and keep ourselves always at the ready, our vision will stay clear, and we won't miss opportunities to be the hands and feet of Christ.

When we reframe the questions, then, we realize that the preparations are part of living in the kingdom. Our life of joy begins now, not in some distant, fearful future. (Sara Shaver)

Lectionary Commentary

Isaiah 1:1, 10-20

God wants a real relationship with the people of Israel. So often, religion becomes a matter of checking off a list of dos and don'ts. The Israelites have settled into the promised land and have begun living a life that has little room for the God who brought them out of slavery. One can imagine the scene at the temple. The people line up with their doves, sheep, bread, whatever they have brought to offer as sacrifice. And as they wait for their turn, they stand talking with those among them—talking not of all that God has done in their lives and in the lives of their people but of the day-to-day events of their community. It is much like the pastor who assures his congregation on Facebook that the worship service on Sunday will be over in time to catch the tip-off in the NCAA tournament basketball game.

Hebrews 11:1-3, 8-16

So many times we want the answers to all our questions, solutions to all the possible scenarios as we make our journey of faith. We are reminded by the author of Hebrews that those who have gone before us chose to live as the old saying goes "one day at a time," trusting that God would provide not only the strength that was needed to face each day but also would grant the wisdom and understanding needed to follow God's path. Like the manna in the desert each day, God's grace is sufficient for our needs. (Sara Shaver)

Worship Aids

Invocation

We gather in your house, O God, because you have called us your children. Enable us to put aside the worries and concerns of the world and focus on you. Open our hearts to the truth of your love that we might be renewed and refreshed.

Prayer of Confession

God of grace and mystery, we confess that we have often failed to keep you as the central focus of our lives. We have turned our backs on our faith because it was inconvenient, it cost us more than an hour on Sunday mornings, and we were unwilling to share our hearts, minds, and souls with you. Forgive us, we pray, and enable us once again to find our rest in you that we might take up our crosses and walk confidently and hopefully as your children. Amen.

Words of Assurance

Turn around! God is waiting to forgive, to love, to send us out to be the body of Christ in and for the world. Amen.

Benediction

And now as we leave this place, we go as people of hope and joy knowing that the love and grace that God has freely given us will sustain us in the days ahead. Amen. (Sara Shaver)

Jesus Tells Us To

First in a Series of Three on Why Christians Do Missions

Matthew 28:19-20

Jesus says, "Go."

Those of us who are members of this church (as well as our guests familiar with this people, place, and what happens here), come into this sanctuary and want to stay a while. We schedule our lives into this time, knowing that worship keeps a rhythm in our faith, a tempo in our spirituality. This is our most sacred shared exchange with God, experienced as community with like-minded folks who know similar struggles and hold common hopes. Here we are wanting to stay a while, and Jesus, the Lord in whose name we gather, the one in whom we find our identity as loved children of God, says: "Go."

Please, may we be honest with ourselves, with God, and with one another? We're not at all sure that we really want to "Go."

It took much courage for some of us to come here, to keep coming as we do, to go to that Bible study, to volunteer to serve on that committee, and to give our hard-earned money. We've made the place relatively comfortable, enough so that we'll probably come back next Sunday; so we are just not real keen upon arriving to meet a Savior who says, "Go."

This sermon is the first of three that will explore why Christians do missions. First of all, we do missions because Jesus tells us to. When Jesus commissioned his first disciples, his instructions were also to you and me together as the church: "Therefore, go and make disciples of all nations, baptizing them . . ."

Jesus says, "Therefore, go . . ." because he just announced that all authority on heaven and earth has been given to him (v. 18). I know, and you know, too, that we're more inclined to stay right where we are. We can rationalize that we affirm his authority simply by being present here together in his name. Before we content ourselves with faithfulness on our own terms, let's remember the biblical witness: Jesus is questioned about his authority when he does something disagreeable to the religious leadership, when his behavior confronts their personally preferred practice and tradition-bound belief. We Christians grant Jesus authority in and over our lives. It is this Lord who loves us, saves us, and whose promised Holy Spirit sustains us. We listen to him. Jesus tells us to "go," and we respond in mission and ministry.

Our going is faith in motion to change the world one life at a time. Doing missions is our living Jesus' instructions to make disciples, teach them what we learned from Jesus, and remember.

Missions work is about making disciples. I remember a missionary's annual visit to my childhood church. He told stories of exotic places and people, of how the church was sharing Jesus there with them. I learned that doing missions is building relationships and showing God's love by serving alongside the indigenous people, meeting their immediate needs, and adjusting social systems to help them live life to its fullest.

The church does missions as a selfless sharing of Christ's caring. We may be blessed with the satisfaction of our altruistic actions, yet missions definitively put us in a place to be like Jesus. Our shared missions work is our living-beyond-ourselves life, in which we find our deepest meaning as children of God.

Missions work is about teaching others what we learned from Jesus. Christians do missions in practical ways. Through our practice, our doing Jesus' life lessons, we model how to love God, our neighbor, and ourselves. This effective way of teaching reinforces what we already know from Christ, opening our hearts and minds to clearly see this world that we share. We become aware of the disparity that oppresses and segregates, and with those learning from us, we show the joyful and powerful reality of the kingdom of God here and now.

In John 17, Jesus prays, asking God for his disciples, "I pray they will be one" (John 17:21).

The church in its differing traditions and tribes disagrees over various points of doctrinal orthodoxy. Doing missions, diverse Christians are united in *orthopraxy*, the physical practice of our faith in which we find our oneness with Christ.

Doing missions, Christians remember and affirm the presence of the Living Christ. Jesus' parting words in Matthew's Gospel are, "Look, I myself will be with you every day..." When we recall something past, bringing it into our present awareness makes it as much "now" as it was "then." The church does missions because Jesus is present in these acts of servant discipleship, now, in the places where we go.

Here we are in the church, wanting to stay a while, and Jesus, the Lord in whose name we gather, the one in whom we find our identity as loved children of God, says, "Go." We're not at all sure that we really want to "go"; yet it is in this place, together, that we hear Jesus, and we know that our lives are better when we listen and follow what he says.

So we Christians go as the church, doing missions because Jesus tells us to. (Dale Schultz)

Worship Aids

A Call to Worship

We come together to remember who we are.
We come together to affirm whose we are.
We worship God in the name of the Christ who calls us to life.
We worship God in the name of the Christ
who sends us out to serve.

Prayer of Confession

Lord, in our selfishness we want to be still and stay in the sacred space, embraced by your Spirit and enveloped in your love. Please, forgive us in our hesitancy to go beyond these halls and walls to live your mission in this world. In Jesus' name we pray. Amen.

Words of Assurance

God knows our hearts and loves us as we struggle. Amen.

Benediction

Now leave this place and let your loving and living be about making disciples of Jesus, sure that Christ is with you always. (Dale Schultz)

AUGUST 18, 2013

Thirteenth Sunday after Pentecost

Readings: Isaiah 5:1-7; Psalm 80:1-2, 8-19; Hebrews 11:29–12:2; Luke 12:49-56

Tough Love

Luke 12:49-56

Every time this text comes up in the lectionary schedule, I am reminded of how much I dislike it. If I weren't a lectionary preacher, I don't know that I would ever choose to preach it. I would much rather elaborate on the second chapter of Luke, where the story is told of Mary and Joseph's journey to Jerusalem, the birth of Jesus and the shepherds seeing the glory of the angels shining all around them. I would like to preach the texts about Jesus that create warm fuzzies in our hearts, the stories in which Jesus reminds us that we are important to him even when we're not important to anyone else, the texts that remind us of the many paintings we see of Jesus with that calm, serene, loving smile.

But instead, we have to deal with this text. It comes immediately after Jesus comforts the crowd, calling them "little flock" and assuring them that it is God's good pleasure to give them, and us, the kingdom. And then Jesus turns around and says, "You think I've come to bring peace? Nope!"

This abrupt change in Jesus' teachings, this no-holds-barred teaching, is like cold water thrown in one's face. I find myself wishing that Jesus had slowly and gently eased into sharing this news. I wish he had said, "You remember when my Father appeared to Moses in a burning bush? Well, he's going to use fire to get our attention again. And after this fire, there might be some times you don't agree with what's happening in the world. You might find that some people won't believe as you do and they might try to stop you living out your faith or ridicule you." But Jesus didn't ease into these difficult words. He didn't hold back, because Jesus doesn't want us to hold back.

Jesus begins by telling us that he came to bring fire to the earth. Fire can be a scary, destructive thing. Many homes and churches have been destroyed by fire. But fire can also cleanse. Where I grew up, the farmers would burn their fields before planting in the spring. It removed all the dead foliage and all the weeds. It cleansed the field so that the new planting season would be fruitful. Jesus came to bring fire to the earth, to cleanse so that God's people might once again be fruitful.

But Jesus doesn't stop there. He promises that there will not be peace, there will be division. This is one of those times that I wish I had been sitting in the crowd so that I could raise my hand and say, "Excuse me. Didn't you promise to give us your peace? Didn't the angels promise peace among those you favor? I came for the peace that passes all understanding."

But Jesus knew and knows that when we do things for his sake instead of for the world, we are going to meet opposition—sometimes a little, sometimes a lot. I think the hardest part of this passage for me is when Jesus tells us that there will be division among our families. Family is where we are supposed to find our source of community, our sense of belonging, and now we hear that if we allow the fire of his love to cleanse us, we will be divided. I live in a place where having a divided family means you root for rival college football teams. These divided families often sport a car tag that denotes this division. Half of the tag is the University of Alabama colors, and the other half is the Auburn University colors. But the division Jesus speaks about is not whether to wear crimson and white or orange and blue. It is whether one puts on Christ, whether we walk the way of the cross rather than the way of the world. It is when we choose, like the prodigal son's father, to forgive those who in the eyes of the world don't deserve to be forgiven, even when it means watching the older brothers refuse to be part of the celebration.

We also know that it's not just our biological families that become divided. Paul's letter to the church of Corinth was written in large part because of the division that church was facing. Churches today also find themselves in the midst of division and strife. "There will be division," Jesus says. But why did Jesus say this to the people? To warn us? To assure us? To prepare us? I would say yes to all three. The thing is, Jesus didn't stop at telling us that there would be conflict and division. He went on to tell us that we need to pay attention to what's going on around us. If we continue reading in Luke, we discover that Jesus teaches that we need to work out our conflict.

I don't like conflict. It makes my stomach hurt; it makes me nervous. I prefer the text where we can kneel at the manger admiring the baby whom God sent to bring peace on earth, goodwill to humanity while the angels sing and the shepherds come to adore him. But the baby has to grow up, and so do we.

We are called to feel the heat of the fire and, like Moses, stand before the Pharaohs of our day—injustice, hatred, poverty—and work to free God's people for God's glory.

We are called to travel together on this journey of faith as we set our sights on the promised land, the land of milk and honey. And like the Israelites did so long ago, we must constantly battle the divisiveness that threatens to rip through the Christian community and set us at odds with one another—becoming stronger and more united as we all seek the same goal, living to bring God all the honor and glory. (Sara Shaver)

Lectionary Commentary

Isaiah 5:1-7

Through the prophet Isaiah's words, God reminds the people of all that they have been given that they might grow and flourish in the land that is provided for them. There is something very fulfilling in preparing the soil and planting seeds or new plants, then eagerly watching as the plants grow, carefully treating them with the appropriate fertilizer, keeping the weeds from overtaking them and choking them out. Several years ago the church I served had a community garden. Every day I would walk through the garden and marvel at the tomatoes, squash, beans, and eggplant as they grew. I was surprised at just how much joy I received in this simple exercise. I also remember the heartbreak in discovering that the beautiful squash blossoms did not produce fruit.

Hebrews 11:29–12:2

The author of Hebrews equates our journey of faith with a race. Runners know that keeping focused on what is ahead enables them to keep going. There is hope and encouragement in seeing the runners that are ahead. I remember my first semester of seminary. The first few weeks of Old Testament seemed insurmountable to me. But I would remind myself of all the students before me who had made it through. Some days it was the only thing that kept me from giving up and going home. The author of Hebrews offers encouragement and hope to readers by reminding them of the faithful who have gone before and the obstacles and struggles that God enabled them to conquer. (Sara Shaver)

Worship Aids

Invocation

Holy Lord, we have gathered as the family of God, each of us coming with our own ideas and understanding. Fill our hearts to overflowing with the power of your Holy Spirit that we might be renewed and refreshed, empowered to walk in your light. Amen.

Confession

God of wonder and mystery, so many times we come to this place of worship without much thought of what it means to be a part of the family of God. We go through the motions of worship; we compartmentalize our Sunday lives so that they don't interfere with the world in which we live. Forgive us, we pray, for seeking safety rather than justice, complacency rather than mercy. Enable us to recommit ourselves, our lives, that we might be faithful to your call on our lives.

Words of Assurance

God hears. God forgives. Thanks be to God.

Benediction

As we leave this place, we go out into the world where you have called us to reflect your light of love. Grant us compassion, wisdom, and courage as we walk in your will. Amen. (Sara Shaver)

Because We Can

Second in a Series of Three on Why Christians Do Missions

2 Timothy 1:1-14

April 1998. A storm system spawned a massive tornado that cut a mile-and-a-half-wide swath through neighborhoods in Norman, Del City, Midwest City, and into the greater Oklahoma City metropolitan area. I was pastoring a church that knew that it could do something to help the storm's victims. Before summer's end the church had sent three mission teams to Oklahoma, teenagers through people in their seventies, most of whom had never done hands-on missions work. In rented vans, with borrowed trailers filled with tools, they went and served because they could.

As the church, we have been changing the world through missions for generations. We know the stories from our grandparents and parents about the missions that we have shared. We collect items for survivors after tsunamis have swept their homes and businesses into history. We give money to help end malaria in our lifetime. We send teams to serve alongside the families salvaging what they can after the storm clouds have cleared and the people have been all but overwhelmed by the hurricane.

This sermon is the second of three that explore why Christians do missions. Our life together as a faith community has been formed and shaped by how we have served others; yet our shared missions work is about more than living a faithful legacy. We have overcome any fear or inadequacy or failure to do what we could in Jesus' name. Christians do missions because we can.

Paul writes to Timothy, "I'm reminded of your authentic faith, which first lived in your grandmother Lois and your mother Eunice. I'm sure that this faith is also inside you." Paul knew Timothy's family and their faith well. From the Acts we learn that Paul probably visited their town of Lystra at least twice. Paul likely received their hospitality and grew to know that Lois brought her daughter, Eunice, to faith. She, in turn, converted her son, Timothy. The women's legacy was Timothy's lasting faith, mentored by Paul, who guided Timothy to recognize and accept his own calling as a Christ-follower. Paul writes to Timothy, "Because of this, I'm reminding you to revive God's gift that is in you through the laying on of my hands. God didn't give us a spirit that is timid but one that is powerful, loving, and self-controlled" (v. 6).

While Paul's reminder is particularly to Timothy, his description of the spirit is true for any disciple of Jesus. Power, love, and self-discipline enable Christians to do missions.

We have power from the Holy Spirit. A spirit of power opens our senses to hear the cries of the pained and to see the emptiness of the needful. This power moves through our creative imagining so that we comprehend the ways that we can ease suffering and relieve distress. It enables us to assess and acquire the resources needed, bringing them into the situation to change the condition of the affected and afflicted. It provides us the incomparable joy of not only witnessing but also participating in efforts that change the world. We are given this power so we can use it.

We have love that creates compassion to care. A spirit of love compels us to be available to others when we become aware of their needs. This love is the practical response of the love we feel from God through Christ. It is the relationship Jesus prescribed for his disciples to have for one another. It is what moves us out of our comfort and complacency to ease the condition of the diseased.

We have self-discipline that guides our own choices. A spirit of self-discipline allows us to do for others without distraction. It clarifies the better options for identifying immediate needs and distinguishing the sequence of our tasks. It strengthens our confidence that as God provides for us, what we give will not diminish what we have. It frees us from ownership of the situation so that we are not patronizing those whom we help.

Christians do missions because we can. Our model is Jesus, who continually sent his disciples and followers to go and do. They did it because they could. We can too.

Christians do missions because we can look down the street to the women's crisis center and keep it supplied with the personal products that victims don't have time to throw into a bag when they have to escape danger. We can give a few hours across town with Habitat for Humanity, constructing a house that will be a family's new home. We can step into the situation a few states away, cleaning the mess after floodwaters recede. We can reach across the planet, helping others dig and build for life basics that we take for granted—clean water for homes and safe schools for children.

As we worship together, I am reminded of your sincere faith, a faith that dwelt first in your grandparents, and then your parents, and now, I am sure, lives in you. For this reason I remind you to rekindle the gift of God that is within you, for God gives us a spirit not of cowardice but rather of power and love and self-discipline. God gives us this spirit to fully live as God's people in this world.

Let this be a week when you prayerfully take an inner inventory. How are you exercising the power that God gives you? How are you using it in missions? How are you responding to Christ's love for you? Are you expressing Christ's caring in missions? How are you practicing self-discipline? How are you living beyond yourself in missions? Christ has called us. Jesus has told us what to do; and God has equipped us so that we can. (Dale Schultz)

Worship Aids

Invocation

This is a holy place, built on holy ground, dedicated and consecrated to the one, true God, whose power is beyond our imagining. God meets us here to receive our praise and to empower our faith, life, and faithful living.

Pastoral Prayer

Holy God, you amaze us with all that you do to and in and for and through us. Your Spirit overcomes our weakness and fear, strengthening us beyond our imagining and expectation. We pray that we may serve you with a confident boldness in the mission work to which you send us. In Jesus' name we pray. Amen.

Benediction

Receive and accept the faithful heritage that is your legacy from the saints who have gone before you. The Light of the World that shone through their lives now shines through yours. Go and serve because you can. (Dale Schultz)

AUGUST 25, 2013

Fourteenth Sunday after Pentecost

Readings: Jeremiah 1:4-10; Psalm 71:1-6; Hebrews 12:18-29; Luke 13:10-17

When Compassion Trumps Law

Luke 13:10-17

During Jesus' day, the temple was still the main place for Jews to congregate and worship on important religious holidays; however, the synagogue was the place where people would gather for the reading of the Law. It was a house of study. Apparently, Jesus was a regular attendee of the local synagogues (Luke 4:16). Picture him sitting among other teachers of the day, listening, asking questions, reading, and interpreting Scripture.

The stooped woman had come to the synagogue for reasons unknown to us. Maybe she wanted to hear Scripture read or interpreted? Maybe she was looking to be healed? Maybe a family member had simply brought her along? Who knows?

Whatever her reasons for coming, it's interesting that the woman makes no request of Jesus to heal her. She is not the one who approaches Jesus. He sees her and calls out healing to her. In other places we hear that someone's faith has helped to heal them. It is intriguing that nothing is said of this woman's faith before or after Jesus heals her.

Jesus takes the initiative and says to her, "Woman, you are set free from your sickness." But when the woman straightens up and begins to praise God after Jesus lays hands on her, the synagogue leader immediately calls foul! His objection is based on the fourth commandment, to remember and rest on the Sabbath.

In Jesus' day, there were certain codes of conduct and laws of appropriate behavior for the Sabbath. The Ten Commandments had been given after the Israelites were freed from slavery in Egypt. These laws were meant to help the new and free Israelite nation become the people of God by living in ways that honored God and built good human relationships. Through the centuries, the teachers of the law added and interpreted the commandments so that they became legal requirements. By Jesus' day, there were many things that one could or could not do on the Sabbath. The synagogue leader reminds Jesus of the rabbinic principle that healing on the Sabbath is allowed only in critical cases, not for chronic conditions. Jesus dodges the whole issue of healing on the Sabbath and focuses on the issue of meeting human need rather than the issue of healing. Jesus focuses on releasing someone from bondage and suggests that in doing so, he honors the Sabbath and keeps the fourth commandment.

Jesus asks those who question his actions to reason with him. He basically says, "If you'd do something for your animal, would you not also do it for another human being? If an animal were bound, would you not untie it from the manger and lead it to water on the Sabbath?" Surely what they would do for an ox, they would do for another human being.

Jesus plays on the Greek words for "bound" and "loose." If the law permitted the loosing of a bound animal for watering on the Sabbath, should it not be permitted for this woman—this daughter of Abraham—who has been bound for eighteen years? Can she not be loosed from Satan's bond? God delivered the Israelites, who had been bound in Egypt as slaves, so isn't the unbinding of this woman also a good thing?

Concern over the suffering of fellow human beings takes precedence over obligations related to keeping the Sabbath. Compassion always trumps law! Jesus challenges the religious community to think about what keeping the Sabbath really means. Does it mean just following the prescribed order of worship each week? Does it mean following the ceremony to the letter of the law no matter what happens? Jesus knows that religious people can be the most rigid kinds of folks when it comes to following a prescribed way of practicing their religion.

Jesus isn't abolishing the Law of Moses, but helping the people in the synagogue have a better understanding of how to apply the law. The laws were given to help enhance life, not stifle it. Compassion will be the rule for all who follow Jesus. Jesus performs an act of service for this woman that was overdue for eighteen years. The announcement of the good news is an invitation to celebrate. Jesus confers on the woman a status of dignity by calling her a "daughter of Abraham." The laying on of hands was a conferral of blessing.

We have our own written and unwritten laws. Christian churches have made rules, laws, regulations, and other prohibitions to try to protect the Sabbath. Laws have even been passed to force people to go to church. But what Jesus suggests is that the real idea behind the Sabbath is positive affirmation of humanity. We confuse the intent of Sabbath-keeping with our own ideas of rest or with that which makes the Sabbath restrictive and unpleasant.

Jesus reminds us that Sabbath is made for humankind and not humankind for the Sabbath. The commandment to remember the Sabbath and keep it holy does not give us exact instructions on how to do it, but Jesus reminds us that the command was not given to stifle life. God's concern for Sabbath-keeping is for the health and well-being of God's people.

Jesus is bold in taking the initiative to release this woman, knowing he will be questioned. We may wonder if we would do something that we knew was right, even if in doing it, we knew it would probably create a crisis or a controversy. Whether we admit it or not, every church has procedures and protocols for what is supposed to happen at church. Breaking with these and doing something to loosen the bonds for human need is not always popular, but it seems to be Jesus' way of remembering the Sabbath and keeping it holy. (Ryan Wilson)

Lectionary Commentary

Jeremiah 1:4-10

This is Jeremiah's call and commissioning from God. Those who have read the rest of the book of Jeremiah know that Jeremiah could never have imagined what lies ahead of him. He will face hardships and speak difficult words to the powers of his day. He will question his calling and discover how hard a task it is to be a prophet for God. His own resources will be found inadequate. But for the moment of his calling, Jeremiah is sure of God's hand in his life, although he still feels like a child. Jeremiah is assured that God will speak for him and that will be enough. How true for all who dare to speak God's prophetic word!

Hebrews 12:18-29

The writer of Hebrews has been making a case that the very same God who spoke to their "ancestors in many times and many ways" (1:1) is the very same God who has spoken through Jesus. In fact, God has spoken most clearly through Jesus, who is the "faith's pioneer and perfecter" (12:2). The revelation in Jesus is superior to the ways God spoke in the past. Now the author encourages the people to choose the path to Mount Zion and not go back to the ways of old. While Mount Sinai was a good place, where the law was given, through the new covenant in Jesus, they are marching on to Zion, the city of God. (Ryan Wilson)

Worship Aids

Call to Worship

Remember the Sabbath and keep it holy
Six days we are to labor and do our work
But the seventh day is a Sabbath to the Lord our God
For in six days the Lord made the heavens and the earth, the sea, and all that is in them
But the Lord rested on the seventh day
Help us remember that we were slaves in Egypt
But the Lord your God brought you out of there with a mighty hand and an outstretched arm
All: Therefore, help us remember the Sabbath and keep it holy.

Pastoral Prayer

Freeing God, thank you for delivering the Israelites from Pharaoh's strong hand of slavery. Thank you for leading them and giving them the Ten Commandments to guide their new life of freedom and responsibility. Help us see those commandments as words that give, and do not hinder, life. Help us view the commandments as words that offer, and do not restrict, freedom. Help us see your wisdom by helping us balance our lives with six days of work and one day of rest and renewal. Teach us how to remember the Sabbath and keep it holy. Teach us how to find rest, not through laziness or inactivity, but through a change from our normal routine. And may we honor it and keep it holy by always holding compassion for human need over any law of the land. In Jesus' name we pray. Amen.

Benediction

Now may the God who brought order out of chaos bring order to our lives. After working for six days, may God grant us a way to find rest on the Sabbath so that our bodies, minds, and souls will be renewed. May we not create laws that become binding and restrictive, but may our laws help us have order for finding life abundant and life eternal. Amen. (Ryan Wilson)

They Need Christ's Caring Now

Third in a Series of Three on Why Christians Do Missions

Matthew 25:31-46

His knock on my office door was so gentle that I almost didn't hear it while talking on the phone. The stranger was soft-spoken, apologizing for interrupting me, assuring me that he wasn't requesting a handout, then humbly asking if he could sit in our chapel and pray. He needed some time with God. Nodding yes, I pointed him in the right direction and finished my conversation.

Hanging up the phone, I felt a familiar nudging of the Holy Spirit and went to find our praying guest. I didn't want to disturb him; yet I did want to offer more hospitality than a curt nod and wave. He sat on the third row, head reverently bowed. I joined him, rustling as I sat so I might not startle him. He looked up, tearfully whispering, "Thank you for having the church open. I didn't know where else to come. I just need a little bit of Jesus right now. My wife's in the hospital. She got sick as we were traveling to see our new grandbaby. When the doctor said that she'll be okay, that she needed some rest, she suggested that I go for a drive to relax. I saw your church. I just need a little bit of Jesus right now. I was so afraid that the cancer was back—but this doctor said that the test shows that it's all gone. I had to come in here and thank God."

This sermon is the third of three that explore why Christians do missions. Every day, in every place, there's more than one somebody who needs at least "a little bit of Jesus." Christians do missions because there are people who need Christ's caring now.

We often recognize need when it affects members of our church family, and we respond through their Sunday school class, ministry team, or other small group that is their close community within the church. We seldom know the strangers' need. They are hesitant to allow us into their world because the church in our culture generally has a reputation of offering more judgment than grace. In spite of being afraid of us, some venture near, holding a hope that they will find something of Jesus on this holy ground.

Leaving for a lunch meeting, I didn't recognize the car parked close to mine. I couldn't see enough of the body slumped over the wheel to recognize the person. With phone in hand, poised to call 911, I approached the driver's side, hard sobs sounding through the open window. Reaching in, I gently touched her shoulder. Angrily, her words spat, "I'm not hurting anybody. Why can't I park here?!"

"You are welcome to park here," I said. "You're welcome to come inside too. Maybe we can help."

"Nobody can help."

"Maybe we can't, but we can sure listen well."

She reluctantly came inside and eased a bit when I asked one of our female staff members to join us. We sat in the office, listening to her cry. When her tears were exhausted, she furtively asked, "Will you really listen? I mean, really listen?"

We did, and we were able to help. She discovered that we really are about grace. That's why Christians do missions: there are people who need Christ's caring now.

Matthew writes this text as part of a private conversation between Jesus and his first disciples. It begins in chapter 24. Addressing their concerns about the "end time," Jesus answers questions about how they might recognize that it is close to the time when he will return to assess their faithfulness. We read and hear it as words between Jesus and you and me.

Listening to his words, we discover that Jesus places importance on faithful living in the here and now. Our faithful living has greater impact and is more important than any unknowable last day. Jesus says, "But nobody knows when that day or hour will come, not the heavenly angels and not the Son. Only the Father knows" (Matthew 24:36). If we live focused on an indeterminate when, then we will be oblivious to immediate needs. Christians do missions because there are people who need Christ's caring now.

We want, we need to ask Jesus: "Lord, when did we see you hungry and feed you, or thirsty and give you a drink? When did we see you as a stranger and welcome you, or naked and give you clothes to wear? When did we see you sick or in prison and visit you?" (25:37-39).

Jesus knows that we feed the hungry at the homeless shelter. We drill wells in the tiny villages of distant countries so that people may have good water to drink. We open our hearts and minds, and the doors of the church so that this sacred space—so that we, as the body of Christ—are available when someone "just needs a little bit of Jesus." We collect clothes for the crisis center. We support the clinics and hospitals around the world so that people have access to medical care. We go into the jails and prisons, loving people who have made less-than-best choices, and we proclaim forgiveness and new life.

And Jesus answers, "I assure you that when you have done it for one of the least of these brothers and sisters of mine, you have done it for me" (25:40).

Christians do missions because there are people who need Christ's caring now. (Dale Schultz)

Worship Aids

Call to Worship

Our need for God has brought us here.
We've come to worship God whose glory is great,
whose love is eternal.
Worshiping, we give our lives to Christ who gave his life for us.
Worshiping, we receive God's Spirit to live our lives for others.

Prayer of Confession

Lord, we confess that we are self-absorbed. Our selfishness fools us into thinking that this world revolves around us, tempting us to believe that you exist to fill our wants and needs. Please, forgive us, Lord. Let us see the world through Christ's eyes. Let us hear with compassion. In Jesus' name. Amen.

Words of Assurance

God forgives. God opens our eyes and our ears to hear the cry of need. Hallelujah!

Benediction

We are the church that lives for others. We are the people of Jesus who care completely. Leave to live as disciples and love well, in the name of the Father, the Son, and the Holy Spirit. Amen. (Dale Schultz)

SEPTEMBER 1, 2013

Fifteenth Sunday after Pentecost

Readings: Jeremiah 2:4-13; Psalm 81:1, 10-16; Hebrews 13:1-8, 15-16; Luke 14:1, 7-14

Guess Who Should Be Coming to Dinner

Luke 14:1, 7-14

When it comes to dinner parties, Jesus is not Miss Manners, but it is not because he did not get enough practice. Jesus and the disciples eat their way through the Gospels. They go from place to place, house to house, one meal after another, always looking for the next invitation. Most of us cannot imagine not knowing where we will eat our next meal.

Even at that, it is surprising that Jesus would eat at a Pharisee's house. The Pharisees criticized Jesus for blasphemy (because he forgave sins), for uncleanness (because he ate with sinners), and for working on the Sabbath (because his disciples plucked grain from a field). As dinner begins, the Pharisees are watching Jesus carefully. Put in Jesus' place, we would be on our best behavior—careful not to talk with food in our mouth or put our elbows on the table. Dinner at a wealthy Pharisee's house—and wealthy Pharisee is redundant—is more than two forks ostentatious. You know the rules. RSVP within a reasonable amount of time. Bring a suitable gift. Do not unfold your napkin until your host does. Use your napkin only to gently blot your mouth when needed. Use your utensils from the outside in. Do not push a plate away when you are finished. Place your knife and fork at ten and four o'clock angles to indicate that you are done. Once you have used a piece of silverware, never place it back on the tablecloth. Do not leave a used spoon in a cup. Place it on the saucer. Never lay a napkin on the table until the dinner is over. The host signals the end of the meal by placing his or her napkin on the table. And do not refold it or wad it up!

As we might picture it, the table is magnificent, the crystal chandelier shining, the servants attentive, the centerpiece impressive, and the champagne chilled. All the "right people" are there—bankers, doctors, lawyers, preachers. Jesus is invited not because he is considered an equal but because he is a curiosity who has been in the news. The esteemed guests are watching closely to see how Jesus fits in. The table talk is polite, as expected, centering on the new director of the symphony and the buy-out of a local factory producing matzo balls.

Jesus decides to offend the guests. This scene becomes a lesson in how to lose friends and alienate people. Jesus has noticed how the Pharisees look for ways to move up the social ladder—or up the table, on this occasion. He has seen how they try to sit at the places of honor.

We have been in those awkward situations when we are a guest in someone's home, standing before the dinner table, not sure where to sit. Most would not take a place at the end of the table, the seat of honor, unless, of course, the host invites us to do so. This kind of common sense would seem to be what Jesus is suggesting, but it is more than that.

Jesus criticizes the guests for striving for status. "When someone invites you to dinner, you take the place of honor. Then when somebody more important than you shows up, you're red-faced as you make your way to the last table and the only place left. You might as well go and sit at the last place in the first place. Then the host might say, 'Come, sit with me.' If you walk around with your nose in the air, you're going to end up flat on your face. Be content to be yourself."

We still live in a classed society. Ethnic groups, immigrants, the poor, the homeless, the addicted, and the mentally ill face uphill battles. Lower class, middle class, upper class—we know the class in which we reside.

When Jesus finishes insulting the guests, he begins to insult the host for who was included and who did not make the list: "The next time you put on a dinner, don't just invite your friends, family, and those you're trying to impress, the kind of people who will return the favor. Invite people who don't have similar interests, who never get invited out, the misfits from the wrong side of the tracks, the least of our sisters and brothers, the poorest of the poor. They won't be able to return the favor, but God will know."

The disciples want to pull Jesus to the side and say, "You might want to back off a little. First you went after the seating protocol, and as if that wasn't rude enough, now you've gone after the guest list. Our host is an influential person. He could do good things for us. All you have to do is act friendly and keep your elbows off the table. We won't have any more dinner invitations if you can't get through the appetizers without infuriating the person who invited us."

Why does Jesus have to stir up trouble? Why does he criticize people who invite him into their homes? Why can't Jesus leave a pleasant-enough dinner party well enough alone? It is because Jesus understands what is at stake. We have to learn that at God's table there is no need to jockey for position, because all are equally welcome. There are no throwaways when it comes to human beings. Christians are to honor the least among us—the poor and marginalized. While the Pharisees were striving to move toward the head of a rectangular table, Jesus' table is a round one where no person is better than another. The character of our guest list—who is on it and who is not—has everything to do with whether or not we are being Christ's church. The followers of Christ have to learn that any table where Jesus is present is a table where everyone is welcome, a foretaste of the heavenly banquet, a foreshadowing of the kingdom where God cares for all and all we can do is give thanks. (Brett Younger)

Lectionary Commentary

Jeremiah 2:4-13

We find it hard to respond positively to harsh criticism, even when it comes from one of God's prophets. A certain sadness lies beneath the harsh tenor of Jeremiah's rebuke. Just before this passage begins, Jeremiah shares God's message: "I remember your first love . . ." (2:2). In forgetting their first love, the people of God committed two evils, forsaking God and searching for "living water" in the deserts of idolatry. Jeremiah calls God's people back to a love that was lost.

Hebrews 13:1-8, 15-16

The writer of Hebrews offers a simple hope: "Let mutual love continue" (v. 1 NRSV). Mutual love requires that you welcome the stranger as if you needed welcome. Love the prisoner as if you were in prison. Cherish your spouse as you desire to be cherished. Love in such a way that never fears to lose, for we will never be lost from the embrace of Christ. The writer of Hebrews reminds us that the church stands as a community to "do not neglect to do good and to share what you have" (v. 16 NRSV). (Brett Younger)

Worship Aids

Prayer of Confession

Gracious God, you searched our hearts. Forgive our self-centeredness. Forgive the way we ignore the hungry and the hurting, even some very close who need our love and concern. Grant us peace and a new opportunity to know your grace. Amen.

Words of Assurance

God knows our hearts, and God forgives. Thanks be to God.

Pastoral Prayer

Let us pray for every person who will die today
because they do not have enough to eat;
God, hear our prayer.
For the nations, that we might repent of policies that tolerate poverty;
God, hear our prayer.
We pray that the priorities on earth might mirror those of heaven;
God, hear our prayer.

Benediction

The blessing of the one who overturns the world and ensures the lowly a high place, the blessing of the God of Life, the blessing of the Christ of Love, and the blessing of the Spirit of Grace be with you always. (Brett Younger)

Remembrance

First in a Series of Two on the Past and Future of the Church

Matthew 28:19

One of the gifts of being a district superintendent in The United Methodist Church is to discover in some depth the rich history of the churches in one's district. Upon worshiping with the congregation at Brownville, Nebraska, I learned that the church was organized in 1854 as the Kansas-Nebraska Territory was being settled. The Brownville history told of the "great meetings" and conversions in its early years. Methodist Classes were formed. The spirit of the early pioneers was evident with each year of history recounted in Brownville.

The history of the Brownville United Methodist Church is typical of many Methodist churches in America. The Brownville Church was organized by a circuit rider from Missouri. Other churches were started with pastors sent out from Indiana. It was a wide-open frontier in geography and in potential converts. The circuit riders would meet people where they were and that was often in the town saloon.

Today, the fruit of the circuit riders can be seen in communities such as Brownville. Traveling through the small communities of Nebraska today, one will almost always see a United Methodist church, a Roman Catholic church, and a bar, even if there is no other business.

I was born and raised Methodist in Cozad, Nebraska, a community of about four thousand when I was in high school. There were eighteen churches in Cozad, and the Methodist church had more than one thousand members. Like many others of my generation, I grew up knowing the church played a significant role in the life of the community.

Lyle Schaller points out that in 1771 one in two thousand fifty North Americans belonged to the Methodist movement. By 1965 one in fifteen Americans belonged to the Methodist Church (Lyle E. Schaller, *The Ice Cube Is Melting* [Nashville: Abingdon Press, 2004], 28). Methodism was growing, along with other mainline churches. The Roman Catholic church and Protestant churches of many denominations were growing rapidly. Traveling down Northwest Highway in Dallas today, one can see monuments to the growth of the institutional church with Southern Baptist and United Methodist church campuses as large as those of many colleges and universities.

The church's growth occurred not only in numbers but also in influence. Clergy and lawyers have long been significant players in shaping U.S. social policy and have held positions of respect and authority in our society. While the U.S. constitution promotes the separation of church and state, the church has long been a successful partner in shaping our culture.

Into the twentieth century the pioneer spirit was evident in the church. Manifest destiny lived alongside Jesus' commandment to "Therefore, go and make disciples of all nations" (Matthew 28:19). The nation's movement west was accompanied by a passionate Christian evangelism.

Peter Cartwright was a Methodist circuit rider with a rugged evangelical pioneer passion. Cartwright was a large man of stature physically and spiritually. Here is a small slice of Peter Cartwright's life, as he tells it himself. In the early days of his itinerant ministry in backwoods Kentucky, there was a tavern kept by a notorious bully. His loud and repeated boast was, "No preacher gets past here." Cartwright was riding circuit in that neighborhood; he had heard the boast, but kept right on riding. News of the preacher's coming was carried to the tavern keeper, who came out as he saw Cartwright approaching. The bully ordered the preacher to turn back or be beaten up. Peter Cartwright never liked to be "ordered" by anyone, not even, in his later years, by all the bishops of the Methodist Episcopal Church! He got off his horse, and the fight was under way. He soon had the tavern keeper on the ground and pummeled him lustily, while singing, "All Hail the Power of Jesus' Name." He made the bully promise to stop interfering with preachers. But Peter had to sing three verses before the man agreed! (Halford E. Luccock and Webb Garrison, *Endless Line of Splendor* [Nashville: United Methodist Communications, 1992], 50–51.)

Peter Cartwright's fervor for spreading the gospel, illustrative of the nineteenth-century Christian spirit in North America, was the kind of fervor that resulted in exponential growth for the church. Just as Christ and his disciples, and the disciples of the first-century Christian church experienced, outward movement of the Spirit resulted in growth in numbers, growth in institutional structure and church buildings, and growth in cultural influence. The pioneer evangelical and missioner spirit, however, has left the church, and the Brownville Church and others like it are dying. It is time for revival! (Dan Flanagan)

Worship Aids

Call to Worship

We come to worship the God of creation,
the God who gave us Jesus Christ, and the God of our church.
Help us worship as our ancestors did, with God at the center.
We open our hearts to the spirit that led our pioneer foreparents.
May we experience their spirit and the Spirit of the living God.

Prayer

We are thankful, Lord, for the church we have inherited. Your spirit has moved your disciples throughout the years, helping many experience and receive the gospel. Your church has flourished through the power of our

Holy Spirit as your disciples have been led to new frontiers. We pray for a rekindling of that spirit through the church of Jesus Christ. Amen.

Benediction

Receive your inheritance. Move out in the power of the Holy Spirit that has nurtured your ancestors. Go and make disciples. (Dan Flanagan)

SEPTEMBER 8, 2013

Sixteenth Sunday after Pentecost

Readings: Jeremiah 18:1-11; Psalm 139:1-6, 13-18; Philemon 1-21; Luke 14:25-33

Counting the Cost

Luke 14:25-33

We would rather assume Jesus thinks what we think than listen and follow when we find what he says to be hard. We learn to compromise because Jesus' way is difficult. We live with one foot in Jesus' world of peacemaking and one in the old world of wanting our own way. We live with one foot in Jesus' world of seeking justice and another in the world that ignores injustice. We live with one foot in Jesus' world, where we are concerned about poverty, and another in the world of greed. We live with one foot in the world of reconciliation and the other in a world, where we just do not care. We allow the pressures of family life to obscure our call to serve the world. We let money seduce us—so enmeshing our lives in things that we miss the purpose of living. We avoid the crosses, problems, and possibilities of genuine discipleship.

The multitudes are following Jesus because they think he is building an empire. They have heard about this new superstar who tells great stories and helps unhappy people. The crowds think the trip to Jerusalem is a parade. It will be a story to tell their grandchildren, "Did I ever tell you about the time I walked with Jesus? What a party that was!"

Jesus knows this is a funeral procession. The crowds think they are following Jesus, so he wants them to know where he is heading. His attitude is the opposite of most preachers. He is distressed when crowds show up, because he assumes they would not be there if they understood the cost. What Jesus has is a church-growth guru's fantasy—a mass of people ready to sign up. All Jesus has to do is to woo them, entertain them, give them tempting glimpses of comfort, success, and happiness, and then he can haul them in. With a little marketing, Jesus could easily break membership records and receive all kinds of praise. Instead, Jesus offends them. People talk about the Roman Road to salvation, but seldom mention the Lukan Road—hate loved ones, carry a cross, and follow Jesus.

Step 1—Hate loved ones. Jesus has a lengthy list of people to hate: father, mother, wife, children, brothers, sisters, and self. Our first reaction is to want to explain why Jesus does not mean what he is saying. We would like to take the edge off these hard words by suggesting that the word translated as "hate" must mean something else. The Greek word is *miseo*. It means hate. This is Jesus at his hyperbolic best. He uses exaggeration to startle the listeners. If it is necessary, you turn your back on your family. He makes us ask, "Do I really want to follow Jesus rather than some less demanding messiah?"

Step 2—Carry a cross. What could be more despicable in the ancient world than carrying in public the instrument of your own death? The Romans reserved crucifixion for slaves and foreigners. The condemned person was first scourged, then forced to carry a cross to the place of execution. Roman soldiers stripped them of their clothing and fastened the victims to the cross with nails. Nothing is more shameful than carrying one's own cross. To bear a cross is to choose the consequences of suffering with Christ—telling the truth when it is hard, working for justice for the poor, loving enemies, listening to the lonely, and caring for the lost.

Step 3—Follow Jesus. Anyone following Jesus needs to know that he is going to Jerusalem to be killed. Christianity is following someone headed in a direction we would not normally go. Jesus is trying to tell us, with absolute clarity, that nothing—not family or work or possessions—can take precedence over God. We are to subordinate our relationships, let go of everything we own, and give up on hearing applause.

Instead of talking about happiness, Jesus talks about towers and wars. Which of you intending to build a tower, does not first sit down and see whether you have enough to complete it? Count the cost before you say that you are going to follow. What king, going to wage war, will not sit down first and consider whether he is able with ten thousand to oppose the one who comes against him with twenty thousand? Jesus is a king making sure that his army is really committed: "Anyone who won't shoulder a cross and follow can't be my disciple."

We may feel as if Jesus is saying that we will never do enough. This talk of counting the cost and fighting the battles would be completely discouraging, except for this—we get Jesus. It is often when it is hardest that we discover that Jesus is with us. Have you ever had a week where everything goes wrong? You know you are trying to do what is right, but nothing is working. Then there is a moment when you feel Christ with you, caring for you, holding you.

When we become utterly dependent upon the grace of God, when we live in partnership with Christ, when we listen to the promptings of the Spirit—then we find our way to hope. God carries us when we cannot carry any more crosses. God nurtures us when family pressures have drained us dry. God keeps seeking, finding, and forgiving us when we get buried in anxious living. God helps us live in the way of Christ, with compassion, an alternative to the jungle of selfishness around us, with generosity, in opposition to the marketplace of greed, with love, treating people as friends and not problems to be solved. Jesus is demanding, but he is also loving, caring, and forgiving. The one who demands everything also gives everything—meaning, comfort, and joy. Costly discipleship is not easy, especially when the world makes counterclaims, but the question becomes, "Are you willing to give up your limited life to truly live in Christ?"

If we follow, that is what we get. We get Jesus. (Brett Younger)

Lectionary Commentary

Jeremiah 18:1-11

The scars and scratches that life gives us may make us look broken and outcast, but God can make us brand-new. God works with the imperfections in our lives like a potter wielding great power. The potter offers another chance for us to turn now and be made new.

Philemon 1-21

Saint Paul was serving one of his periodic sentences behind bars when he met Onesimus—a slave who belonged to a friend named Philemon. When Onesimus had done his time and was about to be sent home, Paul composed a letter for him to give to Philemon. Paul urges Philemon to receive Onesimus not as a runaway slave but as "a dearly loved brother." Philemon has a list of reasons not to set this slave free, but no matter how he rationalizes it, he knows that if he listens to his heart he will always be able to hear the voice of God calling him to see every person as God's child. It used to be easy to think of Onesimus as a slave, but now he has a letter in front of him that says he is a brother. (Brett Younger)

Worship Aids

Invocation

Spirit Divine, open our eyes, ears, and hearts. Help us see one another with your grace, hear your still, small voice calling us to love, and know in our hearts that we are sisters and brothers. Teach us to give our hopes and lives to your church. Amen.

Pastoral Prayer

Look around the sanctuary for someone who seems to be in distress, or just tired or lonely, and in the silence pray that he or she will be surrounded by God's loving presence. (*Pause for silence.*) Ever present, ever loving God, help us pray for one another and learn to love one another. Amen.

Benediction

Go in faith. Go in hope. Go in peace. Go in joy. Go in love. For the source of faith, hope, peace, joy, and love goes with you. (Brett Younger)

Hope

Second in a Series of Two on the Past and Future of the Church

Matthew 28:19

The morning I worshiped in the Brownville Church, there were eight people in worship. This single-roomed, wood-framed church stood as an historical monument in a town rich with history, and sadly represents the state of the contemporary North American Christian church. There were eighty-two members and forty-two probationers in the Brownville Methodist Church in 1874. Today there are fifteen members.

Lyle Schaller notes that the ratio of United Methodists in America dropped from one in fifteen in 1965 to one in twenty-nine in 2000 (Lyle E. Schaller, *The Ice Cube Is Melting* [Nashville: Abingdon Press, 2004], 28). The United Methodist Church has lost more than three million members in the last four decades, and one can find similar trends in all of the mainline denominations. Some nondenominational, more conservative, and evangelical churches have shown growth, but overall, people are generally not choosing institutional Christianity as they were in the early twentieth and late nineteenth centuries. Participation in the Christian church is declining across the board, and the church's influence has also waned. The context for doing church in the twenty-first century has changed, but the church has not.

Gil Rendle argues the conversation for the contemporary church must center around three questions: (1) Who are we? (2) What has God called us to do? and (3) Who is our neighbor? (Gil Rendle, *Journey in the Wilderness* [Nashville: Abingdon Press, 2010], 40) The first is a question of identity, the second a question of purpose, and the third a question of context.

The United Methodist Church has been uniquely diverse theologically and socially, which has been both a blessing and a curse. Who are we today? What gifts do we have to offer one another and the kingdom of God?

The question of purpose is not a call to formulate a plan of activities for the coming year, it is a challenge to discern what God's call is for the church today. The decline in numbers is devouring much of the church's energy presently. We must create a new and hopeful story for the future church. What difference are we called to make in the lives of people? If our purpose can be found in the Great Commission, how do we live out the commandment to make disciples for the transformation of the world?

The answer to the first two questions must come in the context of our mission field, which today is much different than it has been at any time in the history of America. We find the third question addressed in Scripture by the parable of the good Samaritan: Who is our neighbor? Our neighbor is not defined by family ties, national identity, or theological prescription. Our neighbor is the one who is in need.

Our contemporary context for ministry is changing radically. As Thomas Friedman suggests, the world is truly flat. There is clearly a lack of homogeneity within North America's borders, if it ever existed at all. The difference today is not simply language barriers, but also skin color. Our neighborhoods reflect the colors of the rainbow, but our churches remain predominately white.

The church is in the midst of a time of learning. How do we love God and love our neighbor? The evangelical spirit of the pioneers has settled into the comfort of worship services within our buildings. The world outside the church buildings is changing, but it is difficult to change a permanent structure, whether it be the building or the people within.

The future church can learn from Jesus, who worshiped regularly in synagogues or the temple, but whose ministry was itinerant. Jesus pushed the boundaries of his contemporary church, irritating Jews by ministering to Gentiles, challenging Jewish law, and relating to the most vulnerable through table fellowship and healing. Jesus' life of prayer and worship clearly displayed a love of God, and his itinerant ministry reflected a love of neighbor.

If contemporary Christians are to make disciples for the transformation of the world, we must respond to the needs of our neighbors outside the walls of the church. One of the new-start churches in my district, Water's Edge United Methodist Church, has the vision of providing central worship on Sundays but moving into the neighborhoods with small group gatherings to teach the gospel, offer fellowship, and respond to the needs of the community. Another new start in the district, Wesley Pub, gathers at a bookstore in the Old Market area of Omaha for conversation that is theologically based, socially relevant, and attractive to young professionals. Both models are relational, community based, and innovative ways to make disciples for Jesus Christ.

Research shows the younger generations are spiritual, but they are not deeply interested in the institutional church. They are, and I might suggest most people are, interested in how they can make a difference in the lives of their neighbors. Contemporary North Americans remain spiritually hungry, but their passion for ministry will first be played out in the mission field, not the sanctuary.

The future church must regain the pioneer spirit that led to the growth in North American Christianity, and in the early church. We must reclaim the evangelical spirit that led the circuit riders into the lives of pioneers where they were, even in the saloons. Today our new disciples are in the streets, the schools, the local coffee shops, and on the soccer fields of their children. What is God calling us to be? Certainly not a sedentary people in the pews, but a dynamic people in mission to our neighbors. (Dan Flanagan)

Worship Aids

Call to Worship

Like Israel in Babylon, we are a valley of dry bones.
Our church is desperate and cut off.
Our story is one of decline and death.
We come to be renewed,
to reclaim the power of the Holy Spirit,
to create a new story of hope.

Prayer

We are a fearful people. After years of growth our church is fading in numbers and in passion. We have grown self-serving rather than as missioners. The command of Christ to make disciples rings hollow, and our resolve to respond to the needs of our neighbor is diminishing. Move us beyond our walls, O Lord. Help us create a new story around the hope offered through Jesus Christ. Move us into a world that more than ever thirsts for the gospel. Amen.

Benediction

Go forth to serve armed with the same Spirit that led our pioneer ancestors. Claim the hope of a loving God through a church founded by a resurrected Christ. (Dan Flanagan)

SEPTEMBER 15, 2013

Seventeenth Sunday after Pentecost

Readings: Jeremiah 4:11-12, 22-28; Psalm 14; 1 Timothy 1:12-17; Luke 15:1-10

Feeling Lost

Luke 15:1-10

Jesus is having dinner with a crowd that is lost and wants to be found, but has not recognized it yet: tax collectors and sinners (we might say Democrats and Republicans, the low-downs, and the no-accounts). Every once in a while the ones who think themselves the best and brightest complain about the way Jesus treats the worst and dimmest as if they are his long-lost friends, "Why are you eating with these people?"

For the umpteenth time, Jesus tries to explain: "God is a shepherd with a hundred sheep who loses one, because sheep are always wandering off. Ninety-nine out of a hundred sounds pretty good. Most shepherds wouldn't be upset, but God leaves the ninety-nine in the wilderness—where they are vulnerable to wolves, wandering off, and lots of other mischief—to go out in the dark to find the poor lost one. God beats the bushes, because no one is expendable."

This good shepherd tramps about in the chips scattered through the pasture, pushes through the briars, and listens for snakes, while looking for the sheep with the black spot on the right shoulder. He finally hears the "baa" of the lost sheep. He lovingly puts it on his shoulders, as if he is caring for a lost child. One of the neighbors asks, "Why did you risk leaving ninety-nine to go looking for just one?" God replies, "Let's have a party."

Jesus looks at the church people and asks, "Do you get it?" They do not, so Jesus tries again: "God is a woman who has lost a silver dollar. She still has nine left. Losing one isn't going to break her, and yet she acts as if it's all she has. She pulls up the carpet in her living room, moves all of the heavy appliances out of the kitchen and the furniture into the front yard.

She searches relentlessly until she sees the shine of the coin that has rolled into the corner. God runs out into the yard and calls to everybody up and down the street, 'Let's have a party.' "

"Now do you get it?" God's purpose is to drag everybody into the party—saints and sinners alike. Jesus eats with anybody, because everybody is lost and needs to be found. Jesus seldom called people "sinners." What he called them instead was "lost." Lost sounds more like concern than condemnation. Some days we feel more lost than found, more wrong than right. We have acted like unthinking sheep wandering off. We have felt as helpless as lost coins unable to resist the force of gravity. We have felt like the percussionist in a string quartet, or like everybody else knows something we have not figured out, or like we have got lettuce stuck in our teeth and we are the only ones who do not know it, or like we will always fall a few points short on the "are you a good person" test.

So many things make us feel lost: the sudden loss of a job, debts we wonder if we will ever pay, a disabled child, the pain of a broken marriage, a long illness, an unrequited love, the loss of someone we love. We feel lost when we realize that we do not do what we want to do. We feel lost when we get what we thought we wanted and it is not enough. The worst feeling may be when we realize that we do not even know what we really want. We feel lost when we lose our patience, our sense of humor, our integrity, or our sense of purpose. We feel frustrated, weary, and vaguely troubled. We feel lost even when we are at home with the people who love us most. We wander off and cannot think of any reason anybody should come looking for us.

The shepherd is walking through the thickets in the middle of a stormy night. The woman is looking for the needle in the haystack, diligently sweeping the dust out of the way, shining a light in the dark corners. God keeps seeking our company, trying to show us the good life. God looks for us through caring people, sacred stories, prayer, and worship. God is a hope that pursues us, a comfort that gathers us home, and a love that embraces us.

We are never as indifferent to God as we might think, for the "lost" feeling is the longing for grace. We need to pay attention to the whispers of God's love, because we are not deaf to the sound of God's voice. We can live in grace beyond what we understand. When we accept the truth that God accepts us, the parts of us that embarrass us do not usually vanish, but they are changed in the light of grace. We do not suddenly lose our short tempers, vanity, sharp tongues, and talents for self-promotion and self-delusion, but we are found by a goodness that helps us accept all that we are. We learn to rely on God more than we rely on ourselves.

God knows that we have problems letting go of everything of which we need to let go, of doing all that we think we should do, and of becoming all that we think we should be. What we most need is to do nothing at all. What we most need is to let ourselves be loved. We need to let God punch our ticket "forgiven" and join the party. For the one gift that matters ultimately is God's grace.

God cares passionately that we be well and that we find our way home. God keeps searching for everyone who is lost—lost sheep, lost coins, lost insurance agents, lost teachers, lost mothers, lost daughters, lost people like us. We are here because we know what it is be lost, and we know what it is to be found. Our story is of wandering off yet being sought, being wounded yet healed, confused yet cared for, broken-hearted yet loved, foolish yet forgiven, lost yet found. (Brett Younger)

Lectionary Commentary

Jeremiah 4:11-12, 22-28

The word *jeremiad* means a "speech expressing a bitter lament." Jeremiah is the origin of the word. In this passage it is clear how the prophet contributed to that meaning. God's people are "foolish," "thoughtless," and "inept" (v. 22). God's furious anger will make the earth "without shape or form" and with "no light" (v. 23). As bad as it will be, "I will not destroy it completely" (v. 27).

1 Timothy 1:12-17

Paul is trying to encourage his young friend in a new pastorate at the church in Ephesus. If, as some scholars suggest, Paul did not write First Timothy, it was written by someone who had been reading Paul's diary. Paul has been a loving spiritual mentor to Timothy. What does Paul tell his young friend is most important? Paul says that faith does not begin with our capabilities, but with God's grace. It does not matter how smart Timothy is or what he has accomplished. What matters is that God gives him the grace he needs more than he needs anything else. (Brett Younger)

Worship Aids

Call to Worship (Psalm 100:1-3)

We come each Sunday like lost sheep. Listen to one of the hymns that the children of Israel sang as a call to worship:

Shout triumphantly to the LORD, all the earth!
Serve the Lord with celebration!
Come before him with shouts of joy!
Know that the LORD is God—
he made us; we belong to him.
We are his people,
the sheep of his own pasture.

Pastoral Prayer

Loving God, remind us that we are here because you invite us, seek us, come to us, and embrace us. We are here because as a shepherd seeks a lost sheep, you seek us when we are lost. As a woman searches for a lost coin, you rejoice when we are found. Teach us to give thanks. Amen.

Benediction

We followed Jesus in here. We have sung, prayed, and listened, so that we can follow Jesus out of here—to our homes, schools, offices, and neighborhoods. Jesus loves us and the ones who did not join us for worship, so we should love them too. (Brett Younger)

Why Leviticus?

First in a Series of Two on Lessons from Hebrew Law

Leviticus 18:1-5

The Hebrew faith rests firmly on the law, and the book of Leviticus is all about the law. There is nothing historical in the book except the consecration of the priesthood and the punishment of Nadab, Abihu, and Shelomith's son. Because most of the laws are ecclesiastical laws and contain the laws and ordinances of the *Levitical* priesthood, the book is called *Leviticus*. The Levites were primarily charged with living and teaching these laws.

The book of Leviticus is basically divided into the Priestly Code and the Holiness Code. In chapters 1–7 we have laws regarding different types of sacrifices. The practical application of these laws is given in chapters 8–10. Chapters 11–16 are laws concerning purity and impurity.

The Holiness Code is found in chapters 16–27. The commandments found here are not just for the priests but for the whole community. The laws cover: idolatry, the slaughter of animals, and consumption of blood; sexual conduct; miscellaneous things; the priesthood; the Sabbath and annual feasts; the altar of incense; blasphemy, application of the death penalty, children insulting their parents, and prostitution; the Sabbath, Jubilee years, and slavery; a hortatory conclusion including the commutation of vows.

The Hebrew term most frequently translated as "law" in the Old Testament is *torah*, used more than two hundred times. The basic concept of *torah* is that of instruction about how to live. In the Old Testament this came to be known as a way of life for faithful Israelites.

Law is a primary concept in the Bible. The translation of what this means varies. Specifically this can refer to a commandment, a word, a decree, a judgment, a custom, or even a prohibition. The first five books of the Old Testament (the Pentateuch) are known as the books of the Law because they are based on the commandments God revealed to Moses. However, the *Torah* is more than just "laws," it is the story of God's dealing not only with Israel but with humankind as well.

In the Old Testament the idea of *torah* is closely linked with the concept of covenant. The covenant between God and the people at Mount Carmel became the foundation of all Israel's laws. The exodus from slavery in Egypt for the Israelites became God's basis for requiring obedience to his commandments (Exodus 20:2). The specific laws found in Exodus, Deuteronomy, Numbers, and Leviticus cover all areas of life. The *Torah* is seen as God's gift to his people. Furthermore, obeying the Law would result in blessing (Exodus 19:5, 6). Following the Law promised health and wholeness for the covenant community. It should be pointed out that the Ten Commandments summarize all of the Law (see Exodus 20:2-17; Deuteronomy 5:6-21).

Later development in Israel's history brought forth an expanded meaning to the Law. By New Testament times *Torah* came to mean not only the Hebrew Scriptures (the written Law) but its interpretation over time (the unwritten Law) as well. Law then referred both to the will of God in the Old Testament and the "elders' rules" (compare Matthew 15:2; Mark 7:5; Galatians 1:14). In our next lesson we shall look at what the New

Testament says about these laws—particularly what Jesus and Paul believed.

Why should we study Leviticus? First, its Mosaic authorship and divine inspiration are attested by the Lord Jesus. Both Jewish and Christian traditions state this. Second, its purpose reveals Leviticus was written to show Israel how to live as a holy nation in fellowship with God. Israel, like Christians today, had to be taught the holiness of God. This was done in three ways: (1) in the sacrificial system, which insisted that "there is no forgiveness without blood being shed" (Hebrews 9:22; see Leviticus 17:11). This points out the seriousness of sin; (2) the precepts of the Law, which revealed a divine standard of conduct and character; (3) the penalties attached to violations of the Law, which spoke of divine holiness.

How can people know what to do without some standard of conduct? Is conscience enough? Is the human mind an adequate guide? Who would be so foolish as to insist on his or her own private moral thinking as a standard for everyone? If everyone makes their own ethical decisions, not imposing on themselves any other thinking or instruction, the result is disastrous. The period of the Judges reflected this with these words: "each person did what they thought to be right" (Judges 21:25). We must have laws and interpretations of those laws.

There are many references in Leviticus to the importance of keeping the law. We all know that without law, life is chaotic and intolerable. Without law, society is fragmented and tends to destroy itself. Law protects the weak, provides for interaction among the people, makes for social justice, and gives us a sense of identity as God's people. The Law made the people of Israel a distinct people. David emphasized the importance of the Law to the people of God in Psalm 1:2: "these persons / love the LORD's Instruction, / and they recite God's Instruction / day and night!"

When the *Torah* is removed from the holy ark during worship in synagogues today, the worshipers rise. Respect for the Law and the God who gave it is still needed. Although the Levitical priesthood and sacrifices are now gone, the spiritual realities they pictured abide for all time. For this reason the study of Leviticus is helpful to all. (Drew J. Gunnels Jr.)

Worship Aids

Pastoral Prayer

Heavenly Lord, thank you today for the blessings of our relationship with you. You remind us of our failures and lovingly encourage us in our successes. Your Law reminds us of your holiness, and your forgiveness reminds us of your grace. Thank you for such guidance and goodness. In Jesus' name. Amen.

Prayer

May God the Father, the Son, and the Holy Spirit bless, preserve, and keep you; may the Lord's favor rest upon you and may the grace of God be with you today, tomorrow, and forever. Amen.

Benediction

Depart today with a growing appreciation for the law. Remember God's admonition and promise spoken by Moses: "You must keep my rules and my regulations; by doing them one will live; I am the LORD" (Leviticus 18:5). Amen. (Drew J. Gunnels Jr.)

SEPTEMBER 22, 2013

Eighteenth Sunday after Pentecost

Readings: Jeremiah 8:18–9:1; Psalm 79:1-9; 1 Timothy 2:1-7; Luke 16:1-13

Crying God's Tears

Jeremiah 8:18–9:1

Anyone paying attention asks, "Where is God?" from time to time. When someone asks, "Did you read that horrible story in the newspaper?" the response is usually, "Which one?" Pick up any day's paper and it reads much the same. Here an accident, there a murder, everywhere a tragedy: floods and tornadoes, massacres and bombings, household beatings and drive-by shootings, fires, drownings, and death notices for infants in the obituaries. Column after column, page after page laments the news of blood and tears.

And we do not need the newspaper to tell us about broken hearts. When we gather in the sanctuary, we put on our best face, but we bring a variety of heartaches. The daily toll of a parent with Alzheimer's. A sick child. The pain of a broken marriage. The loss of a job. The challenge of a terminal illness. The anguish of an unrequited love. The loneliness that follows the loss of a loved one. Some days your diary reads like the book of Job. Some days it seems as if everyone is dealing with a crisis.

Two thousand six hundred years ago, Jeremiah was in the middle of a crisis surrounded by broken-hearted people. The prophet wrote cheery devotional thoughts like, "The sound of sobbing / is heard from Zion. / We're devastated!" (9:19). He told the women of Jerusalem, "[T]each your daughters to mourn; / teach each other to grieve. / Death has climbed / through our windows" (9:20-21). Jeremiah has good reasons to despair. Judah is in the twilight of her history. The nation is breathing its last. Babylon has demolished most of the city and torn down the temple.

The armies of Nebuchadnezzar have stolen the best stuff and the best people. Jeremiah cries out:

> Is there no balm in Gilead?
>   Is there no physician there?
> Why then have my people
>   not been restored to health?
> If only my head were a spring of water
>   and my eyes a fountain of tears,
> I would weep day and night
>   for the wounds of my people. (8:22–9:1)

Jeremiah cries out, "God, where are you?" We know how it feels not to understand why there is so much suffering. When tragedies strike, we want an explanation for why God is not doing what we want God to do. At times we want to blame God, and at times we want to defend God. God does not keep us from all harm, and yet we want to pretend that divine protection still makes sense. The truth is that accidents take no detours around good people. Sorrow comes as part of the broken, random rhythm of the world.

About twelve years ago I got a call to come to the hospital; a husband had died. When I got there, the widow was crying in inconsolable grief. After a few minutes, I asked if I could pray with her. I began the kind of prayer that ministers pray in the emergency room when someone has died.

"God, thank you for being with us during this difficult time."

She surprised me by responding loudly, "God, I feel so alone."

I thought maybe I was too quiet or too slow or saying the wrong thing, so I tried to pick up the pace.

I prayed, "God, thank you for the hope you give."

She shouted, "God, I don't feel any hope."

I prayed, "God, thank you that in some ways this good man will always be with us."

She screamed, "God, I can't believe you took him."

My prayer was not angry enough. My prayer was not going to do. It was not getting there, and she knew it. She had to take over.

I prayed, "God, thank you that you will get us through these difficult days."

She yelled, "God, I'm ready to go right now."

Our prayer went on for several minutes. I would offer a platitude, and she would speak the truth. She was right. Mine was the prayer of a religious person trying to sound religious. Hers was the prayer of an honest soul, a person whose heart was broken. Like Jeremiah, she had God by the lapels, in both hands, and was crying in God's face, "I don't think you're listening."

When your child gets hurt, you try to comfort the child. You say, "It'll be all right." You do not mean that the child's pain is unimportant, because you know life is hard. You do not mean that everything is going to be all right in this moment, or that everything will work out in this particular circumstance. What you mean is that finally, ultimately, in the biggest picture, eternity is structured in such a way that things will be all right. The pain will not last forever. When we say, "Everything will be all right," it is because we believe that God will love us forever. We do not sing, "Is there a balm in Gilead?" we sing "There is a balm."

God listens to our cries. God hears our problems. God knows our needs. God understands our pain. God feels our anguish. God cares about our troubles. God works on our behalf, bringing joy where there is death, healing where there is illness, peace where there is violence, reconciliation where there is hatred, the presence of the Spirit where we feel all alone. We may not get all of the answers we want, but we get all of God's love. (Brett Younger)

Lectionary Commentary

1 Timothy 2:1-7

Most Christians do not make a habit of praying for government leaders in worship. Christians should entreat God on behalf of believers as well as all people in authority. The author of 1 Timothy suggests this on the basis of monotheism. There is, as this early Christian hymn says, one God and one revelation, Jesus Christ. The gospel is for everyone.

Luke 16:1-13

This parable is not anybody's favorite for good reason. There is not a single good person in this story. The main character, the one Jesus praises, is Bernie Madoff with a pyramid scheme. Biblical scholars have attempted all kinds of contortions to make sense of this story, but maybe it is not that complicated. Jesus tells this story to say that not nearly enough people do anything out of the ordinary. What does Jesus say at the end of his parable? "The people who don't go to church are better at taking chances than most of the people who do. We have a lot to learn from people who use their imaginations." (Brett Younger)

Worship Aids

Call to Worship

We are here to acknowledge God, remember our heritage, and give ourselves to being the people God intends. May God confront and challenge us, inspire our praise, enliven our prayers, move our hearts, our minds, and our wills. Teach us to worship in Spirit and truth.

Pastoral Prayer

God of the ages—past, present, and future—you are with us now in our sorrows and will be with us in eternal joy. Teach us to recognize the signs of your presence. Give us faith to live in the hope that will lead us home. Amen.

Benediction

May God's peace go with you into the worlds in which you live. Be challenged by this time of worship. Be faithful in the time apart. Love and serve by the grace of God. (Brett Younger)

Hebrew Law and the Practicing Christian

Second in a Series of Two on Lessons from Hebrew Law

Romans 7:14-25

Having looked at the Law from the Hebrew perspective in Leviticus, let us turn our attention to the Law from the perspective of the New Testament. Our focus will be particularly what Jesus thought of and taught about the Law, what Paul the apostle thought, and what we as modern Christians have experienced.

The words of our Lord are the appropriate introduction to our subject. That he knew and respected the Law is obvious to any serious student. Some of the Old Testament laws seem to apply only to specific times, places, and people. The Ten Commandments, however, were given not only for the Hebrew people but also for all God's people. They have an abiding quality, revealing duties for all and speaking of the basic morality to which God calls us. As we shall see, Jesus paid particular attention to these laws.

Adding to the complexity of our subject is the realization that Jesus was both a supporter of the Law and a critic of the Law. Jesus repeatedly quoted the Law in his teaching. If one's interpretation of the Law included the "tradition of the elders" or the "oral Law" that had grown up around the Law, then Jesus was sometimes critical of the Law. It is clear in the New Testament that keeping the letter of the Law had become more important than the purpose behind it. Because Jesus pointed this out, his enemies accused him of breaking the Law.

The Pharisees accused Jesus and his disciples of not following the Law with regard to unclean things (see Matthew 15:1-20). They were also disturbed because he ate with tax collectors and sinners (see Matthew 9:11). However, the greatest conflict came over the Sabbath. He rejected their teachings and declared he was Lord of the Sabbath (Matthew 12:8) and the Sabbath was made for people and not people made for the Sabbath (Mark 2:27). In addition, Jesus taught it was permissible to do good on the Sabbath (Mark 3:4). Nevertheless, Jesus taught that he did not come to destroy the Law, but to fulfill it (Matthew 5:17-20). Jesus was more concerned with inward motivation and intention than outward observance. In this sense he moved to a deeper level, affirming the heart and spirit of the Law from the beginning.

Perhaps our Lord's greatest statement about the Law was given when he was asked which commandment was the greatest. Jesus summed up all the Law with a new Law. "You must love the Lord your God with all your heart, with all your being, and with all your mind" (Matthew 22:36, 37). Then he added, "You must love your neighbor as you love yourself" (Matthew 22:39). Finally, and with great importance to our subject, he added, "All the Law and the Prophets depend on these two commands" (Matthew 22:40).

We know true Christian love is not a matter of rules or regulations. If we want to live our lives beyond legalism, we must take the approach to the Law Jesus took and live his kind of love, a love that was ultimately demonstrated on the cross of Calvary. In this way we can obey the Law, spread his message, and live peaceably with God and our neighbors.

In addition to the position of Jesus regarding the Law, Paul the apostle gave significant insight for practicing Christians (Romans 7). In a rather simplistic approach some modern Christians believe and preach you can replace the experience of Paul in Romans 7 with the peace of Romans 8. Exegetical study, however, does not substantiate this viewpoint. For one thing, all the verbs in our text are present tense verbs, indicating this is current experience for Paul at the time of his writing. Paul, like many of us, had a lifetime struggle with the Law. If one could have some dramatic spiritual experience and not have to deal with this inner struggle, Paul never indicated it.

Why would he encourage us to "press on toward the goal" (Philippians 3:14 NRSV) or "Compete in the good fight of faith" (1 Timothy 6:12) if there was no fight? Paul struggled the way we must struggle.

When Paul referred to the Law, he meant the Law of God as contained in the Old Testament. Paul also wrote of a natural law that exists in human beings. For him the "law of sin" (Romans 7:23) means conduct determined by sin. Paul also referred to the "law of faith" (3:28), or conduct determined by faith in God.

Paul acknowledged that the Law had been given for a good purpose, but this Law could not save (see Galatians 3:11; Romans 3:20). He also stated the demands of the Law were not evil but that the Law pointed out sin in our lives. However, because of our sin, the Law became a curse rather than a blessing (Galatians 3:10-13). It is faith that saves, not the Law (Ephesians 2:8).

We all feel the perplexity Paul felt in trying to live the Christian life. From the beginning of the Christian life to its end, we are at war with the gods of this world (see Romans 7:23). Like Paul, we often find we are two people. We are like Dr. Jekyl and Mr. Hyde in Robert Louis Stevenson's writing. We are animal and angel, saint and sinner. We have both horns and halos. In each of us there is the breath of God and the dust of the earth.

The Law, interpreted by the Spirit of God, tells us of our sin. According to Jesus, we hear the sound of God's Spirit, but do not know what it is (see John 3:5-8). The Holy Spirit of God, the wind or breath of God, will convict us. When the error of our ways is pointed out, we must repent. We must seek forgiveness. That we sin is not in doubt because all are sinners. If we repent, we are forgiven (1 John 1:8-9).

For all of us the Law as contained in the Ten Commandments is ours to obey. These ten declarations are not suggestions to be considered but laws to be obeyed. The additional commandment given by Jesus about loving God and our neighbor is just that, a commandment. In this sense the Law is for all people for all time! (Drew J. Gunnells Jr.)

Worship Aids

Pastoral Prayer

Heavenly Lord, when we are confronted with our disobedience to your laws, may we not only repent but also seek diligently to walk in the light of your teachings. We pray that we may live peaceably and be good witnesses of your grace. Amen.

Benediction (1)

May we depart with new allegiance to all the law, especially those commandments given by our Lord. May our focus be to love you supremely and our neighbor as we love ourselves. Amen.

Benediction (2)

O God, remind us that you want for each of us the best life. We realize this is the reason you gave us the Law. May we see your laws as guideposts to free us, not fenceposts to restrain us. Amen. (Drew J. Gunnells Jr.)

SEPTEMBER 29, 2013

Nineteenth Sunday after Pentecost

Readings: Jeremiah 32:1-3a, 6-15; Psalm 146; 1 Timothy 6:6-19; Luke 16:19-31

Hallelu-Yah!

Psalm 146

We enter and exit Psalm 146 with the Hebrew exclamation "hallelu-Yah" that we translate as "Praise the LORD!" Everything is thus framed with praise, and while that affirmation may work in Scripture—for a psalm, a hymn—it does raise some significant questions.

We sing of consistent praise as aspiration, or inspiration. But, if that's the case, then where's the interpretive key that lets us know, "Oh, framing everything with praise isn't a just claim we make but a goal we claim?" Maybe it's just understood: if you sing it, you can exaggerate, saying just a little bit more—or a whole lot more—than is true.

In our study of Scripture, however, we discover that hallelu-Yah is actually an imperative command, not an exclamation or assertion. *Hallel* means "a joyous praise in song, to boast in God"; *u* means "ye"; *Yah* is the first two letters of the name of God, Yahweh (or YHWH)—praise ye the Lord—a command.

And so now we have the idea that everything should be framed in praise, and that feels better. The psalm offers us an interpretive key that praise is a direction in which we should move, whether we do or don't and to whatever extent we have or have not.

That kind of gets our backs up, doesn't it? Seems it's easier to live with an asserted aspiration we may or may not mean than with a command that we either obey or disobey. If hallelu-yah constitutes the beginning and the end, we have to consider what it frames. It suggests that everything is contained therein, well beyond the particulars of this psalm. Everything? And remember—it's a command. More than theological affirmation or spiritual direction, this is spiritual dictate: frame everything with praise. Everything? That's pretty unrealistic. That's pretty naive. Praise with an utter disregard of circumstances? I don't think so.

But the initial command ("Praise the LORD!") is followed by a rather extravagant claim in response to the command—that the psalmist will sing praises to God "as long as I live" (v. 2). We have someone, in other words, claiming to obey the initial command.

That's followed by a warning about trusting political leaders, which is not really all that unusual in the psalms. But here in Psalm 146, we move from the warning about not trusting in princes to not trusting in "any human beings" (v. 3), which is everybody, including us. There's no help there, we're told; they die and their plans die with them (see v. 4).

Trust rather in God. And we're given a beatitude: "the person whose hope / rests on the LORD their God— / is truly happy" (v. 5) We have the contrast established between not trusting in human beings and trusting in God, not trusting in those who die and trusting the eternal one. We are presented with two choices. Choose wisely and well, the psalm suggests.

Then, in the flow of the psalm, God is identified as creator ("the maker of heaven and earth"), as sustainer ("faithful forever"), and as redeemer ("who gives justice . . . bread . . . free[dom] . . . [sight] . . . [love] . . . protect[ion]" (vv. 6-7). God is identified as being that is doing, being made manifest in wondrous deeds on behalf of the oppressed and the hungry. This is the heart of the psalm.

Note the symmetry. Matched with the beatitude of verse 5 is the identification of those blessed by God, whose help and hope is God: the prisoners, the blind, the bowed down, the righteous, the stranger, the orphans, and the widows. Matched with the warning about not trusting mortals in verse 3, we have the wicked brought to ruin in verse 9. If we don't heed the warning—if we do trust in mortals (even ourselves)—then we participate in wickedness.

As we move on to the conclusion, we have the claim—countering or balancing the claim to praise God as long as the psalmist lives—of the eternal sovereignty of God. So we have God's eternity and the finitude of a lifetime, which brings us back to the opening and closing command to praise God. Now, at the end of the psalm, the command is more sober—more realistic. Now we know that praise is most appropriately focused, not on the one who praises, but on the one who is praiseworthy. Here at the end we celebrate the good news that we rely, not on any faithfulness of our own, but on the faithfulness of God. And thus we can praise even within our ever-changing circumstances because of our unchanging God. We can praise with assurance and with trust; and we praise as the consistent expression of our faith.

Learn this, the psalm asks of us. Know this, the psalm demands. At the heart of everything lies who God is. The heart of the psalm is the heart of reality, the heart of God. And who God is, we know in what God has done and in what God does—divine being made manifest in doing. And so we do not rely on what anyone else says or does, not even on what we say or do, but always on who God is and on what God does. Therein we find the power with which to live through all that life brings our way, into the way of God. Hallelu-Yah! (John Ballenger)

Lectionary Commentary

Jeremiah 32:1-3a, 6-15

In all the itemized details of the transaction in which Jeremiah buys a field, we are offered highly symbolic prophetic action. In response to what he understands God wants of him, Jeremiah buys land in the very face of enemy occupation. He invests his money as an expression of trust in God's word that these circumstances too shall pass, that there is a future beyond the very clear and present fear and danger. Jeremiah concretely invests in his faith.

Notice how many times Jeremiah refers to the word of God, grounding his otherwise incomprehensible actions in his understanding of the word of God present to him. This text offers us a worthy focus for our own understanding of our faith: how do I act in concrete ways that are comprehensible only in light of the word of God?

1 Timothy 6:6-19

What a word for our culture! The author of 1 Timothy offers clarity of insight into what it means to be content, pinpointing the risk of locating contentment in anything earthly. In words as relevant today as they ever were, this epistle warns of the senselessness of the desires, of the mindless hunger that drives individuals ever onward, from one thing to another, in the ongoing search for fulfillment.

Oriented appropriately to the surpassing value of claiming eternal life now, we are set free from that which tempts us to use that which could possess us in service to others.

Luke 16:19-31

It's the story of Lazarus. It's Luke's story of Lazarus, the poor man outside the rich man's estate. And they both die. Lazarus goes to heaven.

The rich man does not. In the ensuing conversation between heaven and hell, the rich man in torment asks father Abraham to send Lazarus to his family to warn them about the terrible consequences of how they're living. Abraham dismisses the request, saying, "If they don't listen to Moses and the Prophets, then neither will they be persuaded if someone rises from the dead" (v. 29). It's Luke's story of Lazarus. Because John's story of Lazarus is, of course, the story of someone who does rise from the dead. So does someone need to rise from the dead to bring home the profound significance of how we live? (John Ballenger)

Worship Aids

Unison Call to Worship

Who and how our God is, defines who and how we are to be. So it is that love, with its passionate concern for the other, pulses its transformative power through our living and shapes us ever more into the image of God in which we were created.

Invocation

We praise you, our God, with our whole being. Even our questions and doubts praise the mystery that transcends them. Our deepest hopes praise your promises. Our most profound hungers praise your fulfillment. Our richest commitments praise your dreams, and our entire being praises your love. We praise you, God.

Pastoral Prayer

We want to offer you our praise, God, but the circumstances of our days get in the way: the stresses, the griefs, the busyness, the fatigue. How do we get beyond the preoccupations that haunt us? Can you please be born amidst the specifics of our living and redeem us? (John Ballenger)

Humble to a Fault—Managing Humility

First in a Series of Four on Jesus Speaking on Asset Management

Luke 18:9-14

He or she is "humble to a fault." We have all heard and perhaps used the phrase. Someone is overly gracious, deflects compliments, and seems to try to blend in so that they go as unnoticed as possible, all the while secretly enjoying the praise and adoration and perhaps continuing the behaviors initiating the original praise. They are too humble, abnormally gracious, and suspiciously covert in their good deeds.

This phrase may have been one to describe the Pharisee in our parable. He is a leader in the synagogue and the community; he keeps the laws and often goes above and beyond what is required. He most likely helps his neighbors out on the weekends and apprentices young men in the synagogue to follow in his footsteps. He knows he is a good man. He knows he is living a good life, one much better than that of the tax collector who tries to disappear from view.

In fact, the Pharisee is such a good man that he sees the need to remind God, and all those within hearing distance of his goodness, lest anyone forget. He stands alone, choosing not to pray in community or with others, and so draws attention to himself. His words are egocentric, each sentence tallying his status in society as well as his adherence to the laws. He even goes so far as to remind God that there are some, even in his very midst (isn't that convenient?) who are not nearly as holy and righteous as he is.

This draws our attention to the tax collector, who wants anything but attention. He is also standing off from the crowd, but for a different reason. The tax collector feels he is unworthy to be in the company of someone with the status and assumed righteousness of the Pharisee. He even feels unworthy to be praying, refusing to look toward God in heaven. He beats his chest and names himself a sinner in need of mercy. The two characters in the story could not be more different.

The Pharisee is the one the hearers would expect to be the righteous one in the story. There are high expectations placed on him with respect to his duties and status in the community and synagogue. He knows the laws and the Scriptures; after all, he is reminding God of his adherence to them. However, his humility is overblown. He plays the role of the righteous one too well. He dictates to God with pride and arrogance. All the while, the tax collector is despised from the beginning of the story. Tax collectors took advantage of their public role to openly steal money from their neighbors. This man makes his living to the detriment of others. He is easy to dislike and a likely target to be the "villain" in the parable. And yet, he is immediately interesting because of his humility. It is unexpected, and thus grabs our attention. He suddenly becomes more human. His humility is appealing and inviting, especially after witnessing the arrogance of the Pharisee.

We are left wondering which character is better than the other. We ponder which one we are more like, or who we would rather be. Is it a question of the lesser of two evils? The Pharisee is expected to be gracious and humble because of his knowledge and adherence to the laws and religious customs, and yet his behavior is deplorable. The tax collector is publicly despised, and yet in the synagogue his actions and prayers are authentic and true. So which is better? Would you rather fall short of the expectations set before you in public and boast before God; or is it better to be authentically despicable in public and repentant and genuine before God?

The root of each man's humility is centered in different places. The Pharisee acts as if God owes him for his good deeds, but really, don't we all? Who hasn't prayed, "Why me, God? Why is this happening to me?" The Pharisee lacks a sense of his humanity and sinfulness, insisting rather on his holiness and righteous spirit. The longer he prays, the more obnoxious and arrogant he appears. He inadvertently makes the argument for his sinfulness on his own. The tax collector is very much aware of his shortcomings. He knows he has failed God and neighbor and begs for mercy. His humility appears authentic, perhaps because he is clearly aware of his need for forgiveness, or perhaps because society would likely be unwilling to let him forget his stealing from the community. Regardless, his humility before God invites us to want to be more like him.

The parable is clear in its conclusion. The Pharisee receives his reward by the attention he receives in the synagogue, which is probably what he wants, anyway. The tax collector's request for forgiveness results in his exaltation in the eyes of God.

People are not always as they seem. Motives are hidden and are often misguided. The parable reminds us that we are not the ones to judge others' appearance or actions, that is left up to the heart of God. Humility can be deceiving, especially when it is done to a fault. Amen. (Victoria Atkinson White)

Worship Aids

Invocation

God, we come before you with full lives and even fuller hearts and minds. Help us empty ourselves so that we might leave full of your spirit. We humble ourselves before you as your children, our God and our Lord. Amen.

Pastoral Prayer

Gracious Lord, too often our prideful hearts get in the way of our relationship with you. Help us rely on you for our reward rather than seek the approval and praise of others. Let pleasing you be reward enough for us. Amen.

Benediction

Go in peace, seeking the favor of God so that your deeds may not be exalted here on earth but rather in heaven, for the reward in heaven is eternal and everlasting. Amen. (Victoria Atkinson White)

OCTOBER 6, 2013

Twentieth Sunday after Pentecost

Readings: Habakkuk 1:1-4, 2:1-4; Psalm 37:1-9; 2 Timothy 1:1-14; Luke 17:5-10

Write the Vision

Habakkuk 1:1-4, 2:1-4

Habakkuk starts with a complaint, levied as blame, "Things are not good, and it's your fault, God." It isn't just a matter of believing that as a child of God, the prophet has a peculiar perspective on the world; as a child of the world, he has a peculiar perspective on God. Habakkuk was particularly interested in the issue of justice (or the lack thereof) and understood injustice as both an affront to God (God's character) and a challenge to God (God's authority).

"What else to do," he asks, "with this obscene juxtaposition between you and all I believe you to be and the way things are? What do I do, God, with the contrast between professions of faith and my experience of the faithful?" It's really not so much an angry complaint as the deeply pained cry of a bewildered, confused, and passionate believer.

Given the professed centrality of God in the lives of the people of God, shouldn't that have been the common complaint at the time of Habakkuk—a consistent, public outcry? Instead we get the prophecies of some obscure person, not mentioned anywhere else in Scripture. This cry should have been the people's prophecy—from the armchair, dinner table, barroom stool, car pool, soccer sideline, water cooler at work, sanctuary pew, checkout line prophecy—the people's complaint, grief, bewilderment, and confusion.

But the voices of the people were not raised up. And when "the people" are silent on an issue, it falls to individuals to speak up—individuals who cannot abide the implicit and dreadful contradiction, the awful juxtaposition and the unbearable silence. And so prophecy becomes that of the individual, prophet and preacher only by default.

Habakkuk acknowledged what everyone should have acknowledged and said what everyone should have said. So today, Habakkuk would read our newspapers and demand of God, "Explain homelessness to me. You created, in your own image, a people who send people into space, who build things that have to be seen to be believed, who can do the most amazing things, medically, some of whom can afford virtually any military expenditure they desire—and yet they allow their own sisters and brothers to go hungry. Explain this to me, please. Were you not clear enough about taking care of the vulnerable in society? And given that they are not taking care of the vulnerable, why are you not?"

"Explain to me a budget that can apparently be balanced only on the broken dreams and the broken lives of the most vulnerable. This doesn't reflect well on you, God."

"And let me get this straight, people are at war to promote standards they're willing to break in order to fight the war? How do people justify lowering standards to claim they're protecting a higher standard?"

"And why is it tolerated that race and socioeconomic factors have such an impact on the process of justice? If imbalances in the scales of justice are observed, shouldn't they be corrected? Are you uninterested in justice, God, or just unable to do anything about it?"

But national news, international news, and God are not all part of one conversation for us. We don't believe God manipulates circumstance. The rate of violent crime, the statistics from our prisons, the news from the Middle East—that's not God at work. And if God's not pulling the strings of circumstance, then why bother having God be in on the conversation? Why bother having God expectations impinge upon political realities? It is tricky holding elected officials—or national and international policy—to godly expectations. And yet, it's not that we have such expectations of our elected officials because they are Christian, but because we are.

The principle of separation of church and state has been too much misunderstood as the church not having anything to say to the state—not having legitimate faith-inspired expectations of the state—rather than, more appropriately, that the church shouldn't get any favors from the state, nor the state from the church. The goings-on in the world are not acknowledged as part of the goings-on of God, leading to the perception that God really doesn't seem to have that much going on. If we segregate our faith affirmations and expectations from our day-to-day life and our public life, where do we stop? If we start separating conversations: "Okay, that one can have God in it; that one can't," then what conversations does God remain a part of? And from how many important conversations is God eliminated?

What if we were to invite God back into the conversation? "Things aren't good, God. Not all your fault, we know, but we're going to complain to you anyway. We're going to pray and include you in our assessments of our world, our living, and our hopes. We're going to watch for a word from you." Interesting, don't you think? Watching to see a word?

"Then the LORD answered me and said, / Write a vision" (2:2). Write down a vision of a just society, a world in which people take care of one another. Write a vision of the world and of a God in whose image we are created, whose image we can live up to. Write it down so we have something to which to compare the way things are, something to contrast with what we accept and justify. Write it down so we won't forget the best vision we have. Write it down so we have a word to make flesh. Ah, may it be so. (John Ballenger)

Lectionary Commentary

2 Timothy 1:1-14

According to Acts, Timothy was from Lystra, the son of a Jewish mother and a Greek father (Acts 16:1-3). The beginning to this letter is relationally expansive. We start with one person, Paul, in relation to God through Jesus who is thus related in love and respect to his ancestors and to another person, Timothy, and to Timothy's family—his mother and grandmother. Maybe it's even more expansive than that—encompassing not just people in relation, but faith traditions in relation—respectfully acknowledging different beliefs, while in no way minimizing the difficulty of relating deeply from different perspectives.

Luke 17:5-10

A largely unacknowledged dimension to discipleship is the cultivation of healthy self-esteem. Jesus regularly puts his disciples (then and now) in their place! For, as we learn in this text, on the one hand, we could do so much more than we do, and, on the other hand, what we do is no more than is expected. So it is that amidst our extraordinary calling to God's way of living and loving, Jesus will not allow us to get the big heads! Don't you think Jesus offered his disciples the sayings that comprise today's text with a smile? Part pleasure, part amusement, part affection—all true. (John Ballenger)

Worship Aids

Unison Call to Worship

In the interplay of what God has to teach us about our world and what our world has to teach us about our God, we gather to worship—to cultivate amidst the story we live the story we believe, and to sustain the hope they might converge in Jesus' name.

Invocation

In your word, our God, we most clearly see a vision of creation as it might be, full of mutual respect and acknowledged interdependence. As we invoke your presence and your will, may we invoke, as well, our commitment to that vision in Jesus' name.

Benediction

Go from here in the power of God's word—which shaped all that is, has been in dialogue with humankind from the beginning, was made flesh in Jesus, and seeks still to be made flesh in us—working always toward the redemption of all creation. (John Ballenger)

Approaching Jesus—Managing Loss

Second in a Series of Four on Jesus Speaking on Asset Management

Matthew 9:9-26

The scene is set for chaos. Jesus is sitting at dinner with tax collectors and sinners. The act is unexpected, scandalous, and definitely worthy of our watching. Jesus is breaking bread with the dregs of society, people who would draw attention to Jesus and his disciples because of their lack of status and the general disdain in which they are held. Just as our sensitivities are heightened because of the scene, the first burst of chaos breaks into the story.

A public official interrupts the meal with Jesus and makes an absurd request. He is a leader in the community and has likely been a part of plots to overthrow Jesus. He would hate all that Jesus does and stands for. He lives according to the orthodox customs and appreciates order and the status quo. All of his connections and status in the community cannot help his desperate situation. His daughter has died and naturally, his sense of loss is overwhelming. No parents should have to witness the death of their child. He is at his wits' end, and so he turns to the only hope he has, though he has never before had any hope in Jesus. The grief-stricken father says, "come and place your hand on her, and she'll live" (v. 18). It is as if he is not asking for much—just for Jesus to extend his hand to his daughter.

The next character in the story doesn't think she is asking much of Jesus either, in fact she doesn't even bother to address him. She simply slips behind Jesus and reaches out her hand to touch his cloak. Her act is also one of desperation and grief. She has been hemorrhaging for twelve years and is thus ostracized from the community. She lost the ability to worship in the synagogue because she is considered unclean by the priests. She feels she has lost everything in her estrangement, and she too is at her wits' end. She wants to rejoin her family and friends. She wants her life back. Twelve years is too long to suffer and grieve the life she once had before this illness took over. She has heard of Jesus and his miracles, and so she has hope. Perhaps he could be the one to heal her, save her, bring her back to life. And now she sees Jesus getting up to follow a man whose daughter has died, presumably with the intention of restoring her life. She seizes her chance to have her life restored as well, and she grasps the miracle worker's cloak. She hopes no one will notice; they never do, except to tell her to get out of the way. She just wants to experience a little bit of his power to restore her life. In faith, hope, and desperation, she extends her hand. In an instant her faith heals her. She disappears from the story as quickly as she appears.

The story returns to the public official and his dead daughter. The scene weeps of overwhelming grief and loss. All the accoutrements of a proper grieving process are present. The flute players are wailing their sad tunes while the professional mourners are moaning and crying as if they had known the girl since birth. We might find such pageantry related to death absurd, but it was the custom of the day for those who could afford it. And then Jesus says something unexpected. He commands the mourning to stop. It is not needed. The girl is not dead; she is asleep. The audacity of his words evokes laughter from the crowds. The father, however, did not laugh and did just as Jesus said, dismissing the crowds. As quickly as the hemorrhaging woman was healed in the previous encounter, the girl awakens and gets up. The loss turns into gain alongside awe and jubilation.

These two characters teach us valuable lessons about how and when we approach God. Somehow we have convinced ourselves that we have to be at our very best (ever heard of "Sunday Best"?) before we approach God. We think we need to be freshly forgiven of all our sins and in the right heart and mind before we come to God. The public official and the hemorrhaging woman were hardly at their best. They were, in fact, at their very worst. They had nothing left to lose, nowhere else to turn, and no one who could help them. They had exhausted all their options, so that Jesus was their only hope. They were drowning in their loss.

We find ourselves in a similar spot when we experience loss. We feel we have nowhere to turn and no one to fill the void left by our loved one, our lost health, job, opportunity, whatever it may be. At this point we are kin to the characters of today's scripture. It doesn't matter how or when or why we approach Jesus. Jesus simply beckons us to him. The public official who previously had no faith found it in desperation. The hemorrhaging woman had at least enough faith to seek Jesus out and touch his cloak. Each reached out to Jesus, and Jesus responded. God does not want our lives to be filled with suffering and loss, but with praise, worship, happiness, and fulfillment. God is always ready and waiting for us to reach out with little or great faith so that God can help bear our burdens and restore our lives.

So how are you feeling? When do you approach God? Do you wait until you are in your Sunday best? There is no need to wait. God invites us now and always. Won't you come? Amen. (Victoria Atkinson White)

Worship Aids

Invocation

God, we meet you in this place as your children. We do not boast of being perfect or flawless; rather we seek your guidance and wisdom in becoming more like your Son, Jesus Christ. Fill our hearts and minds as we worship you. Amen.

Pastoral Prayer

God, we come before you in need of greater faith. There are those among us who feel empty because of death, separation, or loss. Let them feel your presence close by so that, as those who have gone before, we may seek you out for healing and renewal. Amen.

Benediction

Come, all who have lost and seek to be found. God beckons those with little faith alongside those with great faith. Go from this place knowing that you can come before God regardless of where you are in your spiritual journey. Amen. (Victoria Atkinson White)

OCTOBER 13, 2013

Twenty-first Sunday after Pentecost

Readings: 2 Kings 5:1-3, 7-15c; Psalm 66:1-12; 2 Timothy 2:8-15; Luke 17:11-19

The Initiating Word

2 Kings 5:1-3, 7-15c

When we encounter the same story repeated with variations in person and place, we expect that the plot will consistently unfold (throughout circumstance and experience).

Our story opens in the kingdom of Aram, where Rimmon, the thunder and weather god was worshiped, and we begin with the mighty and the powerful. Look at the lineup of words to describe Naaman's world of power: a king's general, a great man, highly regarded in high favor, a victor in battle, and a mighty warrior. These are the traits that engender admiration and envy in our world. Yet Naaman had a terrible skin disease.

Within this impressive description of power, we overhear a conversation between a slave girl and Naaman's wife, "... the prophet who lives in Samaria. He would cure him of his skin disease" (v. 3). The wife held the slave girl in enough esteem to tell her husband. He in turn approached the king, who sought to help his valued general by writing a letter to the king of Israel.

As is often the case, the words of the powerless, claimed by the powerful king, are distorted within all the expectations of power. You have to wonder where the message got lost in the translation. The slave girl explicitly said Naaman had to go to the prophet to be cured, and the text says that Naaman told his king exactly what she said, but in the letter, the king of Aram expects the king of Israel to engineer the healing.

The king of Israel reads the letter, tears his clothes, and says more truth than he knows, "Am I God to hand out death and life?" (v. 7). And so this king, who has spent his life pursuing and accumulating power, now stands in torn clothes, terrified that someone might actually expect mighty acts of power from him. And Elisha sends word, "Send Naaman to me. Send him where he was supposed to come in the first place. Send him to me, and let him learn of the power of God."

In the second story within the larger story, Naaman has just been told by Elisha's servant to wash in the Jordan River. He's angry at the insolence of the prophet who doesn't even deign to show his face but sends a servant instead. He's angry at what the servant tells him to do. Naaman's angry he's still sick. He's angry he's got to go back home still sick. He's angry that in spite of everything, he had begun to hope, and his hopes have been dashed. He's angry that the prophet didn't come out, make some strange gestures, mutter some arcane words, even anoint him with some unknown substance, and heal him.

Unlike the king of Aram, Naaman knows he has to go to the prophet; but like the king of Aram, he misunderstands the whole power thing, or he understands God's power in terms of the power he knows—military and political power. In the midst of his ranting, his servants approach him. "Our father, if the prophet had told you to do something difficult, wouldn't you have done it? All he said to you was, 'Wash and become clean'" (v. 13). And Naaman held the words of his servants in enough esteem to wash in the Jordan, and he was healed.

So Naaman, restored to health, makes his way back to the prophet's home. He wants to reward Elisha, but the man of God refuses the riches. Imagine that! Then Naaman asks for dirt. He goes from offering silver and gold to asking for dirt. It's such a rich image. It's Naaman having made a connection to and with the God of Israel, the creator God who so long ago took of the earth and shaped us all, Israelite and Aramean. And as Naaman prepares to go back to his home, he seeks a tangible connection to this God of Israel, now also the God of Naaman.

As he thinks about returning, something else occurs to him. "There is one thing. I need a pardon in advance. I am God's now. I will worship no other. When I get back to Aram though, the king will expect me to accompany him to worship Rimmon, and he will lean on me, as he always has, in his house of worship. Unlike before, it will be only the king who worships, but I know that it matters that I will be where I, as a child of the living God, should not be. Forgive me." And so it is that we end our story with the image of Naaman, initially presented as a man of great power in the world, imaged as servant.

Twice in this story, servants have initiated conversation with their masters and breathed new life, new hope, and new possibilities into circumstance. Twice in this story, servants have channeled the power of God, circumventing the ordinary, expected channels. And thus the story has created the expectation that the plot will consistently unfold throughout circumstance and experience.

Here at the end that may also comprise a beginning in celebration and in hope, the possibility of God's power is evoked for the third time in the most unexpected of ways. For the third time, the opportunity for God's power is evoked in the most unexpected of places. For the third time, the prospect of God's power alive and at work in the works and words of a servant, is evoked in the dramatic role reversal as we imagine what conversations Naaman, child of God, servant of the king of Aram, might now initiate with the king. And Elisha smiles, and says, "Go in peace" (v. 19). (John Ballenger)

Lectionary Commentary

2 Timothy 2:8-15

The consequence of the apostle Paul's faithfulness in living the word of God was his imprisonment and then eventual execution. The writer of 2 Timothy uses the circumstance of Paul's imprisonment to testify to the fact that the word of God can itself never be bound. This fact provided Paul with the assurance that undergirded his commitment through all circumstance and is the same assurance offered the readers of 2 Timothy.

The writer is also aware of how our words about the Word of God—the word of truth—can get in the way of that word. Part of the circumstance we endure as followers of the Word is all the wrangling over its meaning. We must remember that, just as others cannot bind the word of God, neither can we.

Luke 17:11-19

It's the familiar story of the ten men with skin diseases healed and the one who returned to give thanks. Consider though, that the nine who did not return, were on their way to the high priest in obedience to Jesus' command. Consider that the one who returned was a Samaritan. Consider, therefore, that the high priest had nothing to offer him. Consider that in affliction, traditional prejudices and distinctions (Jew and Samaritan) didn't matter. Consider that with affliction removed, the distinctions return. Consider the original, challenging unfamiliarity of what has become so familiar. (John Ballenger)

Worship Aids

Pastoral Prayer

Our God, may we consistently initiate the expression of your words of hope and healing to those in positions of power in our world, even as we discipline ourselves to listen for the words we need to hear from unexpected sources.

Prayer of Confession

We confess, our God, to being overly impressed with those successful in the ways of the world. We confess to coveting wealth and power as the world defines and understands them. We confess to making light of your ways, our God. Forgive us, we pray.

Words of Assurance

God makes light in the darkness. God seeks to illuminate the way before us even as we seek to eliminate God's way before us. And the darkness does not comprehend. Thanks be to God. (John Ballenger)

Gratitude Let Loose—Managing Gratitude

Third in a Series of Four on Jesus Speaking on Asset Management

Luke 7:36-50

One might think the Disney company has a monopoly on the toy and entertainment industry because it seems as if most kids want nothing more than to meet Mickey Mouse and visit Cinderella's castle. It is every child's dream to visit Disney World, isn't it? A series of Disney commercials would lead us to believe this to be true. These ads, which apparently are taken from home video footage, picture children waking up from a good night's rest to hear their parents happily tell them to get dressed because they are going to Disney World—today! The kids are ecstatic. They jump on their beds, screaming, laughing, leaping for joy, and hugging their parents. It's a picture of uncontrollable gratitude.

A friend of mine wanted to pull a similar stunt with his family. He booked a reservation at Disney, purchased airline tickets for the whole gang, and even invited his in-laws to join in on the fun. Like the commercial, he wanted to keep it a surprise for his family until the morning of their departure, but Joe's mother-in-law knew this was not the best idea. She knew her daughter would not appreciate the surprise because Diane likes to plan and prepare. It gives her more time to build up her excitement and find ways to convey her gratitude.

Gratitude is a wonderful asset because it does a world of good for both the giver and the receiver. Words of thanks offer a richness to life that make it more meaningful, and yet there are many different ways people express and manage their gratitude—though the word *manage* may not be the most suitable one to describe what we do with our gratitude. Sometimes we can't control or hold back our thankfulness. We let it loose, like those kids going to Disney World. And then there are those circumstances when we act like Diane, carefully mapping out our expressions of thanks. Both ways are valid because when something good happens, it's natural to leap for joy and hug the person responsible for sharing the good fortune. Yet it's also important that our expressions of gratitude be more than lip service; there should be some substance behind our words.

Both kinds of responses are evident in the example of the woman in Luke 7. Here we find a sinful woman, "a woman from the city" (v. 37), entering the home of Simon the Pharisee, where Jesus is dining. Simon says that it is not good for a man's reputation to be seen with this woman; he says of Jesus, "If this man were a prophet, he would know what kind of woman is touching him. He would know that she is a sinner" (v. 39).

No doubt others held the same view, but not Jesus. He welcomed her intrusion. While he and Simon recline on pillows at the table, she sweeps in to wash Jesus' exposed feet with her tears and proceeds to dry them with her hair and anoint them with perfume. Her gratitude is let loose, and yet, there is an element of preparation in what she has done. She entered the house with an alabaster jar in hand. She came prepared. She had given some thought to what she was about to do before she paid her visit to Jesus, and now she is ready to offer her gratitude. Of course, that leads us to wonder about what she had, in fact, received. Evidently, she had previously learned about Jesus and discovered God's grace. Her life had changed, and she needed to express her thanks. John's Gospel tells us that she was Mary of Bethany, the sister of Lazarus (see John 12:1-8; also see Matthew 26:6-13, where the host is identified as Simon, who had a skin disease).

While the woman's actions may feel over the top, true gratitude is not something that can be faked, because it springs forth as a response to what one has received. The woman in the text was overcome with emotion at having received a great gift. The difference between this woman and Simon is that she willingly received the gift God offered. She knew of her need for forgiveness, so when she received God's grace, she was consumed with gratitude. Jesus emphasizes this point by telling a little parable about a creditor and two debtors. One who owed much and one whose debt was small. Neither had the resources to pay off their debts, and yet, the creditor wiped the slate clean for both. When Jesus asks his host, "Which of them will love him more?" (v. 42), Simon correctly answers, "The one who had the largest debt canceled" (v. 43). He is expected to rejoice more because he had received more, and to the one who is given much, much is expected.

On this matter, actions speak louder than words, for they reveal much about what each person has received. The woman was so thrilled with the gift she received that she bathed the feet of Jesus with tears and kisses, and even poured sweet perfume on them. She received much and offered much in return, but Simon did not even offer the common courtesy of a host, washing the dusty feet of his guests when they enter the house. For whatever reason, Simon had not yet experienced God's grace in his life. Perhaps he wasn't looking for it or maybe he thought he didn't need it, but regardless of the reason, Simon had failed to receive God's gift. Grace wasn't being withheld; Simon had simply not welcomed it into his heart.

When we welcome God's gift into our lives, we will naturally respond with gratitude, which brings joy to God. Jesus was overjoyed at what the woman did, and while Simon was concerned about managing the appearance of a known sinner in his home, Jesus did not worry about his reputation. He defended this woman. He was excited to see her life transformed, and therefore, he didn't discourage her grateful, over-the-top behavior. He sets an example for us. The best way we can manage our gratitude is to share our thankfulness with God and with others. This is more than lip service because it demands that we bring forth our alabaster jars and do something tangible for God and for others. (Mark White)

Worship Aids

Invocation

O Lord, we lift up our hearts and express our gratitude to you, our God. It is indeed right to give you our thanks and praise, for you have set free the captives, you have comforted those who mourn, and you have brought gladness to our hearts. We rejoice in your name and worship you today with thankful hearts. Amen.

Call to Worship

From near and far we come into this sanctuary of worship. We gather to celebrate the mighty works of our gracious God. Out of the busyness of life we center ourselves in the presence of our Lord. We gather to celebrate the mighty works of our gracious God.

Benediction

Go forth to accept and share the blessings of God our creator. Embrace the unending love of our redeemer. Know that the Spirit will be with you for each step of your journey. Go forth in the name of the Father, the Son, and the Holy Spirit. Amen. (Mark White)

OCTOBER 20, 2013

Twenty-second Sunday after Pentecost

Readings: Jeremiah 31:27-34; Psalm 119:97-104; 2 Timothy 3:14–4:5; Luke 18:1-8

Don't Lose Heart

Luke 18:1-8

I have long been troubled by passages of Scripture that cast God in a bad light. It is not necessarily the text itself as much as how a misinterpretation of a text leads to bad theology. It is akin to the jailed man who told me that God gave him a criminal mind to teach him self-control and to help him develop perseverance by means of the U.S. criminal justice system (he was serious)! This is a troubling parable because it has been treated as an allegory by too many interpreters. Preachers and teachers have given it a first-glance reading and then mistakenly taken the story to be a comparison of God to an unjust judge. Worse still, it is a judge who has no respect for either the holy or the human. At its core, this is a powerful parable of Jesus' to teach us to pray with faith, trust, and hope.

From my experience, prayer is the primary spiritual discipline, for without it we have no communication with God. Prayer is the language of the Spirit. It is a conduit between our spiritual self and God, through which we can pour out our feelings and surrender our fears, receiving the strength, solace, and wisdom that stream forth from God in return. Prayer serves to reorient our spirit and mind, which have been disoriented by the chaos, false truth, and materialistic perspective of the world. Through prayer we are reconnected to our spiritual identity and the human need around us. Life may be a physical journey, but it is a spiritual one too, and we are spiritual people who are created to be in contact with our Creator.

Prayer is humbling. Genuine, contrite prayer is the great leveler of people, helping us see the contrasts and similarities of our own needs and the needs of those who share this journey. You cannot look outward in prayer without looking inward with new eyes. Most of all, prayer changes you more than it changes things. The Spirit of God is the change-agent, and we are the ones who stand in need of conversion and transformation.

Particularly in this text, justice does not imply receiving everything that we want but rather realizing righteousness—however that may be manifested. The widow is persistent in seeking justice over her opponent, and it is in her righteous fidelity of this pursuit that victory is found. Whatever our circumstance, this parable points to the need for us to maintain faith, trust, and hope as followers of Christ, regardless of the obstacles that we face. Perhaps we are living in an anxious time due to circumstances of our own choosing. We have taken on more than we can easily do: extra course work, extra volunteer service, a second job, or a second mortgage. Some of these may be out of necessity, while some may be rooted in our own misguided desire to impress others or to be justified by works. Prayer is not a means to guarantee an outcome, Jesus is teaching that prayer is like spiritual breathing (essential for living) and requires steady persistence, "pray continously and not to be discouraged" (v. 1).

There is not room in this brief space to more deeply explore the nature of prayer and the question of "unanswered prayer." Prayers that we place in the category of "unanswered" may be actually answered in ways beyond our ability to perceive and comprehend. I believe that God wants to give us the desires of our hearts—that which we can ask in humility and with spiritual integrity—but that there are circumstances in life that may call us to question this because we miss seeing the larger picture or the greater good.

When a young clergywoman was diagnosed with breast cancer, she was immediately surrounded by friends, colleagues, and parishioners who prayed for her each day, sent cards, and rendered acts of kindness to her family. About the same time, a clergyman learned that he was in need of a heart transplant and that finding a donor in time was unlikely. Again, crowds of faithful lifted him in prayer and embraced the family with encouragement, love, and support during their ordeal. The woman succumbed to cancer; the man found a donor and lives. Did God not answer the prayers of one group? Is God biased by gender, age, or diagnosis? The answer is "Certainly not!" Integrating this truth and the reality of the appearance of injustice is heavy stuff for us to prayerfully contemplate. Still, it is vital for us to do so if we are to strive to grow in our understanding of God, faith, and prayer.

God's faithfulness to everyone in all circumstances does not concern me, and it did not concern Jesus in this parable. Our faithfulness is called into question, with Jesus asking aloud if there will be a faithful remnant when Christ returns after his passion and resurrection. The widow in the story is not a socially compliant old woman (age is assumed with her status, but she could be very young as well) but a feisty, persistent person of faith. She is up against a judge who is either indifferent toward God and people, or the Gospel writer is saying that he is "blind" in rendering justice without regard to status. Either way, it is the woman's belief and determined consistency that results in righteous justice and her vindication.

If prayer is a spiritual discipline—perhaps even an art form—do we practice it and also teach it? Will we see that our children have faith? Will we pass along our spiritual heritage and work to grow "spiritual cedars?" The parable ends with a question for the reader to ponder. When called upon, Jesus observes, God is quick to respond in faithfulness. The question remains, are we? (Gary G. Kindley)

Lectionary Commentary

Jeremiah 31:27-34

The prophet Jeremiah lays out a new vision of how things will be for the people of Judah and Israel. Sin and accountability become personal, which contrasts the old understanding of the sin of the father being cast upon his children (see Ezekiel 18). As it is today, we are responsible and accountable for our actions, regardless of the sin of generations before or our understanding of the original sin of Adam. There will be a new covenant that is different from the covenant of the Exodus. There will be a theological DNA of belonging that is an inherent part of kingdom people. God's people know in their hearts that they belong to God. Even those without spiritual teaching long for something more in life, and they ask, "Is this all there is?" It is a naming and a belonging: "I will be their God, and they will be my people" (v. 33).

2 Timothy 3:14–4:5

It must be noted that both problems with the timeline of Paul's life and contextual issues have left true authorship of Timothy uncertain for many scholars from a variety of traditions. Whether written by Paul or on Paul's behalf, this passage has offered encouragement to countless preachers and biblical teachers for almost two millennia. It uplifts the power of Scripture as a source of teaching and training in righteousness and also encourages those who proclaim the gospel message to be persistent in their vital role as bearers of good news.

One problem with this text is the abuse that has resulted from misinterpretation of verse 16. The statement affirms the ultimate worth of

Scripture, but is not intended to say that each phrase or verse, taken out of context, can be used as some once-and-for-all irrefutable statement of authority. The contrast of 1 Corinthians 14:34 (women should keep silent in the churches) and Romans 16:1 (praise for Phoebe, an ordained deacon of the Cenchrae church), both of which are certainly written by Paul, comes to mind. We should tread cautiously lest our own bias of issues use Scripture as a means of simply proving a point rather than pointing to diversity of valid experiences, understandings, and expressions of the Christian faith. (Gary G. Kindley)

Worship Aids

Call to Worship

Prayer is the language of the Spirit.
Prayer is our connection with God.
Prayer nourishes us, comforts us, and strengthens us.
We need prayer as we need the air we breathe.
Let us gather as a people of hope;
Offering our prayers of praise to God.

Offertory Prayer

God of constant fidelity, Jesus taught us to pray always and not to lose heart. We come today for worship and gather together both who we are and what we have. Accept these gifts, offered in faith, trust, and hope in the name of the One who redeems us—Jesus Christ. Amen.

Benediction

The day is coming when Christ returns. Will he find a faithful remnant of those who call him the Christ? Be that remnant of faith and share the good news so that others might be faithful as well. Amen. (Gary G. Kindley)

We're Not as Loyal as We Think We Are—Managing Loyalty

Fourth in a Series of Four on Jesus Speaking on Asset Management

Matthew 26:31-35

Today's workforce grumbles about companies not being loyal to their employees, and certainly job security isn't what it used to be. There was a time when one could spend an entire career working for the same organization, but for the most part, that day has past. Lifetime contracts no longer exist, and workers complain that their employers have lost a sense of loyalty to their labor force. But are employees as loyal as they say they are? No doubt workers have a right to bemoan unexpected terminations and downsizing, especially when employees have faithfully served a company for twenty or thirty years.

Yet, to be fair in this conversation, it is important to recognize that employees are not as loyal as they once were. True, companies once employed persons for a lifetime, and employees in turn remained committed to one organization, but today's work environment is different. Career advancement is important, and employees seem more interested in loyalty to their careers than to their employers.

So we aren't as loyal as we think we are, and that's the message Jesus delivered to his disciples. Earlier in Matthew 26, Jesus said, "I assure you that one of you will betray me" (v. 21), and then he expands this indictment in verse 31: "Tonight you will all fall away because of me." Peter is adamant that he will remain devoted to his Lord, but none of the disciples, including Peter, are as loyal as they think they are. When Jesus went to Gethsemane to pray, he begged his disciples to stay awake and pray with him, but they fell asleep. Judas betrayed Jesus to the chief priests and the elders for a few coins of silver. When Jesus was arrested, all the disciples abandoned him. And then Peter denied Jesus three times, just as Jesus predicted.

The disciples weren't as loyal as they thought they were, and when it came time for them to stand by their friend, the disciples ran away. But it is not as if this day came as a surprise. Jesus had repeatedly instructed his disciples about his future: "You know that the Passover is two days from now. And the Human One will be handed over to be crucified" (v. 2). But they didn't understand, perhaps because they expected their Messiah to put up a fight rather than lay down his life.

When Jesus predicted that all the disciples would desert him, they scoffed at the idea. "I'm not the one, am I, Lord?" is the way each of them responded (v. 22). "Jesus, you're my friend. I will always be by your side. You can count on my loyalty." Are we any different from the disciples? Jesus is our friend, and we want to be loyal, but we often deny Jesus. We betray our Lord by the way we treat other people, or the way we handle our finances, or through our lifestyles. When it comes time for us to stand firmly by our friend Jesus, we often run away, seeking our own comfort rather than remaining loyal to our Lord.

The good news for us is that even when we betray God, the Lord remains loyal to us. Jesus taught his disciples that the best way they could demonstrate their faithfulness to him was by loving God with all their heart, soul, and mind, and by loving their neighbor as they love themselves. So in this sense, loyalty is rooted in love, and love gets us back on the right track. When we betray God, the Lord doesn't turn away from us. God continues to offer love, which helps us recognize our failures, our sins, and our need for God's forgiveness. Though God is faithful to us, we are given the freedom to either embrace or reject the gift of grace.

Jesus had predicted that all the disciples would betray and reject him, and yet the Scriptures single out Judas and Peter. Judas betrayed Jesus on one occasion, while Peter denied him three separate times. They were not as loyal as they thought they would be, though they recognized and acknowledged the error of their ways. Judas regretted his action almost as soon as he had Jesus arrested, and thus it didn't take long for him to run back to the officials and proclaim Jesus' innocence; he even gave back the bribe money. Peter, likewise, was ashamed by his failure to stand by his friend. He hid in fear, ashamed for what he had done. Jesus, however, was not deterred. After the resurrection, Jesus returned to Peter and the disciples to offer them grace rather than retribution, even though they were not faithful.

The truth is we are not as loyal as we say we are or want to be, but Jesus does not give up on us. The Lord is not put off by our failures and inability to remain loyal. After the resurrection, Jesus came back to Peter and the other disciples one morning as they were enjoying breakfast and he offered them all forgiveness, and specifically, he invited Peter to follow him once again. This act reminds us of an earlier promise Jesus made. He promised his disciples that he would not leave them alone, but that the Father would send the Advocate, the Holy Spirit, and that promise has been extended to us.

We are not as loyal as we say we are. We are not as loyal as we want to be. But God is, and God is pouring out love and forgiveness as a means of inviting us back into a faithful and loyal relationship. The best way we can manage our loyalty to God is through the embrace of God's gifts of love and forgiveness. (Mark White)

Worship Aids

Invocation

Great and wonderful God, may your blessings fall on us this day. As we gather, we are mindful that you have remained loyal to us even when we have gone astray. You have given us the kind of life that provides us encouragement and strength to overcome the obstacles that get in our way. Now we gather to worship you, sing your praises, and listen for your word. Bless this sacred time we have with you and one another. We pray these things in Christ's name. Amen.

Call to Worship

We come together from separate places
for the purpose of worshiping our God.
Lord, we thank you for this sacred time.
We each face unique challenges and struggles,
which weigh on our hearts as we settle into these pews.
Speak to us, O Lord, as we join together
as the body of Christ to praise you, our gracious God.

Benediction

Go forth with confidence knowing that God is with us. Seek guidance from the example of Jesus. Know the Holy Spirit is our guide and will abide with us to the end of our days. Now depart as disciples, ready to serve and devoted to the work of God. Amen. (Mark White)

OCTOBER 27, 2013

Twenty-third Sunday after Pentecost

Readings: Joel 2:23-32; Psalm 65; 2 Timothy 4:6-8, 16-18; Luke 18:9-14

Authentic Disciples

Luke 18:9-14

I believe that it is very difficult to be a true disciple of Jesus without authenticity. There is an essential congruence of belief and practice that is a part of the character of Christ-followers; faith is reflected in word, works, and outlook. In this parable, the tax collector is an unlikely model of repentance and humility. Unlike the Pharisee in the story, his authenticity of character understands what it is to express genuine remorse. He is the only one who demonstrates true contrition, despite his shady profession.

What he did for a living could be described as government-sanctioned robbery. Tax collectors could levy a tax without allowing you any mechanism for appeal, add penalty to that tax at a whim, and then skim a hefty sum from the top before turning in what remained of your hard-earned funds as taxes to Rome. It was a financial shakedown that bred anger and bitterness in the hearts of all those, Jews and Gentiles, who were taxed by the Roman Empire.

Jesus offers this parable with an intended audience in mind. It is for those who trust in themselves as righteous, looking down their noses at those who do not. One wonders if Luke's chronology in relating this parable actually does precede Jesus' encounter with the tax collector, Zacchaeus (Luke 19:1-10). If so, it is a foreshadowing of the story of Zacchaeus, a hated member of society who repents and pays restitution to all whom he has harmed.

There are evidently Pharisees or people of similar theological understanding at both the telling of this parable and the Zacchaeus encounter. Jesus is stirring up trouble, not for the sake of trouble, but because the kingdom of God upsets the status quo and bursts forth with a new paradigm for living and relating to God. This also helps gospel readers better understand why the religious leaders of Jerusalem worked so diligently to plot against Jesus. The nature of Jesus' teaching challenges the very foundation of their religious doctrine and practice.

In the Zacchaeus story, it is a bit ironic that there are onlookers grumbling about Jesus ruining his reputation by associating with sinners. In this text, Jesus is questioning the integrity of those who exalt themselves and regard others with contempt. In the kingdom of heaven, they are the ones with a sullied reputation. Arrogance and self-righteousness are poison to Christian character.

What does it mean to have sincere humility? Sincerity is to have congruence and authenticity in what we believe and what we do. Humility is to hold a perspective that places us contritely before God, recognizing our need to surrender to God's will for our lives. Humble surrender is to move from a place of arrogant, detached independence, to authentic dependence upon God as the source of our hope and salvation. No brokenness we face can ultimately be healed apart from the redemptive power of God.

From a Christian perspective, the only way to achieve the sort of freedom that we call independence is to recognize our interdependence upon God and one another. When we do that, we come to know a new freedom that is grounded in surrender. When we are honest and truly grounded in reality, we start to realize that we need God and one another to make life work together for good. It is not independence but surrender to interdependence that is the key to true freedom.

A friend of mine was talking about his experience in a twelve-step program for addiction recovery. He had eleven years of sobriety and then one day had a slip from his abstinence. When he talked about it, he said that he tried to analyze what exactly went wrong after eleven years of sober living. He finally came to the understanding that he had forgotten the one to whom surrender is essential for redemption to be realized. He was trying to maintain sobriety based on his own merit and self-discipline. As anyone who has had any length of sobriety can tell you, abstinence is never based on self-will but on surrender to God's will.

True surrender involves faith to overcome the natural fear of letting go. It requires the courage of taking a step into darkness and trusting that there is solid ground on which to stand. True surrender, like the location of the tax collector as described in this parable, may require that we stand "at a distance" (v. 13) from the crowd. The Pharisee, lacking compassion and true empathy in his affluent and self-absorbed world, looks at those around and sees how much better he is than the rest. The humble man ignores the crowd, and his contrition is based on his self-awareness of what he lacks apart from God. We are humbled when we accept that we are made in the divine image and fall far short of such grand potential.

Authentic Christian disciples choose not only to pursue the one they claim to follow but also to emulate him. In this instance, the tax collector, even in the role that made him a social pariah, is more Christlike in his true humility, genuine candor, and complete surrender to his reliance upon God than the one who is deeply religious. Let those with ears hear. (Gary G. Kindley)

Lectionary Commentary

Joel 2:23-32

The prophet Joel, like so many of the Old Testament prophets, may have his name on a book of holy Scripture, but little else is known about him. It is his interpretation of events, in this case a plague of locusts, and a call to repentance that characterize this book. The text carries the reader from decimation (the locust swarm), to repentance (the people's acknowledgment of straying from Yahweh), and the restoration of Judah (God's always-faithful response to the cries of God's people), while God judges the nations who stray or attempt to stand against Judah.

We read the prophet's descriptions of signs of God and interpret them in light of our own experience, which is what every generation has done. For us in a nuclear age, there is a unique understanding of pillars of smoke and the moon turning to blood that did not come to mind for the nation of Judah. Certainly, the text could be a launching point for discussing the distinctive differences in Calvinism and Armenianism. It calls us to ask the question, "Is God the agent decimating the crops with an army of nature, or is God the agent who turns something terrifyingly destructive into something marvelously redemptive?"

2 Timothy 4:6-8, 16-18

Verses 7-8 of this text have been used so often at memorial and funeral services, that their context is sometimes lost. Paul, or the one writing in the name of Paul, is jailed. The details of his incarceration and trial are sketchy, which is one reason that definitive authorship of this letter has been questioned for centuries.

Paul praises God for, again and again, defending and saving him from the "lion's mouth" (v. 17). Paul's ultimate mission, to bring the message of the gospel to the Gentiles, remains his constant focus and the task for which he has poured out himself. Whether using metaphors of Greek games or simply stating his plight, Paul is a struggler/competitor who claims victory over evil in the name of the one who sent him forth to preach. (Gary G. Kindley)

Worship Aids

Prayer of Confession

God, be merciful to us! We stand broken and do not know why. We feel empty and are unsure what will satisfy. Forgive that for which we know not to ask absolution. Mend us and fill us that we may be whole. We ask this in the name of the one authentic and great redeemer, Jesus Christ. Amen.

Words of Assurance

God is merciful. God forgives. God redeems. Thanks be to God.

Offertory Prayer (Responsive)

Render to Caesar what is Caesar's and to God what is God's.
How do we know what to give our God?
Give God your whole faith, trust, and hope.
May our faith be reflected in our words, our works, and our worship!

Benediction

We leave this place more alive than when we arrived! Let us be authentic rather than pathetic, sincere and not cavalier! May we be as genuine as heaven and as real as the love of God who saves us! Let the church say, "Amen and Amen!" (Gary G. Kindley)

Let All the World in Every Corner Sing

First in a Series of Three on the Church's Favorite Songs

Psalm 96; Psalm 98; Psalm 100:3

God will always have a people to offer God praise. The preacher suggested a new and more contemporary form of worship. His sermon made it clear that this was truly biblical; the Scripture supported this change. However, changing the worship style seemed sacrilegious. Some of the members wondered if a change in leadership might be better. The young Baptist preacher continued to encourage the change by claiming, "After all, Jesus practiced worship in this manner." Even though not all agreed with their pastor, the majority of his London congregation decided to sing one hymn at the end of worship; until this moment, no church in Europe had included congregational singing for nearly one thousand years.

Can you imagine a time when the church would not include singing as part of worship? We could understand the controversy surrounding instrumental use or whether drums should be included. We can relate to a church that struggles over whether or not to use slides rather than hymnals, but not singing simply seems foreign. From roughly A.D. 500 to 1500, congregational singing stopped. There were professional cantors, but congregational singing simply stopped. When Pastor Benjamin Keach instituted a hymn in the early 1600s, he created so much controversy across England that for the next twenty years he found himself defending his position. He wrote a series of hymns supporting congregational singing, as well as an essay entitled *Breach Repaired in God's Worship* (1691).

The ancient Hebrews worshiped with song. The Israelites, including Miriam, Moses' sister, sang praises after crossing the Red Sea (Exodus 15:1-20). Can't you picture the rejoicing survivors of the exodus dancing as Miriam sings aloud, "Sing to the LORD, / for an overflowing victory!" (v. 21). This is our first resurrection hymn, a song of God's deliverance.

Once again, as the Hebrews crossed into the promised land, Moses instructs them to sing a new song of remembrance when they worship. This song holds the story of their past, their deliverance, and the challenge to never forget that God alone has brought them to a new land with a new song.

Much later, young shepherd David wrote ballads to God, playing his flute for King Saul and singing the passions of his heart. Leaf through the Bible and discover many writers placing God's truths in a hymn because words alone were simply inadequate. By the time of Jesus' birth, the Psalms had become Israel's hymnal. Even without the music, we have the rich and powerful content, reminding us that melody, alone does not make a hymn.

Song has powerful appeal. Most of us can recall where we were when we first heard a particular song. Couples love to remember "our song," as a theme for their love. National anthems bring emotion as the strains remind us of our homeland. The same is true with songs of faith.

What's your favorite church song? Perhaps it holds some memories or experiences. What truths about your life and your relationship with God does it convey? For some the musical quality is most important, while for others the style of music is crucial, and for others personal memories make the significance. Our most cherished songs were generally important at a significant season of our faith development. Favorite church songs almost always speak to our hearts. We shouldn't be surprised when someone whose faith experience differs from ours names a favorite song that is also different.

Martin Luther believed faith should be accessible to everyone. He believed that God's word should be understood by all people, and he insisted on using German, not Latin, in worship. He brought popular music into the church instead of the traditional Gregorian chants. Bridging popular music with worship, he brought the organ out of the beer halls and into the sanctuary, and is reported to have loved asking, "Why should the devil have all the good music?"

Not much later, a rising English poet left his law practice to become a parish priest. George Herbert loved to express his passion and thoughts about God in verse. Entering the priesthood late in life, he too sought to bridge his secular artistic life with a new and rich ministry. In 1633, while walking along a very muddy road, he stopped to help a man whose horse had collapsed in the mud under its heavy load. Normally a very clean and smart dresser, George's friends were surprised to see him covered in mud. He told them that what he had done that day was like music to his soul. He later noted that "I am bound to practice what I pray for . . . and I praise God for this occasion. Come, let's tune our instruments." He went home and wrote verse that was later put to music. Recalling Jesus' words at his triumphal entry, he wrote the hymn: "Let All the World in Every Corner Sing." (*The Evergreen, or Church-Offering for All Seasons; A Repository of Religious, Literary, and Entertaining Knowledge for the Christian Family*, vol. 5 [New York: George W. Mason, 1848], 360).

We live in a time when many question the future of church music. We need not fear. God's people will always sing because we need to sing! God will always have a singing people because God will always have a people. Our songs may change because God is always calling out a new people. Should we sing in Chinese or English? Should our music be Native American or European? Should our songs be traditional or contemporary?

The answer is always yes! Why? Because God has us to worship. Because God has placed a new song in our hearts! Because to know God is to worship and to worship is to sing! Amen. (Guy Ames)

Worship Aids

Call to Worship (Psalm 150 NRSV)

Praise the LORD! Praise God in his sanctuary. . . .
Praise him for his mighty deeds; . . .
Praise him with trumpet sound; praise him with lute and harp!
Praise him with tambourine and dance;
praise him with strings and pipe!
Praise him with clanging cymbals; praise him with loud clashing cymbals!
Let everything that breathes praise the Lord! Praise the Lord!

Call to Worship #2

Make a joyful noise to the Lord!
What if I can't carry a tune?
Let all the world in every corner sing.
What if my world does not know the song?
Let every tongue confess that Jesus is Lord!
What if their tongues are silenced?
What if their music is tone-deaf?
What if we cannot speak the same language?
What if we don't like their music?
What if they are not our people?
How shall the people of God sing songs of Zion in a foreign land?
How can we worship if we do not know the song—
the melody—the words?
Let everything that breathes make a joyful noise!
Babies make noise . . . the ocean roars . . . the crickets chirp
. . . wind whistles through the treetops.
Let all the world make a joyful noise!
Horns blaring . . . donkeys braying . . . geese calling
. . . children squealing . . . mothers calling . . .
Let all the world in every corner sing.
Jesus Christ is Lord, to the glory of God the Father.
Let everything that has breath praise the Lord.
Praise the Lord.

Benediction

Now go from this place letting your life serve as music to the one who brings spring after winter, Resurrection after Good Friday. Tune your instruments that together we might make melodies with our lives and so that the whole world will one day join in singing with us that Jesus Christ is Lord, to the glory of God the Father. Amen. (Guy Ames)

NOVEMBER 3, 2013

All Saints Sunday

Readings: Daniel 7:1-3, 15-18; Psalm 149; Ephesians 1:11-23; Luke 6:20-31

Blessings, Woes, and Saints

Luke 6:20-31

For all of the talk we do about saints, angels, and heavenly hosts, deep down we know that sainthood does not begin with flowing robes and glowing halos, although by tradition it has evolved into that imagery. Saints are people who keep the faith when it is not easy, expedient, or even safe to do so. Disciples are easy to find in pews on Sunday morning but much more sparse in times of religious persecution and spirit-breaking hardship.

The life of a saint is one of blessings and woes, for a saint is someone who lives by faith despite the heartaches and hurdles of life's journey. They remain unwavering when joyous, easier times tempt faith to ebb and spiritual discipline to wane. Luke's account of the blessings and woes of the Beatitudes passage reads like a primer for those seeking God's kingdom. Luke clearly states that Jesus is speaking directly to his disciples. It is especially for those who have little more than their faith and devotion to help them in their quest for redemption. Those who know that they need God are those who understand that life is not meant to be lived "spiritually solo"!

In his listing of woes Jesus calls out to those who do not know what it is that they lack. Those who do not know that they are never truly fulfilled without being filled by Christ's Spirit may not realize the unidentified emptiness that they have masked with "feel good" consolations. When I served an affluent community in a suburb of the Dallas-Fort Worth area, a missionary who was native to the Democratic Republic of Congo was dismayed at the large homes and elaborate gardens he drove past. "It must be very difficult," he said to me, "to minister to people such as these!" He saw the wealth and knew that riches can mask spiritual need with temporary comfort.

The blessings of God are a gift for which we pay no price; that is why both Christ's atoning passion and God's mysterious wonders are considered acts of grace—unmerited and unconditional love. God's love is freely given, but it can be a costly thing to be a Christ-follower. The life of Christian discipleship demands doing that which goes against our nature: love your enemies, wish them good and not harm. It is a fine philosophical treatise, but one that often sticks in the craw when it must be put into practice. I speak from personal experience here.

I wanted to believe that she meant well. It was her opinion that the congregation would be best served by a change of pastor. As the pastor, that was not my opinion, nor was it that of the church leadership. That did not dissuade this parishioner from her mission to see that I vacated, voluntarily or otherwise, my role as senior pastor.

The conversations were rarely easy, the meetings at times were contentious, and the bitter feelings of ill-will brewed into a sour swill. I had a slightly better understanding of Jesus' words, "Father, let this cup pass from me." Who wants to drink such terrible dregs of human conflict? Although I could not see it at the time, I now understand that God used the zeal of the parishioner to challenge my self-complacency and push me to a closer self-examination of my calling, conduct, and direction. I risked charting a new course and grew closer to Christ because of this adversary, this "enemy" who shared the same loaf and cup from God's table at each Communion service. She, too, is a child of God, a daughter of the Most High. Perhaps, in her own way, she is also a saint.

The Chinese festival to honor the dead, "Qing Minq Day," is a traditional time—more than two thousand five hundred years old—to honor the memories of ancestors. It is known as "The Pure Brightness Festival" and focuses on the sun, spring, and the hope that is to come—not the dark things typically associated with death. We can choose to see blessings or woes, and both are at hand. Where we focus our energy is up to us.

A word of caution to those who may attempt to take all of this passage literally: I think that we would be misunderstanding Jesus' point if we did so. It seems to me that Jesus is not encouraging us to enable robbery or ignore injustice. It may also be more Christlike to give a word of admonition to fraudulent beggars, or to offer food and encouragement to those begging for money who are actually attempting to feed an addiction to drugs or alcohol. Verse 31 is key: offer to others what you most want, perhaps giving away what you most need. It is often true that living the Golden Rule is the most saint-like—the most Christlike—choice any of us can make. If a saint is someone through whom one witnesses Christian discipleship, what better expression of the faith than to serve and work for others' well-being in Jesus' name!

Blessed are you whose spirit aches, for your pain leads you to the Source of comfort. Blessed are you who long for something more, for you see beyond the vision of those distracted by riches. Blessed are you who know you need God, for you are closer to truth than the "church lite" preachers whose motivation is flattery and popularity. Blessed are the poor in spirit, for yours is God's kingdom—not a place or land, but a condition of being. To live in the kingdom of God is to live in the truth that no matter what happens nothing can separate us from God. In life, in death, and in life beyond death, God is with us; we are not alone. Thanks be to God! (Gary G. Kindley)

Lectionary Commentary

Daniel 7:1-3, 15-18

The book of Daniel and the Revelation of John both paint visions of the future and end of creation as apocalyptic biblical literature. Daniel is both a prophetic dreamer and an interpreter of dreams. In this passage, Daniel dreams and asks another, an attendant, to interpret his dream for him. It is a time of Jewish persecution (167 B.C.E., Antiochus IV Epiphanes), and the four beasts are commonly thought to reflect the four great kingdoms of the day: the Persians, Greeks, Babylonians, and Medes (*New Interpreters Study Bible* [Nashville: Abingdon Press, 2003], 1243).

Preaching on apocalyptic texts can be tricky because of the very confusing nature of allegory and historical context that often blend together. It demands that the preacher hold integrity with the text, setting it in the context of the day in which it was written, and not use it to extrapolate contemporary interpretations which, although popular, are foreign to true exegesis.

Ephesians 1:11-23

Paul writes the church at Ephesus (now in modern-day Turkey and one of the best restored ancient cities) and addresses Christian Jews along with Gentile converts. Paul praises them for their affection for the "saints" and, as is often Paul's style, expresses his gratitude and tells them that they are remembered in his prayers. This is another letter that (according to 6:20) is written from prison but whose authorship cannot be verified. Whether or not it was actually written by the hand of Paul, it reflects Paul's ethics and teachings, and his desire to encourage and instruct the Christian community, reminding them of God's wondrous design for their salvation. (Gary G. Kindley)

Worship Aids

Unison Invocation

We gather together to remember. We remember those who are no longer with us in body, but whose spirit is as present and palpable in our memories as it was when we shared their pews. Come, let us worship and praise God in memory of these saints of the faith whom we this day recall. Amen.

Pastoral Prayer

Today, Holy God, we surrender to you these saints whom we have named and commend them to your everlasting care. Embrace them in your loving arms so that, empowered by your Spirit, this great cloud of witnesses may continue to inspire and guide us by their legacy and their love. Amen.

Benediction

Go forth, living into your legacy as people called to be saints of the faith. Go forth and be the church! Amen. (Gary G. Kindley)

Singing the Songs of Zion: When We've Been There 10,000 Years

Second in a Series of Three on the Church's Favorite Songs

Psalm 40:2-4; Psalm 51

Early in 2008 leaders with United Methodist Communications put a question to 1,500 Facebook "friends" asking which was their favorite hymn in *The United Methodist Hymnal.* The results noted a growing shift, though some of the "classics" continue to make the top ten. Relative newcomer, "Here I Am, Lord" by Dan Schutte took first place, immediately followed by the Billy Graham favorite, "How Great Thou Art," and John Newton's "Amazing Grace" (Ben Rhodes, "Facebook Fans Rank

Favorite Hymns," The United Methodist News Feed, August 13, 2010, http://tinyurl.com/3tcquav, accessed September 1, 2011). What would you list as your top ten all-time favorites?

No one is surprised that "Amazing Grace" made the top three. In most polls among almost any nationality, "Amazing Grace" comes close to the top. These simple words by this eighteenth-century Anglican priest tell our story. Our favorite songs must always tell our story, both our biblical story and our personal faith journey. Who cannot recall a time when the words "I once was lost but now am found, was blind, but now I see" did not resonate with life? Father Newton's hymn tells the biblical story of a people in need of redeeming and of a God who accepts people just as they are, but whose love demands nothing short of transformation.

What gives "Amazing Grace" the qualities of a classic is that these six simple verses witness to the whole gospel. The gospel in which we acknowledge our sin, admit our helplessness, and seek forgiveness. This gospel reminds us that God's grace can reclaim the most ugly among us. Who can sing these verses and not be at times moved to tears? Why does this old song still reach us? Because we believe the writer has lived the truth of these verses. This is a witness of one who lived to understand the power of God's grace. (Have the congregation sing verse 1.)

As a teenager, Newton rebelled against his father, like the prodigal son. Instead of following his father's plan that he work on a sugar plantation, Newton pursued a career at sea and ultimately joined the crew of a slave ship (biographical details from http://en.wikipedia.org/wiki/John_Newton, accessed April 2011). After sailing from England to Africa, the ship placed as many as eight hundred Africans into the hold as it headed for the West Indies. The conditions were totally inhumane. Africans were mistreated, tortured, and suffered from varying diseases. They were malnourished and dehydrated. On many trips, as many as half died at sea. After delivering the slaves for profit, the captain took on goods bound for England.

Though away from his father, Newton still suffered from a deeply rebellious spirit. He was a continual problem for slavers, who finally left him in West Africa with a slave dealer. John became a slave of an African princess. A sea captain who was asked to search for John by his father found John, rescued him, and brought him home. During his voyage home, a severe storm threatened the ship one night. As the ship filled with water, John fell to his knees. Having been delivered from slavery and now staring into death, he finally called out to God. The prodigal came home—though not quite. (Sing verses two and three.)

Believing that God had saved him, he began a devoted and spiritual life. In 1754, a stroke left him unable to continue in sailing but he continued investing in slaving. He began a serious study for the ministry. In 1764, he began work as a parish priest, but still he didn't speak against slavery. Do you hear the confession in these words? This testimony truly transcends cultures and generations, languages and nations. No wonder "Amazing Grace" has been translated into more languages than nearly any other religious song.

Twenty years as a parish priest had passed when he met William Wilberforce. Wrestling with a call into Christian ministry and inclined to enter the priesthood, Wilberforce sought counsel. Newton advised him not to give up his wealth or his political endeavors and to wait upon God for direction. Wilberforce took his advice and for some thirty years became the leading voice against slavery in all of England. Finally in 1788, thirty-four years after retiring from the slave trade, Newton wrote a serious pamphlet, "*Thoughts Upon the Slave Trade*," describing the horrible conditions and apologizing for "a confession, which...comes too late..." (*The Posthumous Works of the Late Rev. John Newton*, vol. 2 [Philadelphia: W.W. Woodward, 1809], 227).

The Slave Trade Act finally passed in Parliament, due to the tireless efforts of Wilberforce, on March 21, 1807, nine months before Newton died. John Wesley, a friend of both in this fight, wrote the last letter of his life to Wilberforce, urging him to continue the fight (Charles Yrigoyen Jr., *John Wesley: Holiness of Heart and Life*, 56, http://gbgm-umc.org/umw/wesley/wilber.stm, accessed April 2011). (Sing verses four and five.)

Wesley taught conversion as only one step in the order of salvation. Grace seeks us when we are rebellious and keeps after us until we are found. This grace works in us while we are being converted and as we become more and more like Christ. With holy lives as the aim, this grace is finished when "this...moral life shall cease." But the best is yet to come. As he drew his last breath, John Wesley uttered the hope of eternity, "Best of all is, God is with us." (Sing verse 6.) (Guy Ames)

Worship Aids

Call to Worship (Based on Isaiah 61)

Sing to the Lord a new song:

He calls us to proclaim good news to the poor

and has sent us to bind up the brokenhearted,
Sing to the Lord a new song:
Who calls us to proclaim freedom for the captives
and release for the prisoners,
Sing to the Lord a new song:
He calls us to proclaim the year of the Lord's favor,
to comfort the grieving
Sing to the Lord a new song:
Who showers us with amazing grace
so that our mourning has turned to praise
All: Let us sing a new song to the Lord.

Prayer of Confession

Create in us a new and clean heart, O God. Have mercy on us, O God, according to your amazing grace and abundant mercy. Open the inward eyes of our hearts that we might see our true selves even as you see us. Like the apostle Paul we, too, confess that the good we should do seems far from us and the wrong so close at hand. So often we feel powerless over the affairs of our hearts and minds. We have declared at our baptism that we are sinners, but that truth is not in us. The truth is that we do not believe that we are as sinful as our neighbor. Create in us a new and clean heart, O God.

Words of Assurance and Pardon

We worship a God of mercy and amazing grace.
In the name of Jesus the Christ, you are forgiven.
In the name of Jesus the Christ, you are forgiven. Amen.

Benediction

Now, sisters and brothers, by God's mercy go live your lives so that each day becomes a season of worship and each act and word an offering of praise to God for his indescribable grace. Amen. (Guy Ames)

NOVEMBER 10, 2013

Twenty-fifth Sunday after Pentecost

Readings: Haggai 1:15b–2:9; Psalm 145:1-5, 17-21; 2 Thessalonians 2:1-5, 13-17; Luke 20:27-38

Dwell on the Possible and Be Thankful

Haggai 1:15b–2:9

Marian Wright Edelman is famous for telling children, "Don't let anything get in the way of your education," but I am particularly fond of her view of things that people may consider impossible. In today's passage, God instructs Haggai to speak to people returning from exile, who saw the job before them as daunting and impossible. Apparently their anxiety then is much like our anxiety now because leaders like Marian Wright Edelman find it important to write, "So often we dwell on the things that seem impossible rather than on the things that are possible. So often we are depressed by what remains to be done and forget to be thankful for all that has been done" (*Guide My Feet* [Boston: Beacon Press, 1995], 15).

The mainline Christian churches of today are much like the people who looked at the temple, remembered its glory days, and were discouraged by what it would take to restore it to its magnificence. Although Haggai is speaking to a handful of people, I believe his message speaks clearly about God's desire for all people to see the possible.

When Haggai writes,

> The silver and the gold belong to me,
> says the LORD of heavenly forces.
> This house will be more glorious
> than its predecessor,
> says the LORD of heavenly forces.
> I will provide prosperity in this place,
> says the LORD of heavenly forces. (2:8-9)

I believe that many twenty-first century churches are seeing the task of regaining past glory as impossible. I believe that God wants the church to know that the "house will be more glorious / than its predecessor." Today's mainstream, ecumenical churches are led by intelligent men and women well versed in biblical interpretation, and you and I are among the learned. However, we may well be the ones to blame for allowing generations to fall away from continuing to spread our beliefs, our morals, and our faith.

In so many ways our churches are disconnected from the masses of nonreligious and marginally churched people. In so many ways, we have failed to help people understand the joys of the Christian faith and specifically the teachings of Jesus Christ. In so many ways, we lose sight of the calling from Jesus Christ to connect people with God and to connect people with one another. We have reached a point where it is imperative to do a better job of connecting people and churches ecumenically.

Now more than ever, we need to reach across the walls that divide us, and make connections. It is the role of the Christian to make connections across all boundaries, including different views in religion, politics, and physical characteristics.

I believe that all Christian denominations should be in the process of studying and praying about why we are here. We should all be asking, "Why do we exist as a church?" The answers may seem overwhelming and downright impossible on the surface. With diligent prayer, perhaps we will stop dwelling on the impossible and find a whole new focus on the way we approach loving one another and all people in the world. We need to focus on bridging the gaps and narrowing the chasms between young and old, light and dark, conservative and liberal, and among cultures in our neighborhoods.

When we begin to make those connections, we help create understanding and kindle the growth of faith in all people. Churches have a golden opportunity to touch the lives of residents of all ages, races, and socioeconomic statuses. We are positioned to reach students in our school systems, people living in poverty just down the street, and—although it may seem impossible—community leaders in ways that no social or government entity has.

Our vision and action will restore our calling to a place greater than it has been. Churches can provide the comfort of a home to people who feel far from home. We are called to be creative and refreshed by God's call to action. We should know that God calls us, not to long for the past and wish to return to the way things used to be, but to get to work and build a future.

In our passage today, the people were freed from captivity in Babylon and hurried back to Jerusalem to what they remembered as glorious. They were heartbroken as they gazed longingly at what was their beautiful city and temple, their past.

Many Christians look back to the time when churches were filled to capacity, new buildings were required, small groups were actively making differences in the lives of people in the community. It is unfortunate that so much time is spent looking back that we fail to catch a glimpse of what can be ahead. What can be are churches that have small groups actively changing lives, pastors who are spending more time among the people outside the church, and church leaders who understand that the building is not the answer. They will learn that Jesus, the carpenter, never built a building for worship, but saw all of God's creation as holy ground and people everywhere as precious.

Let us all be reminded that we are called to be a connecting church: conservatives with liberals, church members with church members, towns with towns, states with states, nations with nations, cultures with cultures, and most important, everyone with God.

Jesus is at the center of our life together. Jesus is our connection. When we come to the table where we celebrate our connections with God and with one another, may we be reminded of the need to reach out to all God's people. May we see a glorious future and be thankful. Amen. (Ted McIlvain)

Lectionary Commentary

2 Thessalonians 2:1-5, 13-17

It appears that some of the people in Thessalonica are disturbed by a rumor that the day of the Lord has already come. Paul writes, in verses 1-5, to remind the people of what he had told them on a previous visit. Paul encourages them to not be deceived by the "person who is lawless." He predicts destruction of the deceiver and reminds them that they had already had the conversation. Verses 13-17 reveal Paul's message that the people have been chosen for salvation, and he offers them assurance and hope.

Luke 20:27-38

Luke tells the story of Jesus' confrontation with the Sadducees over the Torah. The address to Jesus as "Teacher" indicates that they are asking the Rabbi his interpretation. The scenario about a woman being passed through a variety of marriages and finally dying leads to the real question regarding Jesus' view of the resurrection. His response would have taken the Sadducees off guard because Jesus supported the hope of resurrection for Moses. The answer from Jesus caused the religious leaders to cease questioning him, and they actually complimented him. (Ted McIlvain)

Worship Aids

Call to Worship

O Holy God, we long for what once was.
May we pass from then, to now, to when.
O Holy God, be in our now.
O Holy God, be in our can be.
All: Grant us peace in this worship, let the past be past,
and teach us to find solace and strength in a glorious future.

Unison Prayer of Confession

We confess that we often dwell on what was once heartwarming and comfortable. We have failed to remember that warm hearts and comfort are gifts of your creation. The gifts you have given us are often not acknowledged while we pray for more. We see other people who are different from us and desire that they be the same. We have not taught future generations to tell the stories of your great gifts then and now and in times to come. Help us, dear God, be aware of your guiding light that shines so brightly in the words and actions of Jesus, and teach us to speak and act in that amazing way. Amen.

Words of Assurance

We worship the God of the past, present, and future. Thanks be to God.

Benediction

Go in peace from this place of worship. May you find great comfort in knowing that God is with us now and forevermore. Find peace in all people and show God's love in your being. Be pleased by God's grace and presence in all our lives. Amen. (Ted McIlvain)

I Can Only Imagine: Making Melody to God

Third in a Series of Three on the Church's Favorite Songs

John 4:19-26; Matthew 18:20; Revelation 21:3-4

The fastest growing area of Christian music today is in the contemporary arena. Many churches are shifting to a blended or contemporary style of music. Choirs have given way to praise teams, while organs have given way to keyboards. Some worry that our church music is being lost. We long to pass on our heritage. Yet, just as children may not inherit our faith, neither can new generations necessarily inherit our worship.

Many preachers and churches deal regularly with complaints about worship being dull or boring, or the number one complaint, "I'm not being fed." More emphasis seems to be on the quality of the worship experience. Realizing that this is the priority for many twenty-first-century U.S. churchgoers, one leading church has changed the name of their worship services to "experiences." They tell us that the word *worship* implies dull and boring.

Another major complaint from long-time churchgoers is that worship seems more like entertainment. The changes seem to some more like a concert than a service of worship. Even some among the younger generations agree.

The Samaritan woman at the well tried to draw Jesus into the question of worship styles. "You believe that traditional worship is best done in the temple and that only the Hebrew priests can properly lead worship, but our Samaritan leaders have another view." What led to this division between Samaritans and Jews was the long period of exile in Babylon. Jews who had been taken into captivity tried to remain racially and religiously pure, not allowing any intermarriage. The Jews who were left behind intermarried and developed new religious practices as a part of their survival. When those in captivity finally returned under Nehemiah and Ezra, those who had remained behind were declared "unclean" and their worship on Mount Gerizim was termed sacrilegious. The debate had continued for centuries as Jews and Samaritans remained enemies.

Jesus cut to the heart of the woman's need. Worship does not require either temple or sacred mountain; true worship focuses upon God and not upon the worshiper. What does that say about our contemporary-versus-traditional debates? Jesus' words call us to question our worship. Why does God call us to worship? Why do we sing? Leaf through most hymnals and notice few hymns written in the manner of the psalms. The language of the psalms points attention toward God. Our hymns, contemporary and traditional, often point toward us: our calling, our experience, the testimony of the church.

John Wesley provided directions for congregational singing, which read, in part: "sing spiritually. Have an eye to God in every word you sing. Aim at pleasing him more than yourself. . . . [A]ttend strictly to the sense of what you sing, and see that your heart is not carried away with the sound, but offered to God continually" (*The United Methodist Hymnal* [Nashville: The United Methodist Publishing House, 1989], vii. Used by permission).

Our favorite church songs assist our worship. Some bring praise, and others call to pray. Some hymns declare God's faithfulness, while others call us to serve. Some relay the gospel, and others tell the story of the church. We need hymns that call us to know God, not merely to know about God. When the Samaritan woman tries to divert conversation away from herself by saying that one day the Messiah will come, Jesus simply says, "I Am—the one who speaks with you."

In his revelation, Jesus portrays a picture of heavenly choirs. Throughout the pages, he paints a graphic scene of the heavenly congregation continually in relationship with God, engaging in worship, and bringing praise to the Lamb of God. These worshipers and choristers are in the presence of the Messiah; they need hope no more, for the Messiah has come. Toward the end of Revelation, God completes the redemption of all creation, and God and humanity dwell together. John writes that a loud voice from the throne shouts, "Look! God's dwelling is here with humankind. He will dwell with them, and they will be his peoples. God himself will be with them as their God. He will wipe away every tear from their eyes. Death will be no more. There will be no mourning, crying, or pain anymore, for the former things have passed away" (vv. 3-4). Finally, there are no barriers to our worship, no distractions, no more confusing our need with worship. Finally, all worshipers give full attention to God, our creator. Can you imagine what that will be like?

"I Can Only Imagine" by the award-winning Christian singers Mercy Me, wonders aloud about John's picture of Revelation. What will life be when our complete focus is on the one who is present among us? Written in first person, this is a song sung as a prayer to God. "Surrounded by Your Glory, what will my heart feel?. . . I can only imagine!"

What will you do? Perhaps the question Jesus poses for us today is, what are you doing? If the Christ, our Messiah, has come, if Christ, our Lord, is present today, then how is our worship? Someone says, "But Lord, the music was just not of the quality that you deserve?"

Christ replies, "But my friends in the ghetto sing passionately without any accompaniment."

Another complains, "I just couldn't worship today, Lord, because I just wasn't fed."

Christ answers, "By whom are you expecting to be fed? I was with you. Did I not satisfy you?"

Can you imagine what it might be like when we finally know that Christ is present? Amen. (Guy Ames)

Worship Aids

Call to Worship from Psalm 103

Bless the Lord, O my soul,
And all that is within me; bless God's holy name.
Bless the Lord, O my soul, and do not forget any of God's blessings,
Who forgives every single iniquity and heals all our wounds,
Who redeems our lives,
Who crowns each of us with steadfast love and mercy,
Bless the Lord, O my soul,
And all that is within me; bless God's holy name.

Invocation

O God of truth and Spirit, we come in worship that we might know you and be better known by you. Help us in this hour set aside the noises of our lives that we might listen to your Spirit. Help us set the inward eyes of our spirits on you that our minds might be open to the cleansing and restoring presence of that same Spirit. May even the greetings and conversations beyond this hour continue to serve as an offering of praise that our lives might be an ongoing act of worship to you, almighty God. In the name of Jesus, our Lord. Amen.

Prayer of Confession

O God of all peoples, all nations, all colors, and all languages, we confess to you our selfishness and our self-centeredness. We gather to worship you, but we live as people who do not know you. While we desire true worship and sing praise to you, the true melody of our life is "all about me." Forgive us for allowing our worship to be limited to

only a brief moment in this place, while the sanctuary of our lives calls for a life that worships and honors you. In truth we strain to give you one hour a week as an act of faith. We acknowledge our hypocrisy, O God, and humbly ask that you so inspire us that our singing and our prayers might come alive with passion.

We ask your forgiveness and pray that you will move us to passionate acts of love, and of service, and of devotion for the sake of Jesus, who has never stopped giving all for us. God, call us away from empty worship. Now may your Spirit drive away our feeble songs and unbelieving prayers this day, and call us into renewed worship of spirit and truth. We pray this for Jesus' sake. Amen.

Words of Assurance

God hears and forgives. Hallelujah! (Guy Ames)

NOVEMBER 17, 2013

Twenty-sixth Sunday after Pentecost

Readings: Isaiah 65:17-25; Psalm 98; 2 Thessalonians 3:6-13; Luke 21:5-19

New Heaven, New Earth, New Life

Isaiah 65:17-25

The farming community in the Panhandle of Texas where I grew up is no more. The houses have been bulldozed, debris and foundations are gone. When I go to the area, I make a point to go to the old home place as though it might have become a mansion just waiting for my return. But to the contrary, I cross over the tracks on the small dirt road that led to my family home, and I am met with a vast amount of nothing. When I lived there, the house was run-down, very cold in the winter, vinyl flooring was worn through to the wood planks, and all nine hundred feet was inhabited. Parents, four boys, a few rodents, and an array of family and friends filled the small void.

The house and surrounding barns were far from beautiful or impressive, but I miss the good times there. Wouldn't we all like to return to the home of our youth, where we could play in trees and sheds that seemed so large, hang out with parents who were young and filled with answers for inquisitive minds, and invite friends over to play, and talk, and dream?

But instead, some of our parents' days are spent reliving the stories from their youth, and the friends who were so important live somewhere on the East Coast and do not have time for dreaming anymore. It's true that, as the saying goes, "You can't go home again." As much as we long for the glory road we traveled, we find that the curves in the road are the same but everything along the path is different.

Our story from prophet Isaiah is about God speaking to a people who once had a way of life that is now lost, and like me, they really want to live that way again. Life had been good (or so it seemed) right up to the time Babylonians came to town, killed many of their family and friends, carried off the youngest and the best into a foreign land, occupied their homes and ate heartily from gardens that they, the people of Judah, had cultivated so carefully. The world they had known and loved was instantly destroyed and lost to them for generations.

With the passage of time, they finally returned to their homeland. And in this story, they are a few generations away from their release from captivity. It is fifty years since returning to their beloved Jerusalem, and things have not been restored to the beauty and glory they had kept in their minds and hearts. Campfire stories are about the "good old days of glory," and the children can almost see the grandeur through the enthusiastic voices of older family members.

Efforts to rebuild the temple to the way Solomon had guided the original construction never materialized. Looking at the rebuilding, they see a rather ragged structure with decorations that lack the flair of old. After all that work, it is still not what it used to be.

I can only imagine that their hearts and spirits resemble the rubble they are viewing, and worse yet, they are living where the Babylonians had left their mark. Their lives were invaded, beloved scenes had changed, and despondency has set in.

In many ways, the Christian churches today are like the Jews who dream of the past. So many people remember the glory of the 1950s and 60s, when the mainline churches were full and active, and the people gathered each Sunday for Sunday school and worship, and a picnic on the grounds. But like the Jews, we are struggling to let go and move forward.

I believe that mainline churches are beginning to listen to the promises of God from today's passage. Many of us are turning the tide from the past and looking forward to a reforming Christianity. The term "postmodern" has become a staple in discussions. We speculate about the forms it should take, what the new messages will be, and the expanse of mission work the church should hold close.

This isn't a new dream for Christianity. Parallels with John Wesley's time are remarkable. Wesley believed God had raised the "people called Methodists . . . to reform the nation, particularly the church, and to spread scriptural holiness over the land" (John Wesley, "Minutes of Several Conversations" Q.3, in *The Works of John Wesley*, ed. Thomas Jackson [Grand Rapids: Baker, 1978], vol. 8, 299).

I believe Wesleyans should welcome the reforming church, or the "emerging" church. The reforming leaders are attuned to today's cultural and moral and theological perspectives. I believe that all Christians, regardless of denominational affiliation, should support this emerging church movement. I think that new leaders like you and me are aware of the need to be reforming and not dwelling on the past, just as Wesley did in his time.

When God promises a new temple better than the original, and a new heaven and new earth, the expectation is that Christians will think less of the past and more in the future. We should all be focusing on the church's purposes and values, vision of discipleship, and mission.

We can learn much from Isaiah about this new heaven, new earth, and reforming life. We can look forward to God's promise:

> Look! I'm creating
> a new heaven and a new earth:
> past events won't be remembered;
> they won't come to mind.
> Be glad and rejoice forever
> in what I'm creating,
> because I'm creating Jerusalem as a joy
> and her people as a source of gladness. (65:17-18)

Let us learn to forget what was good before but is not now, and look forward to new life in a new Christian experience. Amen. (Ted McIlvain)

Lectionary Commentary

2 Thessalonians 3:6-13

Paul writes a series of warnings to the people in Thessalonica: "we command you..." (v. 6). With that stern statement, he warns them against idleness. Paul encourages them to imitate him and those who travel with him. He lifts up the model of his own life: "we worked night and day with effort and hard work so that we would not impose on you" (v. 8). Two directives are the focus of this passage: avoid people who are not followers of Paul and his entourage, and avoid unruliness. Paul is critical of their idle actions and encourages them to do what is right.

Luke 21:5-19

Jesus has made efforts to reclaim the temple and has found it necessary to reprimand the leadership. Questions about the temple and the beautiful adornments open the door for Jesus to predict its destruction. The old ways will change as well, and people will experience betrayal from family and friends. Some will die. But he lifts up hope for those who are steadfast and prepared to suffer. (Ted McIlvain)

Worship Aids

Call to Worship

We are strengthened by the living God who is our hope for what is to come. We are encouraged by the God who creates a new heaven and earth and gives new life to all. We are strengthened by God's people and are not alone. Let us worship the God of all creation.

Prayer of Pardon

God is gracious and merciful at all times, even in the face of our failures. God provides comfort and helps us overcome difficult times, even in the face of our doubts. In the name of Jesus Christ and in the presence of the Holy Spirit, we are forgiven. Amen.

Benediction

Do not be caught up in past glories. Go forth with renewed confidence in the future. Know that God is with you, to protect you, to strengthen you, and to give you peace. Amen. (Ted McIlvain)

I, Paul, a Prisoner for Christ Jesus—The Stewardship of Gratitude

First in a Series of Two on Managing Thanksgiving

Ephesians 3:1-2, 7-13

How did he manage? The apostle Paul we know suffered a great deal. People familiar with Paul's writing can predict what's about to come once he mentions that he's a prisoner. He tends to relate how he has suffered all for the sake of the gospel. In 2 Timothy, Paul complains about the treatment he received in Asia (1:15). In Galatians, he details the conflict with the leaders in Jerusalem. In Philippians, Paul laments that there were people preaching Christ out of selfish ambition, and to irritate him (1:17). In 2 Corinthians 11, Paul provides an inventory of the ways that he has suffered: given lashes five times, beaten three times, stoned once, shipwrecked three times—adrift at sea through the night, suffering privation and exposure to the elements (vv. 22-29). It begins to sound like the old response from our parents when we complained: Paul had to walk to school uphill, both ways, barefoot, in the snow, carrying a lard pail of biscuits. Sometimes we read about Paul's suffering and roll our eyes. He starts to sound like that elder uncle at the Thanksgiving dinner table telling us once more about the journey from Willamette to Tiago; we've heard these stories a thousand times. But Paul had truly suffered.

There are others who do not make us roll our eyes but push our eyes wide open as we wonder, "How do they manage?" The single mom with four kids struggling to make ends meet, busier than anyone could imagine. Yet she carries an inner peace that halts anxiety in its tracks. The hospital patient who has lost limbs to the ravages of diabetes but has not lost the capacity to smile and to embrace life. The eighty-four-year-old stroke survivor, sitting in front of a yellow pad—making big A, little *a*, big *B*, little *b*—learning to write again, this time with her left hand. How do they manage?

We expect Paul to belabor his labor and assault us with his assaults, but Paul does not do what we expect him to do. He doesn't drone on about his suffering here. He makes a brief reference to his prisoner status in verse 1 and offers encouragement regarding his suffering in verse 13, and that's it. The section that stands between has been described by scholars as an excursus, diversion, or detour. It does not fit the flow of the argument. But it has the feeling of one suddenly overwhelmed by a truth that transcends the situation. Despite imprisonment, separation, and a career that has stalled, despite the beatings, poor treatment, and exclusion, Paul manages thanksgiving.

It happens for others somehow. Where some mothers see chaos, the peaceful mother sees the beauty of discovery. Where one patient sees discomfort, another sees a community of care. Where some stroke survivors see one bad hand, the persevering one sees another that's been underutilized. This is not to suggest that people who don't respond to adversity in quite the same way have failed somehow. We all must deal with our trials in our own way. But the wisdom pointed to by Paul is the wisdom of responding to prison with praise. These verses standing between two references to imprisonment are not a detour—they are a demolition. They break down the walls of Paul's imprisonment. Instead of focusing on what he lacks, Paul stresses what we have; instead of thinking of how he has suffered, Paul focuses on how we have been blessed.

In a few days, you'll need to be able to answer the question, "What are you thankful for this year?" If you're anything like me, you hope that your kids don't say something totally inappropriate in front of the in-laws (something that will undoubtedly get blamed on your influence). You pray that no one will say something too serious—the sort of thanksgiving that really isn't a thanksgiving but a lament decorated to look like a thanksgiving. You hope that you can say something meaningful and penetrating that will make you look truly reflective of grace but not come off sounding like a sermon. Okay, maybe you don't, but I do. But if Paul were at our table, he might just do what he does here and virtually explode with a litany of blessings that you cannot count one by one, for each one is beyond the next. He gives thanks for divine power. He gives thanks for boundless riches. He gives thanks for new revelation. He gives thanks for eternal purpose. He gives thanks for confident access. In short, to answer the question "How does Paul manage thanksgiving despite his imprisonment?" Paul manages it by the grace of God.

In Greek, there's a curious word that shows up here in our reading, *oikonomia*—the management of the household. Outside the book of Ephesians it occurs a couple of times. But three of the nine New Testament uses of the word occur in the book of Ephesians—two of those coming in this chapter. In verse 2 it's the word the NRSV translates as "commission"—the commission of God's grace. In verse 9 it is translated as "plan"—the plan of the mystery. Look through several versions of the Bible and you'll see different words used there. It's a struggle to know exactly what it means—is it a reference to God's plan or the responsibility entrusted to Paul? Should it be seen as a divine possession or a human directive? Linguistically it's an uninspired out to say "both." Nonetheless, Paul would say "both." It is the human responsibility over the divine possession. And that is why my favorite translation of *oikonomia* is "stewardship." Stewardship at its best is the detour of gratitude that emerges from us whenever we see that what we have in Christ Jesus exceeds the prisons that try to hold us in. (Andy Mangum)

Worship Aids

Invocation

Lord, you did not leave your diverse people divided, but through Jesus Christ you have brought people near through the gracious acts of Christ our Lord. Enable us to be faithful stewards of your gift of unifying grace, we pray. Amen.

Prayer of Illumination

Gracious God, it is through Christ Jesus that we have access to you, and it is in Scripture that we find our witness and access to Christ. Enable us now to live within that access through prayerful meditation on your word.

Benediction

And now, people of God, we have heard once again that Christ restored divided humanity and bridged the gaps between us. Let us now make known to rulers, authorities, and all others who might see or hear that all may have access to God. Amen. (Andy Mangum)

NOVEMBER 24, 2013

Reign of Christ / Christ the King Sunday

Readings: Jeremiah 23:1-6; Psalm 46; Colossians 1:11-20; Luke 23:33-43

God Is Our Refuge and Strength

Psalm 46

"God is our refuge and strength, / a help always near / in times of great trouble. . . . / The LORD of heavenly forces is with us" (vv. 1, 7). Words of assurance and hope! The psalmist's song is a celebration that God will preserve us and give us victory over the challenges that face us. The Almighty is in our midst, and although the nations are in an uproar, and the kingdoms totter, God's voice melts the earth. It is God who makes the wars to cease and the bows to break. God's kingdom of peace will prevail!

In the context of what happens on a daily basis, the psalmist's words come as a sign of relief and strength to the troubled soul. The lists are many, and we could take a long time noting how the nations are in an uproar and the kingdoms totter. We can look out and see what has happened across parts of Northern Africa and the Middle East and notice how nations and peoples have been tottering to and fro. We can look at what has happened throughout the world and see how peoples have dealt with one calamity after another: with earthquakes and tsunamis, with volcanoes and tornadoes. Not only are the nations in an uproar, but the earth shakes and moves and trembles. From whence does our help come?

We can look at our own lives and ask the same questions, dealing as we do with loved ones who are sick or with children who need special attention. We can look close to home and see friends who have lost jobs or a company, or businesses that have gone under. We can look around and ask what we can do. But the message of the psalmist remains: "God is our refuge and strength, / a help always near / in times of great trouble."

One of the most memorable occasions following the 9/11 terrorist attacks was the Service of Remembrance in the Washington Cathedral. At the time, the nation was reeling and in shock, figuring out what had happened and what it was going to mean. During the service the people who had gathered sang the great hymn by Martin Luther "A Mighty Fortress Is Our God." Bellowing through the cathedral was the sound of the organ, calling the people, if not the world, to the truth that God is a "bulwark never failing; our helper he amid the flood of mortal ills prevailing" (*The United Methodist Hymnal* [Nashville: The United Methodist Publishing House, 1989], 110. Used by permission). Luther's hymn, of course, is based on Psalm 46: God's kingdom is forever. Or, to put it another way, in the midst of the city, in the midst of the ruins and pain, in the midst of suffering and death, God's fortress of love is present.

It's a message that goes to the heart of the gospel: that in death there is life. On the cross, God's mercy, while hidden, is revealed in Christ, and gives strength, even during the worst of times. There is help from the one who gives his life in service to all. And, oddly, the only response to what God is doing in the midst of this suffering is to sing! We worship and give thanks to God, who is present, giving us help and hope.

One of the most remarkable scenes I have witnessed as a pastor came during the fall, when the farmers of our church were out in the fields bringing in the harvest. I received a call that one of our farmers had a heart attack and was being taken to the emergency room. Immediately, the family stopped what they were doing. We all met at the hospital, gathered at the side of Greg's bed.

The sounds of crying, of course, could be heard, as well as sobbing. The four boys and mother and grandchildren who had been working in the fields were all there. Greg had died of a massive heart attack. What to do?

As I began to offer prayer, I noticed Greg's wife out of the corner of my eye. She was beginning to kneel by the bed. She was a woman highly devoted to prayer, and she was one of the "prayer warriors" in our church. Without saying another word, I simply moved aside as Joan offered one of the most moving prayers I have ever heard, thanking God for Greg's life and offering Greg to God as a servant of Christ. We all were moved to tears, both of sadness and joy.

I share this story because there, in the midst of death, was God's very present help. God's strength made possible what seemed impossible. Prayers were being offered because of the help we have from God. It reminds us that what Paul says is true: "I can endure all . . . things through the power of the one who gives me strength" (Philippians 4:13); or "[God's] grace is sufficient" (2 Corinthians 12:9 NRSV). God will help us when the morning dawns, for the Lord of hosts is with us.

It's a message we share as we move toward the Advent season, reminding ourselves that God is with us: Emmanuel. On this last Sunday of the Christian church year, we celebrate the presence of the Shepherd King, the one who protects and serves, and the one who gives and provides. The Shepherd King is with us as we worship and sing and prepare for the coming of the Lord, even as we anticipate giving thanks for all that God has given us.

In the midst of trouble and uncertainty, God is here. Or, to put it in the words of the apostle Paul, in the midst of everything that life can throw at us, there is nothing that can separate us from God (Romans 8:39).

It's why we can come to the table with grateful hearts, and it's why we can give thanks for God's goodness: the Lord of hosts, the God of Jacob, is with us. God is indeed our refuge and strength! (Andrew D. Kinsey)

Lectionary Commentary

Jeremiah 23:1-6

This passage is an oracle reproaching Judah's rulers for not attending to the people, or flock, of God. The passage is a charge to the rulers that God will restore Judah and will establish a "righteous descendant" (or "Branch" v. 5 NRSV; see Isaiah 11:1) who will execute righteousness and justice in the land. This king will bring salvation to Judah and will rule responsibly before God, unlike Zedekiah, who served and led irresponsibly before God. Jeremiah, the weeping prophet, longs for the day of God's shalom in the land.

Colossians 1:11-20

There are two parts to this passage: the first is the conclusion of a prayer, asking for God's strength and power; and the second is the magisterial hymn, praising the invisible God for his beloved son. The thrust of the entire passage is on the way Jesus has rescued us from the power of darkness and transferred us to the kingdom of Christ, that is, the kingdom in which we have redemption and forgiveness (v. 13). Christ, the firstborn of all creation, the firstborn of the dead, is the Lord of life, for he is the head of the body, the church. It is in Christ that the fullness of God is pleased to dwell.

Luke 23:33-42

This passage on Christ the King Sunday may sound odd to the ears of those who are preparing for Thanksgiving and moving into the holiday season. Yet the language of kingship runs throughout the text, as Luke shares how the "king of the Jews" (v. 37) cannot save himself from suffering and death on the cross. The irony is present as Jesus welcomes into his kingdom, even in death, those criminals at his side. Remembering Jesus on the throne of the cross is to remember how God is turning the world upside down. This is no ordinary king! (Andrew D. Kinsey)

Worship Aids

Call to Worship

Use *The United Methodist Hymnal* psaltet, p. 780, a responsive reading of the NRSV translation of Psalm 46, with musical response 1, from "A Mighty Fortress Is Our God." (Nashville: The United Methodist Publishing House, 1989).

Invocation

O God, you are our refuge and strength. In you we find hope and assurance, and in you we discover your help. As we lift our hearts to you in this time of worship, may we discover yet again how you are with us and how your love endures forever; in Christ's name we pray. Amen.

Benediction

And now may the God of Jacob, the Lord of Hosts, be with you, and may the strength of God's saving love and care give you peace, as you live in the service of God's blessed kingdom. Amen. (Andrew D. Kinsey)

Getting Tired—Stewardship of Thanksgiving

Second in a Series of Two on Managing Thanksgiving

Ephesians 3:14-21

Last week we looked at the verses preceding our text for this morning. In closing, I mentioned the curious use of *oikonomia*—management, plan, or stewardship. In describing his own work as an apostle, Paul speaks of his stewardship of God's mysteries. Paul believed in the God of Abraham, Isaac, and Jacob, the God of the people of Israel. He had been trained to follow the commands of the Torah and live within the community of fellow Jews. As an adult, Paul had a dramatic moment of conversion. He was moved out of the normal boundaries of his upbringing and was called to share the message of God's grace for people who had been excluded from the promise (Ephesians 2:11-21). This was God's *oikonomia*—God's plan—to expand the reach of the gospel to include everyone. This was the work entrusted to Paul's *oikonomia*—his management.

I never studied management. What little I think I know about management, I've picked up along the way. Somewhere along the way, I learned a little management principle: you can only manage what you can measure. I assume that Paul had also heard this principle, as he writes to his Gentile audience, "I ask that you'll have the power to grasp love's width and length, height and depth, together with all believers. I ask that you'll know the love of Christ that is beyond knowledge so that you will be filled entirely with the fullness of God" (vv. 18-19). It is good to take stock of everything we have received in Christ. We ask people to do that through our stewardship campaigns every year. We ask people to assess the ways they have received provision and blessing from God and then designate a percentage of that as an offering. Stewardship campaigns seem to be the time when people in the church, despite their lack of training, try to measure and manage. We ask people to measure what they will give, because you can only manage what you can measure.

The church where I grew up gave us offering envelopes that asked us to measure our stewardship. It had a check box for "present," which always struck me as odd, since I wouldn't be there to turn in the offering envelope if I weren't. Bible brought—check (you weren't fully dressed unless you had your Bible). "Bible Read Daily"—umh, sure, if for a few days the scripture on the refrigerator magnet qualifies. "Lesson studied"—no, "giving," "worship," and "contacts—prospects or members"; we were expected to make contact with people. I must admit that I didn't take the envelopes seriously at the time. Although it's been over twenty years since I have attended that church, the message of those little envelopes sticks with me—your stewardship involves your presence, your habits, your finances, and your service. That's a good message, but it can become very focused on our actions and fail to see what we have in Christ.

When people who aren't members of the church I serve find out I'm a minister, they often feel compelled to explain their religious views or practices. I try to make sure that I handle these kinds of conversations delicately. The last thing I want to do is to come off as judgmental. A few months ago, I found myself in just such a conversation. My conversation partner was a thoughtful, caring, and intelligent woman in her fifties. Her husband, she explained, didn't believe in God, but he never objected when she wanted to go. Even so, attending church on a regular basis had become difficult over the years.

She spoke of the United Methodist minister she liked to listen to most. He didn't get bogged down, she said, in theology. "In his sermons he just encouraged us to be a little bit better the next week." The message was clean and simple, encouraging and positive. Each week, just work to be a little bit better than you had been the week before. But then she said something very telling: "The problem with trying to be a little better each week is that you get really tired."

The checklist of our own stewardship can become tiring to deal with, which is why I think the checklist on the front of Paul's envelope is quite different. It does not focus on what we need to do for God but on what God has done for us. I think it would say something like this: Do you know God, the maker of every people in heaven and earth—check? Do you perceive God's glorious riches—check? Inner strength? Indwelling presence, rooted in love? Paul asks us whether we have made contacts not with other members or visitors but with the love of Christ. Paul prays that we might comprehend the dimensions of Christ's love.

It reminds me a little of a vision from the prophet Ezekiel as he imagines a restored temple and then a river that flows from the temple to revive the land and turn the Dead Sea into a freshwater lake teeming with life. In the vision, the prophet is given a cord to measure the length of the river, and as he moves, the river grows deeper and deeper until he is submerged from head to foot. On the banks of the river are trees, whose leaves are for healing (Ezekiel 47:1-12). The height and depth and width and length of Christ's love is beyond measure. It is also there for the healing of the divide that sin forged between God's people and within their souls.

Paul quickly adds that we cannot really measure it. The love of Christ surpasses knowledge. And if that wasn't enough for us to get the point, Paul takes it one step further in verse 20: God is able to do "beyond all that could ask or imagine." Why does Paul want us to measure the immeasurable? It is to discover for ourselves that it is immeasurable, that we cannot measure it, and therefore we cannot manage it; we can stand in gratitude before it and be stewards of our own thanksgiving that we might be filled with the fullness of God. (Andy Mangum)

Worship Aids

Invocation

Amazing Lord, you do far more than we could hope, imagine, measure, or calculate. We arrive week by week to express the inexpressible—our gratitude to you. Receive our prayers and songs, and our very lives as well, as we seek to be faithful stewards of your gifts.

Prayer for Illumination

Master and Foundation, we are simply stewards of that which belongs to you. Through the reading and hearing of Scripture, remind us of the nature of your plan and your desires for us who live and serve within it.

Benediction

To the Lord our God who is powerfully at work within us, who does abundantly more than all we can ask or imagine, be glory in the church—through the world and in this very congregation—and may this generation, the last generation, and all generations to come give praise and thanks forever. (Andy Mangum)

NOVEMBER 28, 2013

Thanksgiving Day

Readings: Deuteronomy 26:1-11; Psalm 100; Philippians 4:4-9; John 6:25-35

Whose We Are

Psalm 100

If you ever go to New York City, you will see millions of people. You will see persons from different religious groups and different ethnic groups. You will also probably see Jewish men wearing a skullcap on the top of their heads. Most of the skullcaps are black, but some of them are very festive. Still others have designs embroidered on them. You might wonder why these men go around wearing them. The name for the skullcap is *yarmulke*, and it is typically worn by men during times of prayer and study. It is also worn during worship and meals. It is worn as a reminder of who is God and who isn't.

On a recent trip to New York a friend of mine spoke with a young Jewish man who was wearing a *yarmulke*. My friend asked him why he wore it, and here is what the young man said: "I wear it to remind me that there is someone who is over me and above me. I am not God. I am not the Lord. I am simply one of the sheep in his pasture."

That's a great statement. The image of being a sheep in God's pasture goes back to Psalm 100, a psalm we remember from childhood onward:

> Make a joyful noise to the LORD, all the earth.
> Worship the Lord with gladness;
> come into his presence with singing.
> Know that the Lord is God.
> It is he that made us, and we are his;
> we are his people, and the sheep of his pasture. (vv. 1-3 NRSV)

It's a psalm that captures who God is. God is the creator and giver of life. God is the one above whom no other exists, the awesome Sovereign of the whole universe. And who are we? We are the creatures of God's creation. We are the sheep of God's pasture.

Or to put it another way, there is no life for the one who doesn't know God is God, and who doesn't know that before God we are but mere creatures, mere sheep in God's pasture! That is, when we fail to grasp this point, we begin to think that we are God and that the whole world is supposed to revolve around us. And once we begin to live with this kind of deceit, we begin to fail in our worship of God in truth.

It's why many of us may need to wear a *yarmulke* of some sort to remind us that we are not God and never will be. We are mere creatures of God's creation, mere sheep in his pastures. And it's when we begin to recognize this truth that we can begin to live with gratitude. In other words, when reading Psalm 100, we come face to face with how deeply blessed and how deeply dependent we are on God for our very lives and existence. It's a profound but basic truth, a truth many in our culture have forgotten: that we didn't make ourselves and that we don't sustain ourselves and that even our next breath is not something we can produce or manufacture on our own. In forgetting this truth, we put ourselves and not God at the center.

Maybe it's time we realize the truth that God is God and that we are the sheep of his pasture, that all we have comes from him and is to be returned to him, especially as we remember and celebrate Thanksgiving. Maybe it's time we as a church and as a nation wake up to the truth that we are dependent on God and sustained by God. Maybe it's time we realize who God is and whose we are.

In some ways this message may be a little insulting. After all, a sheep is not a very smart animal. In fact, a sheep is considered one of the dumbest animals in the barnyard. And yet, from the Psalms, and the Scriptures, and Jesus' own ministry, we see that as human beings we are considered as sheep.

Is this an image of gratitude? Being compared to sheep?

Perhaps this is where the gratitude part comes into the picture. Gratitude, after all, is a way of looking at life and living. It is a way of looking at the world and seeing that there is a power beyond us and above us that can make our lives more joyful. There is one who can make our lives into what they were created to be.

It also points out why ingratitude is a sin. In fact, following Jesus' healing of the ten with skin diseases, he points out what can happen when persons fail to give thanks. From Jesus' perspective, ingratitude is life-threatening (Luke 17:11-19). Imagine that! Ingratitude is life-threatening! And it's life-threatening because it fails to see the giver behind the gift.

As people plan to rush the stores on Black Friday, the biggest shopping day of the year, we need to remember whose sheep we are. As we take time to celebrate our gifts and treasures with loved ones, we can do so with a sense of gratitude for all that God has given to us. And in a time of thanksgiving, we can remember, in Paul's words, how we may always be thankful and joyful, no matter what happens (1 Thessalonians 5:14-18). For we are indeed the Lord's sheep, and it is God who made us.

In a season of thanksgiving, let us continue to enter God's gates with singing and God's courts with praise, remembering and knowing whose we are. (Andrew D. Kinsey)

Lectionary Commentary

Deuteronomy 26:1-11

This passage speaks to the rites and ceremonies for offering the first fruits and the tithe to God after the land has been settled. The chapter anticipates the conclusion of Moses' main address in chapter 28. The occasion of this text is the harvest festival, when the people of God thank the Lord for the gift of the land and the generosity of God's goodness. The "starving Aramean" is reference to Israel's nomadic life and takes here the form of a confession of faith, affirming how God's faithfulness is the basis of freedom in the life of faith.

Philippians 4:4-9

It is difficult to imagine a more stunning portrayal of faith's confidence than Paul's expression of joy to the Philippians while in prison. Here is a person who is full of joy because of what Christ has done for him and whose life is grounded in the virtues of Christ's life, death, and resurrection—the life of faithful service. And because of what Christ has done, Paul can express this joy, knowing how close the Lord is and knowing how the peace of God surpasses even our small understandings of faith.

John 6:25-35

Jesus is dealing with a large crowd on the side of the sea. The disciples have gone ahead of him, and the people who had come for bread have followed him. Jesus cautions the crowd and the disciples not to work for food that perishes but for food that endures for eternal life. That's when the disciples respond with a question (v. 28): "What must we do in order to accomplish what God requires?" The question assumes a works-based or rules-based set of expectations. Jesus, on the other hand, has something else in mind: the key is not so much doing as believing, believing in the one whom God has sent. The first responsibility of the follower of Christ is to believe, to trust in the mighty works of God's salvation. (Andrew D. Kinsey)

Worship Aids

Call to Worship (Psalm 100)

Shout triumphantly to the LORD, all the earth!
Serve the LORD with celebration! Come before him with shouts of joy!
Know that the LORD is God—he made us; we belong to him.
We are his people, the sheep of his own pasture.
Enter his gates with thanks; enter his courtyards with praise!
Thank him! Bless his name!
Because the LORD is good, his loyal love lasts forever;
his faithfulness lasts generation after generation.

Invocation

Loving God, we give you thanks this day for all that you have given to us. You fill our lives with joy, and now we return that joy with gratitude. May we in this time of worship give to you our proper thanks and praise as we enter into communion with you and as we share with thankful hearts. In Christ's name we pray. Amen.

Benediction

Go forth with gratitude in your hearts to live with thanksgiving on your lips and to share in the abundance of God's grace and mercy. Know that the Lord is God and that we are his sheep. In the power of Christ's presence we pray. Amen. (Andrew D. Kinsey)

Thankful for the Words of Jesus

Thanksgiving

Luke 19:5-9; John 8:1-11

Thanksgiving arrives as expected but seldom prepared for, every fourth Thursday of November. We will have invited guests and family to our homes for a traditional Thanksgiving feast, and of course some football on TV. My family and I will play a friendly, wild-and-crazy game of flag football on our front lawn. Perhaps many of you have similar traditions that make Thanksgiving special for your family.

I suspect that some of you are asking, "Why do we worship on a secular holiday like Thanksgiving?" After all, there is very little religious significance to the day and certainly no biblical requirement. You know that the commercialism of one of Christianity's most sacred days, Christmas, will be in full swing. Children from their little table strategically placed away from the big people will loudly proclaim how much they want the special toy they plan to mention to Santa Claus.

I am an advocate of being thankful to God three hundred and sixty four days of the year. Setting aside one day a year for gratitude seems to be nothing but ungratefulness. I believe that intentionally thanking God all those other days would make the ungrateful day less egregious.

I am convinced that the words of Jesus will bring about many reasons for being thankful, and today, I want to emphasize the results of Jesus' words from our Bible text. The words of Jesus in conversation with sinners emphasize his understanding of the need to instill a sense of value and dignity not only in Zacchaeus and the condemned woman but every person he encountered.

Let's begin with how he recognized value in a man who was not respected by his family, neighbors, and in fact, the entire community. When Jesus came to the tree the wee little man had climbed, he looked up and saw him, and said, "Zacchaeus, come down at once. I must stay in your home today" (Luke 19:5).

Jesus was inviting himself to the home of someone the Jews detested and certainly did not trust. Their hero from Galilee, whom they had followed on their way to the Passover, was breaking the rules. I do not believe that Jesus was concerned about the rules. He was concerned about how Zacchaeus felt about himself. Then he shocked the disciple's sensibilities and those of the people of Jericho by inviting himself to be the guest of a chief publican who didn't have the best reputation. This Zacchaeus desired to see Jesus, and although that's commendable, the idea of it is surpassed by the fact that Jesus wanted to see him! In that moment, I believe Jesus restored some dignity to the life of one from whom dignity had been stripped.

The Zacchaeus story shows that we should be attentive to people others see as disreputable and recognize there is value in everyone. When we do, we are blessed. On this Thanksgiving Day, I pray, "Thank you, God, for blessing me when I recognize value in everyone I meet."

Let us now consider how Jesus restored dignity to a woman awaiting the punishment of death for the crime of passion. Here we picture a woman standing before her accusers and people eager to throw stones. I see a woman whose head hangs low, her hands bound with straps, and tears staining her cheeks. She has no one to turn to, no one to offer solace to her in this time of punishment. She is alone. She is frightened. She has no sense of dignity.

All of these emotions are forced on her, and the last time I checked, it took two people to commit adultery! If they caught the woman in the very act, then where is the man? She must sense the injustice.

In the midst of her anguish, a conversation between the religious leaders and a man named Jesus gets her attention. It is apparent that the leaders are asking this Jesus questions about her crime. She likely does not comprehend the impact this conversation will soon have. Tears continue to flow. Fear continues to overwhelm her. I believe that with her head bowed, she sees Jesus kneel before her and the questioners, and write in the sand with his finger.

Then suddenly, she is standing before the one who brings peace and justice. After all the public humiliation and the danger of losing her life, she is standing with the savior. Her accusers are gone. She has just witnessed Jesus' piercing insight into their sin and his condemnation of their actions, but how will he deal with her now? Jesus' response is different from what she expected.

Jesus straightens up and asks, "'Woman, where are they? Has no one condemned you?' 'No one, sir,' she [says]. 'Then neither do I condemn you'" (John 8:10-12 NIV).

Jesus does not say, "Sin no more, and then I won't condemn you." Jesus' grace says, "I do not condemn you, now go and sin no more." In that moment, Jesus restored her dignity.

On this Thanksgiving Day, I pray, "Thank you, God, for blessing me when I restore dignity to those from whom it has been stripped."

I find it special that in both passages, when Jesus encountered two people who had lost value and dignity, Jesus "looked up" to Zacchaeus and "straightened up" before the woman in the stoning pit. Jesus never looked down on either person. Even in the presence of the leaders who would condemn and cause his death, he looked up to the people who needed him most.

On this Thanksgiving day, I pray, "Thank you, O God, for blessing me when I restore dignity and recognize value in people from whom self-worth has been stripped." I say, "Thank you, O God, for teaching me to look up to all people and never look down on anyone. Yes, God, I am thankful."

Thanksgiving is more than games and food, it is a time to give thanks to God for allowing us to find blessings in our treatment of others. In those moments, people see Jesus in us. Thanks be to God. (Ted McIlvain)

Worship Aids

Call to Worship

We come here to worship with thanksgiving.
Let us remember that God is the audience
and we are the players.
We come here to be renewed and thankful.
We come here to be gratefully changed.
Teach us to seek people who have lost their value and dignity.
Let us be the source of change that gives them peace.

Pastoral Prayer

Oh God, on this day when we find joy in your creation, we give you thanks. We experience the chill of the air and find warmth in this place where we gather with friends to worship you. Give us vision to identify and change people who have been stripped of value and dignity. We are thankful and amazed by your presence. Amen.

Benediction

Go into your world seeking people you can make new by acknowledging their self-worth. Find joy when you give them solace and comfort. Let their renewed faces show you Jesus, and let their smiles be your peace. Amen. (Ted McIlvain)

DECEMBER 1, 2013

First Sunday of Advent

Readings: Isaiah 2:1-5; Psalm 122; Romans 13:11-14; Matthew 24:36-44

Hype or Hope?

Isaiah 2:1-5

We've all heard the come-ons: four days and three nights in an oceanfront condo—absolutely free! Jewelry at ridiculously low prices. Prescription drugs available at a fraction of the cost. Real estate deals at unbelievable prices. How many of us have been taken in by these enticements? How many have learned their lesson? You know the old saying, "If it sounds too good to be true, it usually is!"

The older we get, the more suspicious we become of the advertisements and the come-ons that seem to defy logic and common sense. At this time of the year, we are especially aware of advertising hype. The retailers are out to make a sale, and most of us are skeptical.

Eight centuries before the birth of Christ, the prophet Isaiah describes a time in the future when peace will prevail throughout the world, a day when God's righteousness and justice will be the law of the land. "Then they will beat / their swords into iron plows, / and their spears into pruning tools," writes Isaiah; "Nation will not take up sword / against nation, / they will no longer learn / how to make war" (v. 4). To a war-weary world, these words sound like the come-on of a fast-talking salesperson or of a politician skilled in the use of appealing rhetoric. Yet for the Judeo-Christian community, these words are not the hype of a persuasive speaker but the hope of the world.

Each year during this season, as the days are growing shorter, and in my part of the world, the nights are growing longer and darker and colder, God breaks through with the story of Jesus, light for our darkness, joy for our sadness, and hope for our despair. Every year we take four weeks to reflect on the meaning of the Christ-event, the baby born in Bethlehem's manger to be the Savior of the world. Of course, every baby's birth—regardless of the circumstances—reminds us of the preciousness of life and the potential of tomorrow. Someone has said that the birth of every baby is God's vote for the future of humanity. Every time I hold a precious little one in my arms, every time I baptize a baby, I think about the promise and the hope that God has for our world.

While the coming of every baby is special and cause for much preparation on the part of family and friends—showers and redecorating and baby furniture and all the rest—the coming of this baby causes special preparation. There are stern warnings and voices of alarm in the Bible for those who are not focusing on the coming of this child, but the promise of this baby is not something to be feared or resisted. His coming will be wonderful! Young parents sometimes say, "We don't know what to do. We've never been parents before!" Advent reminds us that God is coming to be with us. "We've never had God in our lives before," someone might be saying. I remember a little poem we used to learn in Sunday school entitled, "If Jesus Came to Your House." We would gulp and shrink back, because if Jesus came to our house, he would see us being mean to our brothers and sisters or not doing our homework or chores like we were told. But the coming of Jesus is not supposed to be something that we fear, but something for us to rejoice about. Jesus promises to usher in a new day of peace and harmony that will be wonderful. Not hype, but hope for the world!

We of the church believe that the God who once entered Bethlehem's manger will come to this world again and establish God's kingdom forever. When will this take place? It happens every time a person accepts Jesus Christ as his or her Lord and Savior. It happens every time a person meets our Lord on the road of life. It will happen when our lives end, and ultimately, it will happen at the end of time. When will that be? No one knows, the Bible tells us, and it is not ours to predict. We are called, not to predict the future, but to prepare for it. We are called to live as if God is already here with us, because, indeed, God is already here with us. We are called, not to sit and wait for something to happen in the future, but to live lives of hope and joy, right now, today. As Christian believers, we know what time it is, to paraphrase the apostle Paul. It is time to wake from sleep. Now is the acceptable time. Today is the day of salvation.

What does it mean to live in hope during Advent? It means giving up our old ways of doing things. We have lived selfish and self-centered lives for long enough. Now is the time to give up the weapons of mass destruction, the weapons we usually use: dishonesty, pride, quarreling, and jealousy. In their place we are called to "put on the Lord Jesus Christ" (Romans 13:14 NRSV; "dress yourself with the Lord Jesus Christ" CEB), which means to live as he taught us: in love, in joy, and in generosity of spirit.

When you live by hope rather than by hype, your values change and life takes on a different focus. The old weapons lose their power, and they are replaced with a whole new lifestyle. You see, Jesus calls us to live as if the swords have already been beaten into plows and the spears already made into pruning tools. That's what it means to live in hope this Advent season.

Advent should be the most wonderful season of the year, for it lifts up the promise that God is coming to be with us. Not only did God come to Bethlehem's manger, not only will God come at the end of time and at the end of our time, God also comes to us in the everyday situations of life, when we are not looking for God, sometimes when we least expect.

The God who came, who is coming again, comes to us every day. This is not holiday hype, but the promise of hope. May each of us keep awake, keep alert, and live in hopeful expectation this day and every day! (Charlie Yoost)

Lectionary Commentary

Romans 13:11-14

Paul exhorts the Roman congregation to wake up! It is later than they think. In fact, Christ is already in their midst, and they need to act appropriately! Radical change is expected. No longer is it acceptable to mirror the behavior of the rest of the world. Instead, we are to put on the "weapons of light" and live new and exemplary lives of faith.

Matthew 24:36-44

The call to readiness is also sounded in this passage concerning our Lord's return. Matthew is predicting that Jesus will come suddenly, like "a thief in the night" (1 Thessalonians 5:2; see Matthew 24:43-44). Believers are called to be prepared. The passage is a warning both to those who become indifferent toward spiritual concerns and to those who exhibit moral laxity due to the mysterious and unpredictable timing of the Lord's return. Constant vigilance and staying alert are the only acceptable behaviors as we wait during Advent. (Charlie Yoost)

Worship Aids

Call to Worship

What time is it?
It is time to wake from sleep!
The day of our salvation is at hand
Christ is with us, and will lead us forward.
All: Thanks be to God!

Invocation

Dear God, as the ancient Israelites prayed for the peace of Jerusalem, so today we pray for peace for all the peoples of this world, no matter where they dwell. As we begin this season of Advent, may we truly pray that the day will come when all people everywhere will "beat / their swords into iron plows, / and their spears into pruning tools." This we pray in the name of the Prince of Peace. Amen.

Prayer

Dear God, as we sense the urgency of the gospel message today, forgive us for acting as if we have all the time in the world. Help us realize that you are near, that you care, and that you are calling us to follow you ever more closely this Advent season and every day of our lives. Make us alert to your presence and draw us closer to you. In Jesus' name we pray. Amen. (Charlie Yoost)

Zechariah: A Visionary Priest

First in a Series of Six on Unlikely Characters of the Nativity

Luke 1:5-25

There are some biblical characters who fade into obscurity in our memories, especially in stories that are as vivid as the story of the birth of Christ. Given the way that our imaginations have been shaped by the crucial plotline of the holy family encountering "no room in the inn" followed by the adoration of the grubby shepherds and the splendid wisemen from the East, we all too easily forget the many other figures who are not at the manger, yet are central figures in the drama of the nativity.

When these characters are considered alongside Mary, Joseph, and Jesus, one can be forgiven for losing track of them, as they drift in and out of the scene. In cinematic terms, these lesser characters would not be in the running for "Best Supporting Actor/Actress." Rather, we might be tempted to think of them as "extras," playing bit parts that help round out the story or fill the frame. But when we encounter familiar stories, we must remind ourselves that the Bible is not a movie; there are no extras. And we see this principle in action in the nativity when we encounter Zechariah, an old priest with a barren wife and a front-row seat for the mighty acts of God.

Zechariah and his wife, Elizabeth, were getting along in years, and they were childless; this was not by choice. As it is today for so many, their infertility was a defining tragedy for them. They were "that" couple, the couple that some regarded with condescending pity, or worse, with an air of moral suspicion. These were days when children were considered a blessing from God, and by extension, the lack of children was considered a curse. No doubt there were some cruel whispers: "I wonder why God hasn't blessed them with children? He is a priest, after all. Makes you wonder what skeletons are in that closet."

We do not know whether they still hoped for the work of God on their behalf; we only know that Zechariah served as a priest, an advocate who came alongside people as they presented their requests before God. And yet, it seemed that God had not heard his prayers. We know from our own experiences of frustrated prayer that it must have hurt.

Who among us doesn't know the pain of a dream deferred, or a prayer that seems to bounce back before it has even left our lips? Like an old friend who never responds to our attempts to reconnect, ignoring repeated e-mails and phone calls, one might be tempted to politely stop praying about things to avoid the awkwardness and embarrassment of yet another "unwelcome" prayer request.

So, when Zechariah is performing his priestly duties, offering incense in the temple, we can imagine his state of mind when the angel of God appears to him with some stunning news. Gabriel said,

> "Don't be afraid, Zechariah. Your prayers have been heard. Your wife Elizabeth will give birth to your son and you must name him John. He will be a joy and delight to you, and many people will rejoice at his birth, for he will be great in the Lord's eyes. He must not drink wine and liquor. He will be filled with the Holy Spirit even before his birth. He will bring many Israelites back to the Lord their God. He will go forth before the Lord, equipped with the spirit and power of Elijah. He will turn the hearts of fathers back to their children, and he will turn the

> disobedient to righteous patterns of thinking. He will make ready a people prepared for the Lord." (Luke 1:13-17)

Like so many others who were given great promises or daunting commands, Zechariah simply wants a sign to ensure that the offer was real. He wants something that he can have and hold until he holds his son. While his decades-long prayer for a son is honored, his request for a sign is not. The birth itself will be the sign. Instead, the angel decrees a different sort of symbol: Zechariah will be unable to speak until the child is born.

We ought not to see this penalty as excessively harsh. The promised son would still be born in his old age, but now he was forced to practice the difficult spiritual discipline of silence: sitting back in stillness, watching the impossible unfold before his eyes.

And it does unfold, beautifully. He returns home from priestly duties, and before long his wife is found to be pregnant. People talk, speculating about the angelic vision that Zechariah had and the future name of the miracle baby (most likely Zechariah, as custom dictated). When the baby is born and Elizabeth proclaims his name to be John, the crowd won't have this break with tradition. Zechariah, having had much time to ponder the situation, writes on a tablet, "His name is John," just as the angel had commanded. Immediately, Zechariah is able to speak. With his reclaimed gift of speech Zechariah cuts loose with the sort of poetic meditation that can only be formed in a place of silent wrestling with God (Luke 1:76-79).

Zechariah was invited into the drama of the nativity as one who shares so many of our own strengths and weaknesses. He was simultaneously a believing doubter and a doubting believer. He prayed fervently for a son and then balked when the good news came by way of an angelic messenger. But, through his encounter with the divine, and through the forced discipline of silence, he was given a glimpse of the mystery of salvation and his newborn son's role in it. In Zechariah's story we see a connection between the Old Testament and the New; between the Bible's story and ours. May we, too, learn to be patient in hope and to respond in faith to God's good news. (Cameron Jorgenson)

Worship Aids

Collect

Almighty God, who hears our prayers in our times of greatest need: Speak to us this day so that we will be strengthened in faith, established in hope, and perfected in love. We pray this in the name of Jesus Christ our Lord, who lives and reigns with you and the Holy Spirit, one God, in glory everlasting. Amen.

Pastoral Prayer

Loving God, we have much for which we are thankful, yet we have experienced the pain of unanswered prayers. Strengthen us. Heal the broken places. You are the source of life, and hope, and peace. May we receive from you these things in abundance! Amen.

Benediction

Go now in peace, knowing that the one who sends you out is the one who is able to do exceedingly, abundantly, beyond all you could ever ask or imagine. Amen. (Cameron Jorgenson)

DECEMBER 8, 2013

Second Sunday of Advent

Readings: Isaiah 11:1-10; Psalm 72:1-7, 18-19; Romans 15:4-13; Matthew 3:1-12

Spare Change

Matthew 3:1-12

The sign came across my computer screen: "Warning: Low Ink." I ignored the message because I was in a hurry, and I knew from experience that when that warning light comes on, there is still plenty of ink in the cartridge. I printed my document, and it looked just fine. Finally, after several days of ignoring the warning, I clicked the print icon and only blank paper came out!

The warning light lit up on my dashboard, saying that I was low on fuel. I figured I could still go a few miles before I got gas. That was how my old car had worked. I continued my afternoon hospital calling, going from place to place. All of a sudden, my car stopped in the middle of the busiest intersection in the county. I had run out of gas. I had been given ample warning. The light had been on for hours. Now I had to pay the price for my negligence.

Computer printers that run out of ink and cars that run out of gas are problems we all have to deal with. But there are larger warning signs on the horizon than "low on ink" and "low on fuel."

Out in the country, where things are normally peaceful and calm, the voice of a preacher is heard. He is not sharing three points and a poem. He is urging his congregation to repent before it is too late. "Prepare the way for the Lord," he proclaims; "make his paths straight" (Matthew 3:3). We who live on the other side of John's proclamation understand that he was urging the people to prepare their minds and hearts for Jesus, the one whose coming to the world changed everything. A few people listened, but most ignored this strange man who ate weird food and dressed in a rather unusual fashion. After all, if you ignore the warning lights, you can still get along all right—at least for a while.

I am always haunted by people who approach me on the street and ask for money. Typically, a forlorn-looking man or woman will approach me, hand outstretched, saying, "Spare change? Can you spare some change?" When I dig in my pocket and come up with a few coins, is the smile on the face of the beggar a smile of appreciation, or the sly smile of satisfaction that he's found another sucker? I am never quite sure.

It struck me as I was reading this Advent passage about the call to repentance and new life, that many times when we hear these texts, we respond by giving God only what we can spare. When the "low ink" warning pops up on my computer, I should go to the store and buy a new cartridge. When the "fuel" light comes on in the car, it's time to head for the gas station. When we hear the words of John the Baptist, we are supposed to let God change our lives from top to bottom, allowing us to follow Jesus in our care for the poor, our concern for justice and truth, and our commitment to put God above all else. This is not supposed to be a religion of pabulum, where we give God only what we can spare in terms of time and energy and commitment. John the Baptist calls for nothing less than a complete change.

We all need to change at times. Examples: (1) If you don't change your study habits, you'll flunk out. (2) If you don't change your priorities, your marriage will fail. (3) If you don't kick that habit, you'll ruin your health. The problem is, we humans are ambivalent toward change. Some of us are downright resistant! Do you know how many church members it takes to change a light bulb? Change? My grandmother donated that light bulb!

I appreciate the comments I receive on my sermons. I remember the time someone wrote anonymously that most of my sermons ask people to change, to give more, to do more. Why not an occasional sermon affirming us for who we are and what we are already doing? this person wrote. I realize that sometimes we pastors lay the guilt on too thick. But quite honestly, I don't find much in the Bible that supports a sermon on "I'm O.K., you're O.K." I worship a God who tells me that I have a great deal more potential than I am using, a God who says, "You can live a better life if you allow me to be a bigger part of your life." I worship a God who meets me where I am, but always challenges me to go deeper, reach higher, and stretch further.

When I was a boy, I would do something wrong and then say, "I'm sorry." My mother would respond by saying, "If you're really sorry, you won't do it again." We cannot say we are sorry and then go on as if nothing has happened. True repentance leads to fundamental change. We are called to bear fruit worthy of repentance.

What is God calling us to do? I cannot answer that question completely, for it is hard enough for me to discern God's voice in my own life, let alone presume to say what God has in mind for you or for our community of faith. Yet Scripture teaches me that while God meets us where we are, God does not leave us where we are. God is always calling us forward, to take bigger and bolder and more courageous stands as followers of Jesus. We are not talking about spare change, but a complete and total transformation of our lives. Nothing less is adequate. Nothing less will do justice to the words of the prophets and the words of John the Baptist. Nothing less is appropriate as we stand before God, as one day we will.

"Spare change?" he asked. "Got any spare change?" This morning let us think not about what we can spare, but about what God is calling us to experience. It's not a matter of parting with some spare change. It's a matter of letting God change our lives from top to bottom.

The warning light is on! The time has come! Prepare the way of the Lord! (Charlie Yoost)

Lectionary Commentary

Isaiah 11:1-10

Isaiah sings a song of peace, telling the story of Israel's promised restoration. Just as a tree that has been cut down can grow again, so a "shoot" or "branch" (v. 1) will grow following the exile. One will emerge who will later be called God's Messiah. He will be everything that a king is supposed to be, and righteousness and justice will prevail. The weak will be safe, and no one will need to be afraid. It may be difficult to imagine the beasts of the animal kingdom living in harmony with one another. It is even harder to envision a world of nations at peace. But through the eye of faith, Isaiah is able to perceive that ultimate reality.

Romans 15:4-13

In this passage, Paul describes the transformation that results from the new life in Christ. The coming of Jesus is the fulfillment of the hope that was promised to the patriarchs and foretold by the prophet Isaiah. Those who recognize that Christ is the fulfillment of the promises of God are to live in harmony with one another, both Jews (the circumcised) and Gentiles. Each group is to welcome the other, while accepting and respecting each other's differences. Christ, who has welcomed us, is our model. His coming fills us with joy and peace so that we are enabled to live lives filled with hope. (Charlie Yoost)

Worship Aids

Call to Worship (Based on Psalm 72:18-19)

Blessed be the Lord, God of Israel,
God of our Lord Jesus Christ,
God of the church,
God, you alone do wondrous things!
Blessed be God's glorious name forever;
May the glory of God fill the whole earth!

Prayer of Assurance (Based on Romans 15:4-13)

Though we have sinned, we worship a God of steadfastness and encouragement. Therefore, may we abound in hope by the power of the Holy Spirit. May we live in joy and peace, knowing that God has forgiven our sins and cleansed us from all unrighteousness.

Benediction

Receive this blessing first shared by the apostle Paul with the church at Rome: "May the God of hope fill you with all joy and peace in faith so that you overflow with hope by the power of the Holy Spirit" (15:13). Encouraged and empowered by God's word, may you go forth in peace to love and serve the Lord this Advent season and every day of your lives. Amen. (Charlie Yoost)

John: A Prophet in Utero

Second in a Series of Six on Unlikely Characters of the Nativity

Luke 1:39-45, 67, 76-80

At the beginning of the book of Jeremiah, we are invited to hear God's words of calling and affirmation of the timid young man. God says to him: "'Before I created you in the womb / I knew you; / before you were born I set you apart; / I made you a prophet to the nations'" (Jeremiah 1:5).

These words were a reassuring reminder for Jeremiah, who felt too young and otherwise underqualified to serve as a prophet. But in light of the story of the nativity, these words to Jeremiah take on new life, gaining a new layer of meaning, and shedding a whole new light when read alongside the stories surrounding the birth of the great prophet of the New Testament: John the Baptist.

When we think of John the Baptist, we tend to think of the grown prophet, the one crying out in the wilderness, leading an ancient revival of piety and spiritual hunger. We think of the one dressed in a camel hair tunic, eating locusts and wild honey. He was untamed, the epitome of a prophet, and he offered an unrestrained call for repentance in preparation for the coming Messiah. John was the fearless prophet of the "Day of the Lord" that everyone was expecting.

But all of that would come in time. At the nativity we see another John. We see John, the son promised to Zechariah. We see John, the hidden miracle child, as Elizabeth secluded herself for the delicate first five months of the pregnancy. And then, a month later, we see John, the prophet "in utero," proclaiming the Messiah who had come.

When the angel Gabriel announced to Mary that she would be the mother of Jesus, he also mentioned that Elizabeth was already in the sixth month of her miraculous pregnancy. When she heard this, Mary hurried to Elizabeth's house in the hill country of Judea. When Mary arrived and greeted Elizabeth, John leaped in her womb and she was filled with the Holy Spirit. With great joy she returned Mary's greeting, exclaiming:

> "God has blessed you above all women, and he has blessed the child you carry. Why do I have this honor, that the mother of my Lord should come to me? As soon as I heard your greeting, the baby in my womb jumped for joy. Happy is she who believed that the Lord would fulfill the promises he made to her." (vv. 42-45)

No doubt, this scene offers us much to ponder. Perhaps the most obvious place to begin is with these remarkable women who were about to play a central role in redemption by giving birth to the long-awaited Messiah and the prophet who would prepare the way. But there is another facet of the story that is just as astounding as these women and their prophetic words: it seems as though John's work of proclamation was already beginning, even before his birth.

At the sound of Mary's voice, John leaped in the womb. With that leap, John announced Jesus' arrival in their house, and immediately

Elizabeth was filled with the Spirit, speaking a prophetic word of blessing with great boldness. Months before his birth, John is already living into his call as the one who would proclaim the Messiah and prepare the way for the one who would send the Spirit.

The encounter between these two mothers was a profound moment in salvation history. Elizabeth, old and formerly barren, was now carrying the one who would be known as the "Forerunner." Mary, a young virgin, was carrying the God-Man. One mother announced the arrival of the Messiah in her house; the other came, full of grace, singing a song that declared the long history of God's saving acts (Luke 1:46-55). Truly, one can feel the weight of history hanging on this encounter, on this moment before the world would change.

Three months later, things did begin to change. John was born, and in that joyous event another miracle happened. His father, Zechariah, who had been struck dumb in his encounter with the angel announcing John's birth, was suddenly filled with the Holy Spirit, much as Elizabeth had been. Similarly, he spoke a powerful prophecy under the Spirit's influence, announcing the sort of ministry that his son would have. He would be a prophet like Elijah. He would prepare the way for the Lord by preaching repentance and forgiveness of sins. He would fulfill the hopes and longings of Israel's generations past by serving as the forerunner, the way-maker, and the herald of things to come. He would be great, but not as the world considers greatness. These were appropriate words for the newborn prophet resting in his mother's arms.

Over time, John grew. He became strong, tried and tested by life in the wilderness, full of the wisdom of the desert. And soon he would begin the work he was called to do, making straight the way of the Lord. He fulfilled his vocation as a man, but it was a vocation first given and fulfilled when one child in a womb recognized another and a joyous leap became his first sermon.

So, what should we take away from John's life for our own? After all, we might be tempted to despair if we concluded that the only ones following the will of God are those living in the desert on a diet of locusts. Perhaps part of the answer can be found in the words of Søren Kierkegaard: "What I need is a [person] who . . . gesticulates . . . with his entire personal existence" (Søren Kierkegaard, Howard Vincent Hong, et al, *Søren Kierkegaard's Journals and Papers* [Indiana University Press, 1967], 265). John the Baptist could be described in exactly the same way. From his earliest days, with every breath and every action, John pointed toward Christ. While the specific shape of his calling was unique to him, the Christward direction of John's whole existence provides a pattern for us all. May we, each in our own ways, learn to gesticulate with the whole of our existences, and in doing so, may we fulfill the calling on our lives from birth. (Cameron Jorgenson)

Worship Aids

Collect

O God, creator of this world in its majesty, and us, your people, in our diversity: help us hear your call and enable our response; reveal who you would have us to be, then empower us to fulfill that design. Above all, may we be conformed to the image of your son, Jesus Christ our Lord, who lives and reigns with you and the Holy Spirit, our one God, forever. Amen.

Pastoral Prayer

Lord, we confess our desire and our need for our lives to become embodied prayers. May our lives tell of your goodness and grace. May our whole beings point toward Christ, the author and finisher of our faith. Amen.

Benediction

May the God who has called and gifted you lead you out from this place to become living signposts, pointing to the mystery of God's loving presence among us. Amen. (Cameron Jorgenson)

DECEMBER 15, 2013

Third Sunday of Advent

Readings: Isaiah 35:1-10; Psalm 146:5-10; James 5:7-10; Matthew 11:2-11

Where Can I Find God?

Matthew 11:2-11

A little boy stood gazing at a picture of his father, who had been away for several days on a business trip. He turned to his mother and said wistfully, "I wish Daddy would step out of that picture and be with us tonight!" His mother replied, "I know, Son, I do too!" Probably all of us have felt like that at one time or another—that someone we love could somehow be with us, even though they were separated by a number of miles. That little boy expressed in his own way one of the deepest yearnings of the human heart—that God, our heavenly parent, would somehow come and be with us in a real and tangible and vital way.

There are people everywhere seeking God. They are looking in nature; they are practicing meditation and spiritual discipline. People are reading religious books, looking for God in cults and on television and in personal growth groups. For all the searching, most are missing the New Testament's obvious point: that God is already with us. God has made God's presence known in the world through the coming of Jesus Christ, and God continues to reveal himself through creative, life-giving activity in our midst. For those who have invested much time and energy in the search for spiritual peace and happiness, I have good news: God can be found!

In today's Gospel lesson, John the Baptist has been put in prison because of his teachings. There is the report of a very curious conversation. John wants to know: is this man who is going about the countryside preaching and teaching really God's promised Messiah? John has done his best to prepare people for the coming of the "Anointed One." He has spared nothing in order to preach the word as he has understood it. Now, here comes Jesus: not in the judgmental role that John the Baptist has anticipated, but instead as a gentle and kind figure—who spends more time eating with tax collectors and sinners than in condemning them, who accepts gifts from prostitutes rather than scolding them, who is concerned with little children, old people, the powerless, and the disenfranchised, as well as the influential and the affluent. So John sends word to Jesus, "Are you the one who is to come, or should we look for another?" Had Jesus been a commanding presence who took control and really put people in their place, there would have been no need for this question. Had Jesus made John a kind of deputy or assistant Messiah, John would probably not have thought twice about whether he was the one.

But consider the circumstances: Jesus is taking a soft line on sin and wickedness, at least as far as John is concerned. John is in prison for his offensive preaching and his open criticism of everything and everybody. Frankly, John is a little confused. He expected Jesus to come in and pick up where he left off. Jesus is not fulfilling his expectations! Is Jesus really the Messiah? Or has he put his hope in the wrong person?

If we are honest, I think all of us will have to admit that at times we question our religion. Is it really true? Or are we foolish to believe in God? We talk about the coming of Jesus and the angels' message of peace on earth, and yet we are probably no closer to world peace now than we have ever been. We hear that Jesus restored sight to the blind, made the lame to walk, cleansed the sick, and restored hearing to the deaf, yet disease still runs rampant in our world. Jesus preached good news to the poor, yet everywhere we see the hungry, the needy, and the dispossessed, and for every ray of sunshine there is a cloud practically covering the rest of the sky. We try to believe and remain faithful, yet problems and cares and worries weigh us down. Sometimes we get so discouraged we wonder whether there is a purpose to all of our struggles or whether we are just kidding ourselves. Like John, we are not sure Jesus is the one.

Leo Tolstoy's story of Martin the Cobbler, the old man who is promised a visit by Christ himself, yet encounters only ordinary people with common problems from morning until night, is the story of your life and mine. All the while we are looking for the big and the spectacular, overwhelming evidence of the presence and power of God, only to discover in retrospect that God appears in the quiet, the ordinary, even the obscure places of life, when we least expect him. God comes, as Martin learned, through the kind word, the understanding heart, the quiet sharing of a good deed done in simplicity and love. We expect God to come in a big way. But we discover that God is already present in many ways, ways that we sometimes fail to recognize and do not grasp until after the fact.

At an Advent dinner at church, we exchanged names. We asked each person to do something nice for the person whose name they received. "Secret Santas," we called it. While we were eating supper, a little girl came up to an older man, and while he was looking in the other direction, placed a cookie that she had made on his plate, then with a giggle ran out of the room. Someone observed the whole scene and was quick to remark, "She must have gotten his name!" That little girl set off a spark of joy that spread like wildfire throughout the church that evening! We suddenly realized that in that little girl's excitement and joy, and in the giving of herself, we had all experienced something of the presence and power of God.

Where can I find God? If I am looking for the spectacular lightning bolt, heaven-opening experience, I might go a lifetime without finding God. But if I look in the common and the ordinary places, I will see God at work almost every time I take the time to look. May we have eyes to see and ears to hear! (Charlie Yoost)

Lectionary Commentary

Isaiah 35:1-10

In the early sixth century B.C.E., Judah experienced the catastrophe that the prophet Isaiah had threatened, and many people were taken into exile. Now the prophet foretells a coming day when Judah will be restored. The desert wilderness that currently produces only enough grass to support a few sheep will "burst into bloom" (v. 2). People in exile who are discouraged will be delivered. Those who are in despair will have their hope restored. These great acts of God will open the eyes of those who are currently unable to see the hand of God at work, and will cause people to rejoice and praise God. Those who have been cut off from Jerusalem will be able to return safely. Their despair will turn to joy! Like the people of Judah, do we have difficulty seeing God's hand of transformation at work in our world and in our lives? What prophets in our day point to signs of hope?

James 5:7-10

As we wait for the coming of the Lord, our faith is tested. How are we to explain the problem of suffering? The Bible's principal response to human suffering affirms God's eventual and ultimate victory over all the evils that provoke and perpetuate that suffering. In the meantime, we are to wait with patient endurance, knowing that the Lord is near. Indeed, "the judge is standing at the door" (v. 9). Just as the farmer is patient, knowing that he cannot speed the harvest but must wait for rain in order to water his crops, so we are to be patient and not grumble or complain about waiting. Another example of patience is the prophets, who often did not see prophecy fulfilled in their lifetime. (Charlie Yoost)

Worship Aids

Call to Worship (Based on Psalm 146:5-10)

Come worship the Lord,
for happy are those who hope in the Lord our God!
We will worship the Lord,
for happy are those whose help is in the God of Jacob.
The Lord made the heaven and the earth.
The Lord will reign forever.
All: Praise the Lord!

Prayer of Confession

Dear God, we confess that often we are impatient. We grumble about the unfairness and injustice that we see all around us. We complain about the suffering that seems to be so prevalent in our world. Help us see signs of your coming in our midst. Help us trust in you, believing that justice and righteousness will eventually prevail. Let us not lose hope as we anticipate your coming this Advent season! In Jesus' name we pray. Amen.

Words of Assurance

Hear the good news! Jesus is coming! Hallelujah!

Benediction

Be strong! Do not fear! Look no further: the Lord is in our midst! Go forth with joy, and tell everyone that the blind see, the lame walk, the sick are cleansed, the deaf hear, the dead are raised up, and there is good news for the poor. Thanks be to God! (Charlie Yoost)

December 15, 2013

Gabriel: Angelic Messenger

Third in a Series of Six on Unlikely Characters of the Nativity

Luke 1:26-38

Perhaps the angel Gabriel doesn't really seem an unlikely character in the nativity. After all, what crèche would be complete without an angel floating over the holy family? For that matter, what would a Christmas pageant be without a little angel in a white bathrobe announcing to a flock of little shepherds that "Your savior is born today in David's city. He is Christ the Lord" (Luke 2:11)? One could argue that Christmas is the time of year when the winged messengers of God have an acceptable—or even starring—role in the story of our faith.

Yet, while all of that is true, I wonder if we have become all too accustomed to our haloed friends, missing the real wonder that their presence brings. Specifically, I wonder what we could learn from Gabriel, the angel who delivered two birth announcements that would forever change the world. If we could take a step back from the familiar figures on our Christmas cards and tree ornaments, perhaps we could encounter anew the mystery of the nativity and be drawn into a deeper worship of the God who sent this messenger to deliver exceedingly good news.

While there are many angel stories in the Bible, only two angels are called by name. One is Michael the archangel, a commander of the angelic hosts, the armies of God. The other is Gabriel, an angel who appears by name only twice. He first appears in the book of Daniel, where he interprets a rather disturbing vision about the future for the bewildered prophet. The next time we encounter him is in Luke's account of the nativity, where he delivers a message to Zechariah, announcing the coming birth of John the Baptist, and to Mary, announcing the birth of Jesus.

Isn't it fitting that the same angel who helped a prophet understand mysteries about the future is the one who would announce the long-awaited arrival of Messiah and the prophet who would prepare his way? Gabriel is the messenger of mysteries—and these births were full of mystery. They were the culmination of countless hints and fragments of insights throughout salvation history; these births were the mystery toward which all the other mysteries pointed.

For all the mystery that surrounded Gabriel's announcements, one puzzle leaps out at us. What are we to make of Zechariah's and Mary's reactions to the news they were given? More puzzling still, why does Gabriel react so differently to each of them?

When presented with the news that he and his wife, Elizabeth, in their old age, would soon have a son that they were to name John, Zechariah responds by asking how he can be sure of this word (Luke 1:18). Gabriel's answer is to the point:

> "I am Gabriel. I stand in God's presence. I was sent to speak to you and to bring this good news to you. Know this: What I have spoken will come true at the proper time. But because you didn't believe, you will remain silent, unable to speak until the day when these things happen." (Luke 1:19-20)

Zechariah is looking for a guarantee that the word is true, that he could dare to hope that he will soon have a son, and that his hopes will not be dashed yet again. But Gabriel's response makes one thing certain: no such guarantee will be given.

The story is quite different when Gabriel visits Mary. Gabriel greets her as "favored one" (v. 28), and assures her that she has found favor with God. He then presents the stunning news: she will give birth to Jesus, and he will be known as both the Messiah and the son of God. Surely this news is no less shocking than that delivered to the old priest, but Mary's response is quite different. She simply asks: "How will this be since I am a virgin?" She is told that she will give birth to the long-awaited hope of Israel—without the involvement of a man—and all she offers in response is a question of logistics, followed by a pristine yes: "I am the Lord's servant. Let it be with me just as you have said" (v. 38). And with those simple, elegant words, this young woman surpasses the faith of Zechariah the priest and father Abram.

One wonders what Gabriel must think of these events. We have no indication, of course. The last word about Gabriel's involvement in the story is Luke's abrupt stage direction after Mary's affirmation of faith: "Then the angel left her." But perhaps it is fair to ask whether he leaves with a sense of wonder. In his encounters with Zechariah and Mary, he has witnessed two radically different kinds of faith, one far surpassing the other. With Mary, Gabriel witnesses an unconditional yes, despite the risk and cost, setting off a chain reaction of events that fulfills the ancient hopes of the people of faith. Having witnessed real faith, and having seen the mystery of salvation unfold in ways that surpass his own understanding, one can only speculate as to whether he experiences wonder or awe. It seems possible. After all, as 1 Peter says, "even angels long to examine" these things (1 Peter 1:12).

There are many unlikely characters in the nativity, and one of the most fascinating is the one who is overlooked simply because, as the old saying goes, "familiarity breeds contempt." We've become so familiar with domesticated pictures of angels, we may forget that both Zechariah and Mary are frightened by the angel's appearance. But in these stories we encounter the messenger Gabriel, who bears good news of two unexpected births to two people whose responses reveal the nature of faith. One can only wonder what it would have been like to be God's herald, witnessing the mystery unfold. May we who witness the mystery of this season be gripped by awe once again. (Cameron Jorgenson)

Worship Aids

Collect

Loving God, who revealed yourself so powerfully to the world, grant that we may peer more deeply into what you accomplished in your nativity, uniting God and humanity for the sake of our redemption. We pray in the name of Jesus Christ our Lord. Amen.

Pastoral Prayer

Lord, the closer we come to Christmas, the busier our lives become. Help us slow down so we can see what it is that you have done, and are still doing, among us. Give us eyes to see and ears to hear your good news unfolding. Amen.

Benediction

May the Lord bless you and keep you, guiding you into all goodness and truth, on this and every day that is to come. Amen. (Cameron Jorgenson)

DECEMBER 22, 2013

Fourth Sunday of Advent

Readings: Isaiah 7:10-16; Psalm 80:1-7, 17-19; Romans 1:1-7; Matthew 1:18-25

In This (Strange and Surprising) Way

Matthew 1:18-25

Advent teaches us to wait. Of course, during Advent we wait for Christmas, and such waiting is a countercultural discipline in its own right. On a deeper level, Advent forms us to wait for the appearing of the Lord, and perhaps you've noticed that God doesn't always follow our calendar. That was Joseph's experience, and I expect it's yours as well. According to our church and family calendars, today we stand at the doorstep of Christmas. Only a few days remain, ready or not. In today's Gospel, we also stand alongside Joseph, waiting to hear what God is about to do in and through Jesus the Messiah.

You may say, "I've heard it many times before," and perhaps you're lulled by these familiar words: "This is how the birth of Jesus Christ took place" (v. 18). So then, cue the shepherds, the magi, and the angels, and let's get on with the Christmas pageant. Careful readers will see that there's only one angel and no shepherds in Matthew's narrative, but we'll leave that for another day. I'm not so worried about shepherds, but had I written Matthew's Gospel, I might've said, "Now the birth of Jesus the Messiah took place in this strange and surprising way. Mary is pregnant. She and Joseph are not yet married, and this righteous man has a major dilemma. Then God spoke to Joseph, 'Do not be afraid to take Mary as your wife, for the child conceived in her is from the Holy Spirit'" (NRSV). It's strange stuff. Can we believe it? Religious people have blamed all manner of things on the Spirit.

Then the narrator informs us that this development was the fulfillment of prophecy, and so he quotes Isaiah 7:14, amending it ever so slightly: "Look! A virgin will become pregnant and give birth to a son,/...

Emmanuel" (v. 23). Here we see the beginning of a pattern that Matthew follows throughout this Gospel. He describes events in the life of Jesus, and then he connects them with texts from the Old Testament: "This fulfills what had been spoken through the prophet." What's going on here? It's Matthew's way of claiming that God's work in and through Jesus stands in continuity with what God had done before. Our biblical, covenantal faith is based on that continuity. We believe that the God who spoke through Moses on Mount Sinai spoke through Jesus in the Sermon on the Mount, and the same God speaks to us when we hear the scriptures today. We believe that the God who freed the slaves from bondage in Egypt still frees captives today. All of our prayers rise from this dynamic.

So then, "Don't be afraid," right? But remember, this is God we're talking about.

"Don't be afraid" doesn't mean that God's call won't shake us to the very foundations, perhaps delighting us, perhaps rocking our world and changing everything. God spoke and Joseph heard God, and he would never understand righteousness in the same way again; and just wait until Jesus begins speaking. Yes, God is doing what God has been doing. "Don't be afraid," but watch out!

I can't arrive at this fourth Sunday of Advent without thinking of my younger son's first Christmas. It fell on December 24th that year, so it was going to be a full day of church, with services from morning until midnight. In order to lighten the load a bit, we decided to have a youth Christmas pageant in the morning. Could the parsonage family's new son be the baby Jesus? Of course that's what we did. The proverbial good time was had by all, and we have the photographs to prove it. Nevertheless, I can't look at those photos without thinking of what else happened that morning. My father phoned to tell me that my grandmother had suffered a massive heart attack. Grandma had also been a parishioner of mine earlier in my pastoral career and in those days was probably the best baby sitter our oldest son ever had. It was a blow. I managed, of course, as we pastors usually do. Grandma survived for the moment, and we visited her on Christmas Day; but she would die before the week was over.

So we have suffering mixed with joy: birth, new life, and death. That's life. That's the way of faith. That's Advent and Christmas. I wish I could say that believers somehow get to skip such difficulty, but we don't, and you know it. Along with Joseph, we're called to serve Christ in the midst of complicated situations, and we don't know where it all leads. I will grant you that my suffering was garden-variety stuff. No one expects grandmothers to live forever. But that same year, our son's first, the

Oklahoma City bombing occurred only a few short weeks after he was born, just a few days after Easter. That same year, children continued to go hungry and other people lost their jobs and homes. Some had health care and others did not. They suffered and grieved, just as some of you suffer and grieve today, even in the shadows of Christmas.

Yet God appears, and God will appear, even today. Knowing this doesn't make trouble or grief go away. What a disservice we do when we say such things in the name of the gospel! But look, sisters and brothers, "*Look! A virgin will become pregnant and give birth to a son, / And they will call him*, Emmanuel. / (*Emmanuel* means 'God with us.')."

Believe it along with Joseph, even if it doesn't all make sense right now. Believe that God is with us, even today: with us in the breaking of the bread, with us in the sharing of fellowship, with us in words of encouragement, with us in the cancer ward and maternity ward, with us in the hour of our birth and the hour of death. And so we wait, and God continues to make promises that we can trust. (Mark W. Stamm)

Lectionary Commentary

Isaiah 7:10-16

It is important to note that the Isaiah 7:10-16 passage is not merely a free-floating prophecy meant to set up the proclamation of virgin conception and birth in Matthew's Gospel. This prophecy of a "young woman" bearing a son was spoken into a situation filled with conflict and fear. Seeing that, one might also note the political conflict witnessed in Matthew.

Romans 1:1-7

In these opening verses of Romans appointed for today, Paul makes a point similar to that underlying Matthew's Gospel, that the proclamation to the Gentiles of salvation in Christ stands in continuity with the Hebrew Scriptures: "God promised this good news about his Son ahead of time through his prophets in the holy scriptures" (v. 2). Who are the outsiders to whom we need to proclaim and embody the good news? (Mark W. Stamm)

Worship Aids

Call to Worship

Restore us, O Lord God of hosts;
let your face shine, that we may be saved.
Come, Lord Jesus.

Prayers of the People

Let us pray for the nations of the world and those who lead them,
that wars may cease, and peace and justice may be known
in every place.
O come, O come, Emmanuel.
Let us pray for all of those who live in sorrow or any kind of need,
that they may be healed and strengthened.
O come, O come, Emmanuel.
Let us pray for families, that, like Joseph and Mary,
they may care for their children and protect them.
O come, O come, Emmanuel.
Let us pray for the church, that we may welcome Christ
when he appears in our midst,
especially among the hungry, the sick, and the homeless.
O come, O come, Emmanuel.
We offer these prayers through Jesus Christ our Lord.
Amen.

Collect

Come to us, Emmanuel, and by your mercy open our hearts to receive your grace and answer your call, that we may serve faithfully among those who need you most; for with the Father and the Holy Spirit you live and reign, one God, now and forever. Amen. (Mark W. Stamm)

Inn Keeper: Unexpected Servant

Fourth in a Series of Six on Unlikely Characters of the Nativity

Luke 2:1-7

I love interruptions. It probably has something to do with my short attention span, but I'm the kind of person who enjoys detours and unexpected developments. Being interrupted was one of the things that I loved the most about being in church ministry, and that made some of my colleagues hide in their offices with the door shut. I loved the drop-in visits and unexpected phone calls. I loved not knowing whether a visit would require a momentary thank-you for a basket of fresh garden produce or a tissue and an hour of listening. Although I learned over time that sometimes interruptions were just interruptions and that it was important to stay focused, I also learned the powerful opportunities that arise from the ministry of interruption. As a matter of fact, I think God sometimes used those accidental encounters even more than my intentional ones, giving me a glimpse of something unexpectedly sacred along the way.

The story of the birth of Christ is full of sacred interruptions and unintentional encounters. Mary's and Joseph's lives were, for instance, interrupted in a way that they never imagined. The shepherds were no doubt shocked at their angelic interruption. Even those, like Zechariah, Elizabeth, Simeon, and Anna, who were intentionally waiting for the Messiah, were surprised by their providential encounters. Zechariah, who spent his life and work waiting for the redeemer, was so surprised that his initial reaction of unbelief left him silenced for months. God has a way of interrupting our ordinary lives with something extraordinary. Perhaps our greatest challenge is to allow ourselves to be interrupted. There is one nameless participant in the story of Jesus' birth whose ordinary gesture allowed the sacred a place to enter the world.

The most detailed scriptural account of Jesus' birth takes place in Luke 2:1-7. It is the brief description of hurried, anxious parents, lives already interrupted by an unexpected pregnancy, who must make a long journey at absolutely the worst time. Although the journey from Nazareth to Bethlehem to be counted in the census was a journey of less than seventy miles, it would have been a long, treacherous journey by donkey or on foot, particularly for Mary in the advanced stages of pregnancy. The journey was complicated when, upon arriving in Bethlehem, they could find no room in any inn. After probably hours of searching and at the point of near-desperation, a nameless innkeeper allowed the young couple to spend the night in his stable with the animals, since there were no available rooms. Although we know nothing of the innkeeper, I've seen him portrayed many times. Sometimes, he's a heartless man, so concerned with the bottom line that he turns the poor couple away. Most often, he's portrayed as a sympathetic businessman who wishes he had available space, but is so moved with compassion for the young couple that he allows them his stable. Really, no one knows who he was or what he was like. One thing is certain, though. He allowed himself to be interrupted. His inn was full. He had no vacancy. That's really all he needed to communicate to Joseph and Mary. And yet he did more. He found a spot. He thought outside the box and allowed himself to be so moved by his compassion that he found a way to serve the young couple. We never know more about him, although it's probably reasonable to think that he knew at some point that a baby was born that night in his stable. He probably even noticed the band of excited shepherds who arrived and the unusually bright star. I wonder if he knew something significant happened that night.

However the innkeeper's story ended, his small but important role in the savior's birth foreshadowed in many ways the ministry of Christ. The innkeeper allowed himself to be interrupted, to be moved, to show love and grace, even when he had no obligation to do so. Jesus was on a mission. God had a plan for him. He was intentional in what he did and taught, and yet Jesus constantly allowed himself to be interrupted. He had compassion on those he encountered, whether grieving fathers, hurting women, hungry crowds, or even his own doubtful disciples. In many moments when Jesus could have just thrown up his arms in frustration at all he was doing for humanity, he stopped and helped a person in need.

Likewise, I think, we are called to be interrupted. We are called to be mindful of the needs around us. Like the innkeeper, we are called to look outside of our responsibilities and obligations and serve others unexpectedly. We are called to pause on our journeys, like Jesus, when we feel the needs of one tugging on our robe. And even in moments when we feel tired and depleted, we are called to respond to the storms of life and their effects on those around us. We are called to enter those sacred spaces with people, even, and perhaps especially, in those unplanned opportunities of life.

This season we celebrate the birth of our Christ. We celebrate that God allowed God's plan for creation to be interrupted, acknowledging our need for a savior. We celebrate the interruption allowed by those characters in the nativity story, and the ways that their lives were affected by the Christ. We celebrate God's divine interruption of our lives, intervening when we didn't realize we needed intervention. Most of all, we celebrate Christ, who allowed his divinity to be interrupted to experience what it is like to be us, and still loved us so much that he gave his life for us on the cross. May we allow ourselves to be interrupted to show that same love to those around us. (Tracey Allred)

Worship Aids

Prayer of Confession

Our God, we confess to you our shortcomings,
our moments of weakness and wickedness.
Forgive us, O Lord.
We confess our insensitivity to the needs around us,

our ignorance of the interruptions and opportunities to serve.
Forgive us, O Lord.
We confess our forgetfulness of your mercy and sacrifice.
Forgive us, O Lord.

Words of Assurance

O God, we thank you for the assurance of your forgiveness and salvation. We praise you for knowing our hearts and forgiving our sins. We thank you for all your gifts of salvation. Amen.

Benediction

Now, go into the world of interruptions, thankful for the interruptions of Mary, Joseph, the innkeeper, and most of all of Jesus, who allowed himself to be so interrupted by our need that he sacrificed all for us. Go and likewise allow yourself to be interrupted by the needs of others. (Tracey Allred)

DECEMBER 25, 2013

Christmas

Readings: Isaiah 52:7-10; Psalm 98; Hebrews 1:1-4, (5-12); John 1:1-14

The Light Shines in Darkness

John 1:1-14

"The light shines in the darkness, / and the darkness doesn't extinguish the light" (John 1:5). This is a glorious and bold claim. We celebrate it with a joyous festival, with the lighting of candles, with much singing and feasting. We are right to celebrate as we do. This prologue to the fourth Gospel insists that God has not rejected the world, but rather that God has entered it—the cosmos in its entirety—even taking on human flesh. So rejoice, along with all creation; but don't miss the shadows in this text.

Our Gospel doesn't insist that there isn't any darkness in the world. Nor should we hear it as if it were asking us to come to church on Christmas and pretend that all is well even when it isn't. No, the writer insists that darkness remains, although God's light is greater. The Scriptures never ask us to believe in a fairy-tale world in which those who believe the right things can henceforth live "happily ever after." That kind of false gospel has tempted many people over the years, but it doesn't hold up well when trouble comes. The ancient people that the evangelist was addressing would light the evening lamps because night was falling and the darkness was real, not to make it simply go away. Christmas and its well-known texts don't allow us to avoid difficulty. So hear the shadows present in this text and in our world. "The light shines in darkness, and the darkness doesn't extinguish the light."

As I write this sermon in 2011, Japan stands in crisis, in the wake of a devastating earthquake followed by a tsunami followed by potential nuclear meltdown. The death toll continues to rise, and it will never be fully determined, because many bodies will never be found. By the time you read this, sometime in 2013, Japan's recovery process will be far from complete. The crisis in Japan is not unlike the one faced by New Orleans and the Gulf Coast when Hurricane Katrina struck in September 2005. In some ways, Katrina is old news, just like Japan's tsunami will eventually become old news. Nevertheless, the effects are long lasting and the recovery takes years. Sometimes, it never really happens.

When events like these occur, people of faith and goodwill often respond quickly, with gifts, with prayers and hands-on service, and this is appropriate, yet I've often wondered about people in crisis through less newsworthy means, like the person who loses his job when the business fails. Perhaps then he loses his health insurance, then his house, then maybe even his marriage, and family. What about folks like that? For them, there is no international surge of compassion, no front-page articles, just a rather quiet and perhaps unnoticed slide into the darkness. Or what about the woman victimized by an abusive husband? She suffers in silence, perhaps horrified that light will be shined on her darkness, lest neighbors and friends find out. Maybe they'll blame her. Christ's light shines in darkness, and darkness does not overcome it, but it doesn't make the darkness go away.

What can we do about this? Take a cue from John the Baptist, who shows up (yet again) in today's text, just as he did on the second and third Sundays of Advent. The evangelist wrote, "[John] came as a witness to testify concerning the light, so that through him everyone would believe in the light. He himself wasn't the light, but his mission was to testify concerning the light" (vv. 7-8). In some ways, the Baptizer shows us where we stand. We know the darkness, and we know the light who overcomes it. Sometimes the church has acted as if it possessed the light and could distribute it to the world. Join our church, and we'll let you in on the secret. However, we've never possessed the light, and we never will.

Rather, as we listen to this text today, the Baptizer points us toward the light, toward Christ, and he calls us to believe. With him, we point others to the light, calling them to believe. What is at stake here, in this call to believe? "But those who did welcome him, / those who believed in his name, / he authorized to become / God's children" (v. 12). In many ways, we've tamed the meaning of this word *believe* to the point that it means something akin to doctrinal affirmation, like getting the right answer on an exam. "Yes, I believe in Jesus, that he is God Incarnate." Next question, please.

However, when today's text and others throughout the New Testament use this word *believe*, they mean far more than that. To believe means to trust Christ with all your heart, to lean on him in every way, with every fiber of our being. Can you do it? I'm never quite sure that I'm up to the task, and I know I can't do it by myself. But trust doesn't work that way.

Last year, I learned that I would need heart surgery to replace a pair of diseased heart valves. My doctors and I had known about them for years; they had told me that I would need this surgery someday, and finally the day had arrived. Be that as it may, I wasn't eager to do it, and for all kinds of reasons, including the fact that it would disrupt my schedule for a few months. Type A personalities of the world, unite! Even so, I began to share my story and ask for prayers. People I know told me that they were praying for me, and they in turn told others whom I don't know. Eventually I heard that persons in Puerto Rico, in Brazil, and beyond were praying. I'm still hearing the testimonies today. All of those faithful sisters and brothers pointed me toward Christ. They believed for me and with me, and eventually I was able to believe as well, to trust (literally) with all of my heart, or most of it, anyway. The light carried the day.

Look around today, friends, and count those who carry the light and point others to it. The Light is in the world. The glory of Jesus Christ shines in our midst. Together we know it, and no darkness will overcome it. (Mark W. Stamm)

Lectionary Commentary

Isaiah 52:7-10

"How beautiful upon the mountains / are the feet of a messenger / who proclaims peace, / who brings good news" (v. 7). This expected messenger announces God's salvation to "the ends of the earth." What is the nature of this good news? Note that the baring of the holy arm in verse 10 is an image of judgment. With a holy God, good news is never simply an affirmation of the life that we have been living, but it usually includes some measure of judgment. Who are these people who will hear the good news at "the ends of the earth"? Are we ready to be surprised by those whom God is calling?

Hebrews 1:1-12

Hebrews 1:1-12 begins with a short summary of salvation history, including the phrase, "In these final days, though, [God] spoke to us through a Son" (v. 2), that is, in and through Jesus Christ, who reflects the glory of God. Here, again, is strong proclamation of Incarnation. This passage also includes intimations of judgment. This Son who has appeared now sits "at the right side of the highest majesty" (v. 3). He carries a righteous scepter, "righteousness," and hates "wickedness" (v. 9 NRSV). It appears that the Son comes not merely to bless the world but to change and redeem it. In what ways does the proclamation of Christ's appearing call us to turn from sin toward a more abundant life for all people? (Mark W. Stamm)

Worship Aids

Call to Worship

Joy to the world, the Lord is come!
Let earth receive her king.

Prayers of the People

Holy God, in the appearing of your Son,
your love and glory extends to the ends of the earth,
and so we rejoice.
Joy to the world, the Lord is come! Let earth receive her king!
We pray for all those who administer justice in our nation
and the nations of the world.
May they reflect both your truth and mercy.
Joy to the world, the Lord is come! Let earth receive her king!
We pray for victims of natural disasters.
(*Here, one might name specific recent incidents.*)
Extend your compassion to the ends of the earth.
Joy to the world, the Lord is come! Let earth receive her king!
We pray for those who struggle with less visible difficulties . . .
those who are homeless and hungry,
victims of abuse, those struggling with mental illness,
the unemployed, and others.
Defend them and heal them, O God.
Joy to the world, the Lord is come! Let earth receive her king!
We pray for Christ's church.
Strengthen us both to believe the good news
and share it with others.
Joy to the world, the Lord is come! Let earth receive her king!

We offer these prayers through Jesus Christ our Lord.
Amen.

Prayer of Confession

O God, in the appearing of Jesus Christ we see your image, and the image of human life as you intended. We are humbled. Christ offered forgiveness; we have kept a score of offenses. Christ bound up the broken-hearted; we have made war and destroyed many lives. Christ fed those who came to him in the wilderness; we have hoarded your good gifts. Have mercy upon us, O God, and help us turn from sin. By your grace, recreate us in your image; through the same Jesus Christ our Lord. Amen.

Words of Assurance

In the words of Jesus the Christ, you are forgiven.
In the words of Jesus the Christ, you are forgiven. Amen.
(Mark W. Stamm)

Shepherds: Unlikely Guests

Fifth in a Series of Six on Unlikely Characters of the Nativity

Luke 2:8-20

For most Americans, royalty is literally a foreign concept. Although we esteem our leadership and certainly our celebrities, there is something simply mysterious and regal about the countries where royal families still exist. As I write this in 2011, for instance, a huge event, a wedding, is about to take place in England's royal family, and it appears the whole world is watching with great anticipation as details unfold regarding everything from wardrobe choices to food being served to transportation to the big event. A few weeks ago, after wedding invitations were mailed, news reports were buzzing with lists of those included and, more important, those who were snubbed. In a world where there are few princes, princesses, or castles, the opportunity to witness a royal occasion is indeed exciting, even to those of us oceans away.

For centuries, the Israelites awaited a royal event. It wasn't the wedding of a prince. It wasn't a grand social event. It wasn't even an event that most outside the Jewish world considered particularly newsworthy. For those waiting, however, it was the event of a lifetime. The birth of the Messiah, the descendant of David who would come to lead and deliver the Jewish nation, would have been something that generations awaited. It would have been an event with even more speculated hoopla than a royal wedding. And yet, when the baby Messiah, Jesus, was born in Bethlehem, there was no hoopla, no media frenzy, no grand celebration, and perhaps even more surprising, no regal guest list. As a matter of fact, the first group of visitors would have been the last visitors one would expect at a royal birth.

Luke 2 gives the brief, seven-verse account of the birth of the Messiah. It is a simple, quick account of two young, desperate parents who experience the birth of their first child not only miles away from their family but also in a stable surrounded by livestock. It wasn't exactly how Mary and Joseph imagined the birth of their son, the child the angels told them would be the son of God, the savior of their people. The couple had little experience with royal births, but no doubt realized that a stable birth was an unusual royal start. It was probably no great surprise when their first visitors were not the typical royal guests but an excited, dusty group of shepherds.

The shepherds' story is told in Luke 2:8-20. They were as unexpected a part of the birth story of the Jewish Messiah as the teenagers and the stable, and yet their inclusion in the story is an immediate hint at just the kind of savior Jesus would be. In verse 8, the shepherds are in the midst of an average night, as they stand watch over their flock of sheep. Suddenly, in verse 9 and following, an angel appears to them, sharing the good news of the birth of the Messiah, encouraging them to go and see the baby, and joining a heavenly host of angels in singing of praise and peace. All in all, the angelic interruption was probably only a few minutes, and I love to imagine the scene as the angelic host departed and the shepherds were left in the quiet field, wondering what had just happened to them. Although the scripture doesn't elaborate, I bet several minutes passed before finally one of them broke the silence, by saying, "Well, let's go to Bethlehem!" And so they leave the field. They leave their sheep. They leave their very responsibilities, and they go with haste to see the baby, whom they recognize and believe to be the one their people have waited for all their lives. They are so amazed and changed by what they have experienced, that these shepherds, who were probably most comfortable living on the fringe of society, tell everyone they can about the birth of the Messiah. Perhaps even more surprising, their news is so widespread that it eventually makes its way to a king.

The shepherds would not have been included on any royal guest lists. They were, after all, the part of the ancient world that most royalty liked to pretend didn't exist. They were the lowest of the lower class in their society. And yet God saw something so significant in them that God met them where they were and revealed the great news of the birth of the Messiah to them, prompting them to leave everything to go and see the child. Perhaps the choosing of the shepherds shouldn't be surprising, given God's tendency to choose those whom no one else would choose to do something great. After all, two of God's most notable servants in the Old Testament, Moses and David, were chosen by God as they shepherded. In all honesty, Mary and Joseph weren't exactly the royal parents one might expect either, and yet, they were precisely the ones God chose.

It is unlikely that I will ever be invited to a royal wedding, or know anyone who is invited. It is more likely that I will be among the crowd, watching from my couch. Yet the story of the shepherds reminds me that God's perspective on worthiness and potential is far different than the world's. In 1 Samuel 16:7, God gives Samuel the criterion by which God will choose the new king, "the LORD sees into the heart." As we celebrate the birth of the Messiah, the son of God, what a wonderful reminder of God's purpose and plan. God chose to send God's son to save us all, from the shepherds to the kings. Jesus came to break down the barriers that separate us from one another and from God. He came to demonstrate the power of love and sacrifice, even to the cross. This Christmas, celebrate the birth of your savior, who looks at your heart and knows that sometimes shepherds make the best royal guests. (Tracey Allred)

Worship Aids

Call to Worship

We gather today to worship our God, who sent our savior.
Glory to God in the highest heaven,
and on earth peace among those whom he favors.
We celebrate Christ's miraculous birth,
and the joy Christ brings to all who encounter Christ.
Glory to God in the highest heaven,
and on earth peace among those whom he favors.

Invocation

Savior God, we come to you this day with hearts full of celebration for the birth of your son. We celebrate this opportunity to worship you, thanking you for the gift of salvation you offer through your son. Join us here. Fill our hearts and this place. Amen.

Benediction

As you leave this place, know that God has not chosen you based on the criteria of the world, but because of your heart. Go into the world reflecting the love and salvation of Christ toward all you meet. (Tracey Allred)

DECEMBER 29, 2013

First Sunday after Christmas

Readings: Isaiah 63:7-9; Psalm 148; Hebrews 2:10-18; Matthew 2:13-23

Is Christmas Over?

Matthew 2:13-23

Now that it's December 29th, more than a few people will say that Christmas is over; finished, that is, until the beginning of November next year. Christmas is most definitely over at the mall, and it's probably over in more than a few local churches. Listening to the Gospel for this morning, perhaps it seems like it's over here as well, regardless of the white parchments and the title on today's bulletin: "The First Sunday after Christmas."

If Christmas isn't over, as we keep insisting, then at the least today's text may seem like an odd Christmas card that arrived late in the mail. We see the crèche that we've come to love, but everything about it is wrong—the place where Mary and Joseph watched over Jesus has been searched by Herod's secret police, the manger is overturned, and the animals have scattered. Throughout the countryside, one hears the lament of mothers and fathers, distraught over children ruthlessly slaughtered. Listen!

What happened? Alarmed at the mere thought of another king, even a child, Herod sent his henchmen to search diligently, and they did so. Infuriated when he couldn't find the baby, he sent them back "to kill all the male children in Bethlehem and in all the surrounding territory who were two years old and younger" (v. 16). Perhaps the real Christmas isn't over, but the sentimental Christmas of our fantasies is no more. This violent text won't tolerate it.

Our text also shows us that Jesus and the holy family had left Bethlehem. We see them as refugees—indeed, Palestinian refugees—

fleeing their homeland to find safety in Egypt. Of course, there's a desert between Palestine and Egypt, and the holy family crossed it, much like thousands have crossed the Chihuahua desert, trying to find refuge in the United States, much like battered women and their children have fled violent homes to find refuge in shelters. Some flee not knowing where they are going. Hearing today's text, try to imagine the child Jesus among such: "Get up. Take the child and his mother and escape..." (v. 13). Perhaps you don't expect to see Jesus among the refugees, but he's there!

So this text ends the sentimental Christmas, the false one that we constructed. Now the real one can begin. The Incarnation makes a radical claim. We Christians insist that God took on human flesh and appeared in the midst of the world as we know it, not the fantasy world that we might like to build, but the world that we experience right now. As Charles Wesley wrote, "Veiled in flesh the Godhead see; hail th'incarnate Deity, pleased with us in flesh to dwell, Jesus, our Emmanuel" (Charles Wesley, "Hark the Herald Angels Sing," 1739, altered by George Whitefield (1753) and others. *The United Methodist Hymnal* [Nashville: The United Methodist Publishing House, 1989], 240).

The Incarnation means that God has entered every realm of human life, both to bless, and yes, friends, to meddle with it and convert it. God is in the midst of our jobs and our play, our meetings and our parties. God is in the midst of our finances, our families, and our marriages—again, to bless and to convert. And God is in the midst of our suffering as well, and all suffering is to some extent the suffering of Jesus. As the writer of Hebrews proclaimed: "He's able to help those who are being tempted, since he himself experienced suffering when he was tempted" (Hebrews 2:18).

But how is all of that good news? That question isn't easily answered, nor should it be. We need to read the Gospel and allow that to take root in us. Everything in Matthew is heading to the Christ's passion, death, and resurrection. The brutal slaughter of the holy innocents is but the first foreshadowing of that dynamic. It's all through the narrative: Jesus insisted that he would suffer, die, and be raised on the third day. He insisted that his disciples—that's us—would find life in that same way, by taking up the cross. There is no other gospel than that one, even on the first Sunday after Christmas. Frankly, such clarity is a relief. When it's time to flee the violence and seek shelter, a battered spouse needs the truth, not false assurance that the monster kissed will suddenly become Prince Charming. When cancer invades and overturns your tranquil life, you don't want to be told that nothing is wrong. You lament, and then seek refuge in chemotherapy or perhaps palliative care.

I don't have any of my own wisdom about how to deal with such things, but I hear echoes of good news in today's text. Christmas isn't over, much less the gospel. Four different times, we hear "get up" or "got up." The angel said, "Get up. Take the child and his mother and escape to Egypt. . . . Joseph got up" (vv. 13-14). Then later, "Get up . . . and take the child and his mother and go to the land of Israel. . . . Joseph got up" (vv. 20-21). "Get up" and "got up" are translated from the Greek word *egeiro*, the same word Matthew and others use when they refer to the resurrection of Jesus, to his rising from the dead. "He isn't here, because he's been raised from the dead, just as he said" (Matthew 28:6). Our text is the first usage in Matthew, but it's all through the Gospel. After Jesus touches Peter's mother-in-law, "she got up and served them" (8:15). With Jairus's daughter presumed dead, "Jesus went in and touched her hand, and the little girl rose up" (9:25). And so hints of the resurrection show up all through the Gospel of Matthew. Perhaps I'm overinterpreting here. It wouldn't be the first time.

Nevertheless, I'm convinced I'm on to something, and especially as it pertains to your life and to mine. God speaks resurrection. God gets the final word. That's not to minimize tragedy or say that oppression is insignificant—far from it. But God gets the final word in today's text, where Jesus and the holy family are preserved; and God will have the final word in your life as well. In Jesus Christ, God enters creation and suffers with it. But God is also at work redeeming it. (Mark W. Stamm)

Lectionary Commentary

Isaiah 63:7-9

In this text, the prophet praises the name of the Lord for all of God's gracious deeds. Such grace was known in the midst of difficult circumstances, and such remains the testimony proclaimed by many of the faithful. According to the prophet, "[God] became their savior / in all their distress" (v. 8-9 NRSV). Preachers need to make such an affirmation without at the same time minimizing the trials that people face.

Hebrews 2:10-18

We do well to hear this text as commentary on today's difficult narrative found in Matthew 2:13-23. How does suffering relate to the

Incarnation? In Jesus, God would "use experiences of suffering to make perfect the pioneer of salvation" (v. 10) and through death destroys the power of death. Since he shares our humanity, in and through his suffering, he is able to help those of us who suffer, those of us who are being tested. Why read such texts during Christmastide? This text points us toward the Paschal mystery of Christ's dying and rising, and reminds us yet again that Christmas is not a sentimental interlude in the fuller proclamation of the gospel. (Mark W. Stamm)

Worship Aids

Call to Worship (from Psalm 148:13)

God has come among us. Let us rejoice.
Praise the Lord, all creation.
For God's name alone is exalted.
God's glory is above heaven and earth.

Invocation

Merciful God, in Christ you have come among us and we rejoice; yet still the world groans in hope of redemption. Open our hearts to hear you speaking today in and through some difficult texts. By your Spirit give us grace so that we deny neither the sufferings that remain nor the hope that you give us; through the same Christ our Lord. Amen.

Benediction

Go forth to love and serve God in all that you do. In God's strength, comfort the afflicted, stand with those who weep, and defend the oppressed. And may the grace of our Lord Jesus Christ, the love of God, and the fellowship of the Holy Spirit abide with you, now and always, and unto ages of ages. Amen. (Mark W. Stamm)

Simeon: Unexpected Affirmation

Sixth in a Series of Six on Unlikely Characters of the Nativity

Luke 2:25-35

New parenthood is downright scary. I vividly remember the day we brought our oldest child home from the hospital. It was the moment that my husband had left the room to pull the car around. There was a sweet senior adult volunteer helping me get our things together to go home when suddenly, I got an overwhelming sense of panic. I looked at our newborn and realized that I had no clue how to take care of her. I remember asking the volunteer if I could stay longer, and attempting to make a case for my ineptitude as a parent, thinking that she would have some kind of moral responsibility to keep me longer if she realized how clueless I was.

Remembering how petrified I felt that day, I can't imagine how Mary and Joseph must have felt in Bethlehem after the birth of Jesus. After what must have been a traumatic birth experience in the stable, even by ancient world standards, and the unexpected visit from the shepherds, Mary and Joseph probably began their first days of parenthood nervous and uncertain. They were, after all, very young, miles away from home, and caring for the newborn Son of God. In addition to the jitters that come with caring for an infant, there was the reality that their son was the Messiah, a fact that probably not many people knew. Those early days must have been nerve-racking and stressful for Mary and Joseph, as they dealt with their roles as new parents to the one who would one day be their king.

The verses that follow the shepherds' visit in Luke tell the story of Jesus' first few days. In accordance with Jewish tradition, Jesus was circumcised at eight days old and named. After their purification, the parents took the baby Jesus to Jerusalem to offer a sacrifice in the temple. In Luke 2:25-35, the young family encounters Simeon, an old Jewish man who had been waiting many years for the Messiah. The Holy Spirit had revealed to him that he would not die until he had seen the Messiah with his own eyes. While Mary and Joseph were in the temple, the Holy Spirit led Simeon to them. Upon seeing them, Simeon took Jesus into his arms and began praising God, acknowledging that his eyes were indeed beholding salvation, a light of revelation to the Gentiles and glory for Israel. Mary and Joseph were amazed by Simeon's words. Simeon then blessed the young family and gave Mary a final word regarding her young son. In verses 34-35, Simeon tells Mary, "This boy is assigned to be the cause of the falling and rising of many in Israel and to be a sign that generates opposition so that the inner thoughts of many will be revealed. And a sword will pierce your innermost being too."

The young couple had gone through a lot in the past few weeks. They had been visited by angels, decided to marry, traveled to Bethlehem, delivered a son, and were in the throes of early parenthood. While their calling as Jesus' earthly parents had been confirmed by angels, and the shepherds had visited them in the stable, there were probably days that they scarcely could believe that their baby was really the Son of God, and that they were really the parents to the one who would grow up to deliver their people. As a matter of fact, there must have been times when it seemed almost impossible that this child who was born in a stable would some day be the king of the Jews. Given all of this, Simeon's words in the temple would have been especially powerful for the young couple. The affirmation of the wise old man inside the temple would have reminded them yet again of their calling and God's plan for them and their son. In addition to offering affirmation, Simeon's final words for Mary gave them a glimpse of God's plan for Jesus. Even as the parents found comfort in Simeon's affirmation of Jesus as the Messiah, his final words painted a bleak and perhaps different picture of Jesus' role as Savior than they had expected, leaving Mary with the reality that not only would her son be opposed, but that in the end her own soul would be pierced as well.

Simeon's affirmation of the Christ child in the temple came at just the right time for the young parents. Although we do not have scriptural evidence, it would not be surprising if God provided those types of occasional affirmations for the family, at just the right times, to encourage them in their journey. There are a couple of powerful lessons we can learn from Simeon's story. First of all, God called Simeon to bless this young family, and Simeon did. He came to the temple, and Simeon spoke words of affirmation to them. There are times in our lives when God calls us to do the same thing. I don't mean that God necessarily has a prophetic word for us to speak, but there are times that God calls us to affirm and bless another person. It's really important not to ignore that calling, as the blessing of affirmation is a powerful one.

The second thing I think we learn from Simeon's story is that the reality of the cross is part of the Christmas story. So often we are so lost in the sweetness of the nativity scene that we forget that this sweet baby will indeed grow up to be despised and opposed, and ultimately crucified. This baby who came so miraculously will grow to be an adult who will sacrifice all for the sins of all humanity. I think Simeon understood that even as he held the baby Jesus. This Christmas, as we celebrate the birth of God's greatest gift, may we remember that Jesus' gift would carry the highest imaginable cost. Indeed, thank you, God, for sending your son. Amen. (Tracey Allred)

Worship Aids

Call to Worship

Let us enter God's gates with thanksgiving
and God's courts with praise.
For the Lord is good;
and God's steadfast love endures forever.
As Simeon entered the temple to worship the young Messiah,
We will worship the Lord with gladness;
and come into God's presence with singing.

Invocation

Holy God, we acknowledge your power and goodness as we enter this place. O Lord, we seek to meet you here, to worship you, to honor you for the great gift of your Son. Meet us here. Accept our attempts at glorifying you. Amen.

Benediction

As we leave this place, let us go into the world offering and accepting the affirmation of all that God has called us to do, and acknowledging the high cost of the greatest gift of all, Jesus Christ. Amen. (Tracey Allred)

III. APPENDIXES

APPENDIX A. CLASSIC SERMON

The More Excellent Way

John Wesley

[*The Bicentennial Edition of the Works of John Wesley, vol. 3, Albert C. Outler, ed.* (Nashville: Abingdon Press, 1986), *Sermon 89,* 263–277. Notes from *The Works of John Wesley, Vol. 3, Sermons* © 1986 Abingdon Press. Used by permission.]

"Covet earnestly the best gifts; And yet I show to you a more excellent way (1 Corinthians 12:31)."

1. In the preceding verses, St. Paul has been speaking of the extraordinary gifts of the Holy Ghost[1]; such as healing the sick, prophesying, (in the proper sense of the word; that is, foretelling things to come) speaking with strange tongues, such as the speaker had never learned, and the miraculous interpretation of tongues. And these gifts the Apostle allows to be desirable; yea, he exhorts the Corinthians, at least the teachers among them (to whom chiefly, if not solely, they were wont to be given in the first ages of the church) to "covet" them "earnestly," that thereby they might be qualified to be more useful either to Christians or heathens. "And yet," says he, "I show unto you a more excellent way"—far more desirable than all these put together, inasmuch as it will infallibly lead you to happiness both in this world and in the world to come; whereas you might have all those gifts, yea, in the highest degree, and yet be miserable both in time and eternity.

2. It does not appear that these extraordinary gifts of the Holy Ghost were common in the church for more than two or three centuries. We seldom hear of them after that fatal period when the Emperor Constantine[2] called himself a Christian, and from a vain imagination of promoting the

Christian cause thereby heaped riches, and power, and honour, upon the Christians in general; but in particular upon the Christian clergy. From this time they almost totally ceased; very few instances of the kind were found. The cause of this was not (as has been vulgarly supposed) "because there was no more occasion for them,"[3] because all the world was become Christian. This is a miserable mistake; not a twentieth part of it was then nominally Christian.[4] The real cause was, "the love of many"—almost of all Christians, so called, was "waxed cold."[5] The Christians had no more of the Spirit of Christ than the other heathens. The Son of man, when he came to examine his Church, could hardly "find faith upon earth."[6] This was the real cause why the extraordinary gifts of the Holy Ghost were no longer to be found in the Christian church—because the Christians were turned heathens again, and had only a dead form left.[7]

3. However, I would not at present speak of these, of the extraordinary gifts of the Holy Ghost, but of the ordinary; and these likewise we may "covet earnestly," in order to be more useful in our generation. With this view we may covet "the gift of *convincing* speech," in order to "sound the unbelieving heart;"[8] and the gift of *persuasion*, to move the affections, as well as enlighten the understanding. We may covet *knowledge*, both of the word and of the works of God, whether of providence or grace. We may desire a measure of that faith which, on particular occasions, wherein the glory of God or the happiness of men is nearly concerned, goes far beyond the power of natural causes. We may desire an easy elocution, a pleasing address,[9] with resignation to the will of our Lord; yea, whatever would enable us, as we have opportunity, to be useful wherever we are. These gifts we may innocently desire: but there is "a more excellent way."

4. The way of love, of loving all men for God's sake, of humble gentle, patient love, is that which the Apostle so admirably describes in the ensuing chapter. And without this, he assures us, all eloquence, all knowledge, all faith, all works, and all sufferings, are of no more value in the sight of God than sounding brass or a rumbling cymbal,[10] and are not of the least avail toward our eternal salvation. Without this, all we know, all we believe, all we do, all we suffer, will profit us nothing in the great day of accounts.

5. But at present I would take a different view of the text, and point out "a more excellent way" in another sense. It is the observation of an ancient writer, that there have been from the beginning two orders of Christians.[11] The one lived an innocent life, conforming in all things, not sinful, to the customs and fashions of the world; doing many good works,

abstaining from gross evils, and attending the ordinances of God. They endeavoured, in general, to have a conscience void of offence[12] in their outward behaviour, but did not aim at any particular strictness, being in most things like their neighbours.[13] The other sort of Christians not only abstained from all appearance of evil, were zealous of good works[14] in every kind, and attended all the ordinances of God, but likewise used all diligence to attain the whole mind that was in Christ,[15] and laboured to walk, in every point, as their beloved Master. In order to this they walked in a constant course of universal self-denial, trampling on every pleasure which they were not divinely conscious prepared them for taking pleasure in God. They took up their cross daily.[16] They strove, they agonized without intermission, to enter in at the strait gate.[17] This one thing they did,[18] they spared no pains to arrive at the summit of Christian holiness; "leaving the first principles of the doctrine of Christ, to go on to perfection;"[19] to "know all that love of God which passeth knowledge, and to be filled with all the fullness of God."[20]

6. From long experience and observation I am inclined to think, that whoever finds redemption in the blood of Jesus, whoever is justified, has then the choice of walking in the higher or the lower path. I believe the Holy Spirit at that time sets before him "the more excellent way," and incites him to walk therein, to choose the narrowest path in the narrow way, to aspire after the heights and depths of holiness, after the entire image of God. But if he does not accept this offer, he insensibly declines into the lower order of Christians. He still goes on in what may be called a good way, serving God in his degree, and finds mercy in the close of life, through the blood of the covenant.[21]

7. I would be far from quenching the smoking flax,[22] from discouraging those that serve God in a low degree. But I could not wish them to stop here: I would encourage them to come up higher,[23] without thundering hell and damnation in their ears, without condemning the way wherein they were, telling them it is the way that leads to destruction,[24] I will endeavour to point out to them what is in every respect "a more excellent way."

8. Let it be well remembered, I do not affirm that all who do not walk in this way are in the high road to hell. But thus much I must affirm, they will not have so high a place in heaven as they would have had if they had chosen the better part.[25] And will this be a small loss? The having so many fewer stars in your crown of glory?[26] Will it be a little thing to have a lower place than you might have had in the kingdom of your Father?

Certainly there will be no sorrow in heaven: there all tears will be wiped from our eyes.[27] But if it were possible grief could enter there, we should grieve at that irreparable loss! Irreparable then, but not now! Now, by the grace of God, we may choose the "more excellent way." Let us now compare this, in a few particulars, with the way wherein most Christians walk.

I. To begin at the beginning of the day. It is the manner of the generality of Christians, if they are not obliged to work for their living, *to rise*, particularly in winter, at eight or nine in the morning after having lain in bed eight or nine, if not more hours. I do not say now (as I should have been very apt to do fifty years ago) that all who indulge themselves in this manner are in the way to hell. But neither can I say they are in the way to heaven, denying themselves, and taking up their cross daily.[28] Sure I am, there is "a more excellent way" to promote health both of body and mind. From an observation of more than sixty years, I have learned, that men in health require, at an average, from six to seven hours' sleep, and healthy women a little more, from seven to eight, in four and twenty hours. I know this quantity of sleep to be most advantageous to the body as well as the soul. It is preferable to any medicine which I have known, both for preventing and removing nervous disorders.[29] It is, therefore, undoubtedly the most excellent way, in defiance of fashion and custom, to take just so much sleep as experience proves our nature to require; seeing this is indisputably most conducive both to bodily and spiritual health. And why should not you walk in this way? Because it is difficult? Nay, with men it is impossible. But all things are possible with God;[30] and by his grace all things will be possible to *you*. Only continue instant in prayer, and you will find this not only possible, but easy: Yea, and it will be far easier to rise early constantly, than to do it sometimes. But then you must begin at the right end: if you rise early, you must sleep early. Impose it upon yourself, unless when something extraordinary occurs, to go to bed at a fixed hour. Then the difficulty of it will soon be over; but the advantage of it will remain for ever.

II. The generality of Christians, as soon as they rise, are accustomed to use some kind of *prayer*; and probably to use the same form still which they learned when they were eight or ten years old. Now I do not condemn those who proceed thus (though many do) as mocking God, though they have used the same form, without any variation, for twenty or thirty years together. But surely there is "a more excellent way" of ordering our private devotions. What if you were to follow the advice given by that great and good man, Mr. Law,[31] on this subject? Consider both your outward and inward state, and vary your prayers accordingly. For instance: Suppose your outward state is prosperous; suppose you are in a state of health, ease, and plenty, having your lot cast among kind relations, good neighbours, and agreeable friends, that love you and you them; then your outward state manifestly calls for praise and thanksgiving to God. On the other hand, if you are in a state of adversity; if God has laid trouble upon your loins;[32] if you are in poverty, in want, in outward distress; if you are in any imminent danger; if you are in pain and sickness; then you are clearly called to pour out your soul before God in such prayer as is suited to your circumstances. In like manner you may suit your devotions to your inward state, the present state of your mind. Is your soul in heaviness, either from a sense of sin, or through manifold temptations?[33] Then let your prayer consist of such confessions, petitions, and supplications, as are agreeable to your distressed situation of mind. On the contrary, is your soul in peace? Are you rejoicing in God? Are his consolations not small with you?[34] Then say, with the Psalmist: "Thou art my God, and I will love thee: Thou art my God, and I will praise thee."[35] You may, likewise, when you have time, add to your other devotions a little reading and meditation, and perhaps a psalm of praise, the natural effusion of a thankful heart. You must certainly see that this is "a more excellent way" than the poor dry form which you used before.

III. 1. The generality of Christians, after using some prayer, usually apply themselves to the *business* of their calling. Every man that has any pretence to be a Christian will not fail to do this; seeing it is impossible that an idle man can be a good man, sloth being inconsistent with religion.[36] But with what view? For what end do you undertake and follow your worldly business? "To provide things necessary for myself and my family." It is a good answer as far as it goes; but it does not go far enough. For a Turk or a Heathen goes so far, does his work for the very same ends. But a Christian may go abundantly farther: His end in all his labour is, to please God; to do, not his own will, but the will of him that sent him into the world—[37] for this very purpose, to do the will of God on earth as angels do in heaven.[38] He works for eternity. He "labours not for the meat that perisheth," (this is the smallest part of his motive)—"but for that which endureth to everlasting life."[39] And is not this "a more excellent way?"

2. Again: In what *manner* do you transact your worldly business? I trust, with *diligence*, whatever your hand findeth to do, doing it with all our might;[40] in justice, rendering to all their due,[41] in every circumstance of

life; yea, and in mercy, doing unto every man what you would he should do unto you.[42] This is well: But a Christian is called to go still farther—to add piety to justice; to intermix prayer, especially the prayer of the heart, with all the labour of his hands. Without this all his diligence and justice only show him to be an honest heathen—and many there are who profess the Christian religion, that go no farther than honest heathenism.

3. Yet again: in what *spirit* do you go through your business? In the spirit of the world, or the Spirit of Christ? I am afraid thousands of those who are called good Christians do not understand the question. If you act in the Spirit of Christ you carry the end you at first proposed through all your work from first to last. You do everything in the spirit of sacrifice, giving up your will to the will of God; and continually aiming, not at ease, pleasure, or riches; not at anything "this short enduring world can give;" but merely at the glory of God. Now can anyone deny that this is the most excellent way of pursuing worldly business?

IV. 1. But these tenements of clay[43] which we bear about us require constant reparation, or they will sink into the earth from which they were taken, even sooner than nature requires. Daily food is necessary to prevent this, to repair the constant decays of nature. It was common in the heathen world when they were about to use this, to take meat or even drink, *libare pateram Jovi*;[44] to pour out a little to the honour of their god—although the gods of the heathens were but devils, as the Apostle justly observes.[45] "It seems," says a late writer, "there was once some such custom as this in our own country. For we still frequently see a gentleman before he sits down to dinner in his own house, holding his hat before his face, and perhaps seeming to say something; though he generally does it in such a manner that no one can tell what he says."[46] Now what if instead of this, every head of a family, before he sat down to eat and drink, either morning, noon, or night, (for the reason of the thing is the same at every hour of the day) was seriously to ask a blessing from God on what he was about to take; yea, and afterward, seriously to return thanks to the Giver of all his blessings. Would not this be a more excellent way than to use that dull farce which is worse than nothing; being, in reality, no other than mockery both of God and man?

2. As to the *quantity* of their food, good sort of men do not usually eat to excess. At least not so far as to make themselves sick with meat, or to intoxicate themselves with drink. And as to the manner of taking it, it is usually innocent, mixed with a little mirth, which is said to help digestion. So far, so good. And provided they take only that measure of plain,

cheap, wholesome food, which most promotes health both of body and mind, there will be no cause of blame. Neither can I require you to take that advice of Mr. Herbert, though he was a good man:

> Take thy meat; think it dust; then eat a bit
> And say with all, Earth to earth I commit.[47]

This is too melancholy: it does not suit with that cheerfulness[48] which is highly proper at a Christian meal. Permit me to illustrate this subject with a little story. The King of France one day, pursuing the chase, out-rode all his company, who after seeking him some time found him sitting in a cottage eating bread and cheese. Seeing them, he cried out: "Where have I lived all my time? I never before tasted so good food in my life!" "Sire," said one of them, "you never had so *good sauce*[49] before; for you were never hungry." Now it is true, hunger is a good sauce;[50] but there is one that is better still; that is, thankfulness. Sure that is the most agreeable food which is seasoned with this. And why should not yours at every meal? You need not then cast your eye on death, but receive every morsel as a pledge of life eternal. The Author of your being gives you in this food, not only a reprieve from death, but an earnest that in a little time "death shall be swallowed up in victory."[51]

3. The time of taking our food is usually a time of *conversation* also, as it is natural to refresh our minds while we refresh our bodies. Let us consider a little in what manner the generality of Christians usually converse together. What are the ordinary subjects of their conversation? If it is harmless, (as one would hope it is) if there be nothing in it profane, nothing immodest, nothing untrue, or unkind; if there be no talebearing, backbiting, or evil-speaking, they have reason to praise God for his restraining grace. But there is more than this implied in "ordering our conversation aright."[52] In order to this it is needful, first, that "your communication," that is, discourse or conversation, "be good;"[53] that it be materially good, on good subjects; not fluttering about anything that occurs; for what have you to do with courts and kings? It is not your business to

> Fight over the wars, reform the state;[54]

unless when some remarkable event calls for the acknowledgment of the justice or mercy of God. We *must* indeed sometimes talk of worldly things; otherwise we may as well go out of the world.[55] But it should only be so far as is needful; then we should return to a better subject. Secondly, let your conversation be "to the use of edifying;"[56] calculated to edify either the speaker or the hearers, or both; to build them up, as each has particular need, either in faith, or love, or holiness. Thirdly, see that it not only gives entertainment, but, in one kind or other, "ministers grace to the hearers."[57] Now, is not this a more excellent way of *conversing* than the harmless way above-mentioned?

V. 1. We have seen what is the "more excellent way" of ordering our conversation, as well as our business. But we cannot be always intent upon business; both our bodies and minds require some relaxation. We need intervals of diversion from business. It will be necessary to be very explicit upon this head, as it is a point which has been much misunderstood.

2. Diversions are of various kinds. Some are almost peculiar to men, as the sports of the field—hunting, shooting, fishing—wherein not many women (I should say, ladies) are concerned. Others are indifferently used by persons of both sexes; some of which are of a more public nature, as races, masquerades, plays, assemblies, balls. Others are chiefly used in private houses, as cards, dancing, and music; to which we may add the reading of plays, novels, romances, newspapers, and fashionable poetry.

3. Some diversions indeed which were formerly in great request, are now fallen into disrepute. The nobility and gentry (in England at least) seem totally to disregard the once fashionable diversion of *hawking*; and the vulgar themselves are no longer diverted by men hacking and hewing each other in pieces at *broadsword*. The noble game of *quarterstaff*, likewise, is now exercised by very few. Yea, *cudgelling* has lost its honour, even in Wales itself. *Bear-baiting* also is now very seldom seen, and *bull-baiting* not very often. And it seems *cock-fighting* would totally cease in England, were it not for two or three right honourable patrons.

4. It is not needful to say anything more of these foul remains of Gothic barbarity,[58] than that they are a reproach, not only to all religion, but even to human nature. One would not pass so severe censure on the sports of the field. Let those who have nothing better to do, still run foxes and hares out of breath.[59] Neither need much be said about horse-races,[60] till some man of sense will undertake to defend them. It seems a great deal more may be said in defence of seeing a serious *tragedy*. I could not do it with a clear conscience; at least not in an English theatre, the sink of all profaneness and debauchery;[61] but possibly others can. I cannot say quite so much for *balls* or *assemblies*, which are more reputable than *masquer-*

ades, but must be allowed by all impartial persons to have exactly the same tendency. So undoubtedly have all public dancings. And the same tendency they must have, unless the same caution obtained among modern Christians which was observed among the ancient heathens. With them men and women never danced together, but always in separate rooms. This was always observed in ancient Greece, and for several ages at Rome,[62] where a woman dancing in company with men would have at once been set down for a prostitute. Of playing at *cards* I say the same as of seeing plays.[63] I could not do it with a clear conscience. But I am not obliged to pass sentences on those that are otherwise minded.[64] I leave them to their own Master: to him let them stand or fall.

5. But supposing these, as well as the reading of plays, novels, newspapers, and the like, to be quite "innocent diversions;" yet are there not more excellent ways of diverting themselves for those that love or fear God? Would men of fortune divert themselves in the open air? They may do it by cultivating and improving their lands, by planting their grounds, by laying out, carrying on, and perfecting their gardens and orchards. At other times they may visit and converse with the most serious and sensible of their neighbours; or they may visit the sick, the poor, the widows, and fatherless in their affliction.[65] Do they desire to divert themselves in the house? They may read useful history, pious and elegant poetry, or several branches of natural philosophy. If you have time, you may divert yourself by music, and perhaps by philosophical experiments.[66] But above all, when you have once learned the use of prayer, you will find that as

> that which yields or fills
> All space, the ambient air, wide interfused
> Embraces round this florid earth;[67]

so will this, till through every space of life it be interfused with all your employments, and wherever you are, whatever you do, embrace you on every side. Then you will be able to say boldly:—

> With me no melancholy void,
> No moment lingers unemploy'd,
>   Or unimproved below:
> My weariness of life is gone,
> Who live to serve my God alone,
>   And only Jesus know.[68]

VI. One point only remains to be considered; that is, the use of money.[69] What is the way wherein the generality of Christians employ this? And is there not a more excellent way?

1. The generality of Christians usually set apart something yearly, perhaps a tenth or even one-eighth part of their income, whether it arise from yearly revenue, or from trade, for charitable uses. Few I have known who said like Zaccheus, "Lord, the half of my goods I give to the poor."[70] O that it would please God to multiply these friends of mankind, these general benefactors! But,

2. Besides those who have a stated rule, there are thousands who give large sums to the poor; especially when any striking instance of distress is represented to them in lively colours.

3. I praise God for all of you who act in this manner. May you never be weary of well-doing! May God restore what you give sevenfold into your own bosom! But yet I show unto you a more excellent way.

4. You may consider yourself as one in whose hands the Proprietor of heaven and earth and all things therein has lodged a part of his goods, to be disposed of according to his direction. And his direction is, that you should look upon yourself as one of a certain number of indigent persons who are to be provided for out of that portion of His goods wherewith you are entrusted. You have two advantages over the rest: The one, that "it is more blessed to give than to receive;"[71] the other, that you are to serve yourself first, and others afterwards. This is the light wherein you are to see yourself and them. But to be more particular: First, if you have no family, after you have provided for yourself, give away all that remains; so that

> Each Christmas your accounts may clear,
> And wind your bottom round the year.[72]

This was the practice of all the young men at Oxford who were called "Methodists."[73] For example: One of them had thirty pounds a year. He lived on twenty-eight and gave away forty shillings. The next year receiving sixty pounds, he still lived on twenty-eight, and gave away two-and-thirty. The third year he received ninety pounds, and gave away sixty-two. The fourth year he received a hundred and twenty pounds. Still he lived as before on twenty-eight; and gave to the poor ninety-two.[74] Was not this a more excellent way? Secondly, if you have a family, seriously consider before God, how much each member of it wants, in order to have what is needful for life and godliness. And in general, do not allow them less, nor much more, than you allow yourself. Thirdly, this being done, fix your purpose, to "gain no more." I charge you in the name of God, do not increase your substance![75] As it comes daily or yearly, so let it go; otherwise you "lay up treasures upon earth."[76] And this our Lord as flatly forbids as murder and adultery. By doing it, therefore, you would "treasure up to yourselves wrath against the day of wrath and revelation of the righteous judgment of God."[77]

5. But suppose it were not forbidden, how can you on principles of reason spend your money in a way which God may *possibly forgive*, instead of spending it in a manner which he will *certainly reward*? You will have no reward in heaven for what you *lay up*; you will, for what you *lay out*. Every pound you put into the earthly bank is sunk: it brings no interest above.[78] But every pound you give to the poor is put into the bank of heaven. And it will bring glorious interest; yea, and such as will be accumulating to all eternity.

6. Who then is a wise man, and endued with knowledge among you?[79] Let him resolve this day, this hour, this moment, the Lord assisting him, to choose in all the preceding particulars the "more excellent way;" and let him steadily keep it, both with regard to sleep, prayer, work, food, conversation, and diversions; and particularly with regard to the employment of that important "talent," *money*. Let *your* heart answer to the call of God, "From this moment, God being my helper, I will lay up no more treasure upon earth: This one thing I will do, I will lay up treasure in heaven;[80] I will render unto God the things that are God's;[81] I will give him all my goods and all my heart."

Notes

1. Cf. No. 4, *Scriptural Christianity*, §4 and n. [This and similar citations refer to other sermons and works of John Wesley, also published in the *Bicentennial Edition of the Works of John Wesley*; hereinafter referred to as *Works*.]
2. Cf. No. 61, "The Mystery of Iniquity," §§27–28 and n.
3. An echo from Richard Graves, *The Spiritual Quixote?* Cf. I.55: "They [our modern itinerant reformers] are planting the gospel in a Christian country; they are combating the shadow of popery where the protestant religion is established; and declaiming against good works in an age which they usually represent as abounding in every evil work."
4. Cf. No. 15, *The Great Assize*, II.4 and n.
5. Cf. Matt. 24:12.
6. Luke 18:8 (*Notes*).
7. An interesting note here that the possibility of "the extraordinary gifts of the Holy Ghost": stands open, in principle, in any age of the church.

8. Cf. John Wesley, "On the Descent of the Holy Ghost at Pentecost," *Hymns and Sacred Poems* (1739), p. 186 *Poet. Wks.*, I.166). This was altered from Henry More's poem in *Divine Dialogues* (1668) which Wesley had read in 1733. Later, Wesley prepared two hymns from this poem for his *Collection* of 1780 (Nos. 444–45; see 7:623–65 in *Works*). The quotation is from st. 8:

The spirit of convincing speech,
Of pow'r demonstrative impart,
Such as may ev'ry conscience reach
And sound the unbelieving heart.

9. Cf. *Directions for Pronunciation and Gesture* (*Bibliography*, No. 161, Vol. 15, *Works*).
10. See 1 Corinthians 13:1; but see *Notes, loc. cit.*, where Wesley had followed the consensus of Wycliffe, Tyndale, Cranmer, Geneva, Rheims, and the AV in translating ἀλαλάζον as "tinkling." In No. 36, "The Law Established through Faith, II",: III.1, we find "tinkling," but in No. 91, "On Charity," III.1, Wesley uses "rumbling" again. Wesley had no precedent for this in Poole's *Annotations*, or Henry's *Exposition*—and has had no imitators in later translations. See also Arndt and Gingrich, and Liddell and Scott, *Greek-English Lexicons.*
11. This distinction is at least as old as *The Shepherd of Hermas*, but was developed more explicitly by Clement of Alexandria; cf. *The Instructor*, I.i–vii, and *Stromateis*, II.xix–xx, IV.xxi–xxii, V.i–iv. It was then summed up by Eusebius in his *Demonstratio Evangelica*, I.viii.
12. Acts 24:16.
13. Still another deprecating reference to the *General Rules*. Cf. No. 22, "Sermon on the Mount, II," II.4 and n.
14. Titus 2:14.
15. See 1 Corinthians 2:16 and Philippians 2:5.
16. See Luke 9:23.
17. Luke 13:24; cf. No. 17, "The Circumcision of the Heart," II.7 and n.
18. See Philippians 3:13.
19. Cf. Hebrews 6:1.
20. Cf. Ephesians 3:19.
21. See Hebrews 13:20.
22. See Isaiah 42:3.
23. See Luke 14:10.
24. For another example of this striking change in the doctrine of assurance, cf. No. 106, "On Faith, Hebrews 11:6," I.11.
25. See Luke 10:42.
26. Cf. No. 57, "On the Fall of Man," II.8 and n.
27. See Revelation 7:17; 21:4.
28. See Luke 9:23.
29. Cf. "Thoughts on Nervous Disorders," §7, AM (1786), IX.94–95, where Wesley discusses intemperance in sleep being one cause of "lowness of spirits"; see also No. 93, "On Redeeming the Time," *passim*.
30. See Matthew 19:26.
31. The reference here is to A *Serious Call*, ch. xiv, and Wesley's own published *Extract* of it (see *Works* Bibliography, No. 86). But Law had also published *The Spirit of Prayer*, and for Wesley's comment on it see JWJ, July 20, 1749. Wesley's estimates of Law varied

according to circumstances and contexts; e.g., his attitude here represents a mellowing of the late Wesley. For his earlier criticisms of Law, cf. Wesley's letter to him, May 14, 1738, as well as a later one, Jan. 6, 1756; and see the letter to Dorothy Furly, May 18, 1757: "Mr. Law...betrays deep ignorance both of Scripture and the inward work of God. You are more liable to receive hurt from his late writings than from any other which I know." Cf. also No. 20, *The Lord Our Righteousness*, II.16.
32. See Psalm 66:10 (*Book of Common Prayer*).
33. 1 Peter 1:6.
34. See Job 15:11.
35. Psalm 118:28 (*Book of Common Prayer*).
36. Cf. No. 111, *National Sins and Miseries*, II.6 and n.
37. See John 6:38.
38. See Matthew 6:10.
39. Cf. John 6:27.
40. See Ecclesiastes 9:10.
41. See Romans 13:7.
42. See Matthew 7:12.
43. Cf. No. 28, "Sermon on the Mount, VIII," §21 and n.
44. "To pour out a libation bowl to Jove"; cf. Virgil, *Aeneid*, vii.133: "...*nunc pateras libate Jovi*."
45. See 1 Corinthians 10:20.
46. A vague recollection of an anecdote from Law, *Serious Call* (*Works*, IV.41); cf. another anecdote in this same vein in *The Spectator*, No. 380, May 16, 1712.
47. Cf. George Herbert, *The Temple*, "The Church Porch," ll. 131–32.
48. In Wesley's "holiness-happiness" equation cheerfulness is emphatically included; cf. the younger Wesley's letter to Mrs. Chapman, March 29, 1737 ("...holiness cannot be without cheerfulness..."), and the older Wesley's letter to his niece, Sarah, August 18, 1790 ("Perpetual cheerfulness is the temper of a Christian,...which is in one sense to rejoice evermore").
49. π; source unidentified.
50. Quoted by Cervantes in *Don Quixote*, II.5; and earlier in Cicero, *De Finibus [bonorum et malorum]* (*On the Purpose of Good and Evil*), II.xxviii.90, where it is credited to Socrates.
51. Cf. 1 Corinthians 15:54.
52. Cf. Psalm 50:23.
53. Cf. Matthew 5:37; Ephesians 4:29.
54. Prior, "The Ladle," l. 96.
55. See 1 Corinthians 5:10.
56. Ephesians 4:29.
57. Ibid.
58. Pope, in *The Guardian*, No. 61 (May 21, 1713), had used this phrase as from the Abbé Claude Fleury's *Les Moeurs del Israélites* in the context of Fleury's comparison of the ancient Israelites with those of "*les Francs*." The pejorative use of the adjective "Gothic" had, however, already become a commonplace (cf. *OED*).
59. This had appeared in quotation marks in No. 79, "On Dissipation," §12; cf. n. there.
60. Cf. No. 143, "Public Diversions Denounced," III.2.
61. In his Oxford days Wesley "had a passionate interest in plays and in the theatre....There was a histrionic streak in his character" (Green, Wesley, 72, 114 [see

Bibliography, *Works*]. And his delight in plays continued even after he had come round to the views of Jeremy Collier (*A Defense of the Short View of the Profaneness and Immorality of the English Stage* [1699]) and William Law (*The Absolute Unlawfulness of the Stage-Entertainment Fully Demonstrated* [1726]); cf., e.g., his comment on John Home's recent tragedy, *Douglas* (JWJ, June 9, 1757). Notice the extraordinary range of his quotations from various dramas; his reading in them was extensive (clearly, he distinguished "seeing" plays in a theatre from *reading* them). Cf. George Farquhar's description of a typical "first night": in his *The Inconstant: Or, the Way to Win Him* (1702), Act IV, sc. 3; see also No. 94, "On Family Religion," III.14.
62. A doubtful inference from Lucian, "The Dance"; Atehnaeus, *Deipnosophistae*, I.14–22; and Plato, *The Laws*, VII.814E–816D; cf. Chambers's *Cyclopaedia*, *loc. cit.*
63. The young Wesley had also played cards; cf. diary, Dec. 30 1736 ("played at ombre"); Jan. 7, 1727 ("played loo"); Jan. 10, 1727 ("played cards and lost"); on June 20, 1729, he played cards and lost twelve shillings.
64. More evidence of the mellowing late Wesley; cf. No. 39, "Catholic Spirit."
65. See James 1:27.
66. Cf. Chambers's *Cyclopaedia*, "Experimental": "Experiments are of the last [i.e., highest] importance in philosophy. . . . In effect, experiments within these past fifty or sixty years, are come into such vogue that nothing will pass in philosophy [i.e., natural science] but what is founded on experiment or confirmed by experiment. . . . The new philosophy is almost altogether experimental." The chief sponsor of this new philosophy was The Royal Society of London for Improving Natural Knowledge, which was founded in 1660; cf. Thomas Sprat, *History of the Royal Society* (1667).
67. Cf. Milton, *Paradise Lost*, vii.88–90; No. 55, *On the Trinity*, §9 and n.
68. Cf. Charles Wesley, *Hymns and Sacred Poems* (1749), II.136 (*Poetry Works*, V.279), which was reprinted separately in *Hymns for the Watch-night*:

With us no melancholy void,
No moment lingers unemployed,
Or unimproved below;
Our weariness of life is gone,
Who live to serve our God alone,
And only thee to know.

69. See No. 87, "The Danger of Riches," II.8 and n.
70. Luke 19:8.
71. Acts 20:35.
72. Cf. Prior, "An Epitaph," ll. 47cn48:

Each Christmas they accounts did clear,
And wound their bottom round the year.

Orig., "your accounts," altered by Wesley's errata; see also No. 87, "The Danger of Riches," II.7 and n.
73. Cf. No 53, *On the Death of George Whitefield*, III.2 and n.
74. Tyerman regarded this as Wesley's reference to himself; cf. *JW*, I.71–72. But see Green's comments on Wesley's income at Oxford in *Wesley*, pp. 100–1, 320–21. Thus, this is either a romanticized memory of those early days or, just possible, a reference to some other member of the Holy Club (John Clayton?).
75. Another flat prohibition of surplus accumulation; see No. 50, "The Use of Money," intro., I.1, and n.

76. Matthew 6:19.
77. Cf. Romans 2:5.
78. A notable contradiction of the famous "Weber-Tawney" thesis that it was the Protestant work ethic that served as the prime sponsor of capitalism and its presuppositions as to the legitimacy of capital accumulation by means of interest. By contrast, Wesley here reaffirms his agreement with the classical and medieval condemnation of "interest"; cf. the summation of that tradition in Thomas, *Summa Theologica*, II–II, Q. 78, Arts. 1–4. Clearly, there is a need for a more careful and complete study of Wesley's economic notions and for a more careful critique of the "Weber-Tawney" thesis itself; cf. Max Weber, *The Protestant Ethic and the Spirit of Capitalism* (London, G. Allen and Unwin, 1930), and R. H. Tawney, *Religion and the Rise of Capitalism* (London, J. Murray, 1926).
79. James 3:13.
80. See Matthew 6:19-20.
81. Matthew 22:21.

APPENDIX B. PRE-SERMON AND OFFERTORY PRAYERS

David N. Mosser

Pre-Sermon Prayers

1

As we journey into the sacred story, help us along the path toward faithfulness. Create in our lives a place for faith, hope, and love. In the name of Jesus we pray. Amen.

2

When we hear the word proclaimed from your holy book, O Lord, may it inspire us as you have inspired it. Give us the vision and discernment to understand the word offered us today and send your spirit to enthuse our preacher. Amen.

3

As we sit before your holy texts and as we contemplate what it means to be "under authority," O God, guide us to your paths which lead to you. Help us stand under Scripture and thereby understand it. We pray in Christ's holy name. Amen.

4

In holy writ O God, you issued to us a decree. Your decree puts into words what the life of Christ might look like as lived out in every group of people. Help us be ready on that day to take advantage of the grace you offer us in the written word. Amen.

5

O Lord of All, we pray that as John's Gospel tells us that you might "sanctify [us] in the truth; your word is truth" (John 17:17 NRSV). May we have the vision to see your truth in the word delivered in our worship today. Amen.

6

Gracious One, as we gather to ponder our lives before you, help us reflect on the connection between believers and the Divine that Scripture gestures toward. Make us like Damaris and Dionysius as Paul preached them nearer the realm of divinity. Let us listen to your holy word. Amen.

7

The word is sacred O God and may it be so for us. As we share the story of faith in Jesus, help us appropriate the discipleship called for and give us the will to enact it. In the name of the one who said it all! Amen.

8

We need to hear the good news of the gospel, O Lord of All. Send us not only the preacher, but also the spirit of vision and discernment to apply your sacred writ to our lives—all in the name of Christ. Amen.

9

As we come to your altar, Lord, let us bow before you as creator of all. As we wade into the story of faith which we find in our holy Scripture, remind us that we share this story with saints around the world and through the centuries. Connect all of us in Jesus. Amen.

10

As our Heavenly Parent, O God, remind us that our models for faith can meet us in Scripture. When we try to put into practice faith ideals such as forgiveness and mercy, help us remember that there are biblical exemplars from whom we can gain wisdom and daring. In the name of Christ we pray. Amen.

Offertory Prayers

1

Gracious God, as we gather today to worship your holy name, make us mindful of the manifold resources that we control by our will. Give us the volition and good judgment to be your people and offer our gifts to those in need. Help us follow Jesus. Amen.

2

O God, as people who have been blessed beyond our comprehension, help us recognize that what you have given to us you intend for us to share with others. May we dare to share! In the name of Jesus, we pray. Amen.

3

As our Absolute Monarch, O God, remind us as we gather in Jesus' name to serve others as you have served us in Christ. You have saved us from sin—now save us for service as stewards of your gifts. In your holy name we pray. Amen.

4

Paul writes to the church at Corinth: "Each of you must give as you have made up your mind, not reluctantly or under compulsion, for God loves a cheerful giver" (2 Corinthians 9:7 NRSV). Lord, help us follow Paul's guidance as we are followers of Jesus, in whose name we pray. Amen.

5

God who gives and gives and gives to your children, give again to us grateful hearts and remind us of what the Psalter tells us: "the righteous are generous and keep giving" (Psalm 37:21). Amen.

6

We need ways in our day-to-day lives, O Lord, to offer back the generosity that you have placed in our hearts through Jesus. Help us reach out to others in compassion as Jesus reached out to us. We pray this in the name of the one who gave all for us. Amen.

7

O God, in whom we move and live and have our being, guide us toward having glad and generous hearts as did the earliest church. Remind us that we only pass along what you have first given us as a sanctified gift. Make us worthy to be called Christians and give us bountiful hearts. Amen.

8

O God, while it may be true that "Many seek the favor of the generous, / and everyone is a friend to a giver of gifts" (Proverbs 19:6 NRSV), strike a memory chord in us that speaks words of truth: We give only because you first gave to us. In Jesus' name we pray. Amen.

9

God of divine benevolence, teach us not only how to pray but also how to give with glad and generous hearts. We want to be charitable, but sometimes we are afraid. Remind us that you provide all we will ever need in Jesus, in whose name we pray. Amen.

10

God of Wisdom, may you inspire us once again to become openhanded givers in this world of "looking out for #1." Offer us the courage to be compassionate toward others and forgiving in spirit. Remind us that others gladly come to our aid, and help us pay that generosity forward. Amen.

APPENDIX C. PASTORAL PRAYERS

David N. Mosser

New Year's Day

Dear Lord, as we stand at the portal of a new year, remind us that we are not only stewards of our financial resources—although we are that—but we also are responsible for the time you give us to spend. It is too easy to speak about wasting time or killing time. Yet we pray for your help to make us mindful that you give each of us twenty-four hours every day. We pray that we might control these precious hours as if you watched us each and every moment. Give us tasks that not only challenge us, but can build up your realm here on earth.

2

Remind us as well, O Lord, that as we enter a new year we are also leaving an old one. As we move into the future, may your forgiving grace help us let go of a past that clings to us so. Let us leave old obligations with a sense that we have offered our best as we move toward new obligations that will call forth the best of us. Most of all let the pioneering spirit of the Living Christ guide our steps as we once again move into the future which you hold firmly in your hands. We pray this in Jesus' name. Amen.

The Season of Epiphany

God of light, who has overcome the darkness of the forces of malevolence and evil, open us to the word that offers us a challenge to go into the world in Christ's name.

2

O God who is Creator of all, help us be faithful in our worship of you all the days of our lives. Make your heavenly kingdom manifest in our world. Give us sustenance for the day and let anxiety for tomorrow wait until its proper time. May we help feed all who are hungry and find our mission in our life's orbit and in our time. Help us discover who we truly are as we walk in your light and attempt to be your disciples. Amen.

3

We must confess before the church and as the church that we have not walked in the light—at least not often enough. Too often our congregation has little reflected the opulent assortment of people in our neighborhood. As we witness to the world, make our lives testify to your redeeming power. We pray in Christ's holy name. Amen.

Baptism of the Lord Sunday

As we pray for each other, O Holy God, may be worthy of Christ's promises. We pray that as you baptized Jesus and the voice from heaven came: "This is my Son, the Beloved, with whom I am well pleased" (Matthew 3:17 NRSV) that you, God, might be well pleased with our ministry as well. Almighty, eternal God, as you revealed Jesus as your child at the Jordan, reveal to us that we too are your children. Make us, like Jesus, be those who are born of the water and the spirit.

2

May we who share Jesus' incarnation see the Christ's humanity ever as much as we desire to partake of the Christ's divinity as we seek to be disciples in the realm of God. Give us the wherewithal to become what you, O God, have created us to be—those in perfect covenant promises with you. All this we ask through our Lord Jesus Christ, who lives and reigns with You and the Holy Spirit, one God forever and ever. Amen.

Transfiguration Sunday

Gracious God, who before Ash Wednesday, Lent, and Holy Week, encouraged our Lord as he suffered at the hands of ignorant people. This son of the divine, the only-begotten Son, revealed his divine glory on the holy Mount of Transfiguration. Help us as modern, twenty-first-century servants be wiser and more courageous than were Peter, James, and John as they stood gaping at the glory before them.

2

Grant to us your servants, O Lord, that our faith may behold the light of Jesus' countenance and that you may strengthen us to bear our crosses prepared for us by this mystery we call life. May your spirit change us into the likeness of Jesus as we worship the Christ during this Sabbath of revelation. Through the name of Jesus Christ our Lord we pray. Amen.

Ash Wednesday

O Almighty and eternal God, we come into your presence with weeping and mourning over our disobedience and lack of a righteously managed life. As disciples we ironically display little discipline. So here on Ash Wednesday we come to worship and pray that Scripture, music, liturgy, and the spoken word will remind us of what we already know—we are from the dust and to the dust we will return.

2

As we confess our sin, we are also mindful that you provide loving-kindness for our lives. Remind us that we never earn your grace or mercy, but rather they are always and everywhere given to human creatures because it is your nature to offer mercy and forgiveness for your wayward children. Bring us to repentance and that as we embrace your grace we might indeed become again the people you created us to be in Christ. Amen.

The Season of Lent

O God of all creation, as we enter this season of Lent prepare our hearts to take a spiritual journey with Jesus. You know we have a lot of explaining to do—yet it is within your realm to be merciful to your children lost and adrift. So to begin today, Lord, we simply need to confess much and get a lot off our chests. For one thing, we care more about our favorite pastimes than we do the starving people of the world. Forgive us, Lord, for our indifference and lack of nerve to speak out for those many people who are continuously wronged.

2

As you offer us glimpses of your glory in the life of Jesus, help us be Christ's disciples as we surrender to divine authority spelled out in the teachings, miracles, and life of Jesus our Christ. May we revere the ministry of Jesus to the poor, the outcast, and the ones on society's edges. Give us a sense of awe and reverence for the gift of grace and mercy you so willingly offer to us. May we receive what we need from your divine hand in Jesus Christ. Amen.

Holy Thursday

Lord, whatever our circumstance, we pray that you give us knowledge of you. Help us come to an honest assessment of who we are as people who seek a deeper and more abiding relationship with you through Jesus our Christ. On this night of nights, remind us that Jesus becomes our Passover lamb and that we must acknowledge his surrender on our behalf. In our most honest moments we confess that we are full of fear and anxiety.

2

We know that deep down even your assurance does not always quiet our restless spirits and fearful hearts. Help us overcome our doubt and let us trust in your grace once again. As Jesus is broken for us, may we in turn be broken for the world. Help us be those who heed the authority and surrender to the witness of the prophet who commands us to "do justice, and to love kindness, / and to walk humbly with your God" (Micah 6:8 NRSV). We pray this all in the name of our Messiah. Amen.

Good Friday

Compassionate God, Father and Mother of us all, in your gracious love you have embraced us even though we have run amuck. In sending Jesus to be our Christ and savior, you have given us the hope that can sustain us all the days of our lives. As we contemplate the divine gift given this Good Friday, help us come to ourselves and confess our sin before you. Give us the courage not only to face ourselves and our sin but also to face others who have failed to be just to the last, the lost, and the least.

2

In Jesus' own suffering may we be reminded of the consolation in our redemptive suffering and helped to find meaning therein. Let our sickness of soul push us to cling to Jesus in order to allow your divine spirit to heal us. We pray in the name of Jesus the Lord. Amen.

The Season of Easter

O God, in whom we trust our very being, thanks be to you for raising your Son and our Messiah from the grave to assure us of eternal life. In Jesus' life and ministry we learn what it is to be fully human as well as fully divine. May we partake of the sanctified Jesus so as to elevate the lives you have given us as a sacred responsibility.

2

By Jesus' glorious resurrection you have delivered us from human creatures' final enemy—the power of death. Unlike those "Galileans whose blood Pilate had mingled with their sacrifices" or "those eighteen who were killed when the tower of Siloam fell on them" because of your resurrection of Jesus we get a second chance. Thank you for your abounding grace revealed at an empty tomb. In Jesus' name we pray. Amen.

The Day of Ascension

O Lord of the Holy Spirit, we thank you for raising our Jesus at the resurrection and taking him unto your self as the ascension. As we see Jesus' essence ascend into heaven, we know that in his physical place he has promised us an Advocate who will encourage us and guide us in all of the ways of truth. Make this Advocate be for us the one who comforts us all the days of our lives.

2

By the power of your Holy Spirit, O God, connect us with the divine life that makes our lives worth living and fills them with meaning and value. As your spirit breathes in and out of us, may it truly inspire us to be the people you created us to be. Guide our feet onto the true pathway of abundant life—the life completely found in you. Help us, O Divine Master, in our search for genuineness in action and purity of thought. Grant that through the endowment of your Holy Spirit we may act in truth as we attempt to guide others into the peace which you alone can give. Amen.

The Season of Pentecost

Almighty God, author of everlasting life, as we experience the story of Pentecost from the book of Acts—as we hear those words—"When the day of Pentecost had come," inspire us as you inspired them. Help us as the church truly be all together in one place. Let us hear that sound like the rush of a violent wind which came from heaven. May you fill our sanctuary with your spirit as we strive to be people alive to your mighty wind.

2

As you give us life and we see creation's groaning, may we again understand the whole fullness of nature—in the wind, water, land, and animals, both great and small. Let your blazing spirit burn increasingly within us until that day when you gather all things unto yourself. Until that day, however, let us be faithful to the tasks you set before us and good stewards of your holy time. We pray this and everything in the grandeur of Jesus' name. Amen.

Trinity Sunday

O Holy and Triune God, your endless magnificence we see wherever we have the spiritual discernment and vision to see. On this Trinity Sunday we rest and remember on this Sabbath day that your essence is so much wider and grander than we can ever imagine. When we ponder your dominion and grace, we can only capture a trifling of the truth of the universe that you encapsulate in your holy being. And yet we try.

2

In Jesus' flesh you reveal the incarnation of divine love in human form. Jesus shows us how to be fully human and yet imbued with your fundamental nature. It is this nature that not only moved you to create the world and all that is in it. This nature also made you the divine caretaker of the entire world of nature. In the Holy Spirit you disclose the Advocate who comes from you and testifies to Jesus. Inspire us to love and care for the world of your creation as perfectly as you do. And remind us that we are indeed our sister's and brother's keepers as well. Give us the courage to do this in the name of our Messiah, Jesus the Christ. Amen.

All Saints Day

Great God, we sometimes sing of you as a mighty fortress. This day we sing of you as the one who has provided for us all the saints . . . who from their labors rest. Across the eons you have dispatched to us more witnesses than we could know, yet their testimony has made all the difference for us. Help us continue to sit at their metaphorical feet and learn from them. They knew the joy of total dependence on your grace, and therefore we pray, encourage them to surround us like witnesses and teach us as well.

2

May our Saints' resources for faith be transmitted to us so that we too might partake of your divine wisdom incarnate in their lives. Gracious Lord of all, help us unearth the strength, insight, and bravery to face hunger, crooked politics, ignorance, prejudice, and all of the afflictions that bedevil our world—which is in reality still your garden. In the name of Jesus, make us all servants of you O God on High. Amen.

Reign of Christ/Christ the King Sunday

On this Reign of Christ/Christ the King Sunday may we as your sacred congregation, O God, recall that in Jesus you made the King of Glory. As the Apocalypse of Saint John the Divine tells us: "On his robe and on his thigh he has a name inscribed, 'King of kings and Lord of lords'" (Revelation 19:16 NRSV). Thus as this Christ was so for the first-century believers, may he be so for us—the Lord of lords, and King of kings. In this sacred vein, Lord, we pray that your Kingdom will be in power forever, both in our hearts and in your world.

2

As far as monarchs go, O God, we Americans know very little. But from what we do know, we thank you for sending Jesus, who shows us an unusual side of being King. He as king is a "Wonderful Counselor, Mighty God, Everlasting Father, [and] Prince of Peace" (Isaiah 9:6 NRSV). May we honor such a sovereign today as a reflection of your love, compassion, concern, and mercy toward us, your wayward children. May this sovereign begin a reign of peace and of spiritual prosperity in our lives today—and forever. Amen.

Thanksgiving Day

O God, our Parent in Heaven—or wherever, we offer you thanks for this day and all it represents in our individual lives but also in the life of this congregation. We thank you for our being able to gather to worship in our land of freedom. As we sit down to enjoy the bounty of nature and agriculture, we thank you for the food that we enjoy day by day. We thank you for those who care so much for us that they prepare these delicious meals that give us the strength to live our lives in a productive manner.

2

Our prayer today as thankful people is that we might pass along our good fortune to others. We pray for the health and strength of those who are not so blessed with health and strength in these days. Help them, O Lord, carry on and live as those who have a blessed future—as perhaps their past has been so blessed by your graciousness. On this Thanksgiving Day we ask all things in the name of Christ as we offer our thanks and praise. Amen.

The Season of Advent

O God of Incarnation and Increase, we pray that you might give us a spirit of patience as we honestly confront those things necessary the next four Sundays to prepare for the coming of Christ. O Lord, you know patience is not our strong suit. We, like our little children, are ready to get to Christmas TODAY, and for that reason our tolerance for letting time unfold naturally is not what it might be. Forgive us for our rushing the revelation and not journeying with Mary and Joseph to see the beauty of the Christ-child.

2

As you sent John from the wilderness to prepare the way of the Lord, so too prepare our hearts for Jesus' coming. Remind us that to get ready for the Messiah's arrival we can repent from our sin and turn toward the salvation you offer us in the babe in a manger. Remind us that inherent in this tiny baby is the key to our forgiveness from sin and death. You loved us so much that you gave us your only son, "so that everyone who believes in him may not perish but may have eternal life" (John 3:16 NRSV). Thank you, God. Amen.

Christmas Eve

On this night of nights, O God, instill in us the wonder of your spirit of grace, mercy, and forgiveness. As we anticipate the birth of the one we have awaited, give us the good sense to recognize him when he comes. This tiny baby is the "the Alpha and the Omega." He is the one "who is and who was and who is to come, the Almighty" (Revelation 1:8 NRSV). In this baby we place the hopes of the world. Please, Lord, do not let us turn loose of this truth to grab another drumstick or glitzy present.

2

We need the hope that Jesus offers us. He gives us a reason to move into an unknown future, and for this, O Gracious God, we give you thanks. Help us witness to the truth of Christ, which in theory is easier for us at this sacred time of the year than at virtually any other time. May peace and tranquility come over our hearts, and may we begin to forgive others—and ourselves—as a sign and ensign of the season. Help us walk with humility as we move forward in life. May your creation thrive and may we be a part of this new movement. In the name of the Messiah, our Christ, we pray. Amen.

CONTRIBUTORS

Chuck Aaron
Whaley United Methodist Church
Gainesville, Texas

Tracey Allred
Greensboro, North Carolina

Guy Ames
Ardmore, Oklahoma

Chris Andrews
First United Methodist Church
Baton Rouge, Louisiana

John Ballenger
Woodbrook Baptist Church
Baltimore, Maryland

Dave Barnhart
Birmingham, Alabama

Lawson Bryan
First United Methodist Church
Montgomery, Alabama

Scott Bullard
Marion, Alabama

Jacquetta Johnson Chambers
Fort Worth, Texas

Mike Childress
Louisville, Kentucky

Dan R. Dick
Wisconsin Annual Conference
Sun Prairie, Wisconsin

Neil Epler
Frazer United Methodist Church
Montgomery, Alabama

Amber Essick
Lexington, Kentucky

John Essick
Lexington, Kentucky

Dan L. Flanagan
Saint Paul's United Methodist Church
Papillion, Nebraska

Travis Franklin
Salado United Methodist Church
Salado, Texas

Drew J. Gunnells Jr.
Mobile, Alabama

Cameron Jorgenson
Buies Creek, North Carolina

Gary G. Kindley
Dallas, Texas

Andrew Kinsey
Community United Methodist Church
Vincennes, Indiana

Mike Lowry
Central Texas Conference of The UMC
Fort Worth, Texas

Timothy Mallard
Blythewood, South Carolina

Andy Mangum
First Christian Church
Arlington, Texas

Ted McIlvain
William C. Martin United Methodist Church
Grapevine, Texas

David N. Mosser
First United Methodist Church
Arlington, Texas

Raquel Mull
Saint Paul's United Methodist Church
Socorro, New Mexico

Bill Obalil
United Methodist Church of Geneva
Geneva, Illinois

Bob Pierson
Tulsa, Oklahoma

Dale Schultz
Round Rock, Texas

Sara Leitnaker Shaver
Monroeville, Alabama

Mark W. Stamm
Perkins School of Theology
Dallas, Texas

Arlene Turner
Chatfield United Methodist Church
Chatfield, Texas

Mark White
Richmond, Virginia

Victoria Atkinson White
Mechanicsville, Virginia

Darren Williams
Seneca, South Carolina

Jessica Williams
Trinity Baptist Church
Seneca, South Carolina

Ryan Wilson
Trinity Baptist Church
Seneca, South Carolina

Harris Worcester
First United Methodist Church
Wortham, Texas

Julie Worcester
First United Methodist Church
Wortham, Texas

Sandy Wylie
Bella Vista, Arkansas

Charles Yoost
Church of the Saviour
Cleveland Heights, Ohio

Brett Younger
McAfee School of Theology
Atlanta, Georgia

Marti Zimmerman
Holladay, Utah

SCRIPTURE INDEX

Old Testament

Proverbs

Isaiah

Jeremiah

Daniel

Hosea

Joel

Amos

Habakkuk

Haggai

New Testament

Matthew

Mark

Luke